LAWRENCE SAGER

Guide to Passing the PSI Real Estate Exam

EIGHTH EDITION

President: Dr. Andrew Temte
Executive Director, Real Estate Education: Toby Schifsky
Development Editor: Rosita Hernandez

GUIDE TO PASSING THE PSI REAL ESTATE EXAM EIGHTH EDITION

Published by DF Institute, Inc., d/b/a Dearborn Real Estate Education
332 Front St. S., Suite 501
La Crosse, WI 54601

Printed in the United States of America

First revision, November 2019

ISBN: 978-1-4754-8725-1

DEDICATION

For my wonderful wife Adrienne with love and gratitude, and for always being there for me.

CONTENTS

PREFACE

All states require applicants for real estate licenses to pass a state license exam, and most states currently employ professional testing organizations to aid them in the development and administration of licensing examinations. One of these organizations is PSI Examination Services, of Glendale, California, which has developed widely used licensing exams for real estate professionals.

The focus of this study guide is preparation for PSI's real estate salesperson and broker licensing examinations. Of the existing books devoted to preparing for real estate licensing exams, this was the first study guide geared specifically to the current format of the PSI examination. The PSI exam is distinctive and challenging. As such, it warrants the specialized focus of *Guide to Passing the PSI Real Estate Exam*, hereafter referred to as the *Guide*.

This book is intended to guide prospective licensees in their preparation for the exam; it is intended to *direct* their effort. The study aids presented will help the student make the best use of his or her preparation time. It is hoped that this study guide will enable the prospective salesperson or broker to achieve success not only on the licensing exam but ultimately in the dynamic field of real estate.

ACKNOWLEDGMENTS

My thanks to all those who participated in the preparation of this text. I am especially grateful for the comments and advice of: Tim Meline, GRI, DREI, e-pro, Iowa Real Estate School; Daniel Conte, Appraisal and Real Estate School of Connecticut; Keith Donaldson, Donaldson Educational Services; Darlene Mallick, J.D., LL. M., Anne Arundel Community College, REALTOR® and broker, Mallick & Associates, Maryland and Pennsylvania; Sue Miranda-Rosensteel, CDEI, DREI; Farhad Rozi, Training Director and Instructor, Long & Foster Institute of Real Estate; Teresa Sirico, Teresa Sirico REALTOR® LLC, Greater New Haven Association of REALTORS®; Donald White, DREI, Gambrills, MD; and Alton E. "Tony" Duncanson, Long & Foster Institute of Real Estate. (Note: All designations current as of the time of the review.)

ABOUT THE AUTHOR

Lawrence Sager is a licensed real estate broker, certified residential appraiser, AQB-certified USPAP instructor, and REALTOR®. He holds a master's degree in urban land economics from the University of Illinois and was Real Estate Coordinator at Madison College. His writings have appeared in numerous publications on real estate and related fields.

Larry has acted as a research consultant for Madison College, the University of Wisconsin, and other public and private organizations. He is a Certified Fair-Housing trainer and has served as president of the Community Reinvestment Alliance. He has worked with the Wisconsin Real Estate Examining Board as a course writer and as the assistant executive secretary in the certification of educational programs for real estate licensure. He is a member of the Professional Standards committee of the REALTORS® Association of South Central Wisconsin and served for nine years on the Governor's Council on Real Estate Curriculum and Examinations. Previously, he has held membership on the Appraiser Application Advisory Committee of the Wisconsin Department of Regulation and Licensing and on the Advisory Committee on Continuing Assessor Education of the Wisconsin Department of Revenue. He currently serves as an expert witness in the areas of real estate practice and law, as well as competency of real estate licensees.

Use of the Manual

The intent of this manual is to prepare you on as many levels as possible to pass the real estate licensing examination compiled by the PSI Examination Services, Glendale, California. The *Guide* addresses two primary aspects of test taking:

- The structure and format of the exam
- The content of the exam

The organization of the *Guide* follows these two basic concerns. In addition to suggesting the most efficient use of this manual, Chapter 1 provides specific information about the PSI organization, testing procedures, and the test itself. Chapter 2, Examination and Study Strategies, is intended to familiarize you with the *format* of the questions in the PSI exam and suggests a strategy for optimizing test scores. Several studies have shown that given two examinees of equal ability and subject knowledge, the one who is more familiar with the form and style of the test will consistently score better than the other. Accordingly, Chapter 2 discusses the mechanics and the strategies of a test. It explains, for example, the parts of a question and how a typical question is developed. It illustrates how to analyze a question for clues to the right answer and how to determine what skills the question is intended to measure. Particular attention is given to the types of questions used by PSI in its real estate licensing examinations.

Chapter 2 also presents a strategy for optimizing test results by using the diagnostic exams following the content outlines presented in Chapters 3 through 12. Chapter 13 is a test of real estate calculations.

Chapter 14, Salesperson Examinations, and Chapter 15, Broker Examinations, afford an opportunity to take sample exams to measure your knowledge and the test-taking skills you have gained.

The Glossary is a reference list of real estate terms and definitions.

EXAMINATION INFORMATION

The PSI salesperson exam contains 80 one-point, multiple-choice questions. Ample time is allowed to complete the test.

The exam has two parts. The first part is an 80-question national test that measures your understanding of real estate practices and principles common throughout the country.

The second part of each exam (30 to 40 questions) is the state test. These questions focus on real estate regulations and practices and state statutes that are unique to that state. More information on the content of this part of the exam can be obtained from your real estate commission and the PSI candidate bulletin for the state.

All questions on the broker and salesperson examinations are multiple choice, with four alternatives. (Formats are discussed in detail in Chapter 2, "Examination and Study Strategies.") Objective, or multiple-choice questions, are advantageous, because they can accurately test several different levels of an applicant's knowledge in a limited amount of time and can be scored quickly. An important change in the broker examination is the introduction of a higher level of cognitive processing, evaluation, and synthesis. This requires candidates to integrate and evaluate complex information to formulate and specify a course of action and evaluate a conclusion or outcome.

Each answer has the same value—no penalty is imposed for wrong answers. This means that it will benefit you to answer all the questions on the exam as best you can.

Examinees must pass both the national section and the state section of the test. The required percentage of correct answers varies from one licensing Commission to another; this information is available from your local school, commission jurisdiction, or in the PSI candidate handbook for your state. Upon completion of both sections of the test, the computer screen displays a score report. Each of these reports indicates the examinee's scores on each of the two major sections of the exam (national and state), as well as on the various content areas in each major section. The scores represent the examinee's performance on a scale of 0 to 100. PSI does not allow an applicant to review her or his actual examination or the questions that were given.

All PSI exams are administered via computer. Candidates may fill out the special accommodation form if they are in need of a paper examination. However, they need to attach a letter from a professional stating the reason for this request. Most states require two forms of identification, and non-programmable calculators are allowed.

Standard instructions and procedures are part of the written exam booklet and probably will be read to you by a test supervisor before you begin the exam. When you get your test booklet, read the directions completely.

Taking the PSI examination by computer is simple; neither computer experience nor typing skills are required for taking the test, which requires you to use fewer than 12 keys. Upon being seated at the computer terminal, you will be prompted to confirm your name, identification number, and the examination for which you are registered.

Prior to your starting the exam, an introduction to the computer and keyboard appears on the screen. The time allowed for this introduction will not count as part of your exam time.

The introduction includes a sample screen display telling you to press 1, 2, 3, or 4 to select your answer or to press ? to mark for a later review. You then press the enter key to record your answer before moving on to the next question. You may change your answer as often as you like before pressing the enter key. Note that during the examination, the top of the screen displays the time remaining for your examination and is updated as you record your answers. If you have time remaining after you have answered every question in the examination, you will be given the opportunity to review all of the questions in the examination. You also will have the choice of reviewing only those questions that you marked for review or ending your examination and seeing your results. You may change your answers during the review options, and you may repeat the review options as time allows.

For further examination information, you may visit the PSI website at www.psiexams.com.

SALESPERSON EXAMINATION

The content order in Chapters 3 through 13 of this text follows the organization of the basic areas of PSI's national broker and salesperson test.

Chapters 3 through 13 end with a brief examination of the topics covered in each section. These pretests, called diagnostic tests, will help you determine your particular strengths and weaknesses and thus indicate which section of the examination needs additional review. They will identify the specific real estate concept, terminology, or application that you do not fully comprehend. The answers for each pretest are keyed to the page with the information you need to know for that subsection. The recommended procedure for using these sections is to take the diagnostic tests, then check your answers against the answer key provided at the end of the pretest. If your evaluation of your wrong answers indicates that you misunderstand the topic, study the chapter again. If your evaluation on the pretest indicates that you understand the concept but missed the question because of its structure, then reread Chapter 2, Examination and Study Strategies. If math is a problem area, check Chapter 13 for a basic real estate calculations review.

When you feel sufficiently prepared, turn to the 80-question sample exams in Chapter 14 (for salesperson) or Chapter 15 (for broker). These exams closely approximate an actual PSI exam in content and format and offer an opportunity to thoroughly test your knowledge and test-taking skills. The answer key and its explanations will help you identify your problem topics, which are based on the results of your diagnostic tests and the sample exam. Consider consulting real estate principles and practice texts if you missed a significant number of questions that relate to the specific topic.

PSI Test Specifications for Salespeople

In the national portion of the real estate licensing examination for salespersons, PSI has defined its testing priorities and outline as follows:

- **Property Ownership** (8%, approximately 6-7 questions) covers real versus personal property, conveyances, land characteristics and legal descriptions, encumbrances and effects on property ownership, and types of ownership.
- **Land-Use Controls and Regulations** (5%, approximately 4 questions) covers government rights in land, government controls, and private controls.
- **Valuation and Market Analysis** (7%, approximately 5-6 questions) covers appraisals, estimate value, and competitive/comparative market analysis.
- **Financing** (10%, approximately 8 questions) covers basic concepts and terminology, types of loans, and financing and lending.
- **General Principles of Agency** (13%, approximately 10-11 questions) covers agency and nonagency relationships, agent's duties to clients, creation of agency and nonagency agreements, disclosure of conflict of interest, responsibilities of agent to customers and third parties (including disclosure, honesty, integrity, and accounting for money) and termination of agency.
- **Property Disclosures** (6%, approximately 4-5 questions) covers property condition, environmental issues requiring disclosure, government disclosure requirements (LEAD), and material facts and defect disclosure.
- **Contracts** (17%, approximately 13-14 questions) covers general knowledge of contract law, contract clauses (including amendments and addenda), offers/purchase agreements, and counteroffers/multiple offers.
- **Leasing and Property Managemen**t (3%, approximately 2-3 questions) covers basic concepts/duties of property management, lease agreements, landlord and tenant rights and obligations, property managers' fiduciary responsibilities, ADA and fair housing compliance in property management, and setting rents and lease rates (broker only).
- **Transfer of Title** (8%, approximately 6-7 questions) covers title insurance, deeds, escrow or closing, tax aspects of transferring title to real property, special processes, and warranties.
- **Practice of Real Estate** (13%, approximately 10-11 questions) covers trust/escrow accounts, federal fair housing laws and the ADA, advertising and technology, licensee and responsibilities, and antitrust laws.
- **Real Estate Calculations** (10%, approximately 8 questions) covers basic math concepts, calculations for transactions, and calculations for valuation and rate of return (broker only).

BROKER EXAMINATION

While the salesperson exam contains 80 one-point, multiple-choice items, the broker exam is composed of 75 one-point, multiple-choice items and five two-point, multiple-choice items. Beginning January 1, 2019, longer versions of the salesperson and broker examinations will be available for states to adopt. The longer version of the salesperson examination is composed of 100 one-point, multiple-choice items. The longer version of the broker examination is composed of 80 one-point, multiple-choice items and 10 two-point, multiple-choice items.

Chapters 3 through 12 provide outlines and diagnostic tests to help prepare for material on the exams. The math review in Chapter 13 and the sample exams in Chapters 14 and 15 should be of considerable study value to the prospective broker in preparing for the exam.

PSI Test Specifications for Brokers

In the national portion of the real estate licensing examination for brokers, PSI includes the same categories covered in the salesperson exam. The difference between the two national tests is the proportion of questions in each category. The distribution in the broker exam is as follows:

- **Property Ownership** (10%, approximately 8 questions)
- **Land-Use Controls and regulations** (5%, approximately 4 questions)
- **Valuation and Market Analysis** (7%, approximately 5-6 questions)
- **Financing** (8%, approximately 6-7 questions)
- **General Principles of Agency** (11%, approximately 8-9 questions)
- **Property Disclosures** (7%, approximately 5-6 questions)
- **Contracts** (18%, approximately 14-15 questions)
- **Leasing and Property Management** (5%, approximately 4 questions)
- **Transfer of Title** (7%, approximately 5-6 questions)
- **Practice of Real Estate** (14%, approximately 11-12 questions)
- **Real Estate Calculations** (8%, approximately 6-7 questions)

The state supplement exam for brokers contains approximately 25 to 50 questions and is based on a state's statues, rules, and contractual forms.

Examination and Study Strategies

The PSI real estate examinations are achievement tests that candidates must pass before they can work as salespeople or brokers in their states. An achievement test measures an individual's proficiency in a given field. The ultimate objective of the license exam is to maintain the standards of the industry and to protect the public from persons not qualified to practice real estate sales and brokerage. The exam, therefore, tests

- the knowledge applicants have gathered through license-preparation courses and individual study, and
- the ability of the applicants to use that knowledge in real estate applications.

PREPARING FOR THE EXAM

Mental and Physical Preparation

Multiple-choice tests demand a special type of mental preparation. While memorizing definitions, terms, and formulas, keep in mind that some questions also will require you to apply your knowledge to novel situations. Concentrate on real estate principles as you study, and try to *apply the principles and facts to real-life situations.*

An excellent method of preparing for an exam is to take similar tests prior to the actual exam. You can gain important percentage points simply by being an experienced test taker. The more similar to the actual exam the practice test is in content and format, the more you will benefit. This is the strategy behind the presentation of the diagnostic tests and the salesperson and broker exams in this manual. You will earn a better score if you are in top physical and mental shape the day of the test. It is a good idea to review your notes within the 48 hours before the exam. Get your normal amount of rest the night before the exam; it is *not* wise to stay up all night in a panic-stricken effort to cram. Eat normally, but do not have a heavy meal before going to the test.

Your *attitude* is at least as important as your metabolic state. You should be prepared, determined, and positive. A small amount of anxiety is natural—it can even help you do your best—but too much anxiety is a handicap.

Taking the Exam

Upon checking in for the examination, you will be required to show the necessary identification. (Two separate pieces of ID—one of them government-issued and with a photo—are required.). You may not take purses, bags, water, or food into the test room. Cell phones must be left in the car. The proctor will then present the candidate information screen. Review the information and ensure its accuracy, and immediately report any errors.

In exchange for one of your IDs, you will be given a piece of scratch paper and asked to sign and date the top. You may have as many pieces as you need, but you must turn in each used piece to get a new sheet. You will then be assigned a seat, and the proctor will generate the exam. You will then be directed to enter the testing room and go to an assigned seat and begin the exam. When you actually begin the exam, carefully read the directions and questions. Be sure you understand each question completely before answering, and read each question twice to make sure of the question being asked.

A major cause of test errors is simply failure to think. Many tests measure judgment and reasoning, as well as factual knowledge. Always try to choose the *best* answer to a question; more than one alternative may be partially correct. Do not look for trick questions; choose the most logical answer to the premise of each question. Statistically, your first answer is likely to be the correct answer, so do not change it unless you are absolutely sure you have made an incorrect answer.

Words used in the questions will have their standard meanings unless they are special real estate terms. It sometimes helps to rephrase a question if you are not sure of the answer. For example, you may suspect that **4** is true in the following item:

> In holding a deposit delivered with a purchase contract, which of the following would be the *BEST* place to put the money, provided you had no instructions to the contrary?
> 1. In your office safe
> 2. In a neutral depository in the buyer's name
> 3. In your checking account
> 4. In a neutral depository

By rephrasing mentally, "The best place to put a deposit delivered with a contract would be in a neutral depository," you can clarify your thoughts about **4** being the correct answer. Be careful, though, not to change the meaning of the question when you rephrase it.

Pacing

Work through the exam at a comfortable rate. You are allowed ample time to finish the exam; however, you should work as rapidly as you can without sacrificing accuracy. Budget your time before you begin the exam. Plan on having more than half the questions answered before half the exam time has elapsed.

You may want to take a short break halfway through the exam. If you are ahead of schedule, you can afford to look up from the computer screen; take several deep, slow breaths; stretch your legs; relax in your seat; and rest for a minute or two. This breaks physical and mental tension and helps prevent mistakes.

As you work through the exam, answer the easy questions first—they are worth the same number of points as the hard ones, and they will build your confidence. Mark difficult items and time-consuming calculation problems and return to them later. You may find clues in later questions; or, if time runs out, you will have all the sure points. Do not give hurried answers just because you are intimidated by the number of questions. Most objective items are not very time consuming. Do not become discouraged if the exam seems difficult; no one is expected to get a perfect score.

DEVELOPING TEST QUESTIONS

The PSI exams are the result of collaboration by real estate experts and educators. How the tests for salespeople and brokers are organized and how many questions are associated with each topic of the exam were covered in Chapter 1, Use of the Manual. This section discusses the mechanics of test building.

Both the broker and the salesperson exams are completely multiple choice. Each test usually includes two types of questions. The first type tests your knowledge of general real estate, and the second tests your ability to apply this knowledge to specific real estate situations. The parts of a typical multiple-choice question are shown in the following examples:

> When a claim is settled by a title insurance company, the company acquires all rights and claims of the insured against any person who is responsible for the loss. This is called
>
> 1. escrow.
> 2. abstract of title.
> 3. certificate of title.
> 4. subrogation.

Note: The answer is **4**.

The Stem

The first step in developing a question is to write the *stem*, or *lead.* The stem provides all the information necessary to determine the correct response. It usually does not include irrelevant or extraneous information; the exceptions generally are items dealing with mathematics.

The stem can be an incomplete statement, as in the preceding example, or a question.

A lease provides a minimum rent of $250 per month plus 5% of annual gross income over $100,000. If the tenant did $145,000 in business last year, what total rent was paid?

1. $3,000
2. $5,250
3. $4,500
4. $7,250

The answer is **2.** Although the direct question lead tends to be somewhat less ambiguous than the incomplete statement, it usually is slightly longer and contains fewer clues to the correct response.

The Alternatives

The distractors then are written, with the correct keyed response embedded among the alternative choices. In the PSI exam, the alternatives are presented in a multiple-choice format. The multiple-choice format, as illustrated in the preceding example, supplies four separate alternative answers. In this format, you are asked to consider four possible answers, alone and in combination. Study the following example:

Listing agreements include which of the following?

1. An open listing only
2. An exclusive-right-to-sell listing only
3. An open listing and an exclusive-right-to-sell listing
4. A contract for deed

The answer is **3.** The purpose of distractors is to differentiate between well-prepared examinees and those who do not know the subject. Test developers often use popular misconceptions or even true statements that do not apply to the stem as distractors. Questions that do use true statements as distractors test not only your knowledge but also your judgment concerning the relevance of that knowledge. The difficulty of a question depends on the quality, or plausibility, of the distractors. In the worst case, where you have no idea which answer may be correct, the chance of answering it correctly is 25% because, theoretically, one out of four questions could be answered correctly just by guessing. Answering the question becomes much easier, and the odds of guessing correctly much higher, if one or two responses can be immediately eliminated.

SAMPLE QUESTIONS

The questions on the exam are not intended to trick you. You will, however, encounter several exam questions on the broker's exam that are more complex than the majority of the questions. Such questions are usually in a situational (story) format. You will need to read each question carefully to know exactly what is being asked before you begin to formulate your answer.

Several examples of questions that seem to be the most difficult for examinees are illustrated in this section. These include questions involving superfluous facts, reading comprehension, multistep math, value judgments, and best answer.

Superfluous Facts

Exam questions frequently contain superfluous facts that are not needed to answer the questions.

For example:

A family paid $50,000 for their home five years ago, making a $10,000 down payment. Their monthly payment, including interest at 7.75%, is $286. The interest portion of their last payment was $225.27. What was the approximate loan balance before their last payment?

1. $29,480.64
2. $34,880.52
3. $44,283.87
4. None of these

The answer is **2.** The only facts needed to answer this question are the amount of the last interest payment and the rate of interest. To solve, multiply the amount of the monthly interest, $225.27, by 12. Then, divide the result by the interest rate, 0.0775, to get the approximate loan balance.

Reading Comprehension

Another type of question you may find on the test requires that you carefully read each word for comprehension.

For example:

Closing of a transaction for a residential property is set for April 19, 2015. The seller has a three-year insurance policy that expires June 25, 2016. The seller has prepaid a three-year premium of $555. The buyer is to take over the policy as of the date of closing. The amount credited to the buyer at closing is

1. $185.00.
2. $202.99.
3. $231.25.
4. None of these

The answer is **4**, because the prorated amount of the prepaid insurance would be *debited* to the buyer.

Multistep Math

A type of question that may appear on PSI exams involves mathematics problems that require several steps.

For example:

A woman bought a house at exactly the appraised value. She negotiated a loan through a savings-and-loan association at 75% of the appraised value. The interest rate was 9%. The first month's interest was $405. What was the approximate selling price of the property?

1. $54,000
2. $60,000
3. $72,000
4. None of these

The answer is **3**. To answer this question, first multiply $405 by 12 to get the approximate annual interest ($4,860). Then, divide $4,860 by the interest rate, 0.09, to get the amount of the loan ($54,000). Finally, divide $54,000 by 0.75 to find the appraised value ($72,000), which is the same as the purchase price. Sometimes, a candidate who understands the mathematical process can use the answer key and work backward.

$72,000 × 75% (0.75) = $54,000 × 9% (0.09) = $4,860 ÷ 12 months = $405

Value Judgments

A few questions on the exam may require you to make value judgments.

For example:

A broker listed a small house for $86,000, obtaining an executed sales contract on it within six weeks at $85,000. The broker learned there was an existing $75,000 first mortgage and a $5,000 second mortgage on the property. The broker knew the real estate could be refinanced on a new $70,000 first-mortgage loan. The holder of the second mortgage told the broker he was willing to discount his $5,000 note, selling it for $4,500. The buyer has $20,000 cash and qualifies for a new $70,000 first-mortgage loan. The broker should

1. say nothing to the seller about refinancing and allow the transaction to close.
2. tell the seller the second mortgage can be paid off at a $500 discount.
3. tell the holder of the second mortgage the property is sold and, therefore, he or she should demand the full amount of $5,000.
4. buy the second mortgage himself at the $500 discount.

The answer is **2**. As an agent of the seller, the broker must act in the seller's best interest.

Best Answer

You will frequently be asked to choose the best answer from alternatives when the ideal answer is not present.

For example:

A broker listed a beachfront home at $263,000. Three weeks later, the broker was fortunate to obtain a full-price offer on the beach house. Stopping by the house after the sales contract was executed and in force, the broker was appalled to see a large foundation crack. Two days later, the broker noticed the crack had been carefully repaired. The broker knew the seller was unaware of the crack, because she had extremely poor eyesight. The broker suspected that the crack had been fixed by the seller's son-in-law, a building contractor. The broker should

1. disclose the fact of the crack to the buyer.
2. immediately cancel the sales contract.
3. keep quiet about the crack, because it has been repaired.
4. confront the son-in-law with his suspicions and threaten to sue.

The best alternative available here is **1**. It would be ideal to inform the seller of the crack, requesting permission to inform the buyer, but that alternative does not appear here. Note that this question also asks you to make a value judgment.

HOW TO ANALYZE A QUESTION

Apparent Content

In general, the PSI exams are designed to measure your real estate knowledge and skills. Multiple-choice questions can test much more than your recall of specific facts. The PSI exam will, in fact, test how well you understand a given concept; whether you can apply rules to real-life situations; and how well you can analyze, synthesize, and evaluate information, then arrive at a correct conclusion. If you can determine what ability the question is trying to measure, it will help you become a more effective test taker. The levels of skill the PSI exam seeks to measure are illustrated by the following examples:

Example 1
How many acres are there in a section?
1. 16
2. 36
3. 200
4. 640

The answer is **4.** This is an example of *recall*, or recognition. The point of the question is to determine if you know this fact about sections—logic does not help much in determining the answer. The *factual question* is the easiest type to recognize.

Example 2
Brokers owe their primary fiduciary duty to which of the following?
1. The principal
2. The lender
3. The public
4. The real estate commission

The answer is **1.** This type of question seeks to measure your understanding of the concept of fiduciary duty—and who it involves. *Comprehension questions* such as this often require you to identify real estate principles, laws, or practices.

Example 3
An investor leases a 20-unit apartment building for a net monthly rental of $5,000. If this figure represents a 7.5% return on investment, what is the original cost of the property?
1. $80,000
2. $200,000
3. $800,000
4. None of these

The answer is **3.** Multiply the monthly rental by 12 to get the rental income ($60,000). Then, divide $60,000 by 7.5% (0.075) to get the investment cost

($800,000). *Application questions* such as this are one level higher than comprehension questions. They ask you to use recall or understanding to solve a new real-estate-related problem. Knowledge of real estate laws, regulations, principles, and practices must be applied to concrete situations encountered on the job. Math problems are usually of this type.

Example 4
Which of the following types of financing would be the most appropriate for a young veteran who has just used most of his savings to complete his degree in engineering and now would like to buy a house for his family?
1. A conventional mortgage
2. An installment contract
3. A VA mortgage
4. An FHA mortgage

The correct answer is **3.** At this point, you are being tested not only on the concept of financing but also on your ability to weigh each of the options and come up with the best answer. *Analysis items* gauge your ability to identify parts of a whole, understand the relationships among the parts, or identify the way that these elements are organized. You may have to differentiate between reasons and conclusions or indicate the relative importance of causes or factors. This question involves more than recall, because all of the options are true. You must take your thinking one step further.

Example 5
Which of the following types of listing agreements affords the broker the most protection?
1. An open listing
2. An exclusive-agency listing
3. A net listing
4. An exclusive-right-to-selling listing

The correct answer is **4.** *Evaluation questions* such as this one test your ability to determine the best solution or to judge value in some manner. Often, you must use recall, comprehension, analysis, *and* synthesis to arrive at the answer.

Studies show that items testing the lower levels of cognition (recall or recognition) are easier than application, comprehension, and higher-level questions. However, items testing the higher cognitive functions often can be solved by using general intelligence rather than specific real estate knowledge. Your score can be improved simply by exercising logic. You can turn this to your advantage by reasoning through difficult problems using the following seven steps:

1. Read the items carefully to determine the general subject that the item is testing and exactly what is asked.
2. Reread the question for essential facts and qualifiers.
3. Eliminate answers that you know are incorrect.
4. Rephrase the problem (often helpful).

5. Determine what principles or formulas are necessary and how to solve the problem.
6. Apply relevant information to arrive at a solution.
7. Reread the question and check the answer.

Try this item for practice:

If an offer to purchase is received under certain terms and the seller makes a counteroffer, what is the prospective purchasers' legal position?
1. They are bound by the original offer.
2. They must accept the counteroffer.
3. They are relieved of the original offer.
4. They must split the difference with the seller.

The answer is **3.** How do you use the seven steps to arrive at that answer? In step 1, you determine that the subject is whether an offer is binding under certain circumstances. In step 2**,** you reread the question to determine that the prospective purchasers make an offer and the seller makes a counteroffer. In step 3, you eliminate any obviously incorrect answers—in this case, response **4.** Step 4 suggests rephrasing the problem: "If the buyers make an offer under certain terms and the seller makes a counteroffer, the buyers. . ." Step 5 is performed so automatically for this type of question that you may not be conscious that you are doing it. You need to know that an offer is not binding on the prospective purchasers once a counteroffer has been made. In step 6, you determine that alternative **3** is correct. Step 7 ensures that you have understood the question and have marked the right answer.

Although this logical process may seem long or complicated, your mind will accomplish it automatically within a few seconds once you train yourself to think or reason through questions.

EXAM STRATEGY

Many people study diligently and simply show up at the examination site without having given any thought to a strategy for taking the test. To maintain your confidence, poise, and positive mental attitude, you should start the examination with a game plan for taking the test.

We suggest that you develop your own strategy for completing the test. Following is an example of an exam strategy:

Read each question once to determine the particular subject matter of the question. Read the question a second time, and concentrate on determining the correct response. If you are uncertain of the correct answer, eliminate obviously incorrect responses. If you still are uncertain of the single best answer, mark the question for review and move on to the next question. By doing this, you divide the test into two parts:

- The part you know, which you answer quickly and efficiently and remove from further consideration.
- The part you do not know but have managed to isolate, to which you can devote the remainder of your test time.

Multiple-choice items often test not only your knowledge of specific points, but also your ability to relate other information to the point. Many important topics have more than one question allotted to them. The correct answer to one question often can be found in some portion of another, so jot down the numbers of the questions that you think contain clues. This will help you in rechecking answers or answering questions you skipped.

There will be approximately five to seven math questions on the exam. Math problems often use varying units that must be converted. You may have to change income per month to income per year before applying a formula, or you may have to convert square feet to acres before proceeding with a calculation. If you really have no idea how to solve a math problem and must guess, eliminate the two most extreme numerical answers and mark one of the remaining choices. This tactic is not always correct, but the odds favor it.

If math is not your strength, do not let yourself be intimidated by the calculation problems. A good approach to math questions is to estimate the answer before actually working the problem. Figure neatly and carefully—this reduces error; then compare your answer with your original estimate. If they are different, you may have misplaced a decimal or used the wrong equation. If you cannot tell from the problem what equation to use, make up a simple, similar problem and determine the equation from that. If you cannot solve a problem, or if you obtain an answer that is not one of the options, check to see if you used all the figures given in your calculations. If you cannot solve a math problem in the usual way, you sometimes can find the correct solution by working backward from the given answers.

After completing every question on the exam, proofread your answers to ensure that you did not misread any of the questions, and that you marked the answer you intended for each item. By using extra time to correct any careless mistakes, you may boost your score significantly. Do not change an answer unless you are sure the new one is correct. An examinee's first response usually is correct and changes may decrease the score.

By developing an exam strategy similar to this, you should have command of the examination.

Exam Strategy

- Remember that questions are industry-related; know the vocabulary.
- Read all questions and answers thoroughly before choosing the best answer.

- Eliminate answers that are incorrect.
- Do not go back and change answers; do not second-guess yourself.
- First, complete the questions to which you know the answers, then return to the questions of which you are unsure.
- Psychologically prepare yourself.

STUDY STRATEGY

The following gives you a strategy for studying and incorporating the diagnostic tests and outlines of concepts to understand in Chapters 3 through 13.

Chapters 3 through 13 correspond to testing areas on the PSI exam for salesperson: Property Ownership, Land-Use Control and Regulations, Valuation and Market Analysis, Financing, General Principles of Agency, Property Disclosures, Contracts, Leasing and Property Management, Transfer of Title, Practice of Real Estate, and Real Estate Calculations. Each chapter begins with an Outline of Concepts to Understand for the subject area. This is followed by the Diagnostic Test, its Answer Key, and a test score box. Take the diagnostic test and analyze your results before reviewing the content outline. If your progress score suggests that you need improvement, use the test results to establish your priority areas for study.

Remember that the outline format of the concepts is designed primarily to organize your real estate knowledge concisely. If you are having difficulty with a particular topic, consult real estate practice and theory texts for a comprehensive explanation of the topic. Modern Real Estate Practice (published by Dearborn Real Estate Education) provides a solid core of information.

How to Use the Progress Score

After completing and correcting the diagnostic test, count the number of questions missed and enter that number in the box under Your Score after Total Wrong. Then, subtract the number of incorrectly answered questions from the total points. Finally, analyze your results by finding where your score of correct answers falls in the Range column; the rate corresponding to your score describes your progress. Your score will fall under Good, Fair, or Needs Improvement.

For example:

PROPERTY OWNERSHIP			
Rating	**Range**	**Your Score**	
Good = 80% to 100%	31–39	Total Number	39
Fair = 70% to 79%	27–30	Total Wrong	– 8
Needs improvement = Lower than 70%	26 or less	Total Right	31

Passing Requirement: 26 or Better

If your score on a diagnostic test is rated Good, this area is one of your strengths. However, we suggest that a student should strive for 90% before taking the actual exam. A rating of Fair or Needs Improvement in a subject suggests this is an area on which you need to concentrate.

Developing a Strategy for Studying

After you have pinpointed the areas that need particular study, you can begin studying the material in the concepts-to-understand outline. To increase the effectiveness of your study time, we suggest that you follow these rules.

Organize your study time. Educators suggest that the regular short study periods are better than lengthy cram sessions. You should study when you are at your best mentally and physically; this may be early in the morning. The following chart will help you organize your study time in relation to the specific areas on the examination.

SCHEDULED HOURS FOR STUDY

NATIONAL EXAM	M	T	W	Th	F	Sa	Su	Total
Property Ownership								
Land Use Controls and Regulations								
Valuation and Market Analysis								
Financing								
General Principles of Agency								
Property Disclosures								
Contracts								
Leasing and Property Management								
Transfer of Title								
Practice of Real Estate								
Real Estate Calculations								

STATE EXAM	M	T	W	Th	F	Sa	Su	Total
Real Estate Law								
Rules and Regulations								
Special State Considerations								

Study in depth. You cannot simply read the text in preparation for successful completion of the exam; you must arrive at a thorough understanding of the subject matter. This can be achieved by writing a sample test question to yourself about the paragraph you have just read. It is a good practice to outline the thoughts of the paragraph in your own words or develop relationships between items. In other words, create mental images that will help you recall difficult concepts. Acronyms are useful when memorizing a series of items. (For example, the six duties that an agent owes to a principal are COLDAC: care, obedience, loyalty, disclosure, accounting, and confidentiality.) During this stage, you should work alone.

Regularly review material studied. In many cases, this can be accomplished by having a study partner assist you in reviewing your knowledge of vocabulary words, concepts, and relationships. This also can be achieved by taking regular exams on the subject matter. The following are some other tips:

- Make flash cards with terms on the front and definitions on the back.
- Tape-record terms: say the term, pause, then give the definition.
- Encourage group or one-on-one discussion.

Property Ownership

OUTLINE OF CONCEPTS

I. Property Ownership

A. Classes of property
  1. Real versus personal property
     a. Real property—the land and anything permanently affixed to it; includes the interests, benefits and rights inherent in the ownership of real estate.
     b. Personal property—movable objects (chattels) that do not fit into the definition of real property; conveyed by bill of sale.
  2. Defining Fixtures
     a. Fixture—an item of personal property that has been converted to real property by being permanently affixed to the land or building. Fixtures can be either attached or annexed.
     b. A fixture that is permitted to be and is detached from the land or the building would revert to personal property (severance).

B. Land Characteristics and Legal Descriptions
  1. Physical characteristics of land
     a. Immobile—the geographic location of a parcel of land is fixed—can never be changed.
     b. Indestructible—the long-term nature of improvements plus permanence of the land tends to create stability in land development.
     c. Unique or nonhomogeneous—all parcels differ geographically and each parcel has its own location.
  2. Economic Characteristics of Land
     a. Scarcity—although there is a substantial amount of unused land, supply in a given location or of a specific quality can be limited.
     b. Improvements—placement of an improvement on a parcel of land affects value and use of neighboring parcels of land.
     c. Permanence of Investment—Improvements represent a large fixed investment; some such as drainage and sewerage cannot be dismantled or removed economically.
     d. Area preference, or situs—this refers to people's choices and desires for a given area.

3. Types of Legal Property Descriptions
   a. Metes and Bounds
      (1) To locate a property boundary requires two permanent reference markers.
      (2) The boundary is measured from a specific point of beginning (POB) and proceeds around the boundaries using reference to linear measurements and directions.
      (3) Boundaries may be established on the basis of actual distance between monuments (fixed objects).
      (4) A boundary must return to the point of beginning (POB) so that the land described is fully enclosed.
   b. Rectangular (Government) Survey
      (1) Based on measurements from base lines and principal meridians.
      (2) Base lines run east and west; principal meridians run north and south.
      (3) Designed to set up checkerboard pattern of identical squares over specific area.
         a. Parallel vertical lines six miles apart divide land into strips east and west of the principal meridian that are referred to as ranges.
         b. (Parallel horizontal lines six miles apart divide land into strips north and south of the baseline that are referred to as tiers.
         c. The grid that divides the land into townships is formed by superimposing these two sets of lines.
            (i) A township is six miles square (36 square miles).
            (ii) A township contains 36 sections; each section is a square mile and contains 640 acres (one acre = 43,560 square feet).
            (iii) Sections are numbered from the northeast corner; the first row of six sections runs east to west, the second runs west to east, and so on, with section 36 located in the southeast corner of the township.
            (iv) The land description is based on references to either a section or some portion of a section, such as one quarter—section (160 acres) or one half section (320 acres).
            (v) A typical description—the NE ¼ of the SW ¼ of Section 4, Township 3 North, Range 2 east of the Principal Meridian.
            (vi) To determine the number of acres in a rectangular survey legal description, multiply all the denominators and divide the result of this multiplication into 640 acres. NW ¼ of the SW ¼ = 4 × 4 = 16 divided into 640 = 40 acres.
   c. Subdivision Plats
      (1) Location of an individual parcel is indicated on a map of the subdivision, which is divided into numbered blocks and lots.

(2) Each parcel is referred to a lot, block, subdivision name, city, and state.

(3) Street Address: an informal reference too unreliable for a legal description because you cannot walk the boundaries.

4. Usage of legal property descriptions—in order for a claim to any property to have any value, it must be accompanied by a verifiable and legal property description.

5. Physical descriptions of property and improvements—calculations of land and building area are discussed in Chapter 12.

6. Mineral, air and water rights.

a. Mineral rights.

(1) Mineral rights may be owned by the owner of the surface rights or by separate third party owners of subsurface rights, such as natural gas or oil companies, as well as by the developer or the homebuilder.

(2) Homebuyers should determine who owns the mineral rights when purchasing a home.

(3) If the subsurface rights are owned by an oil company, the landowner could find an oil well on his property over which he or she would have little or no control.

b. Air Rights

(1) The right to occupy, use, or control the space above a property, such as a homeowner purchasing the air rights above a neighboring home to protect his view.

(2) Air rights are frequently utilized in larger cities, such as a developer buying the air rights above a large parking lot to build a skyscraper condominium building in the center of a city.

c. Water Rights

(1) Ownership of water and land adjacent to it is determined by state law, which is based on either the doctrines of the riparian and littoral rights or on the doctrine of prior appropriation; owners of water rights generally have the right to use water so long as they do not pollute or interrupt the flow.

a. Riparian rights—rights granted to owners along a non-navigable river or stream.

b. Littoral rights—rights granted to owners along an ocean or large lake.

c. Prior appropriation—the right to use water is controlled by the state rather than by the adjacent landowner. A person must show the first beneficial use for the water, such as crop irrigation, in order to secure water rights.

C. Encumbrances and effects on property ownership—a charge, claim, or liability that attaches to, and is binding on, real estate.

1. Liens (types and priority)

a. Liens—affect the title

(1) A lien is a charge against property that provides security for a debt or obligation of the property owner.

(2) If the debt is not repaid, the lien holder has the right to have it paid out of the debtor's property, generally from the proceeds of a court or foreclosure sale.
(3) A specific lien relates to specific real or personal property; a general lien, such as a judgment or court decree, applies to all of the debtor's property both real and personal as well as all assets.
(4) Possible specific liens against an owner's real estate include real estate taxes, mortgages, and mechanics' liens.
(5) Real estate property taxes and special assessments usually take priority over all other liens, regardless of date of recording.
(6) In some states, mechanics' liens may be given priority over previously recorded liens (not property tax liens) because mechanics' liens revert to the date the work was started, not to when the lien was recorded.

b. Encumbrances that affect the physical condition and/or use of the property include encroachment, easements, and restrictions.
   (1) Deed restriction—a deed restriction or restrictive covenant is a private limitation on the use of property. Developers use it to make their new neighborhoods appealing to certain buyers. These restrictions can be enforced by a court injunction.

2. Easements and Licenses
   a. An easement is a right acquired by one party to use the land of another party for a specific purpose.
      (1) Easement appurtenant
         a. Gives the easement beneficiary the right to use another's property.
         b. Requires that there be two tracts of land, either contiguous or noncontiguous, owned by different parties.
         c. The tract over which the easement runs is known as the *servient tenement*; the tract that benefits from the easement is known as the *dominant tenement*.
         d. Appurtenant easements "run with the land" and are not terminated by the sale of either the servient or dominant tenement.
      (2) Easement in gross—a personal interest in or right to use the land of another, such as the right of way for a utility company; there is no dominant tenement, just a servient tenement.
      (3) Easement by necessity—arises when there is no other access to a property by a street or public way, and the easement is required by necessity rather than for convenience.
      (4) Easement by prescription
         a. Acquired when the claimant has use of other's land for the prescriptive period, generally from 5 to 20 years.
         b. Claimant's use must have been continuous, without the owner's approval, visible, open and notorious. Successive periods of use by different parties may establish

a claim for an easement by prescription through the process of tacking.

b. License
   (1) Permission to enter the land of another for a specific purpose, such as permission to park in a neighbor's driveway or to go hunting on another's property.
   (2) Differs from easement in that it can be canceled or terminated by licensor at any time and does not run with the land.

3. Encroachments—illegal extension of a building or some other improvement, such as a wall or fence, beyond the boundaries of the land of its owner and onto the land of an adjoining owner.

D. Types of Ownership

1. Interests in real estate—feudal versus allodial rights
   a. Feudal—system of land ownership in which the king or government held title to the land; the individual was merely a tenant who held rights of use and occupancy at the sufferance of the overlord.
   b. Allodial—system in which an individual can hold property free and clear of any rent or service due the government; system under which land is held in the United States.
2. Limitations on ownerships—individuals' ownership rights are subject to certain rights of government:
   a. Police power—power of the state to establish legislation to protect public health and safety and promote general welfare.
   b. Eminent domain—right of government to acquire private property for public use while paying just compensation to the owner through a process known as condemnation.
   c. Escheat—reversion of real estate ownership to the state after a statutory time period has elapsed, as provided by state law, when an owner dies and leaves no heirs or no will disposing of the real estate, or when the property is abandoned.
   d. Taxation—charge on real estate to raise funds to meet the public needs of the government.
3. Estates and Land
   a. Refers to degree, quantity, and nature of ownership that a person has in real property for a lifetime (life estate) or forever (inheritable freehold).
   b. Freehold estates—estates of ownership for indeterminable length.
   c. Fee simple absolute
      (1) Maximum interest in real estate recognized by law.
      (2) Holder entitled to all rights incident to property.
      (3) Continues for indefinite period and is inheritable by heirs of owner.
   d. Fee simple defeasible (qualified fee, conditional determinable)
      (1) Continues for an indefinite period; may be inherited.
      (2) Estate extinguished on the occurrence of a designated event, the time of such occurrence being uncertain.

4. Life estate
   a. Limited ownership for the duration to life of life tenant, or life or lives of some other designated person or persons.
   b. Not an estate of inheritance, because estate terminates at the death of the life tenant or the designated person
   c. May be created for the life of another person (estate pur autre vie).
   d. Future interests in the property after the death of the life estate owner.
      (1) Remainder interest—if the deed or the will names a third party to whom title will pass on the death of the life estate owner, then such party is said to own remainder interest.
      (2) Reversionary interest—if the deed does not convey remainder interest to a third party, then upon the death of the life estate owner, full ownership reverts to the original fee simple owner or, if he or she is deceased, to heirs.
      (3) Usually limited to the lifetime of the owner of the life estate (life tenant). An exception would be an estate pur autre vie.
5. Life tenant
   a. Interest in real property is time-ownership interest.
   b. Generally not answerable to the holder of future interest (remainderman).
   c. Has limited rights; that is, can enjoy the rights of the land but cannot encroach upon the rights of the remainderman.
   d. May not commit waste (permanently injure the land or property).
   e. Entitled to possession of the property and to all income and profits arising from property during the term of ownership. Tenant must pay the taxes and other expenses of ownership.
   f. Life interest may be sold, leased, mortgaged, or gifted but may be of little value, because all interest must be forfeited at the death of the life tenant; remainder interest cannot be encumbered by the life tenant.
6. Homestead
   a. Tract of land owned and occupied as the primary residence.
   b. In states with homestead-exemption laws, a portion of the area or value of land is exempted, or protected, from judgment for unsecured debts.
7. Adverse Possession
   a. The continuous, open, hostile, notorious, and adverse possession of another's property without his or her permission. Statutory possession periods vary from state to state and are a factor used in determining this involuntary transfer of title.

E. Freehold Estates—Forms of Ownership
   1. Ownership by natural persons
      a. In severalty—one owner
      b. In co-ownership—two or more owners
         (1) Tenancy in common
            a. All owners have equal right of possession. May hold equal or unequal shares.

- b. Each owner can sell, convey, mortgage, or transfer his or her interest without the consent of the other co-owners.
- c. Upon the death of a co-owner, the individual interest of the deceased passes to heirs or devisees according to the will; there is no right of survivorship.
- d. Tenants in common may partition the land.

(2) Joint Tenancy
- a. All owners must have equal shares and possession. If one owner/tenant dies, this share is automatically transferred to the other owners without going through probate.
- b. Four unities—title, time, interest, and possession—are required to create a valid joint tenancy.
- c. Termination results from the destruction of any of the four unities.
- d. Joint tenants may partition the land.

(3) Tenancy by the entirety
- a. Owners must be husband and wife and live in a state that recognized this type of ownership.
- b. Owners have the right of survivorship.
- c. Title may be conveyed or encumbered only by the deed signed by both parties (one party cannot convey a one-half interest).
- d. Usually no right of partition.

(4) Community property—in certain states (marital property)
- a. Husband and wife may have sole ownership of the separate or individual property if it was owned solely by either spouse before the marriage or was acquired by gift or inheritance after marriage.
- b. Husband and wife are equal partners in the community or marital property (property acquired during the marriage).
- c. Upon the death of one spouse, the survivor automatically owns one-half of the community property, the other half being distributed according to the deceased's will.
- d. Antenuptial agreements are contracts (prior to marriage) that preserve separate property ownership.

(5) Partnerships
- a. Association of two or more persons to carry on business as co-owners and share in the profits and losses of that business.
- b. Types of partnerships
  - (i) General—all partners participate in the operation of the business and may be held personally liable for business losses and obligations.
  - (ii) Limited
    - (a) Includes general as well as limited, or silent, partners.
    - (b) General partner runs the business.

(c) Although limited partners do not participate, they may be held liable for business losses, but only to the extent of their investment unless they take an active role in management.

(6) Corporations
   a. Ownership in severalty—corporations are considered by law to be a single entity.
   b. Each stockholder's liability for losses generally is limited to the amount of investment.

(7) Syndicates—joining together of two or more parties to create and operate a real estate investment.

(8) REITs—a Real Estate Investment Trust is the ownership of real estate by a group of individual investors who purchase certificates of ownership in the trust. The trust invests in real property and distributes the profits back to the investors free of corporate income tax.

F. Leasehold Estates
   1. Types of Leasehold Estates—estates of possession
      a. Tenancy or estate for years—lease for a definite period of time terminating automatically without notice by either party.
      b. Tenancy from year-to-year or periodic estate—lease for an indefinite period of time without a specific expiration date; notice must be given to terminate.
      c. Tenancy at will—lease that gives the tenant the right to possess with the consent of the landlord for an indefinite period of time; terminated by either party giving notice or by the death of either the landlord or the tenant.
      d. Tenancy at sufferance (holdover tenancy)—tenant continues to hold possession without the consent of the landlord.

G. Common Interest Ownership Properties
   1. Cooperatives
      a. Title to the land and the building are held by the corporations whose sole interest is the property.
      b. Each purchaser becomes a corporate stockholder and receives a proprietary lease.
      c. Taxes and the mortgage are liens against the corporation generally given to the shareholders.
      d. Owners-occupants may be forced to pay expenses for the shareholders who are unable to pay, to prevent foreclosure on the entire building.
   2. Condominiums
      a. Generally created under a horizontal property act.
      b. The owner holds fee-simple title to one unit and a specified share in the common elements as a tenant in common.
      c. Default in payment of taxes, mortgage payments, or monthly assessments by one unit owner may result in a foreclosure sale of that owner's unit; this does not affect the titles of the remaining owners.

3. Time-share ownership
    a. Allows multiple buyers to buy interests in real estate with each buyer receiving the right to use the facilities for a specified period of time.
    b. Owners' use and occupancy is limited to the contractual period that was purchased.
    c. Each owner is assessed for common expenses and maintenance based on the ratio of the ownership period to the total number of ownership periods in the property.
    d. Time-share estate includes a fee-simple interest in condominium ownership or a leasehold estate.
    e. Time-share use is a contractual right under which the developer owns the real estate. This may be a deeded interest.

H. Bundle of Rights
1. Legal concept that gives the owner of the land all legal rights to land, such as possession, disposition and exclusion.
2. Ownership rights are not unlimited in that some of the rights may have been taken away or sold.
3. Private limitations on rights could result from owner agreeing to a deed restriction.
4. Public limitations would result from a city's power to tax the owner's land or through the city's zoning ordinance, which would control the use of the property.

I. Square footage calculations
1. Measuring structures
    a. The America National Standards Institute (ANSI) provides standards for measuring and calculating the residential square footage of a house. The ANSI standard is voluntary.
    b. ANSI may be used in proposed, new, or existing single-family homes of any style or construction but does not apply to apartment or multi-family buildings.
    c. Individual multiple listing services generally establish guidelines for measuring and calculating square footage of a house. However, there currently is no uniformity in guidelines among MLS throughout the country.
    d. Square footage is generally taken from exterior measurements.
    e. Agents frequently cut the floorplan into rectangles and multiply length times width.
    f. Agents sometimes use floor levels to explain features such as 1½ stories or a finished lower level.
    g. Calculations of land and building area are discussed in a later chapter.
2. Livable, rentable, and usable area
    a. Livable area is generally defined as legal square footage that is suitable for year-round living.
    b. Rentable area is generally used in marketing office space and usually includes more square feet than will be occupied by a tenant.
        (1) Commercial rentable area includes the usable square feet of the rentable area plus a proportionate share of common areas in the building, such as lobbies, restrooms, and corridors.

3. Usable area generally means that specific amounts of square footage will be required by a tenant to do business, including any storage and private restrooms.

J. Other Important Terms
1. Accession—acquiring the title to additions or improvements to real property as a result of accretion of alluvium or annexation of fixtures (including accession of trade fixture not removed by the tenant prior to lease termination).
    a. Accretion—increase in land resulting from soil deposited by the natural force of water.
    b. Alluvion—actual soil-increase deposit resulting from accretion.
    c. Avulsion—a sudden tearing away of land by the action of natural forces.
2. Appurtenances—rights belonging to land.
3. Assignment—transfer of rights and/or duties under a contract.
4. Attachment—procedure by which property of debtor is placed in the custody of the law and is held as security, pending the disposition of a creditor's suit.
    a. Rights can be assigned, unless the contract expressly forbids assigning them.
    b. Obligations often can be assigned, but the original party is secondarily liable for them.
5. Benchmark—permanent metal marker embedded in cement, which is used as a reference to indicate the elevation above sea level and actual physical location.
6. Cloud on title—any claim that may impair the title to a property.
7. Cul-de-sac—street open at only one end and generally with a circular turnaround at the other end.
8. Erosion—gradual washing away of soil caused by flowing water or air.
9. Fixtures—personal property that has been affixed to and becomes part of the real property.
10. Lis pendens (Latin term for action pending)—recorded document that creates constructive notice that an action relating to a specific property has been filed in court.
11. Novation—also a transfer of rights and/or duties under a contract.
    a. Original contract canceled.
    b. New contract negotiated and drawn, with the same parties or a new second party.
    c. Original party, if replaced, not liable.
12. Quiet-title action—court action to establish the title to a specific property, for example, where there is a cloud on the title.
13. Statute of frauds—law that requires that certain contracts be in writing and signed by all parties.
14. Statute of limitations—law that refers to the length of time within which a party may sue.
15. Sublease—a lease agreement in which the tenant transfers less than the leasehold interest in the property.
16. Waste—abuse by one holding less than a fee estate that results in permanent injury to the land or property.

17. Writ of attachment—writ filed during a lawsuit that prevents the debtor from transferring title to the property involved in the suit.
18. Statute of descent and distribution—the surviving spouse is frequently allowed to take a specific portion of estate in free, rather than life, estate.
19. Trade fixture—an item installed by a commercial tenant according to the terms of a lease and removable by the tenant before the expiration of the lease—personal property. If not removed, the trade fixture becomes real property of the building owner by accession.

K. Property ownership held in trust (broker only)
   1. An estate-planning tool allows the heirs to avoid probate.
   2. Avoiding probate allows for the assets placed in a trust to be transferred to heirs without the heirs having to deal with court costs or delays.

CHAPTER 3 QUIZ

1. The owner of a life estate in property
   1. does not pay real estate taxes.
   2. is entitled to possession of the property.
   3. may not receive income from the property.
   4. is not responsible for all repairs to the property.

2. Three individuals own a motel as tenants in common. One of the individuals decides to sell all of her assets. She may legally
   1. sell, because a tenant in common may sell her portion of assets if a majority of the co-owners also agree to sell.
   2. not sell, because a tenant in common's interests always remain encumbered.
   3. sell, because a tenant in common has an undivided interest in real property that is transferable.
   4. not sell, because there is a right of survivorship.

3. Which of the following statements is *FALSE*?
   1. Fixtures that are purchased, paid for, and installed after the execution of a mortgage are subject to liens of the mortgage.
   2. When a landowner tears down a fence, with the intention that it be permanently removed, and piles the material on the land, such material is real property.
   3. Generally, trade fixtures that were installed by the tenant are personal property.
   4. A water heater installed on the property becomes a fixture.

4. Specific liens would include all of the following *EXCEPT*
   1. mortgage liens.
   2. judgments.
   3. real estate taxes.
   4. mechanic's liens.

5. A farmer purchased land with no access to a street or public way. After an unsuccessful attempt to gain access through negotiation, he was able to gain access through an
   1. easement appurtenant.
   2. easement in gross.
   3. easement by necessity.
   4. easement by prescription.

6. A woman built a fence that extended beyond the boundary of her property onto her neighbor's property. This is an example of
   1. laches.
   2. an easement by necessity.
   3. an encroachment.
   4. an appurtenant easement.

7. A grandmother owned a life estate measured by her own life in residence. She leased the property for five years using a standard lease contract. Shortly thereafter, she died. The lease was
   1. valid only as long as she was alive.
   2. valid for five years.
   3. invalid because she, as an owner of a life estate, cannot lease property.
   4. valid for up to one year after her death.

8. An electrician did some rewiring in a home for which he has not yet been paid. One month after the work was completed, the electrician drove by the home to discover a For Sale sign on the property. The electrician should
   1. file a mechanic's lien.
   2. offer to purchase the house.
   3. obtain injunctive relief.
   4. sue the listing broker.

9. Included among the legal requirements of taking title to real property as tenants in common is that
   1. ownership interest must be equal.
   2. each co-owner may have unequal shares in the property.
   3. a co-owner cannot will his interest in a property.
   4. the last survivor owns the property in severalty.

10. A homeowner employed a contractor to build a swimming pool on his property. Upon completion of the swimming pool, the contractor filed a lien to receive payment of the contract fee. Such filing could be considered any of the following *EXCEPT*
    1. a specific lien.
    2. an encumbrance.
    3. a general lien.
    4. a mechanic's lien.

11. A family buys a 40-year-old house, and the broker tells them the garage was built 30 years ago. Because the buildings are located on a "postage-stamp–sized" lot, the family hires a surveyor who tells them the garage extends six inches onto the neighbor's lot. Because the husband has taken a real estate course, he realizes that this might be a prescriptive easement and through court proceedings could become
    1. a dominant easement.
    2. a license.
    3. a servient easement.
    4. adverse possession.

12. A man has an unrecorded claim affecting the title to another man's property. The owner has been trying to sell the property, and the man with the claim is concerned about the possibility of it selling before a judgment of some kind is obtained. To protect himself, the man with the claim should
    1. file a lis pendens, which means litigation pending.
    2. publish a notice in the newspaper.
    3. bring a quick summary proceeding.
    4. notify the owner that any attempt to sell the property will be considered fraud.

13. Garcia and Johnson own adjoining parcels of real estate. Garcia has granted Johnson an easement over his property for ingress and egress. If Johnson decided to sell his land to Davis, which of the following would be *TRUE*?
    1. The status of the dominant and servient tenements will not change.
    2. The easement will be terminated, for Johnson no longer is the owner of the property.
    3. Garcia may sell the easement to the new owner.
    4. To be valid, the deed of conveyance of Johnson to Davis must specifically mention the easement.

14. Legal seizure of property to be held for payment of money pending the outcome of a suit to enforce collection is
    1. a lis pendens.
    2. an attachment.
    3. a writ of execution.
    4. an abstract of judgment.

15. Two individuals bought a building and took title as joint tenants. One of the owners died testate. The remaining owner now owns the building
    1. as a joint tenant with rights of survivorship.
    2. in severalty.
    3. in absolute ownership under the law of descent.
    4. subject to the terms of the deceased owner's will.

16. A husband and wife own property as tenants by the entireties. The husband dies and his will names their son as inheritor of the property. Which of the following statements is *CORRECT*?
    1. The son and his mother own the property as tenants in common.
    2. The son owns the property in severalty.
    3. The son and his mother own the property as joint tenants.
    4. The son has no interest in the property.

17. Two brothers may take title to income property in unequal shares under which of the following?
    1. Severalty
    2. Tenants by the entirety
    3. Joint tenants
    4. Tenants in common

18. Legal descriptions may *NOT* be based on
    1. the government survey.
    2. metes and bounds.
    3. a street address.
    4. a survey.

19. A land description that begins at a specific point and proceeds around the boundaries of a parcel by reference to linear measurements and directions is based on
    1. metes and bounds.
    2. the rectangular survey.
    3. a subdivision plat.
    4. a survey.

20. In the government survey system
    1. base lines run east and west.
    2. principal meridians run east and west.
    3. base lines run north and south.
    4. a township contains 26 sections.

21. You and your sister own a house. Your sister would like to sell her interest in the house to your cousin. You and your sister own the house under which of the following?
    1. Tenancy by the entirety
    2. Tenancy at will
    3. Tenancy in common
    4. Estate for years

22. A plumber sells his home, in which he has installed washerless faucets. After the contract has been executed, he decides to replace the faucets with standard faucets. Which of the following is *TRUE*?
    1. The plumber may remove the faucets at any time.
    2. Standard faucets are a good replacement.
    3. The plumber can be held liable for removing the faucets, because they are fixtures that were in place before the contract was signed.
    4. This question should be decided by the broker who took the listing.

23. Which of the following forms of ownership may only be held by a wife and husband?
    1. Tenancy in common
    2. Tenancy by the entirety
    3. Tenancy at will
    4. Joint tenancy

24. Johnson sold his house; it included a water softener, which he had bought the previous year. Johnson's water softener would be classified as
    1. chattel.
    2. personalty.
    3. a trade fixture.
    4. a fixture.

25. You bought a property that measured ½ mile by ½ mile. How many acres did you purchase?
    1. 17.78 acres
    2. 36 acres
    3. 92.83 acres
    4. 160 acres

26. You are traveling directly from Section 6 to Section 36 of the same township. You are traveling
    1. northeast.
    2. southwest.
    3. northwest.
    4. southeast.

27. Charles holds a life estate in a house measured against his life. Charles' life estate is
    1. an estate of inheritance.
    2. an example of a future interest.
    3. limited in duration to the life estate owner's life.
    4. a non-freehold estate.

28. A man and woman own their house as tenants by the entirety. Which of the following statements would *NOT* correctly describe the status of their ownership?
    1. Each owner has the right of survivorship.
    2. The owners must be husband and wife.
    3. Either owner may convey a one-half interest in the house to a third party.
    4. Title may be conveyed only by a deed signed by both parties.

29. The county zoo holds title to its land with the condition that if it charges admission fees, the title will revert to the original grantor of the estate. This is an example of a
    1. fee-simple estate.
    2. defeasible fee estate.
    3. legal life estate.
    4. conventional life estate.

30. A farmer purchased a parcel of agricultural land described as the N ½ of the SW ¼ and the S ½ of the NW ¼. How many acres are in this legal description?
    1. 10 acres
    2. 80 acres
    3. 160 acres
    4. 320 acres

31. Which of the following would not generally be included in the definition of real estate?
    1. Air rights
    2. Chattels
    3. Mineral rights
    4. Water rights

32. You purchased the right to live in an apartment in a resort for the 32nd complete week of each calendar year for the next 30 years. The type of interest you have is called a(n)
    1. joint tenancy.
    2. time-share estate.
    3. tenancy in common.
    4. estate for years.

MATCHING QUIZ

The column on the right contains brief memory links to important terms in Chapter 3.

Write the letter of the matching term on the appropriate line.

A. Trade fixtures
B. Meridians
C. Township
D. Specific Lien
E. Servient Tenement
F. Appurtenance
G. Dominant Tenement
H. Prescriptive Easement
I. License
J. Escheat
K. Remainderman
L. Lis pendens
M. Tenancy in Common
N. Joint Tenancy
O. Novation
P. Valuable Consideration

1. _______ Revocable permission to use another's land
2. _______ A commercial tenant's removable fixtures
3. _______ No right of survivorship where the heirs inherit the deceased person's percentage of ownership
4. _______ New contractual substitution of obligations from one party to another
5. _______ Latin for "litigation pending"
6. _______ Ownership with the right of survivorship
7. _______ Something "in addition to," such as a right of way across someone else's property. Anything that attaches to and runs with the land
8. _______ Money or commodity used in a contract
9. _______ An easement created by open, notorious, hostile, and continuous usage
10. _______ Easement is placed on this tenement
11. _______ No heirs; therefore, the government becomes owner of the real property
12. _______ 36 sections with each section having 640 acres
13. _______ Tenement easement user
14. _______ The person to whom a life estate goes upon the death of the life tenant
15. _______ A special assessment
16. _______ Parallel vertical lines (N and S) six miles apart used in a government survey legal description

CHAPTER 3 QUIZ ANSWERS

1. **(2)** The life estate owner is responsible for paying real estate taxes and is entitled to all income and profits as well as being responsible for all repairs on the property. (26)

2. **(3)** Tenants in common have the right to sell their interest in a property without the consent of the other co-owners. (26–27)

3. **(2)** The fence material has been severed from the real estate and returned to personal property status. This is called severance. (21)

4. **(2)** Judgments are general liens; mortgage liens, real estate taxes, and mechanic's liens are specific liens. (24)

5. **(3)** An easement by necessity is acquired when the property is landlocked. An easement appurtenant requires two parcels, a dominant and a servient tenement. An easement in gross involves one parcel. Buried utility lines are examples of easements in gross found on a single parcel. (24)

6. **(3)** *Laches* refers to the inability to enforce a right because of undue delay in asserting it. Easements are rights to use the land of others. An encroachment is the unauthorized use or intrusion onto the property of another. (24–25)

7. **(1)** A life estate may be leased, but that interest is forfeited upon the death of the life tenant or the person whose life is the measurement. (26)

8. **(1)** The electrician cannot prevent the property from being sold; however, he can file a mechanic's lien to protect himself from not being paid. (23–24)

9. **(2)** The other answers are legal requirements of joint tenancy. (26–27)

10. **(3)** A mechanic's lien is a specific lien and an encumbrance. A general lien would apply to all of the homeowner's property. (23–24)

11. **(4)** A prescriptive easement is similar to adverse possession in that if one uses another's property for a statutory period of time, one may acquire a real property interest. The difference is that a prescriptive easement gives one the right to use; while through adverse possession, the courts can grant ownership of the land that has been adversely occupied. (26)

12. **(1)** The claimant cannot prevent the property owner from selling his property. A lis pendens provides public notice that a lawsuit affecting title to the property has been filed in court. (30)

13. **(1)** An appurtenant easement has been created and is considered a real property interest. Once created, the status of the dominant and the servient tenement remain the same. The easement runs with the land, and therefore, is not considered separate from the property. As a result, Davis acquires the easement. (24)

14. **(2)** Lis pendens was previously described. A writ of execution is a court order directing the county sheriff to seize and sell the property of a debtor. An abstract of judgment is a summary of judgments that have become public record. (29)

15. **(2)** The remaining owner automatically takes title to the property under the right of survivorship. The joint tenancy is effective only until one owner remains; the surviving owner then holds title in severalty. (26–27)

16. **(4)** Tenancy by the entirety is characterized by the right of survivorship. The husband has no right to transfer his interest by will. The wife will hold an interest in severalty. (27)

17. **(4)** Severalty refers to one owner, while tenancy by the entirety requires the owners to be husband and wife. Joint tenancy requires equal shares of ownership. (26–27)

18. **(3)** A street address does not tell a surveyor how large the property is or where it begins and ends and, therefore, is not acceptable as a legal description. (23)

19. **(1)** Metes and bounds is an accepted method of legal description. (22–23)

20. **(1)** Principal meridians run north and south, while a township contains 36 sections. (20)

21. **(3)** Tenants by the entirety must be husband and wife. Tenancy at will and estate for years are types of leases. (26–27)

22. **(3)** Unless otherwise agreed, the faucets are considered fixtures that would be included in the selling price. (21)

23. **(2)** Tenants in common and joint tenants do not have to be related. A tenancy at will is not a form of ownership. (27)

24. **(4)** The water softener is a fixture or real property. The other answers are personal property. (21)

25. **(4)** $\frac{1}{2} \times \frac{1}{2} = \frac{1}{4}$
640 acres × ¼ = 160 acres (22)

26. **(4)** Section 6 is in the upper-left corner, and section 36 is in the lower-right corner. (22)

27. **(3)** A life estate is a freehold estate that terminates upon the death of the owner of the life estate. (26)

28. **(3)** Tenants by the entirety may not convey their property unless they both agree and sign the deed. (27)

29. **(2)** A defeasible fee estate may be terminated upon the violation of a condition found in the deed. (25)

30. **(3)** The solution requires an understanding of the word *and*. *And* means "addition." In this problem we have two legal descriptions that need to be added together: N ½ of the SW ¼ **AND** S ½ of the NW ¼. To find the solution, multiply the denominators and divide the results into 640 (total number of acres in a section). 2 × 4 = 8; 640 divided by 8 = 80; **AND** 2 × 4 = 8; 640 divided by 8 = 80. The answer is 80 + 80 = 160. (22)

31. **(2)** Chattels are personal property, while air, mineral and water rights are real property. (21, 23)

32. **(2)** A time-share use is a right under which the developer owns the real estate; a time-share estate is a fee simple or leasehold interest in condominium ownership. (29)

TEST SCORE

PROPERTY OWNERSHIP			
Rating	**Range**	**Your Score**	
Good = 80% to 100%	26–32	Total Number	32
Fair = 70% to 79%	23–25	Total Wrong	–
Needs improvement = Lower than 70%	22 or less	Total Right	

Passing Requirement: 23 or Better

ANSWER KEY: MATCHING QUIZ

1. **I**
2. **A**
3. **M**
4. **O**
5. **L**
6. **N**
7. **F**
8. **P**
9. **H**
10. **E**
11. **J**
12. **C**
13. **G**
14. **K**
15. **D**
16. **B**

CHAPTER 4

Land-Use Controls and Regulations

OUTLINE OF CONCEPTS

I. **Government Rights in Land**

   A. Property taxes and special assessments.

      1. Taxation on real estate

         a. Taxation—power to tax real estate to meet the public needs of the government.

         b. Real estate property taxes take priority over other liens.

         c. Ad valorem tax (Latin for "according to the value")—includes taxes levied on real estate by various governmental units and municipalities.

         d. Assessment—appraisal of value for tax purposes by an assessor representing the municipality in which the property is located.

         e. Equalization factor—used in some states to correct general inequalities in statewide tax assessment.

         f. Computation of property tax rate

            (1) The taxing district adopts a budget that identifies the amount of income to be raised from real estate taxes.

            (2) To arrive at the property tax rate, divide the amount of money required for the budget by the total assessed value of all properties within the taxing district. For example, if the taxing district must raise $600,000 from real estate property taxes and the total assessed value is $10,000,000, the property tax rate would be $600,000 ÷ $10,000,000 = 0.06, or 6%.

            (3) The property tax rate may be expressed in mills. For example, 40 mills = 4% of the taxable value; 45 mills = 4.5% of the taxable value.

            (4) The property tax bill for a property is calculated by applying the property tax rate to the taxable value of the property; for example, a home assessed for tax purposes at

$200,000 and using a tax district rate of 45 mills, or 4.5% of the taxable value, would be required (annually) to pay $9,000. Divided by 12, the monthly tax obligation would be $750.

(5) Special assessments—special taxes levied on real estate; require property owners to pay for improvements that specifically benefit their real estate (installation of curb and gutter, streets, water system, sewers, etc.) are second in priority after property tax liens.

B. Eminent Domain, Condemnation, Escheat
   1. Eminent domain—power of the government to acquire private property for public use while providing just compensation (condemnation) for the property owner.
   2. Condemnation—a judicial or administrative proceeding or process to exercise the power of eminent domain.
   3. Escheat—state laws that provide for ownership of real estate to revert to the state when the owner dies intestate and leaves no heirs or when the property is abandoned.

C. Police power—power of the state to promulgate laws aimed at promoting the general welfare and protecting public health and safety; examples of the use of police power include zoning, building codes, environmental protection; enabling acts are created by states to grant zoning power to municipal governments.

II. Public controls based on police power

A. Zoning and master plans.
   1. Zoning—zoning laws are local laws that regulate and control the use of land in the community, generally pertaining to the height, bulk, and use of the buildings.
      a. Nonconforming use—use in existence prior to the passage of a zoning ordinance and allowed to continue even though it does not conform.
         (1) If property that exists as nonconforming is destroyed, it cannot be rebuilt without the approval of the zoning authority.
      b. Variance—approval by a zoning authority that allows an individual to deviate from the zoning requirement.
      c. Conditional use permit—allows for a use that does not conform with existing zoning but is necessary for the common good, such as locating a medical clinic in a primarily residential neighborhood.
      d. Downzoning—land zoned for residential or commercial use is rezoned for conservation only; it also applies to changes from dense to less-dense usage. The state generally is not responsible for compensating property owners for any loss of value unless the court finds that a "taking" of value has occurred, such as land being rezoned from residential to conservancy.
      e. Buffer zone—a land area that separates one land use from another; a park that separates a residential neighborhood from a shopping center.

f. Spot zoning—reclassification of a small area of land for use that does not conform to the zoning of the rest of the area.
g. Planned unit development (PUD)—planned mix of diverse land uses, such as housing and recreation in one comprehensive plan.
h. Density zoning—ordinances that restrict the average maximum number of houses per acre that may be built within a particular area. As communities expand, urban sprawl becomes a concern, because extensive community growth often leads to issues involving traffic congestion, overcrowding of schools, and loss of open space.

2. Master plans—city plan specifications used to guide the physical development of a community.

B. Building codes—ordinances that specify standards for construction, maintenance, and demolition to protect the public health and safety of communities.

C. Environmental Impact Reports
1. A study of the impact that a proposed development would have on the environment.
2. The report is required by many states to be submitted to a state or local governmental unit prior to a proposed public or private project being approved.
3. The report will typically deal with the determination of whether there is any possible liability for current or future environmental contaminants and can include up to three phases.
a. Phase 1—environmental site assessment, which is aimed at providing an overview of the potential for current or future contamination.
(1) Typically includes an analysis of past and present users as well as a physical inspection of the property.
(2) The existence of a gas station or land fill in the immediate area could result in the need for a Phase 2 analysis.
b. Phase 2—involves an actual site analysis to identify evidence that the site is contaminated, such as drilling.
c. Phase 3—development of a plan to explain how the land can be remediated or safely used.

III. Regulation of Special Land Types

A. Flood zones
1. Any land area susceptible to being inundated by flood waters from any source.
2. Floodplain zoning is a procedure used to identify areas of varying flood hazard.
3. Mortgages insured by the federal government, such as FHA, require either certification that the property covered is not in a flood zone, or that a flood insurance policy is covering the property.
4. The National Flood Insurance Program created by Congress provides protection for millions of families.
5. Homeowners insurance generally doesn't cover floods.
6. Flood insurance backed by the federal government may be obtained from insurance agents.

B. Wetlands
   1. Overview
      a. Every wetland is different since wetlands perform unique functions.
      b. Wetland functional values are determined by parameters such as biological, physical, and chemical components.
      c. Wetlands can provide a place for water storage and assist in flood prevention, as well as protection of water quality.
      d. Wetlands can also provide a habitat for wildlife.
      e. Wetlands also provide recreational opportunities for bird watching, hunting, fishing, and boating.
      f. Regulation of wetlands are among the top obstacles for creating economic development in the country.

C. Coastal Regulation
   1. The Coastal Zone Management Act (CZMA) created a voluntary coastal zone enhancement program for states to implement program changes in one or more of the nine areas of coastal zone enhancement.
   2. Funds for the enhancement programs come from Section 309 of CZMA and are aimed at preventing, or significantly reducing, threats to life and property by eliminating development and redevelopment in high hazard areas and managing development in other hazardous areas.
   3. Coastal hazards include flooding, earthquakes, and shoreline erosion.
   4. Programs deal with areas such as wetlands, coastal hazards, and public access.

IV. Regulation of environmental hazards

A. Abatement, mitigation and cleanup requirements
   1. Two federal laws require disclosure; as well as abatement, mitigation and cleanup requirements for environmental hazards where applicable.
      a. The Comprehensive Environmental Response Compensation and Liability Act (CERCLA) was created in 1980.
         (1) Established fund of $9 billion called Superfund to clean up uncontrolled hazardous waste dumps and respond to spills.
         (2) Created a process for identifying liable parties and ordering them to take responsibility for cleanup.
         (3) Liability under Superfund consideration to be strict, joint and several, and retroactive.
            a. Strict liability—owner is responsible to the injured party without excuse.
            b. Joint and several liability—each individual owner personally responsible for the damages in whole; if only one owner is financially able to handle the total damage, that owner will have to pay all of it and attempt to collect the proportionate share of the rest from the owners.

c. Leaking Underground Storage Tanks (LUST) regulations—established in 1984
    (i) Governs the installation, maintenance, monitoring, and failure of underground storage tanks.
    (ii) Aimed at protecting groundwater in the United States through release prevention, detection and correction.

d. Superfund Amendments and Reauthorization Act (SARA)—created in 1986
    (i) Established stronger cleanup standards for contaminated sites
    (ii) Substantially increased the funding of the Superfund
    (iii) Attempted to clarify the obligation of the lenders
    (iv) Created the concept called innocent landowner immunity

e. In 2001-2002, The Brownfields Revitalization and Environmental Restoration Act, and subsequent Small Business Liability Relief and Brownfields Revitalization Act, were enacted to further reduce the risk of innocent landowners who purchased once environmentally contaminated real estate. This legislation helped to rejuvenate many deserted, defunct, and derelict toxic industrial sites by diminishing the innocent landowner's liability exposure and providing them with the opportunity to expense cleanup costs rather than capitalize them.

B. Federal regulations on lead-based paint disclosure

1. Lead poisoning—lead is a mineral that has been used extensively because of its pliability, its ability to impede water flow, and its rust resistance.
    a. Becomes a health hazard when ingested.
    b. Sources of lead poisoning
        (1) Peeling or flaking paint
        (2) Water supply systems
2. Owners of residential properties built before 1978, when the use of lead-based paint was banned, will have to disclose to buyers or renters the presence of known lead-based paint hazards, if known to owner (seller) or landlord.
3. A lead-based paint disclosure statement must be attached as a separate item to all real estate sales and lease contracts on pre-1978 residential properties.
4. Sellers must distribute to buyers and renters a federal lead hazard pamphlet but are not responsible for ensuring that people read and understand the brochure.
5. Buyers will have up to 10 days to have a lead-risk assessment performed on the property, if they want one.
6. Exemptions from the regulations are provided for housing for the elderly and disabled, provided children are not regularly present; for vacation homes and short-term rentals; for foreclosure sales; and for single-room rentals within dwellings.

7. Children under six years of age are most vulnerable to exposure to lead-based paint.

C. Restrictions on sale or development of contaminated property
   1. Pollution and environmental risks in real estate transactions
      a. Increasing public awareness of, and concern about, pollution problems and their health and economic effects, which have had significant consequences on real estate sales and values.
      b. The actual dollar value of real property can be affected significantly by both real and perceived pollution.
      c. The cost of cleaning up and removing pollution may be much greater than the dollar value of the property before pollution occurred.
      d. In some areas of the United States, mortgage and title insurance approval may depend on the inspection of the property for hazardous substances and proof of their absence.
   2. Role of real estate licensees regarding environmental risks in real estate transactions
      a. Be alert to the possibility of pollution and hazardous substances on the property being sold.
      b. Ask clients about the possibility of hazardous substances associated with the property.
      c. Expect increasing numbers of questions from customers concerned about pollution.
      d. Consider the consequences of the potential liability in real estate transactions where hazardous substances may be involved.
      e. Contact government agencies and private consulting firms for information, guidance, and detailed study; real estate licensees often, however, do not have the technical expertise required to determine whether hazardous material is present on or near the property.
      f. Be scrupulous in considering environmental issues and exercise a high degree of care in all real estate transactions.

D. Types of hazards and potential for brokerage firm or seller liability.
   1. Hazardous substances of concern to real estate professionals
      a. Radon gas—an odorless radioactive gas produced by the decay of radioactive materials in rocks under the earth's surface.
         (1) Radon is released from the rocks and finds its way to the surface; usually it is released into the atmosphere. Radon comes into a house through holes in the foundation or basement or crawl space.
         (2) Long-term exposure is believed to cause lung cancer.
         (3) The U.S. Environmental Protection Agency (EPA) has established radon levels that are thought to be unsafe.
         (4) Testing techniques have been developed that allow homeowners to determine the exact quantity of radon in their homes.
         (5) If a home is determined to have radon gas, the seller may, if the contract requires, be obligated to mitigate the hazard, whether the danger is actual or only perceived.

(6) Most homes with elevated levels of radon can be fixed for between $500 and $2,500, with an average cost of about $1,200.

b. Asbestos—material used for many years as insulation on plumbing pipes and heat ducts and as general insulation because it is a poor heat conductor; also was used in floor tile and roofing material.
   (1) Relatively harmless if not disturbed; can become life-threatening during its removal because of accompanying dust.
   (2) Exposure to asbestos dust may exist if
      a. The asbestos ages and starts to disintegrate. This disintegration is referred to as being friable.
   (3) Remodeling projects include the encapsulating or abating asbestos shingles, roof tile, or insulation that can cause the dust to form in the air and expose people in the area to the health hazard.

c. Urea-formaldehyde foam insulation (UFFI)—a synthetic material generally used to insulate buildings prior to 1978. It was banned because of its toxic out-gassing. The toxicity known as volatile organic compounds (VOC) escaped into a dwelling for several years after its application. Today, insulators use a nontoxic spray to insulate buildings.
   (1) UFFI was typically pumped between walls as a foam that later hardens and acts as an insulating material.
   (2) UFFI became dangerous because of gases released from the material after installation.

d. PCBs (polychlorinated biphenyls)—used in the manufacture of electrical products, such as voltage regulators, as well as in paints and caulking materials
   (1) PCBs haven't been used since 1977; however, they still are dangerous, because many of the products containing them are still in operation.
   (2) An environmental consultant can assess the property and recommend procedures for cleanup.

e. Waste-disposal sites—landfill operations
   (1) Landfill—a specific site that has been excavated and should be lined with either a clay or a synthetic liner to prevent leakage of waste material into the local water system.
   (2) Construction and maintenance of a landfill operation is heavily regulated by state and federal authorities.
   (3) Landfills at improper locations and improperly managed sites have been sources of major problems; for example, landfills constructed in the wrong type of soil will leak waste into nearby wells, causing major damage.
   (4) Real estate licensees must be aware of such facilities within their areas and take appropriate steps when working with potential clients.

f. Underground storage tanks—used in residential and commercial settings for many years.
   (1) In the United States there are an estimated 3 million to 5 million underground storage tanks that hold hazardous substances, such as gasoline.
   (2) Risk occurs when the containers become old, rust, and start to leak.
   (3) Toxic material may enter the groundwater, contaminate wells, and pollute the soil.
   (4) Sources of pollution
      a. Older gas stations with steel tanks that develop leaks through oxidation (rusting).
      b. Underground containers used to hold fuel oil for older homes
   (5) Recent federal legislation calls for removal of such tanks and all the polluted soil around them.

g. Groundwater contamination
   (1) Groundwater includes runoff at ground level as well as underground water systems that are sources of wells for both private and public facilities.
   (2) Sources of contamination
      a. Waste-disposal sites
      b. Underground storage tanks
      c. Pesticides and herbicides typically used in farming communities
   (3) The major protection for the general public against water contamination is government regulation.
   (4) Once contamination is identified, its source can be eliminated; the process often is time-consuming and may be very expensive.

h. Electromagnetic fields (EMFs)—generated by movement of electrical currents.
   (1) High-tension power lines reflect a major concern with EMFs.
   (2) The potential for EMFs being a health hazard is a source of controversy; however, they are suspected of causing cancer and related health problems.
   (3) Real estate licensees should be aware of continuing research on EMFs.

i. Mold—an organism that may cause allergic reactions. Annual maintenance checks (around toilets, showers, and sinks) help to detect mold in its early stages. Dehumidifiers, proper ventilation, perimeter drainage, and sump pumps help avoid mold by removing water from the property. Most homeowners' insurance companies set dollar limits for mold claims or make mold problems an exclusion to the homeowner's policy.
   (1) Common varieties of mold can cause allergic reactions, as well as asthma episodes, infections, and other respiratory problems, but they do not emit toxins.
   (2) Very little is known about toxic molds like Stachybotrys chartarum, often referred to as "black mold." In suffi-

cient amounts, this mold can be dangerous and has been associated with severe health problems and substantial contamination of buildings.

(3) Disclosure of mold contamination is not currently required by the federal government.

(4) The EPA has established guidelines to remediate mold problems for schools and commercial buildings.

j. Agencies administering federal environmental laws

(1) Environmental Protection Agency (EPA)

a. Toxic Substance Control Act

b. Resources Conservation and Recovery Act

c. Federal Clean Water Act

(2) U.S. Department of Transportation—administers the Hazardous Materials Transportation Act.

(3) The Occupational Safety and Health Administration (OSHA) and the U.S. Department of Labor—administer standards for all employees working in the manufacturing sector.

(4) Federal government encourages state and local governments to prepare legislation in their areas.

k. Pollution and environmental risks in real estate transactions

(1) Increasing public awareness of, and concern about, pollution problems and their health and economic effects, have had significant consequences on real estate sales and values.

(2) The actual dollar value of real property can be affected significantly by both real and perceived pollution.

(3) The cost of cleaning up and removing pollution may be much greater than the dollar value of the property before pollution occurred.

(4) In some areas of the United States, mortgage and title insurance approval may depend on the inspection of the property for hazardous substances and proof of their absence.

l. Agents' Responsibilities

(1) Most state laws do not hold the real estate professional to a standard of discovery. This is why most states have passed a seller's property disclosure act. With this new legislation, the burden to disclose both known and latent (hidden) property defects (to the buyer) is shifted to the seller. However, if a broker or salesperson knows or has been made aware of the material defect, they must obviously disclose what they know. A buyer's representative is held to the same standard. Discovery, no. Disclosure, yes.

V. Private Controls

A. Deed restrictions

1. Deed restrictions can restrict the way in which a property can be used.

2. Deed restrictions generally include conditions, such as the owners of units in a condominium are not allowed to own dogs over a certain weight.
3. Deed restrictions could require a minimum square foot requirement for homes built in a subdivision.

B. Covenants, Conditions and Restrictions (CC&Rs)
1. Rules and limitations placed on housing development, such as planned unit developments or condominium projects
2. CC&Rs can impose various types of restrictions depending on the agreement of the people composing them.
3. CC&Rs can require that houses be painted a certain color, or that trailers not be parked in the driveway overnight.

C. Homeowners Association (HOA) Regulations
1. Regulations and rules established by a HOA to protect the common interest of the residents in a condominium.
2. Rules generally relate to the use and the operation of the property and are enforced by the association.

CHAPTER 4 QUIZ

1. When the county board acquires land for a freeway, it is exercising the power of
   1. zoning.
   2. environmental protection laws.
   3. escheat.
   4. eminent domain.

2. One example of the use of police power by a city is
   1. taxation.
   2. eminent domain.
   3. laches.
   4. environmental protection laws.

3. A building housing an insurance agency existed before the property was rezoned residential. The insurance agency building has now been grandfathered in. This is an example of
   1. a variance.
   2. a nonconforming use.
   3. spot zoning.
   4. a planned unit development.

4. Radon generally enters a house through the
   1. roof.
   2. basement floor.
   3. chimney.
   4. windows.

5. A mineral used for many years as insulation on heat ducts is
   1. asbestos.
   2. lead.
   3. urea-formaldehyde foam.
   4. radon.

6. Which of the following was an insulating material pumped between the walls of a house and banned from use in the 1970s?
   1. Asbestos
   2. Radon
   3. Urea-formaldehyde foam
   4. Lead

7. All of the following may be sources of groundwater contamination *EXCEPT*
   1. underground storage tanks.
   2. waste-disposal sites.
   3. pesticides used on farms.
   4. cement.

8. All of the following requirements generally are covered by building codes *EXCEPT*
   1. fire-prevention standards.
   2. electrical wiring.
   3. sanitary equipment.
   4. minimum number of square feet of land area per apartment unit.

9. Strict liability means that
   1. an owner is responsible to an injured party without excuse.
   2. each owner is personally responsible for damages as a whole.
   3. liability extends to people who have owned the site in the past.
   4. an owner is not responsible to an injured party.

10. Which of the following terms refers to a dangerous health hazard that can occur when asbestos ages and starts to disintegrate and become airborne?
    1. Radon
    2. Friable
    3. Bacteria
    4. Oxidation

11. Which of the following *BEST* describes a buffer zone?
    1. An industrial park located between a shopping center and a residential neighborhood
    2. A highrise apartment complex located between a commercial development and a townhouse subdivision
    3. A recreational area located between a residential area and an office park
    4. A sound barrier located alongside a major highway

12. Police-power controls include all of the following *EXCEPT*
    1. city plan specifications.
    2. building codes.
    3. zoning.
    4. deed restrictions.

13. A tire company has a manufacturing plant located in an area that recently has been zoned residential. The company is allowed to operate under the new zoning ordinance. However, if the plant is completely destroyed by fire, the company may
    1. appeal for an exculpatory provision.
    2. not construct another tire plant in the neighborhood without being granted a zoning variance.
    3. not construct another tire plant in the neighborhood under any conditions.
    4. reconstruct the tire company in the same neighborhood.

14. Which of the following provides for monetary compensation to an owner in the event that the owner's property is taken to build a new freeway?
    1. Taxation
    2. Condemnation
    3. Escheat
    4. Police power

15. A property is assessed at $300,000, the taxing body uses a 52% assessment ratio (rollback percentage), and 40 mills is the tax rate. What is the monthly property tax?
    1. $520
    2. $1,200
    3. $1,560
    4. $6,240

16. A buyer made an offer on a building subject to an inspection. During the due diligence period, disintegrating airborne asbestos fibers were discovered. This condition is called
    1. encapsulating.
    2. friable.
    3. disintegrating.
    4. radon.

17. A potential homeowner should have a certified inspector check around toilets, showers, sinks, and basement walls to detect what kind of problem?
    1. Radon
    2. Carpenter ants
    3. Methane gas
    4. Mold

18. Which statement correctly describes mold as an environmental concern?
    1. Common varieties of mold emit toxins.
    2. Disclosure of mold contamination is required by the federal government.
    3. Stachybotrys chartarum in sufficient amounts has been associated with severe health problems.
    4. The Environmental Protection Agency (EPA) has not established guidelines for schools and commercial buildings to remediate mold problems.

19. Which of the following statements does *NOT* reflect the wetlands in the United States?
    1. Wetland functional values are determined by parameters such as chemical components.
    2. Wetlands can provide a place for water storage.
    3. Regulation of wetlands are among the top obstacles for creating economic development in the country.
    4. All wetlands perform similar functions.

MATCHING QUIZ

The column on the right contains brief memory links to important terms in Chapter 4.

Write the letter of the matching term on the appropriate line.

A. Eminent domain
B. Condemnation
C. Nonconforming use
D. Variance
E. Flood Plain
F. Ad valorem
G. Building code
H. Radon
I. Friable
J. Lead
K. Deed restrictions or Restrictive covenants
L. EPA
M. CERCLA
N. Wetlands

1. _______ Land areas used for conservation
2. _______ Law that determines the height and length requirements for stairs
3. _______ The only commercial building in a residential neighborhood said to have been "grandfathered in"
4. _______ "According to value"
5. _______ Method by which government takes and pays for private property
6. _______ Restrictions requiring all neighborhood homes be painted earth tones
7. _______ Oversees federal environmental issues
8. _______ Odorless radioactive gas
9. _______ Permission from the city government to build closer to a lot line than normally allowed by zoning
10. _______ Land susceptible to being inundated by water
11. _______ Right of the government to take private property for public use or benefit
12. _______ The characteristic name for disintegrating asbestos
13. _______ Known as the "Superfund"
14. _______ In the bloodstream, this can cause mental retardation

CHAPTER 4 QUIZ ANSWERS

1. **(4)** Eminent domain is the right of the government to take private land for public use or public benefit. The property owner has a right of appeal and must be paid just compensation. Zoning and environmental protection laws do not provide monetary compensation in the event that a property owner suffers a loss in value. Escheat is a law that provides for title to real estate to pass to the state when an owner dies intestate and leaves no heirs or abandons the property. (42)

2. **(4)** Taxation and eminent domain are not exercised under the police power. Laches refers to the equitable doctrine that bars a legal claim because of undue delay in asserting the claim. (42)

3. **(2)** A nonconforming use property is one that existed before the zoning classification changed. It was there first, hence the name *grandfather clause.* A variance allows one to deviate from the zoning ordinance. Spot zoning allows for reclassification of land for nonconforming use. A planned unit development (PUD) creates a special zoning district for a developer. (42)

4. **(2)** Radon also may enter the house through the basement walls, crawlspace, or uncovered sump pit areas. (46)

5. **(1)** Lead was used in paint and plumbing systems. UFFI was used to insulate buildings. Radon was previously discussed. (47)

6. **(3)** Asbestos was used as insulation on heating pipes and ducts, as well as in floor tile and roofing material. Radon is an odorless radioactive gas that generally enters through the basement of a house. Lead was used in water pipes and paint. (47)

7. **(4)** Leaking underground storage tanks are a major source of groundwater contamination. Pesticide use and waste disposal also may contaminate groundwater. (48)

8. **(4)** The minimum number of square feet of land area per apartment unit would be regulated by the local zoning ordinance. (42)

9. **(1)** For example, an individual who knowingly buys contaminated land also can be liable for damages even though she had no involvement in the events leading up to the contamination. (44)

10. **(2)** Friable is the term that describes the dangerous condition that exists when asbestos begins to deteriorate and becomes airborne. Radon is a radioactive by-product of radium. Various forms of bacteria are found in water. Oxidation is another name for rust. (47)

11. **(3)** A buffer zone is a land area that separates one land use from another, such as residential from commercial, as when a recreational area is located between a residential area and an office park. (42)

12. **(4)** Police-power controls are public land-use controls. Deed restrictions are private land-use controls. (42, 49)

13. **(2)** If a nonconforming use is destroyed, as in the case of the tire manufacturing plant, it cannot be rebuilt without the approval of the zoning authority. (42)

14. **(2)** Eminent domain is the right or the authority of the government to acquire private property for public use or public benefit. Condemnation is the process for actually acquiring the property. Escheat is a state law that provides that, if a decedent dies intestate and has no heirs, the decedent's property reverts to the state. Taxation is a process by which the government raises funds necessary for it to operate. The police power is the right of the government to protect the public welfare through such measures as zoning and building codes. (42)

15. **(1)** $300,000 × 52% = 156,000 × 4% = $6,240. $6,240 divided by 12 = $520 monthly tax (41–42)

16. **(2)** Friable describes deteriorating asbestos. Encapsulation remedies the problem by painting over the non-friable asbestos with a heavy latex paint. (47)

17. **(4)** Mold is the end result of a moisture problem. Once mold dries, it can become airborne, and then it poses a health threat to those allergic to the mold spores. (48)

18. **(3)** *Stachybotrys chartarum*, or black mold, in sufficient amounts has been associated with substantial contamination of buildings. (48–49)

19. **(4)** Every wetland is unique because wetlands perform different functions. (44)

TEST SCORE

LAND-USE CONTROLS AND REGULATIONS			
Rating	**Range**	**Your Score**	
Good = 80% to 100%	16–19	Total Number	19
Fair = 70% to 79%	14–15	Total Wrong	–
Needs improvement = Lower than 70%	13 or less	Total Right	

Passing Requirement: 13 or Better

ANSWER KEY: MATCHING QUIZ

1. **N**
2. **G**
3. **C**
4. **F**
5. **B**
6. **K**
7. **L**
8. **H**
9. **D**
10. **E**
11. **A**
12. **I**
13. **M**
14. **J**

Valuation and Market Analysis

OUTLINE OF CONCEPTS

I. Financial Institutions Reform, Recovery, and Enforcement Act (FIRREA) and the Appraisal Industry

A. The collapse of many savings and loan associations as a result of the surge into unsound investments was at least partly the consequence of questionable property appraisals.

B. Congress introduced appraisal regulation by passing FIRREA in 1989.

C. Appraisals are required for all federally related transactions (any transaction with a value greater than $250,000), must comply with state and federal standards, and must be performed by a state-licensed appraiser.

D. State appraiser licensing requirements and appraisal standards must meet minimum levels set by the Appraisal Standards Board and Appraisal Qualifications Board of the Appraisal Foundation, which is a national group of representatives of major appraisal and related organizations.

II. Appraisal and Value

A. Appraisal—an opinion of value; a detailed estimate of a property's value by a professional appraiser.

B. Purpose and use of appraisals for valuation

1. An appraisal is needed to estimate the market value of a residential property, such as a house, or a commercial property, such as an office building; the appraisal provides information for potential buyers or sellers to make a decision.
2. Mortgage lenders such as banks require appraisals to determine the values of the real estate that will serve as collateral for a mortgage loan.

C. Competitive market analysis (CMA)—used by the broker or the salesperson to help the seller determine a listing price for the property; basically, a comparison of prices of recently sold and currently-for-sale properties that are similar in location, style, and amenities to the property of the listing seller. CMA will generally estimate market value as likely to fall within a range of figures. CMAs also can guide a purchaser in formulating an offer. Similar to a CMA is a broker price opinion, which may be more detailed. However, many states require a statement added to a CMA or BPO that the document is not an appraisal.

III. Situations Requiring Appraisal by a Certified Appraiser

A. All transactions of $1,000,000 or more

B. Non-residential and residential (other than one- to four-family) transactions of $250,000 or more

C. Complex residential transactions of $250,000 or more

1. A regulated institution may presume that appraisals of one- to four-family residential properties are not complex, unless the institution has readily available information that a given appraisal will be complex.
2. The regulated institution is responsible for making the final determination of whether the appraisal is complex.
3. An example of a complex appraisal would be an appraisal of a commercial property in the center of a residential neighborhood.

IV. Value

A. Market value and market price

1. Market value
   - a. Most probable price a property will bring in a competitive market, allowing for reasonable time to find a knowledgeable purchaser.
     - (1) The buyer and seller are not under pressure to act.
     - (2) Payment is made in cash or equivalent.
   - b. Typical goal of an appraiser, although a property may have different values at the same time
   - c. Estimated price (compare to market price, which is the actual selling price)

B. Value—defined as the present worth of future benefits arising from the ownership of real property.

1. Types and characteristics of value
   - a. Types of value
     - (1) There are various types of value including
       - a. Assessed value—a locally determined percentage of market value, which is used by a municipality to establish a property tax.
       - b. Insurable value—replacement cost of a building minus the land value
       - c. Book value—value of an asset less depreciation
       - d. Salvage value—estimated value of an asset at the end of its economic life
     - (2) Characteristics necessary for a property to have value in the real estate market include "DUST":
       - a. Demand—need supported by purchasing power
       - b. Utility—capacity to satisfy human wants and needs
       - c. Scarcity—finite supply
       - d. Transferability—transfer of ownership rights with relative ease

b. Principles of value
   (1) Highest and best use—most profitable use to which a property may be adapted and given legal constraints.
   (2) Substitution—the value of a property tends to be set by the cost of purchasing an equally desirable and similar property.
   (3) Supply and demand—the price of a property increases if the supply decreases, and decreases if the supply increases.
   (4) Conformity—maximum value is realized if the land use conforms to existing neighborhood standards.
   (5) Increasing and decreasing return—improvements to land and structures produce a proportionate increase in value until some point beyond which the impact of improvements begins to decrease.
   (6) Competition—high levels of profits attract competitors into an industry; increase in competition results in decreased profits throughout the industry.
   (7) Change—no economic or physical condition remains constant.
   (8) Contribution—the value of any component of property consists of what its addition contributes to the value of the whole property.
   (9) Anticipation—value can increase or decrease in anticipation of some future benefit or detriment that will affect the property.
   (10) Balance is achieved when adding improvements and structures that will increase the property value.
   (11) Regression—the principle between dissimilar properties: the worth of the better property is affected adversely by the presence of the lesser-quality property.
   (12) Progression—the worth of a lesser property tends to increase if it is located among better properties.

2. Market Cycles and Other Factors Affecting Property Value
   a. Market cycles reflect overall condition of the economy.
   b. Economic—Stable employment and salaries enhance demand for housing and commercial real estate, resulting in an increase in the value of real estate.
   c. Physical and environmental—physical conditions, such as building over known earthquake fault lines or over land containing hazardous substances, can result in substantial declines in property values. Environmental conditions, such as climate, can affect property values.
   d. Social—an aging population can increase the development of housing aimed at satisfying the needs of seniors.
   e. Government and legal—zoning, as well as other land use controls, can impact the cost as well as the availability of housing alternatives.

C. Methods of Estimating Value/Appraisal Process
  1. Market data approach (sales comparison or direct sales).

CONTRIBUTORY VALUE			
Square Footage	$25 per square foot	**Full and ¾ Baths**	$3,500
Brick	4% more than frame construction	**½ Bath**	$1,500

	SUBJECT BETTER: ADD	COMPARABLE BETTER: SUBTRACT	SBA AND CBS
Subject Property	**Comparable # 1 $200,000 (SOLD)**	**Comparable #2 $212,000 (SOLD)**	**Comparable #3 $205,000 (SOLD)**
1,500 Sq. Ft. Ranch	1,300 Sq. Ft.	1,600 Sq. Ft.	1,600 Sq. Ft.
Frame Construction	Frame Construction	Brick	Frame
1¾ Bathrooms	1 Bath	1¾ plus ½ Baths	1½ Baths
Adjust for Sq. Footage	200 × 25 = $5,000 **add**	100 × 25 = $2,500 **subtract**	100 × 25 = $2,500 **subtract**
Adjust for Brick	No Adjustment	$210,000 × 4% = 8,400 **subtract**	No Adjustment
Adjust for Bathrooms	$3,500 **add**	½ Bath = $1,500 **subtract**	½ Bath = $1,500 **add**
Adjusted Value	$208,500	$199,600	$204,000

a. A value estimate is obtained by comparing the subject property with recent sales of comparable properties through adjustment of sales prices of comparables. Comparable properties used in an analysis should be "arm's length" or a normal market transaction involving willing buyers and willing sellers, as opposed to a foreclosure sale, an auction, or a sale to a relative.
b. Four areas of adjustment
   (1) Date of sale
   (2) Location
   (3) Physical characteristics
   (4) Terms of sale

c. The adjustment process involves three basic steps:
   (1) Adjust the price of the comparable for any difference between the comparable and the subject property (the property being appraised). With your dollar adjustments remember to always mirror your subject property.
   (2) C.B.S—*Comparable better subtract* from the comparable the difference between the comparable and the subject property.
   (3) S.B.A—*Subject better add* to the comparable the difference between the comparable and the subject property.

d. Considered the most reliable of the three approaches in appraising residential property.

2. Replacement cost or summation approach
   a. Based on the principle of substitution
   b. Steps of cost approach
      (1) Estimate the land value.
      (2) Estimate the replacement or reproduction cost of the improvements.
      (3) Estimate the depreciation.
      (4) Deduct the depreciation from the replacement cost.
      (5) Add the land value to the depreciated cost of improvements—do not depreciate land.
   c. Depreciation—generally applies to a wasting asset, such as a building
      (1) Physical deterioration (wear, tear, poor maintenance)—may be curable or incurable.
      (2) Functional obsolescence—may be curable or incurable (outdated items, poor design).
      (3) External obsolescence (economic, environmental, or locational)—loss of value due to factors outside the property; is always incurable.
      (4) Most reliable approach for special-purpose buildings, such as churches and schools.

3. Income approach
   a. Based on the present value of the rights to future income
   b. Steps in the income approach
      (1) Estimate the annual potential gross income.
      (2) Deduct the vacancy and rent loss to arrive at the effective gross income.
      (3) Deduct the annual operating expenses to arrive at the annual net operating income.
      (4) Estimate the capitalization rate.
      (5) Apply the capitalization rate to the annual net income.
   c. Formula for capitalization rate: net income ÷ capitalization rate = value.
   d. As risk increases, the rate of return increases and the value decreases; and as the risk decreases, the rate of return decreases and the value increases.

e. Gross rent multiplier (GRM)
   (1) Used as a substitute for the income approach in appraising a single-family home.
   (2) Formula for GRM: sales price ÷ monthly rental income = GRM.
   (3) Monthly rental income × GRM = estimated market value.
f. Gross income multiplier (GIM)
   (1) Used as quick way to appraise commercial and industrial properties.
   (2) Formula for GIM: sales price ÷ annual rental income = GIM
g. Most reliable approach for income-producing property.

4. Steps in the Appraisal Process
   a. State the problem.
   b. List the types of data deeded and the sources.
   c. Gather, record, and verify the general data.
   d. Gather, record, and verify the specific data.
   e. Gather, record, and verify the data for the valuation approach needed.
   f. Analyze and interpret the data.
   g. Reconcile the data for the final value estimate.
   h. Prepare the appraisal report.
5. Neighborhood Analysis
   a. Neighborhood—homogeneous grouping of individuals or businesses within, or as part of, a larger community.
   b. Residential neighborhoods general pass through four stages: growth, stability, decline, and revitalization.
   c. Factors to consider in analysis
      (1) Physical—street pattern, relation to the rest of the community
      (2) Economic—rent levels, new construction
      (3) Social—population density, frequency of crime
      (4) Governmental—zoning, special assessments
6. Basic appraisal terminology (e.g., replacement versus reproduction cost, reconciliation, depreciation, kinds of obsolescence).
   a. Replacement versus reproduction cost
      (1) Replacement cost—construction cost at current prices of property that would not necessarily be an exact duplicate of the subject property but would serve the same purpose or function as the original.
      (2) Reproduction cost—construction cost at current prices of an exact duplicate of the subject property.
   b. Reconciliation—final step in the appraisal process, in which the appraiser reconciles the estimates of value received from the different approaches to arrive at a final estimate of the market value for the property being appraised. The most relevant approach receives the greatest weight in determining the opinion of value.
   c. Depreciation—a loss of value in property due to all causes, including physical deterioration, functional obsolescence, and economic obsolescence.

d. Kinds of obsolescence
   (1) Physical deterioration—gradual wearing out of a building.
   (2) Functional obsolescence—a loss in value due to a deficiency in the floor plan or design of a property, such as a two-story house with four bedrooms upstairs and just one bathroom located on the first floor.
   (3) External obsolescence—a loss in value due to changes outside the property, such as a recession reducing the demand for the property's neighborhood.

D. Competitive/Comparative Market Analysis (CMA)
  1. Selecting and adjusting comparables
     a. A CMA analysis is based on:
        (1) Properties that were recently sold
        (2) Properties competitive with the subject property that are currently on the market
        (3) Expired or withdrawn listings that did not sell
        (4) A CMA generally groups comparables to indicate a range of values, which serve as the basis for a seller choosing a list price or a buyer choosing an offering price.
     b. An appraisal generally analyzes only properties that are actually sold and then adjusts from the comparables to the subject property (the property being appraised) to arrive at an estimate of the value of the property.
  2. Contrast CMA and Appraisal
     a. Price per square foot
        (1) Price per square foot is used in both a CMA and an appraisal.
        (2) An appraiser will compare square feet of comparable properties to the square footage of the subject as one part of the sales comparison approach to value. The appraiser will then adjust the value of the appraised property up or down, if necessary, based on differences between the subject property and comparable properties and will then use the sales comparison approach to arrive at an opinion of value.
        (3) A real estate professional will provide a list of comparables using price per square foot but will not provide a specific opinion of value; the professional will provide the price per square foot in the form of a range of values for selected comparables and then negotiate a list price with the seller.
     b. Gross rent (GRM) and gross income multipliers (GIM)
        (1) Both a GRM and GIM can be used in a CMA or an appraisal.
        (2) A GRM is seldom used by real estate agents in a CMA since the majority of homes are not rented. An appraiser uses a GRM as a substitute for the income approach in estimating the value of a single family home that is being rented.
        (3) The GRM or GIM could be used in both a CMA and an appraisal if comparable rents were available for a four

unit or for five units or more, which would be considered commercial.

c. Capitalization rate
   (1) Appraisers use the capitalization rate to estimate the value of an income-producing property; real estate agents also can use cap rates but seldom do since the CMA is generally used to provide a range of value for single family homes.

E. Other Important Terms
   1. Amenities—the tangible and intangible neighborhood benefits beyond the property's boundaries description. Examples include proximity to schools, transportation, other homes of equal to or greater value, parks, etc.
   2. Capitalization—a mathematical process for estimating a property's value using a proper rate of return on investment and anticipated annual net income.
   3. Capitalization rate—the rate of return a property will produce on the owner's investment.
   4. Comparables—sold properties listed in the appraisal report generally equivalent to the subject property.
   5. Subject property—property being appraised
   6. URAR—Uniform Residential Appraisal Report
   7. Plottage—the combining of two or more parcels of land which results in the combined parcels being worth more than the individual parcels.
   8. Assemblage—the combining of two or more adjoining parcels into one larger parcel in order to create a value which is frequently greater than the value of each of the smaller parcels.

CHAPTER 5 QUIZ

1. The characteristics required for a property to have value include all of the following *EXCEPT*
   1. effective demand.
   2. scarcity.
   3. depreciation.
   4. transferability.

2. You own land worth $40,000 and your building has a replacement cost of $160,000. What would be the value if the appraiser used a depreciation rate of 30%?
   1. $148,000
   2. $152,000
   3. $188,000
   4. None of these

3. Which of the following does *NOT* apply to the definition of market value?
   1. Both buyer and seller must be well informed.
   2. Market value is the average price that a property will bring.
   3. Both buyer and seller must act without undue pressure.
   4. Payment must be made in cash or its equivalent.

4. The annual net income for an office building is $20,000. If an owner realized a 9% return on her investment, the value of the building would be
   1. $1,800.
   2. $22,222.
   3. $222,222.
   4. $285,714.

5. You look at four similar houses for sale in the same area and choose the house with the lowest asking price. You probably are basing your decision on the principle of
   1. highest and best use.
   2. substitution.
   3. contribution.
   4. conformity.

6. A builder developed a subdivision in which the demand for homes was great. He sold the last lot in his subdivision for a much higher price than that for which he had sold the first lot in the area. This example illustrates the principle of
   1. highest and best use.
   2. substitution.
   3. conformity.
   4. supply and demand.

7. In appraising a special-purpose building such as a post office, the most reliable approach to an indication of its value would generally be the
   1. cost approach.
   2. market/data approach.
   3. income approach.
   4. sales comparison approach.

8. Which of the following is an example of locational obsolescence?
   1. Termite damage
   2. Negligent care of property
   3. A zoning ordinance allowing a decrease in the minimum lot size
   4. Poor architectural design

9. Economic obsolescence results from all of the following *EXCEPT*
   1. adverse zoning changes.
   2. a city's leading industries moving out.
   3. an inharmonious land use in a neighborhood.
   4. outdated kitchens.

10. Depreciation generally applies to
    1. the building only.
    2. the land only.
    3. both the land and the building.
    4. the net income of the building.

11. A principal factor for which adjustments must be made in using the market/data approach is
    1. depreciation.
    2. the date of sale.
    3. the amount of real estate taxes.
    4. the cost of replacement.

12. An appraiser is estimating the value of a building that has a net income of $5,000 per quarter and a capitalization rate of 8%. What is the value of this property?
    1. $25,000
    2. $62,500
    3. $250,000
    4. $312,500

13. An appraiser is using the gross-rent-multiplier (GRM) method to estimate the market value of a single-family home. The home has an annual gross income of $7,200, with quarterly expenses of $900. The recognized GRM for the neighborhood is 110. The appraiser's estimate of value is likely to be
    1. $22,000.
    2. $33,000.
    3. $66,000.
    4. None of these

14. The GRM is used in the
    1. market/data approach.
    2. income approach for office buildings.
    3. cost approach.
    4. income approach for single-family homes.

15. In determining the value of a 20-unit apartment building, the appraiser has established the gross income from rents. After deducting the loss for vacancies and collection losses from this gross income, the appraiser would have established the
    1. net income.
    2. spendable income.
    3. gross income.
    4. effective gross income.

16. What is the first step an appraiser would take to arrive at an estimated value using the income approach?
    1. Determine annual potential gross income.
    2. Determine operating expenses.
    3. Determine effective gross income.
    4. Determine the vacancy rate.

17. An airport routing was changed, with the result that airplanes flew over a residential area. The subsequent loss in value caused by the airplane noise would be *BEST* described as
    1. physical depreciation.
    2. functional obsolescence.
    3. external or economic obsolescence.
    4. eminent domain.

18. Which of the following factors would be considered in the market/data or sales comparison approach to value?
    1. Conditions under which property was sold
    2. Annual gross income
    3. Replacement cost
    4. Original cost

19. Outmoded plumbing fixtures are an example of
    1. curable physical deterioration.
    2. curable functional obsolescence.
    3. incurable physical deterioration.
    4. curable external obsolescence.

20. In the income approach to appraisal, if the net income was $42,000 and the capitalization rate was 12%, to find the value of the property, the appraiser would
    1. multiply the income by the capitalization rate.
    2. multiply the capitalization rate by the net income.
    3. divide the net income by the capitalization rate.
    4. divide the capitalization rate by the net income.

21. Denise lived in a house with a well. The groundwater entering the homeowner's well became contaminated and lessened the value of Denise's home. The loss in value is an example of
    1. physical deterioration.
    2. external obsolescence.
    3. functional obsolescence.
    4. regression.

22. Which of the following reflects the stages through which a neighborhood passes?
    1. Growth, decline, stability, and revitalization
    2. Growth, stability, decline, and revitalization
    3. Decline, growth, stability, and revitalization
    4. Decline, growth, revitalization, and stability

23. Gross rent multipliers are generally used in appraising
    1. forms.
    2. shopping centers.
    3. single-family homes.
    4. hotels.

24. You purchased an apartment building for $600,000 nearly 6 years ago. The building accounted for 80% of the purchase price. If the building's economic life is estimated to be 60 years, what is the current total depreciation of the property?
    1. $36,000
    2. $48,000
    3. $60,000
    4. $72,000

25. Ramon purchased an office building with an annual effective gross income of $208,000 and expenses of $74,000. What capitalization rate was used by Ramon to arrive at a value of $1,576,470?
    1. 7.5%
    2. 8.5%
    3. 9.5%
    4. 10.5%

26. Maria was appraising a three-bedroom house. Maria had a comparable with four bedrooms that sold for $160,000. Maria makes an adjustment of $5,000 to the comparable for the difference in the number of bedrooms. The adjusted sales price of the comparable will be
    1. $155,000.
    2. $165,000.
    3. $170,000.
    4. None of these

27. If the house you are appraising has central air conditioning valued at $2,500 and your comparable does not, you will adjust the sales price of the comparable by
    1. – $2,500.
    2. + $2,500.
    3. – $1,250.
    4. None of these

28. A home's value is increased because of its proximity to schools, parks, and transportation lines. These neighborhood sites are referred to as
    1. features.
    2. benefits.
    3. amenities.
    4. attachments.

29. A bike trail that enhances the value of a neighboring home is called
    1. a feature.
    2. a benefit.
    3. an amenity.
    4. None of these

30. A comparable property sold for $250,000, and it has 200 more square feet than a subject property. If square footage contributes $30 per square foot, what is the adjusted value of the comparable?
    1. $250,000
    2. $260,000
    3. $244,000
    4. $256,000

31. An appraiser is told by a lender that if he can appraise a house for $250,000, he will be given the assignment. The appraiser should
    1. accept the assignment if he thinks he can appraise the house for $250,000.
    2. accept the assignment, but tell the lender that he will do his best to come close to $250,000.
    3. accept the assignment, but tell one of his employees to do the appraisal for $250,000.
    4. not accept the assignment, because it violates his professional ethics.

32. Which of the following statements does *NOT* correctly describe a CMA?
    1. A CMA generally groups comparables to indicate a range of values.
    2. A CMA does not consider expired or withdrawn listings that did not sell.
    3. A CMA can use both a GIM and GRM.
    4. A CMA does not provide a specific opinion of value.

33. Which of the following situations would *NOT* require an appraisal by a certified appraiser?
    1. A one- to four-family residential property
    2. A transaction of $1,000,000 or more
    3. A residential transaction or $250,000 or more
    4. A residential transaction of $275,000 or more

MATCHING QUIZ

The column on the right contains brief memory links to important terms in Chapter 5.

Write the letter of the matching term on the appropriate line.

A. CMA
B. Scarcity
C. Substitution
D. Diminishing returns
E. Contribution
F. Arm's length or most
G. Progression
H. Land
I. Physical deterioration
J. Functional obsolescence
K. External obsolescence
L. Capitalization
M. GRM
N. Reconciliation
O. Amenities
P. Comparables

1. _______ Weighing all three appraisal approaches to determine an indicated value
2. _______ Results from building in excess of the value of the neighborhood
3. _______ The principle of value that underlies all three approaches to value, which appraisers use to determine maximum value by comparing equally desirable substitutes
4. _______ Essential to creating value
5. _______ The process when net income is divided by an investor's desired percent of return
6. _______ A cracked foundation wall
7. _______ Value is enhanced by a home's proximity to a beautifully shaded park
8. _______ Diminished value due to airplane landing routes over a neighborhood
9. _______ A three-bedroom two-story home with only one bath
10. _______ Reporting tool to help real estate professionals determine a price range for a property
11. _______ Phenomenon that happens when buying the least expensive home in the most expensive neighborhood
12. _______ Sales not influenced by unusual circumstances used to determine the market value of a property
13. _______ In the cost approach, this is added back after subtracting depreciation from replacement cost new
14. _______ A name for sold homes used in a CMA
15. _______ Principle used to determine if improvements add or subtract from the value of the property
16. _______ Sold price divided by monthly rents

CHAPTER 5 QUIZ ANSWERS

1. **(3)** Depreciation is used in the cost approach to value. (58)

2. **(2)** Replacement cost of building
   $160,000
   Depreciation of 30%
   × 30
   Depreciation $48,000

   $160,000 Replacement Cost
   – Depreciation of $48,000 = $112,000
   Added land value = $40,000
   Value = $152,000
   (61)

3. **(2)** Appraisers do not average to determine market value. Appraisers work from comparable transactions to arrive at an estimate of market value for the subject property. (60–61)

4. **(3)** Income ÷ Rate = Value
   $20,000 ÷ .09 = $222,222 (61)

5. **(2)** The principle of highest and best use deals with the most profitable use. Contribution refers to cost and benefits of a particular improvement. Conformity is a factor in the stability of property values; zoning is an example of conformity. (59)

6. **(4)** A limited supply combined with a great demand will result in a higher price for lots. (59)

7. **(1)** The cost approach is most applicable to the appraisal of a special-purpose building. (61)

8. **(3)** Decreasing lot size is locational obsolescence. Termite damage and negligent care are physical deterioration. Poor architectural design represents functional obsolescence. (61)

9. **(4)** Economic obsolescence is a loss in value due to factors outside the property. Functional obsolescence is a loss in value due to a deficiency in the floor plan or design of a building. (61)

10. **(1)** Land is not depreciated; it is assumed that the land value will be recovered at the end of the economic life of the building. (61)

11. **(2)** Time, location, physical characteristics, and terms of sale are factors considered in the market or sales comparison approach. (60–61)

12. **(3)** $5,000 per quarter × 4 = $20,000 annual net income
    $20,000 ÷ .08 capitalization rate = $250,000 value (61)

13. **(3)** $7,200 gross ÷ 12 = $600 × 110 = $66,000 value (62)

14. **(4)** The GRM is used as a substitute for the income approach in appraising a single-family home. (62)

15. **(4)** The gross income would be reflected in the first step of the operating statement. Annual net income is the bottom line in the operating statement and serves as the basis for capitalization of the income stream. (61)

16. **(1)** Annual potential gross income is based on 100% of economic or market rent plus other income, such as income from vending machines. Effective gross income is annual potential gross income minus vacancy and rent loss. Operating expenses include fixed expenses, such as real estate taxes and variable expenses, such as management expenses. Use the vacancy rate to calculate effective gross income. (61)

17. **(3)** External or economic obsolescence is a loss in value from factors external to the property. (61)

18. **(1)** Conditions under which the property was sold would be used in the market/data approach. Cost would be used in the cost approach; annual gross income would be used in the income approach. (60–61)

19. **(2)** Functional obsolescence is a loss in the value due to deficiency in the floor plan or design of a building. The obsolescence would be curable if it were economically feasible to update the plumbing fixtures. Economic or external obsolescence is assumed to be incurable only because it is caused by factors outside the property. (61)

20. **(3)** The capitalization approach was previously discussed. (61)

21. **(2)** This is an example of external obsolescence, which would generally be incurable, depending on the cost to cure. (61)

22. **(2)** There are numerous examples in cities like Chicago and New York where neighborhoods have gone through the entire process, resulting in higher-than-ever property values. (62)

23. **(3)** Use the gross rent multiplier as a substitute for the income approach in the appraisal of a single-family home. (62)

24. **(2)** $600,000 × .80 = $480,000 value of building

    $480,000 ÷ 60 years = $8,000 annual depreciation charge

    $8,000 × 6 years = $48,000 current total depreciation. (61)

25. **(2)** $208,000 annual effective gross income – $74,000 expenses = $134,000; $134,000 ÷ $1,576,470 = .085 = 8.5 (61)

26. **(1)** C.B.S.—Comparable Better Subtract $160,000 price of comparable – $5,000 adjustment for one bedroom = $155,000 adjusted sales price of comparable (61)

27. **(2)** S.B.A.—Subject Better Add. The subject property is better than the comparable; thus you add the value of the air conditioning to the sale price of the comparable. (61)

28. **(3)** Amenities are neighborhood facilities and services that enhance a home's value but always are outside of the property. Swimming pools, 3-car garages, decks, etc. that are on the property are called features. (64)

29. **(3)** An amenity is always outside the confines of the property, but it adds value because of its proximity. (64)

30. **(3)** 200 sq. ft. × $30 sq. ft. in contributory value = $6,000. Then take the sold price of $250,000 and subtract the square footage amount of $6,000 to arrive at the adjusted value of $244,000. In other words, if everything else was the same between the two properties, the subject property would most likely sell for $244,000. (60)

31. **(4)** An appraiser's comparison cannot be dependent upon the reporting of a predetermined opinion of value. (57)

32. **(2)** A CMA considers expired or withdrawn listings as well as comparables that have sold or are currently for sale. (63)

33. **(1)** A regulated institution may use an appraisal by a licensed appraiser unless the institution determines that the appraisal is complex. (58)

TEST SCORE

VALUATION AND MARKET ANALYSIS			
Rating	**Range**	**Your Score**	
Good = 80% to 100%	27–33	Total Number	33
Fair = 70% to 79%	24–26	Total Wrong	–
Needs improvement = Lower than 70%	23 or less	Total Right	

Passing Requirement: 22 or Better

ANSWER KEY: MATCHING QUIZ

1. **N**	5. **L**	9. **J**	13. **H**
2. **D**	6. **I**	10. **A**	14. **P**
3. **C**	7. **O**	11. **G**	15. **E**
4. **B**	8. **K**	12. **F**	16. **M**

Chapter 6

Financing

OUTLINE OF CONCEPTS

I. General Concepts

A. LTV ratios, Points, Discounts, Broker commission

1. LTV ratios—the relationship between the amount of the mortgage loan and the value of the real estate being pledged as collateral.
2. Points—a percentage of the principal loan amount charged by the lender. Each point is equal to 1% of the loan amount.
3. Origination fees—fee charged by a lender to cover costs of originating the loan; it is frequently 1% of the loan amount.
4. Discounts—A fee paid by the borrower to lower the interest rate on a loan and increase the lender's yield.

B. Private Mortgage insurance (PMI)—Privately insured

1. Depending on the buyer's credit score, the buyer may obtain a conventional loan for up to 97% of the property's appraised value.
2. The buyer is charged the market rate of interest plus reasonable mortgage insurance premium costs.
3. The borrower's mortgage insurance protects the lender against loss on the upper 20 to 25% portion of the loan.
4. PMI insurance premiums are made a part of the borrower's monthly payments.
5. As property values rise and the loan-to-value ratio become 80% or less, the PMI insurance may be dropped.

C. Lender requirements, equity, qualifying buyers, loan application procedures

1. Lender requirements—lender must determine whether a particular borrower and the subject property meet the minimum requirements established by the lender, investor, or secondary market in which the loan will probably be sold.
2. Equity—the interest or value that an owner has in a property over and above any mortgage indebtedness.

II. Types of loans and sources of loan money

A. Term or straight loans—allows for payments of interest only with a lump-sum balloon payment of principal at a stop date (specified time).

B1. Fully amortized loan, or fixed payment—equal monthly payments credited first to interest due, then applied to the loan balance.

B2. Partially amortized loans—payment of some principal and interest with a larger-than-normal final payment of a mortgage loan resulting from the amount of the mortgage loan not having been amortized in full.

C. Adjustable rate mortgage (ARM) loans
   1. Contains interest provision related to a selected index.

D. Conventional versus insured
   1. Conventional
      a. Payment of the debt based solely on the borrower's ability to pay, with security provided by the mortgage; neither insured nor guaranteed by government agency.
      b. Lender sets the terms subject to many of the rules established by the secondary mortgage market. Loans originated by some institutions are sold in the secondary market.
      c. If the loan-to-value ratio exceeds a given level, 80% for example, the lender may require private mortgage insurance (PMI) and escrows for property taxes and homeowner's insurance.

E. Reverse mortgages, equity loans, subprime and other nonconforming loans
   1. Reverse mortgage
      a. A loan that allows older homeowners to convert part of the equity in their home to tax-free income without having to sell, give up title, or take on a new monthly mortgage payment.
      b. The homeowner must be at least 62 years of age and occupy the property as his or her primary residence.
      c. Most of the reverse mortgages are insured by FHA under the Home Equity Conversion Mortgage (HECM) program authorized by congress.
      d. Anyone applying for a HECM loan is required to attend counseling sessions conducted by trained counselors.
      e. Homeowner is not required to repay loan, interest, and other fees until the surviving homeowner has left home.
   2. Equity loan—loan on a home using the equity in the home as collateral for the loan, which is generally a line of credit. Equity is the difference between the value of a home and how much the homeowner owes on the home, which is usually in the form of a mortgage.
   3. Subprime loans—loans to borrowers with a weakened credit history who have a greater likelihood of default. The lender compensates for the greater risk by charging higher fees and interest rates than those on traditional loans.
   4. Other nonconforming loans—a loan that does not conform to the guidelines for qualification established by Fannie Mae and Freddie Mac, such as a loan that does not meet the requirements for down payment; a loan that exceeds the maximum loan limits is nonconforming and is known as a jumbo loan.

F. Seller/owner financing—the seller of the real estate provides financing for the sale by taking back a secured note in the form of a purchase money mortgage, contract for deed, or land contract.

G. The Money Market—Primary market and sources of financing.

1. The Primary Money Market
   a. General characteristics
      (1) Money may be viewed as a means of payment, storehouse of purchasing power, standard of value.
      (2) Money market is regulated by the federal government through the Federal Reserve System (FED)
   b. Federal Reserve System (FED)
      (1) Regulates the flow of money through member banks by controlling reserve requirements and discount rates.
      (2) Tempers the economy through open-market operations.
   c. U.S. Treasury
      (1) In effect, our nation's fiscal manager
2. The primary mortgage market—the market in which mortgages are originated by lenders, such as commercial banks.
3. Sources of Real Estate Financing—The primary market
   a. Savings and Loan Associations
      (1) Principal function: to promote thrift and home ownership.
      (2) Regulated on the national level by the Office of Thrift Supervision.
      (3) Deposits are insured by the Federal Deposit Insurance Corporation (FDIC) for up to $250,000 per depositor.
      (4) Local in nature
   b. Commercial banks
      (1) Prefer short-term loans but have been significant participants in residential mortgage lending.
      (2) Deposits are insured by the Federal Deposit Insurance Corporation (FDIC) for up to $250,000 per depositor.
   c. Mutual savings banks
      (1) Primarily savings institutions in the northeastern United States
      (2) Active in mortgage market
      (3) Prefer FHA and VA loans
   d. Life insurance companies
      (1) Prefer long-term commercial, industrial loans.
      (2) Seek equity position in projects financed.
      (3) Regulated by state law.
   e. Mortgage banking companies
      (1) Originate loans with their own money and money belonging to other institutions and from other sources (pension funds, private individuals).
      (2) Service loans they originate.
   f. Mortgage brokers—originate loans for other lenders but do not service loans.
   g. Mortgage banker—may lend its own money and/or serve as a broker.

H. Secondary Mortgage Market
   1. Market in which loans are bought and sold after they have been originated and funded.
   2. Warehousing agencies play a major role in the secondary market by purchasing a number of mortgage loans and assembling them into packages for resale to investors.
   3. Major warehousing agencies
      a. Federal National Mortgage Association (FNMA)—Fannie Mae
         (1) Publicly traded corporation authorized to purchase conventional as well as FHA and VA loans.
         (2) Raises funds to purchase loans by selling government-guaranteed FNMA bonds at market interest rates.
      b. Government National Mortgage Association (GNMA)—Ginnie Mae
         (1) Federal agency designed to administer a special assistance program and to work with the FNMA in secondary market activities.
         (2) Can join forces with the FNMA in times of tight money and high interest rates; through a tandem plan, the FNMA can purchase high-risk, low-yield loans at full market rates, while the GNMA guarantees payment and absorbs the difference between low-yield and current market prices.
         (3) Government agency authorized to purchase government-insured FHA mortgages; government-guaranteed VA mortgages; and government-subsidized Rural Development Mortgages from intermediaries in the secondary mortgage market.
      c. Federal Home Loan Mortgage Corporation (FHLMC)—Freddie Mac
         (1) Government-chartered corporation created to provide secondary mortgage market for conventional loans.
         (2) Has the authority to purchase conventional, FHA, and VA mortgages; pool them; and sell bonds in the open market with mortgages as security.

I. Down payment assistance programs
   1. Down payment assistance is available through government programs at the federal, state and local levels, as well as through charitable organizations.
   2. Government grants are available to first-time home buyers as long as the family income meets the stipulated minimum, which varies according to the median income for the area as well as the number of dependents.
   3. Government down payment assistance programs are generally interest free and do not require a monthly payment.
   4. Some of these grants take the form of a second mortgage that does not have to be repaid until the house is sold; in many of these programs, the grant will not have to be repaid if the home is owned for a specified number of years.

III. Government programs

A. Federal Housing Administration (FHA) insured

1. FHA insures approved lenders against loss on loans made on new or existing one-to-four unit family housing.
2. Interest rates float with the open market.
3. The borrower finances an up-front FHA insurance premium of 1.75% (which may be partially refundable); borrower then pays a monthly [nonfinanceable insurance premium (MIP)], based on 1.35% of the mortgage for the life of the loan.
4. Mortgaged property must be appraised by an FHA-approved appraiser.
5. FHA does not allow a prepayment penalty.
6. FHA mortgages are assumable with qualification.
7. Discount points are generally used to reduce the interest rate (1 point = 1% of the loan balance); these are generally negotiated between the seller and the buyer.

B. Department of Veterans Affairs Guaranteed (VA loan)

1. VA does not allow a prepayment penalty.
2. A VA loan may be assumed by a veteran, qualified non-veteran, or by a qualified un-remarried surviving spouse.
3. VA guarantees home loans for eligible veterans or an un-remarried surviving spouse with required down payment.
4. The interest rate is set by the lender.
5. VA does not charge the borrower for the guarantee; however, the borrower may have to pay up to a 3.3% funding fee based on usage and his or her military category, whether the veteran is a first-time or subsequent loan user, and whether the veteran makes a down payment.
6. Mortgaged property must be appraised by a VA-approved appraiser.
7. VA sets no limitation on how much a veteran can borrow to finance a home. VA will, however, guarantee only a maximum of 25% of the county loan limit for loans over $144,000. If the selling price is higher than $417,000 the lender may require a down payment.
8. Discount points generally are negotiated between the lender and the buyer.
9. In some cases, the VA will make direct loans to eligible veterans or through the Native American direct loan program.
10. VA requires appraisers to complete a Certificate of Reasonable Value (CRV); the VA guarantee is based on either the amount of the CRV or the selling price, whichever is less.
11. National Guard members and reservists with at least six years of service are eligible for VA-guaranteed loans.

C. Other federal programs

1. Department of Housing and Urban Development (HUD) and the Department of Treasury provide programs that help make homes more affordable, which helps struggling homeowners get mortgage relief through a variety of programs, such as Rural Americans Housing Assistance.

2. Federal Housing Finance Agency recently extended the Home Affordable Refinance Program (HARP), which is focused on helping homeowners who are current on their mortgage but have little to no equity to refinance their mortgage into a lower interest rate.
3. Rural Development provides loans to help families purchase or improve single-family homes in rural areas and operates under the Farm Service Agency.
4. The Farm Service Agency (a federal agency) offers programs to help families operate or purchase family farms.

IV. Mortgages/deeds of trust

A. Mortgage/deeds of trust and promissory note as separate documents
   1. Mortgage—a document by which the mortgagor (borrower) places a lien on his or her property in favor of the mortgagee (lender) as security for debt.
   2. A deed of trust is a three-party instrument used in place of a mortgage in some areas of the country.
      a. Conveys real estate as security for a loan to a third party, which is the trustee.
      b. Trustee holds the title on behalf of the lender, known as the beneficiary; the trustee is the legal owner, and the beneficiary is the holder of the note; the borrower retains the equitable title to the property, and the deed of trust becomes the lien against it.
      c. The trustee may commence a foreclosure action if the borrower (trustor) defaults;
         (1) a reconveyance deed returns title to trustor when trust deed has been paid in full.
   3. Promissory Note—promise to repay debt; a negotiable instrument.

B. Mortgage or deed of trust clauses (assumption, due-on-sale alienation, acceleration, prepayment, release)
   1. Buying subject to versus assuming—if the property is sold "subject to" the mortgage, the buyer is not personally liable to pay the entire debt (the seller remains liable); if the buyer assumes the mortgage, he or she becomes personally liable for payment of the entire debt. The seller is secondarily liable.
   2. Due-on-sale clause—if the borrower sells the property, the lender has the choice of either declaring the entire debt due and payable or allowing the buyer to assume the loan.
   3. Alienation—the act of transferring property to another. Alienation may be voluntary, such as by sale, or involuntary, such as through eminent domain.
   4. Acceleration clause—a provision in a written contract, such as a mortgage or note, which states that in the event of default, all of the principal and interest may be immediately declared due and payable.

5. Prepayment clause—a clause in a mortgage that states the terms on which the mortgagor (borrower) may prepay the entire balance of the mortgage principal prior to the due date.
6. Release—to relinquish an interest on, or a claim to, a parcel of property.

C. Lien theory versus title theory
1. Lien theory—the mortgage is viewed as a lien on real property in many states.
2. Title theory—the lender is viewed as the conditional owner of mortgaged land in some states.
3. Intermediate theory—a number of states allow the lender to take possession of the mortgaged real estate on default.

V. Financing/Credit laws

A. Lending and disclosures
1. Truth in Lending Act (TILA)—Regulation Z
   a. Disclosure requirements
      (1) Require disclosure of cost in credit transactions.
      (2) Customer has the right to rescind in some types of credit transactions under certain conditions; for example, a second mortgage.
   b. Coverage of Regulation Z
      (1) Loans to individuals are covered for all real estate credit transactions for personal, family, and household purposes, regardless of the amount involved.
      (2) Loans to individuals are covered for non-real-estate credit transactions for personal, family, and household purposes up to $25,000.
   c. Requirements on finance charges
      (1) All finance charges, as well as the true annual percentage rate (APR), must be disclosed to the customer before the transaction is completed.
      (2) Finance charge must include interest, loan fees, points, service charges, finder's fees, and property and credit insurance.
      (3) The finance charge must be stated as the Annual Percentage Rate (APR)
   d. Requirements regarding liens on residences
      (1) A "cooling off" period is required when liens such as a refinance or home equity loan will be placed on a principal residence; the borrower has the right to rescind the transaction up to midnight of the third business day following the transaction or until delivery of the disclosure statement, whichever is later.
      (2) The right to rescind does not apply to loans to finance the purchase or initial construction of a house.
   e. Advertising
      (1) Specific credit terms (trigger terms) may not be advertised unless the ad includes full disclosure of these terms:
         a. Amount of down payment
         b. Amount of loan or cash price

c. Finance charges as annual percentage rate
d. Number, amount, and due dates of payments
e. Total of all payments except where advertisement relates to first mortgage

f. Penalties for noncompliance
(1) Violation of an administration order enforcing Regulation Z is $10,000 for each day the violation continues.
(2) Engaging in an unfair or deceptive practice may result in the imposition of a fine of up to $10,000.
(3) A creditor may be liable to a consumer for twice the amount of the finance charge, from a minimum of $100 to a maximum of $1,000, plus court costs, attorney's fees, and any actual damages.
(4) Willful violation constitutes a misdemeanor and is punishable by a fine of up to $5,000 or one year's imprisonment or both.

2. Real Estate Settlement Procedures Act (RESPA)
a. Created to ensure that the buyer and seller have knowledge of all the settlement costs before closing.
b. Requirements
(1) Lenders must give a copy of the special information booklet—Settlement Costs and You, to each loan applicant.
(2) The borrowers must be provided with a good-faith estimate of the settlement costs by the lenders no later than three business days after the receipt of the loan application.
(3) The loan closing expenses must be prepared on a Uniform Settlement Statement (HUD form 1).
(4) RESPA explicitly prohibits the payment of kickbacks and prohibits referral fees when no services are actually rendered.
(5) RESPA regulations apply only to transactions involving new first-mortgage referral loans for one-family to four-family dwellings generally financed by the federally related mortgage loan.

3. Equal Credit Opportunity Act—a federal law that prohibits discrimination against credit applicants on the basis of race, color, religion, national origin, sex, marital status, age, or because the applicant gets public assistance. (It requires that all rejected credit applicants be informed, in writing, of the reasons for credit denial within 30 days.)

B. Fraud and lending practices
1. Mortgage Fraud
a. Fraud perpetrated through acts such as the use of identity theft and false documents, and the occasional willing or unwilling assistance of professionals in real estate. Examples include the following:
(1) Fictitious or stolen identity—false identity is used on a loan application without the true person's knowledge.
(2) Inflated appraisals—an appraiser works in collusion with a borrower or a lender to provide a misleading appraisal

report to the lender by inaccurately stating an inflated property value.

b. Mortgage fraud is investigated by the FBI and is punishable by up to 30 years in prison, a $1 million fine, or both.

2. Predatory lending practices (risks to clients) and laws
   a. Predatory lending practices—any practice in which lenders try to coerce consumers into agreeing to loans that are unaffordable and violate industry standards. Predatory lenders often target low-income people, immigrants, and the elderly as their potential victims.
      (1) Examples of predatory lending practices include:
         a. Offering only loans with interest rates that the borrower cannot afford and including fees that are unnecessary mortgage charges.
         b. Moving a borrower from one loan to another near the end of the payment schedule to extend interest payments and add to the overall cost of the loan by having the borrower refinance prior to the expiration of the payment schedule, and requiring borrowers to buy more insurance than legally required or needed by the borrower.
3. Federal lending laws
   a. Truth in Lending Act, which requires disclosure of loan terms as well as APR.
   b. The Home Ownership and Equity Protection Act was created in 1994 under the Truth in Lending Act and was aimed at identifying potential predatory mortgage loans and limiting their terms.
   c. Many states have passed anti-predatory lending laws.
   d. The Dodd Frank Law assigns the Consumer Financial Protection Board (CFPB) the authority to write rules to protect consumers from unfair or deceptive financial products, acts or practices, as well as responsibility for major consumer laws including RESPA, TILA, HOEPA and the HMDA.
4. Underwriting
   a. Debt ratios
      (1) Ratio of debt to income used by lender is part of loan approval process.
      (2) Most lenders use 43% as the highest debt-to-income ratio in order for a potential borrower to qualify for a mortgage loan.
   b. Credit scoring
      (1) Credit scores are provided by Trans Union, Equifax, and Experian credit reporting agencies.
      (2) Credit scores are used by lenders as part of their loan-making decisions.
      (3) Trans Union, Equifax, and Experian also provide credit history for lenders to use in their loan-making decisions.
5. TILA/RESPA Integrated Disclosure (TRID) Rule
   a. The Truth in Lending Act (TILA)/Real Estate Settlement Procedures Act (RESPA) Integrated Disclosure Rule is also

known as TRID. The rule is more frequently referred to as the *Know Before You Owe* rule.

b. Changes being implemented by TRID include the following:
   (1) Consumer disclosures are now easier to read since the loan estimate forms allow the borrowers to determine if they would like to proceed with the transaction.
   (2) Consumers must be given a copy of their Closing Disclosure at least three business days prior to closing to allow them to ask any questions they might have. The loan originator can then give them additional information.

6. Consumer Financial Protection Bureau (CFPB)/TRID rules
   a. The CFPB is a federal agency that helps consumer finance markets work.
   b. The CFPB is making rules more effective by consistently and fairly enforcing the rules.
   c. The CFPB empowers consumers to take more control over their economic lives.
   d. There are several financing and risky loan features that are addressed by the CFPB.
7. Usury laws—charging interest on a loan that is above the maximum rate allowed by state law. All states have some form of usury law. The purpose of the law is to set a maximum rate for loans, as well as rules regarding loan provisions, such as prepayment penalties and late payment charges.
   a. Non-qualified mortgages
      (1) Mortgages that do not comply with the federal lending requirements, such as a mortgage loan that is for more than 43% of the borrower's income.
   b. Qualified versus non-qualified mortgages
      (1) Qualified mortgages provide lenders with safe harbor protection from being sued by borrowers.
      (2) Non-qualified mortgages do not provide the lender with safe harbor protection against lawsuits filed by borrowers.
      (3) Safe harbor protection means that if the lenders comply with the Ability to Repay (ATR) rule, they have substantial immunity from consumer lawsuits.

VI. Other Important Terms

A. Fully amortized mortgage (direct-reduction loans)—regular monthly payments, applied first to the interest, with the balance to the principal, over the term of the loan.

B. Balloon payment—final payment of the loan; larger than previous payments and repays the debt in full.

C. Equity—value of the owner's interest in the property; the difference between the value of the property and all the liens on the property.

D. Subordination agreement—changes the order or priority of the liens between two creditors.

E. Usury—charging a rate of interest in excess of the maximum rate allowed by state law.

F. Seller financing—the seller of the real estate provides financing for the sale by taking back a secured note in the form of a purchase-money mortgage, land contract, or deed of trust.
G. Hypothecation—pledging property as security for the loan without losing possession of it.
H. Lender's Impound or escrow account—trust account created by the lender for the borrower to set aside funds for the future needs of a property; for example, to provide funds for the payment of real estate taxes and renewal premiums for insurance.
I. "Underwater" mortgage—a mortgage on a home in which the home is worth less than the amount owed to the bank that holds the mortgage on the home; often referred to as a negative equity or an "upside down" mortgage.
J. Satisfaction of mortgage—document acknowledging the payment of the mortgage.
K. Alienation clause (due on sale clause)—if the borrower sells the property, the lender has the choice of either declaring the entire debt due and payable or allowing the buyer to assume the loan.
L. Blanket mortgage—covers more than one property or lot; generally includes a partial release clause.
M. Package mortgage—includes real estate and all fixtures and appliance located on the property.
N. Leverage—the use of borrowed money to finance the bulk of an investment.
O. Escalation clause—permits an increase or decrease in the amount of payments due on contracts such as leases.

CHAPTER 6 QUIZ

1. All of the following statements concerning real estate financing are correct *EXCEPT*
   1. the mortgage generally is considered a lien.
   2. the mortgagee is the lender.
   3. an owner of property by whom the mortgage is executed is called a mortgagor.
   4. a promissory note is security for a mortgage.

2. A promissory note is *NOT*
   1. a negotiable instrument.
   2. evidence of debt.
   3. a document in which the debtor agrees to repay the stated loan.
   4. evidence of title.

3. Which of the following payment plans allows for periodic payments of interest only, with the principal due as a lump sum payment at maturity?
   1. Amortized
   2. Flexible
   3. Straight
   4. Partially amortized

4. All of the following are participants in the secondary mortgage market *EXCEPT*
   1. FHLMC.
   2. FNMA.
   3. FDIC.
   4. GNMA.

5. All of the following are characteristic of a conventional loan *EXCEPT*
   1. it is neither insured nor guaranteed by public agency.
   2. security rests on the borrower's ability to pay and the collateral pledged.
   3. it is never insured by a private agency.
   4. the ratio of the loan to the value of the property usually does not exceed 80% without private mortgage insurance.

6. Which of the following is *NOT* characteristic of a Federal Housing Administration (FHA) loan?
   1. A mortgage insurance premium is charged.
   2. The lender is insured against loss.
   3. The maximum mortgage debt is determined by a formula.
   4. The FHA provides the money for the loan.

7. Which of the following is *NOT* a characteristic of a VA loan?
   1. The loan is guaranteed.
   2. Only an eligible veteran or eligible dependents of veterans, as well as reservists and National Guard members who have served for six years, may qualify for the loan.
   3. The loan is insured.
   4. Little or no down payment is required.

8. Granting a conventional loan requires that the borrower provide the lender with which of the following?
   1. Sales contract and hypothecation instrument
   2. Mortgage and promissory note
   3. Deed of trust and sales contract
   4. Mortgage and letter of intent

9. The process by which a mortgagor regains his or her interest in a property is called
   1. foreclosure.
   2. redemption.
   3. a deficiency judgment.
   4. laches.

10. Which of the following statements about FHA mortgages is *FALSE*?
    1. FHA mortgages require a larger down payment than VA mortgages.
    2. There is no prepayment penalty.
    3. FHA mortgages are assumable provided the new borrower qualifies.
    4. FHA mortgages are not assumable.

11. On the FHA loan, the buyer would *NOT* be required to
    1. provide mortgage insurance to protect the lender.
    2. meet FHA credit standards.
    3. find an approved lender willing to make the loan.
    4. make a 20% down payment on the loan.

12. Disclosure of total cost of credit in a loan transaction is required by
    1. RESPA.
    2. Regulation Z.
    3. the Federal Equal Credit Opportunity Act.
    4. the 1968 Federal Fair Housing Act.

13. Funds for VA loans usually are provided by
    1. HUD.
    2. the secondary mortgage market.
    3. Freddie Mac.
    4. approved lenders.

14. Charging a rate of interest in excess of the maximum rate allowed by law is
    1. laches.
    2. hypothecation.
    3. subordination.
    4. usury.

15. A veteran buys a home with a VA-guaranteed loan. Two years later, the veteran sells the home to a buyer who, with the lender's approval, assumes the veteran's loan. In this situation, the veteran is
    1. responsible for paying an insurance fee charged by the VA.
    2. responsible for paying the loan origination fee.
    3. no longer financially responsible if the buyer defaults six months later.
    4. financially responsible if the buyer defaults six months later.

16. If a lender charges a borrower two discount points on a $60,000 loan, what will be the charge for the points?
    1. $120
    2. $1,200
    3. $2,400
    4. None of these

17. "Trigger terms" relates to
    1. the ADA.
    2. federal fair housing laws.
    3. RESPA.
    4. Truth-in-lending.

18. You are receiving a mortgage from your local bank. Truth-in-lending requires your bank to disclose
    1. your right to rescind within three business days.
    2. the amount of your closing costs.
    3. the annual percentage rate.
    4. penalties to the bank if they do not comply with the laws.

19. A buyer purchased a home and asked the seller to pay 2½ discount points equaling $4,000. How much money did the buyer want to borrow?
    1. $100,000
    2. $160,000
    3. $170,000
    4. None of these

20. A lender makes a loan to a borrower with a poor credit history and charges a higher interest rate because of the greater risk involved in the loan being paid back. This would be an example of a
    1. straight loan.
    2. subprime loan.
    3. short sale.
    4. graduated payment loan.

21. FHA mortgage insurance makes it possible to lower a down payment to as little as
    1. 1%.
    2. 2.5%.
    3. 3.5%.
    4. 5%.

22. A loan that allows older homeowners to convert part of their equity in their home to tax-free income without having to sell, give up title, or take on a new monthly mortgage payment is called a
    1. purchase-money mortgage.
    2. blanket mortgage.
    3. wraparound mortgage.
    4. reverse mortgage.

23. A mortgage on a home in which the home is worth less than the amount owed to the bank that holds the mortgage is called a(n)
    1. wraparound mortgage.
    2. purchase-money mortgage.
    3. underwater mortgage.
    4. reverse mortgage.

24. Which of the following companies does *NOT* provide credit scores?
    1. Trans Union
    2. Capital One
    3. Equifax
    4. Experian

25. The TRID rule requires that consumers must be given a copy of their closing statement at least how many days prior to closing?
    1. One
    2. Two
    3. Three
    4. Four

MATCHING QUIZ

The column on the right contains brief memory links to important terms in Chapter 6.

Write the letter of the matching term on the appropriate line.

A. Mortgagor
B. Mortgagee
C. Balloon payment
D. Secondary mortgage market
E. FHA
F. VA
G. Discount point
H. Hypothecation
I. GNMA
J. Usury
K. Subprime loan
L. Equity
M. Nonconforming loan
N. Regulation Z
O. CFPB
P. Amortized
Q. "Underwater" mortgage
R. Primary mortgage market

1. _______ Fixed P&I payment where the principle increases with each payment
2. _______ Government-insured loan
3. _______ Market in which loans are originated by lenders
4. _______ Value of the owner's interest in her property
5. _______ Charging interest on a loan that is above the maximum rate allowed by law
6. _______ The borrower in a mortgage loan transaction
7. _______ Consumer Financial Protection Bureau
8. _______ Pledging something as collateral without giving up possession of it
9. _______ The holder of the mortgage
10. _______ Purchases government insured and guaranteed loans on the secondary market
11. _______ Regulation that requires disclosure for the cost of credit
12. _______ Negative equity mortgage
13. _______ Market in which loans are bought and sold after having been originated
14. _______ Jumbo loan
15. _______ Final and larger payment of loan
16. _______ Loan to borrower with greater likelihood of default
17. _______ Computed as a percent of the loan
18. _______ Government guaranteed loan

CHAPTER 6 QUIZ ANSWERS

1. **(4)** In some states, the mortgage creates a lien on the property; the note is the promise to repay the debt. (78)

2. **(4)** The promissory note is evidence of the debt but not evidence of title. Deeds are the instruments that convey title and provide evidence of ownership interest. (78)

3. **(3)** The amortized, flexible, and balloon all provide for payment of principal. (74)

4. **(3)** The FDIC insures checking and savings accounts up to $250,000 per account. (74)

5. **(3)** Conventional loans may be insured by a private agency. (74)

6. **(4)** The FHA will not provide money for a loan. However, the VA will provide the money for a loan where the supply of money is scarce. (77)

7. **(3)** An FHA loan provides public mortgage insurance for which the buyer pays an insurance premium. The VA does not charge the veteran for the guarantee of the loan. (77)

8. **(2)** A deed of trust is used in place of a mortgage in states such as California. A mortgage or deed of trust and a note are required for a conventional loan. The mortgagee creates a lien on the property as security for the debt. The note is a promise to repay the debt. (78)

9. **(2)** Foreclosure is related to the redemption period, which may end with the foreclosure sale (equitable redemption) or after the foreclosure sale (statutory redemption). If the lender does not recover what is owed by the borrower, it may sue for a deficiency judgment. Laches was previously discussed. (155)

10. **(4)** FHA and VA mortgages are assumable with qualification. (77)

11. **(4)** The cash investment on an FHA-insured loan is 3.5% of the sales price or appraised value plus closing costs. Gift letters may be used for the required down payment. The maximum mortgage formula for houses over $50,000 is 97.75%. (77)

12. **(2)** RESPA provides consumer protection with regard to closing procedures and costs. The Federal Equal Credit Opportunity Act prohibits credit providers from discriminating against members of certain protected classes. The 1968 Federal Fair Housing Act prohibits discrimination in the sale or rental of housing. (79)

13. **(4)** Freddie Mac functions in the secondary mortgage market; HUD is a regulatory agency. (77)

14. **(4)** Subordination allows a lender to agree to consent to a subsequent mortgage having legal priority, thus placing the original lender in a lesser position. Laches refers to the inability to assert a legal right because of undue delay in asserting it. Hypothecation is pledging property as security for a loan without giving up possession of the property. Usury is charging an interest rate higher than that allowed by state law. (82)

15. **(3)** Both the VA and FHA require buyers who assume existing mortgages to be qualified to do so. Therefore, the original buyer's liability is assigned to the new buyer in a process called novation. (77)

16. **(2)** One point is 1% of the loan amount. $60,000 × 0.02 = $1,200. (73)

17. **(4)** Brokers advertising credit terms must fully disclose terms of credit if they use "trigger terms." (79)

18. **(3)** Regulation Z requires lenders to inform borrowers of the true cost of credit, which includes the Annual Percentage Rate (APR). Kickbacks or referral fees are prohibited. (79–80)

19. **(2)** $4,000 is 2.5% of the borrowed amount. $4,000 ÷ 2.5% = $160,000. (73)

20. **(2)** The lender charged the higher interest rate because of the greater risk of pay-back. A short sale occurs when a lender agrees to take less than the full amount of the debt owed by the borrower. A straight loan is an interest-only loan. A graduated payment loan allows for smaller payments in the early years of a loan. (74)

21. **(3)** FHA mortgage insurance allows for a down payment as small as 3.5%. (77)

22. **(4)** The RAM is repaid when the owner sells, transfers her interest, or no longer occupies the home as her primary residence. (74)

23. **(3)** An underwater mortgage is also known as a negative equity or an "upside down" mortgage. (83)

24. **(2)** Credit scores are provided by Trans Union, Equifax, and Experian. (81)

25. **(3)** The TRID rule is more frequently referred to as the Know Before You Owe rule. (82)

TEST SCORE

VALUATION AND MARKET ANALYSIS			
Rating	**Range**	**Your Score**	
Good = 80% to 100%	20–25	Total Number	25
Fair = 70% to 79%	18–20	Total Wrong	–
Needs improvement = Lower than 70%	17 or less	Total Right	

Passing Requirement: 17 or Better

ANSWER KEY: MATCHING QUIZ

1. **P**
2. **E**
3. **R**
4. **L**
5. **J**
6. **A**
7. **O**
8. **H**
9. **B**
10. **I**
11. **N**
12. **Q**
13. **D**
14. **M**
15. **C**
16. **K**
17. **G**
18. **F**

General Principles of Agency

OUTLINE OF CONCEPTS

I. Nature of Agency Relationships

A. Common law of agency sets up the fiduciary obligations for all agents, not just real estate professionals.
   1. This set of laws sets the basic fundamentals.

B. State laws define how agency or non-agency relationships will be implemented. For example, common law defines dual or implied agency, but state laws may disallow one or both of these to be practiced.
   1. The brokerage business has typically been one of agency; the brokerage firm is authorized by the principal (seller, buyer, tenant or landlord) to act as his or her agent.
   2. Agency refers to the nature of the relationship between the agent and the parties to whom brokerage services are provided; traditional agency involves a principal and an agent.
      a. The brokerage firm is considered to be an agent who consents to represent the interest of another party (the principal) who delegates authority to him or her.
      b. The principal is the party who delegates to the agent the authority to represent the principal's interest in a transaction.
      c. Fiduciary is the common law term typically used to describe the nature of the agency relationship as that of trust and confidence between the principal and the agent.
         (1) The broker (agent) is often referred to as a fiduciary in common law, although the duties owed by the broker in actual practice depends upon the specifics of any agency agreement and state law; common law refers to legal principals passed down on court decisions.
         (2) Fiduciary obligations typically include care, obedience, accounting, confidentiality, loyalty, and disclosure.

d. Under an agency agreement, the principal is the client for whom the agent has agreed to provide a service, typically assistance in a transaction such as the purchase or sale of a home.
e. The principal, or client, agrees to cooperate with the agent, compensate the agent, and not to hinder the agent's ability to provide services. A broker's commission is negotiable.
f. A customer is a person, not under an agency agreement, for whom brokerage services may be provided.
g. A broker may be engaged in a variety of agency relationships to parties in a given transaction, depending upon state law.
    (1) Types of agents, agencies (special, general, designated, subagents, etc.)
        a. Special agent
            (i) A special agent is authorized to represent the principal in a transaction; a real estate brokerage with a listing contract is typically considered a special agent.
            (ii) A broker is a special agent when the broker is employed by the seller to find a buyer for the seller's property or when employed by the buyer to assist in the acquisition of a given property.
            (iii) As a special agent, the real estate broker is not authorized to bind the principal (i.e., is not authorized to sell the principal's property or bind the buyer in a purchase contract).
        b. General agent
            (i) A general agent is one authorized by another to represent that party's interest in a given range of matters.
            (ii) A property manager could be an example of a general agent, if authorized to represent the principal in all matters concerning one area of the principal's interest.
        c. Universal agent
            (i) A person who is given the authority to represent the principal with virtually unlimited authority.
            (ii) A power of attorney is generally required to create a universal agent.
            (iii) A real estate broker typically does not have this scope of authority as an agent.
    (2) Other agency options
        a. Designated agent
            (i) Designated agency, if permitted under state law, allows for two different agents from the same brokerage to each represent a separate buyer—client and a separate seller-client in the same transaction.
            (ii) In the absence of designated agency, or its equivalent, the representation of a client on each side of a given transaction would be prohibited, or would be permissible only under a dual agency situation.
            (iii) Both dual agency and designated agency require disclosure and consent of the parties involved.

b. Subagent
   (i) A subagent is an agent of the agent.
   (ii) The allowance of subagency typically requires the principal's consent.
   (iii) If authorized by the principal, the agent may delegate some of the agent's authority or responsibility to another agent (subagent) to assist the agent in carrying out the agent's services to the seller.
   (iv) A subagency relationship in real estate brokerage may be created through an offer of cooperation made in the multiple-listing service (MLS), where other brokers agree to assist the listing brokerage in locating a ready, willing and able buyer for the listing broker's seller's property. Note that although MLS rules provide for such subagency, mere membership in the MLS does not by itself create subagency.
   (v) Depending on state laws, cooperating agents would owe their duties to the agent creating the subagency, and ultimately to the principal.

(3) Fiduciary responsibilities
   a. Fiduciary is a common law term that describes a relationship of trust and confidence between principal and agent.
   b. Brokers often are referred to as fiduciaries, but the actual duties of a broker to a client in any state will be set by law and the contract of employment, effectively modifying or supplanting what would be traditional common law duties.

(4) Client
   a. A client is a principal in an agency situation; this is the person to whom the agent gives counsel and advice.
   b. Most states require that agreements creating the agency relationship must be in writing.

(5) Customers
   a. A customer is a party for whom a service is provided in the course of the agent's execution of his duties to the principal; the customer is not a client.
   b. Customers are those receiving brokerage services by the agent, but without having entered into an agency agreement.
   c. Under common law, the agent would still owe a customer the duty to be honest and fair in his/her dealings with the customer, or such duties as may be prescribed in state law, such as confidentiality.

C. Creation and disclosure of agency and agency agreements (general, not state-specific).
   1. Creation of an agency relationship may be expressed or implied.
      a. Express agency
         (1) An express agency relationship is created verbally or in writing by a formal agreement or contract. Under common law, state laws, such as Statute of Frauds, require

the representation agreement be in writing to be enforceable so a commission can be collected.
(2) A written listing contract between a seller and a broker is an example of an express listing contract; the seller is authorizing the brokerage to find a buyer for his or her property.
(3) A written buyer representation contract also is an example of an express contract; a buyer is authorizing the broker to find a property that meets his or her needs and, typically, to negotiate on behalf of the buyer in that transaction.

b. Implied agency
(1) The implied agency relationship may be created when the actions indicate they have mutually consented to an agency relationship.
(2) The creation of implied agency may be unintentional or inadvertent; for example, the actions of a subagent of the listing broker in dealing with a potential buyer could cause the buyer to believe that the subagent is treating the buyer as a client, thus creating an implied agency. This is typically is a volition of license or other state laws.

2. Disclosure when acting as principal or other conflict of interest.
a. Full disclosure to all parties, and consent, lessens the likelihood of a conflict of interest problem.

D. Responsibilities of agent/principal
1. Duties to client/principal (buyer, seller, tenant or landlord)
a. Under common law of agency, the brokerage owed a fiduciary duty to the principal, whether seller, buyer, lessor, or lessee of property.
b. Generally, an agent's duties to the principal may be referred to as "COLDAC" (Care, Obedience, Loyalty, Disclosure, Accounting, Confidentiality).
(1) Care—agents must exercise a reasonable degree of care, applying the agent's required level of skill and expertise, on behalf of the principal, such as helping a seller to determine a reasonable listing price or helping a landlord to determine an appropriate level of rent.
(2) Obedience—agents must act in good faith and obey legal instructions by the client/principal related to the service being provided by the agents. Agents cannot obey illegal instructions, such as being told by a landlord to refuse rental to a prospective tenant because the prospective tenant is a member of a protected class, or such as refusing to disclose material adverse facts, at a seller's request, when such disclosures are mandated by state law.
(3) Loyalty—agents are required to place the principal's interests above non-principal's interests, including the agent's own self-interest. The agent is an advocate for the principal.
(4) Disclosure—agents are required to disclose to the client or principal any material facts that might affect the client's decision. Most states now require licensees to disclose

adverse material facts to all parties. An adverse material fact is generally defined as a fact that the buyer doesn't know about and can't discover through a reasonably vigilant observation, such as damage from a fire or significant water damage.

(5) Accounting—agents are required to report the status of all funds received from or on behalf of a principal, and typically, state laws require agents to maintain accurate copies of documents created for the principal in any given transaction.

(6) Confidentiality—an agent owes the principal confidentiality. For example, a listing agent could not disclose the client or principal's willingness to accept less than the listing price, or to disclose that a buyer client is under a tight moving schedule (if that would undermine the buyer's bargaining position) unless authorized by the client or principal. However, as noted, most states now impose confidentiality duties on brokers in all agency capacities. A key element traditionally is confidentiality, although state brokerage laws and ethics impose certain duties of confidentiality in all brokerage agency relationships.

2. Traditional common law agency duties; effect of dual agency on agent's duties.
   a. Historically, real estate agents represented only the sellers of real estate, and under traditional common law, all duties would have been owed to the seller.
   b. Subagency, as traditionally applied, meant that even though "working with" the buyer, the subagent owed duties only to the seller (as a subagent of the listing broker).
   c. The development of buyer agency, and designated agency, along with non-agency relationships, allowed real estate professionals to represent buyers as principal/clients.
   d. Most states have now implemented laws allowing client/principal relationships on both sides of a given transaction provided the disclosure and consent requirements are met.
   e. Dual agency, if permitted by state law, could arise by express or implied agency, but to be lawfully employed, requires disclosure and consent from all parties.
   f. The National Association of REALTORS® Code of Ethics long ago imposed ethics duties of fairness and honesty to all parties, and since then, many states have required licensees to observe various duties owed to all parties to a given transaction, and to provide timely disclosure of these duties to all parties.

E. Responsibilities of agent to customers and third parties, including disclosure, honesty, integrity, accounting for money.
   1. Disclosure—contrasted to traditional common law, most states now define the duties owed by agents to all other parties in the transaction. For example, most states now require that agents disclose adverse material facts known to the agent that may not be known by the various parties. The duties owed to third parties,

if any, would require the agent to conduct him/herself consistently with the agency representation engaged in by the agent.

2. Honesty
    a. Agents are responsible for dealing fairly and honestly with customers and/or third parties, within the scope of the agency relationship.
3. Integrity
    a. Agents must be honest and ethical and not make false or misleading statements about a property being sold or being considered by a customer.
4. Accounting for money
    a. The broker may be required to deposit all funds entrusted to her or him in a trust account, or do what all parties agree should be done with the funds, and may not commingle such funds with the broker's own funds.
5. Termination of agency
    a. Expiration of the agency agreement according to its own terms.
    b. Completion/performance—achievement of the objective for which the agency was created.
    c. Termination by force of law, if applicable.
    d. Destruction of property to be sold and/or death of the principal.
    e. Death of the principal or agent (brokerage firm)—not of the salesperson or broker associate
    f. Mutual agreement—agent and principal agree to extension or termination of the contract.

F. Non-agents (transaction, facilitation)
    1. A nonagent, if allowed under state law, assists the parties without having a principal—agent or client relationship with either of the parties.
    2. A nonagent in real estate could be a transactional broker, facilitator, or intermediary, and in some states could assist both the buyer and the seller in the transaction without having an agency relationship with either of the parties.
    3. The nonagent, as all real estate professionals and agents, is expected to treat all parties honestly, competently, and equally, and would not disclose confidential information to either party and would not negotiate or advocate for either the seller or buyer.

G. Other Important Terms
    1. Blind ads—Ads that do not identify the broker as the advertiser; broker generally is prohibited from placing blind ads
    2. Commission sharing agreements—real estate brokers may share a commission only with their own salespeople or with other licensed brokers.
    3. Broker recourse if seller refuses to pay commission—some states allow broker to sue for commission and place lien on property if not paid.

CHAPTER 7 QUIZ

1. Adam agrees to buy Beatrice's real estate for $123,000. Beatrice signs a sales contract and the $12,300 earnest money check is deposited with Beatrice's broker, Cornelius. Beatrice is unable to show good title, and Adam demands the return of his earnest money from Cornelius, as provided in the contract. What should Cornelius do?
   1. Deduct the commission and return the balance to Beatrice
   2. Deduct the commission and pay the balance to Beatrice
   3. Return the entire amount of earnest money to Adam
   4. Pay the entire amount to Beatrice to dispose of as Beatrice sees fit

2. A broker employs several salespeople at her office. Early one day, one member of the sales staff submits a written offer with an earnest money deposit on a house listed with the broker. Later the same day, another salesperson submits a higher written offer on the same property, also including an earnest money deposit. The broker, in accordance with the policy of her office, does not submit a second offer unless the first has been presented and *rejected* by the seller. In this case, the seller accepts the first offer, so the seller is not informed of the second offer. In the situation, the broker's actions are
   1. permissible, provided the commission is split between the two salespeople.
   2. permissible, if such arrangement is written into the salespeople's employment contracts.
   3. not permissible, because the broker must submit all offers to the seller.
   4. not permissible, because the broker must notify the second buyer of the existence of the first offer.

3. An owner listed her home for $98,000, and the listing broker told the prospective buyer to submit a low offer, because the seller was desperate. The buyer offered $96,000, and the seller accepted. In this situation,
   1. the broker was unethical, but because no one was hurt, the broker's conduct is not improper.
   2. the broker violated the agency relationship.
   3. the broker's action was proper in obtaining a quick offer.
   4. any broker is authorized to encourage bidders.

4. Which of the following is generally required to create a universal agent?
   1. A listing contract
   2. An offer to purchase
   3. A subagency relationship with a listing broker
   4. A power of attorney

5. A doctor listed his home with a broker under an exclusive-right-to-sell contract. The listing salesperson and her broker signed the listing contract. All of the following are true about the relationship among the parties *EXCEPT*
   1. the broker has a fiduciary relationship with the seller.
   2. the salesperson has a fiduciary relationship with the broker.
   3. if the salesperson dies, the listing contract will be terminated.
   4. if the broker dies, the listing contract will be terminated.

6. A real estate broker is usually
   1. a special agent.
   2. a universal agent.
   3. a general agent.
   4. an ostensible agent.

7. All of the following are true concerning a real estate broker *EXCEPT*
   1. all offers must be presented by the broker to the principal.
   2. brokers may place blind ads.
   3. a fixed place of business must be maintained by the broker.
   4. the broker's commission usually is specified in the listing contract.

8. You are a broker who has listed a home for a neighbor. Which of the following terms describes your relationship with the seller?
   1. You are a subagent of the seller.
   2. The seller is your client.
   3. The seller is your customer.
   4. The seller is your agent.

9. You are a broker acting as a facilitator in the sale of a house without being an agent of either party. You are a
   1. buyer's broker.
   2. cooperative broker.
   3. listing broker.
   4. transactional broker.

10. The responsibilities of a broker in an agency relationship include
    1. managing the property.
    2. providing financing.
    3. accountability for funds received.
    4. accepting an offer for the seller.

11. The listing broker owes fiduciary duty to the
    1. buyer.
    2. lender.
    3. seller.
    4. buyer's attorney.

12. When a broker lists a property, the broker may
    1. reject an offer for the seller's property.
    2. bind the seller to a contract.
    3. advertise the seller's property.
    4. offer legal advice to the seller.

13. Which of the following is a violation of the broker's fiduciary relationship with a seller?
    1. The broker charges no commission.
    2. The broker charges a 40% commission.
    3. The broker tells a prospective buyer the lowest price the seller will accept.
    4. The broker tells a prospective buyer the highest price the seller will accept.

14. All of the following are true of a fiduciary *EXCEPT*
    1. a fiduciary owes loyalty to the principal.
    2. a fiduciary must conform to the principal's legal instructions.
    3. a fiduciary is an agent.
    4. a fiduciary is a neutral third party.

15. A salesperson is working under a broker. The salesperson may
    1. work under the broker as an independent contractor.
    2. place an ad without identifying the broker.
    3. receive a commission directly from a seller.
    4. receive a commission directly from another broker.

16. A special agent is *BEST* described as someone who
    1. has power of attorney.
    2. has authority to sell a property.
    3. has authority to represent a principal in a specific transaction.
    4. has authority to represent a principal in all matters concerning an area of the principal's interest.

17. A broker presents a seller with a written offer to purchase. The broker is responsible for
    1. explaining the advantages or disadvantages of the offer to the seller.
    2. explaining the legal implications of accepting the offer.
    3. binding the seller to the offer.
    4. preparing the title search once the offer is accepted.

18. A broker is listing her neighbor's home. The commission should be determined by
    1. the size of the broker's firm.
    2. rates approved by the Real Estate Commission.
    3. rates approved by the local Board of REALTORS®
    4. negotiation with her neighbor.

19. A brokerage has earned a commission on the sale of a listing by another broker. The listing broker may pay part of her commission to
    1. the selling brokerage.
    2. the selling salesperson.
    3. the out-of-state salesperson who referred the seller to her.
    4. the buyer's attorney.

20. A broker has just received an earnest money payment on an offer to purchase. The broker must place the earnest money in his
    1. trust account.
    2. business account.
    3. personal checking account.
    4. savings account.

21. What is the listing broker's legal responsibility to a prospective purchaser?
    1. The broker must not use fraud or deceit.
    2. The broker must help the buyer get the lowest price possible.
    3. The broker is only a middleperson. Neither the buyer nor the seller can charge her or him with avoiding a legal duty.
    4. There is none at all.

MATCHING QUIZ

The column on the right contains brief memory links to important terms in Chapter 7.

Write the letter of the matching term on the appropriate line.

A. Principal
B. Delegated authority
C. Consent to act
D. Fiduciary
E. Loyalty
F. Dual agency
G. Commingling
H. Universal agent
I. Single agency
J. Subagent
K. Puffing
L. Fraud
M. REALTORS® Code of Ethics
N. Special agent
O. Implied agency
P. Client
Q. Customer
R. Obedience
S. Care
T. General agent

1. _______ Standard of ethical behavior for REALTORS®
2. _______ Unlawful mixing of the broker's money and his or her client's funds
3. _______ The person or entity that delegates authority in order to create an agency relationship
4. _______ A property manager who has several duties to perform for his or her principal
5. _______ A duty to a principal that includes confidentiality
6. _______ Giving a seller an estimate of proceeds to determine their net before listing their home is an example of this agency duty
7. _______ A relationship where an agent represents only one party
8. _______ With permission, representing both sides of the same transaction
9. _______ Agent authorized to represent principal in a transaction
10. _______ Agent's exaggerated opinion
11. _______ Intentional misrepresentation
12. _______ An agent's agent
13. _______ Generally requires power of attorney to create
14. _______ The principal's act that creates agency
15. _______ Type of duty required of an agent when asked by an owner not to place a For Sale sign in the yard
16. _______ To create agency, the principal delegates authority, and the Broker must do this
17. _______ A type of relationship based on trust and confidence
18. _______ Creation may be intentional or inadvertent
19. _______ Someone with whom you work
20. _______ Someone for whom you work

CHAPTER 7 QUIZ ANSWERS

1. **(3)** Beatrice has breached the contract because she could not produce clear (marketable) title. Therefore, the earnest money should be returned to the buyer, Adam. (94)

2. **(3)** Brokers are responsible for submitting all offers to clients. (94)

3. **(2)** The broker owes loyalty to the client as part of the fiduciary responsibilities. The broker should encourage the buyer to make his or her highest and best offer. (94)

4. **(4)** A power of attorney is generally required to create a universal agent; a broker generally doesn't have this type of authority. (92)

5. **(3)** The salesperson works on behalf of the broker but is not necessarily a party to the contract prepared by him. While the listing contract is taken by the salesperson, the contract is between the doctor and the broker. Unless there is an agreement to the contrary, listings are considered the property of the broker. (95)

6. **(1)** A special agent has a specific responsibility as compared to a general agent who has greater responsibilities, such as a property manager. A universal agent has newly unlimited authority. (92)

7. **(2)** Blind ads are prohibited. (96)

8. **(2)** The listing broker is the agent of the seller. (91)

9. **(4)** A transactional broker also is referred to as a nonagent whose job is to help the parties with the paperwork and procedure required to complete the transaction. (96)

10. **(3)** Accountability is part of the fiduciary relationship. (96)

11. **(3)** The listing contract creates an agency relationship and thus a fiduciary duty to the seller. (94)

12. **(3)** The listing broker is responsible for marketing the property. The broker would not have the authority to respond to an offer for the client or to offer legal advice. (91)

13. **(3)** Commissions are not part of the fiduciary obligations of an agent. A buyer's broker could suggest that the client offer the lowest price a seller might accept; a listing agent making this suggestion is in violation of the fiduciary obligations owed the principal. (95)

14. **(4)** The broker has a fiduciary duty to work in the best interest of his or her client. (95)

15. **(1)** Blind ads are prohibited. A salesperson may receive a commission only from the broker for whom he or she is working. (96)

16. **(3)** The incorrect answers reflect the authority of a universal agent. (92)

17. **(1)** A broker may not give legal advice nor bind a seller to an offer. A title company licensed by the state insurance commission, an attorney, or a title insurance abstractor would do the title search. (92)

18. **(4)** Commissions are negotiable. A rate approved by more than one broker would be a violation of antitrust law. (92)

19. **(1)** Commissions must be shared on a broker-to-broker basis. (96)

20. **(1)** Brokers are required to set up a trust account for earnest money payments unless otherwise agreed to by the buyer and seller. (96)

21. **(1)** The listing broker must treat the customer fairly but is required to get the seller the highest price possible. (95–96)

TEST SCORE

GENERAL PRINCIPLES OF AGENCY			
Rating	**Range**	**Your Score**	
Good = 80% to 100%	17-21	Total Number	21
Fair = 70% to 79%	16	Total Wrong	–
Needs improvement = Lower than 70%	15 or less	Total Right	

Passing Requirement: 16 or Better

ANSWER KEY: MATCHING QUIZ

1. **M**
2. **G**
3. **A**
4. **T**
5. **E**
6. **S**
7. **I**
8. **F**
9. **N**
10. **K**
11. **L**
12. **J**
13. **H**
14. **B**
15. **R**
16. **C**
17. **D**
18. **O**
19. **Q**
20. **P**

Property Disclosures

OUTLINE OF CONCEPTS

I. Property condition disclosure

A. Property owner's role regarding property condition

1. The majority of states have seller disclosure laws, which require sellers to provide buyers with a written property disclosure.
2. Under disclosure laws, the seller is generally responsible for disclosing any known defects regarding personal safety and structural soundness, as well as any known latent (hidden) defects; e.g. a leaky basement.
3. Latent (hidden) defects are any defect that is not visible and would not be uncovered by a normal inspection.

B. Licensee's role regarding property condition

1. Licensee's responsibility will vary among states; many states require the listing broker or salesperson complete a visual inspection of the property.
2. States with written seller property disclosures require the listing broker or salesperson supply the seller with the required disclosure document and have the seller, never the licensee, complete the form, which will be given to potential buyers.
3. The broker or salesperson is required to disclose any known material facts concerning the property to potential buyers even if the seller requests the licensee not disclose; failure to do so could result in liability for the brokerage and listing licensee, as well as the seller.
4. This does not include stigmatized property issues. Each state's law is used to determine what must be disclosed.

II. Warranties

A. Purpose of home or construction warranty programs

1. Home warranty programs—used for previously owned homes
   a. Home warranty program often is purchased by seller to provide reassurance to potential buyers regarding the condition of items, such as the plumbing, major appliances, and the heating system.

b. Each warranty company has a different contract and coverage so buyers should be fully informed about what is and is not covered.
c. Home warranty programs provide for the replacement or repair of a home's mechanical systems and major built-in appliances in the event of a breakdown due to normal use.

2. New home construction warranty programs
   a. All states have some form of a new construction warranty protecting buyers due to defects caused by faulty workmanship and defective materials due to noncompliance with building standards.
   b. Builders also may provide additional warranties on new homes backed either by the builder or purchased by the builder from an insurance company.
   c. Warranties generally provide limited coverage on workmanship and materials in components, such as heating, air conditioning, and windows; the coverage duration varies with the component of the house.
   d. Coverage can extend up to ten years on certain parts of the home.
3. New construction warranty programs
   a. New construction warranty programs can provide protection for up to ten years on major construction defects resulting from noncompliance with building standards.

III. Need for a home inspection and obtaining/verifying information

A. Explanation of property inspection process and appropriate use
   1. Most states include inspection contingencies in their offer to purchase contracts, or a buyer may add this contingency to any offer.
   2. A licensed home inspector will look for problems, such as mechanical, structural, or electrical issues.
   3. The buyer is seeking an informed opinion to determine if he or she should continue with the purchase of the house.
   4. The inspection process can take up to three or four hours; the buyer should, if possible, accompany the inspector and ask questions.
   5. The buyer can ask for repairs to be made or can use the inspection contingency language to reject the offer.
   6. The home inspector cannot tell a buyer every deficiency in the house but can recommend that other more specialized inspectors be brought in by the buyer, such as a plumber or electrician.
   7. The use of a home inspection contingency is a vital step in the buyer determining whether to purchase a house. The previous comments also apply to the purchase of a new house.

B. Real estate professionals have a responsibility to inquire about "red flag" issues.
   1. A red flag issue is any indication that a property may have a problem, or that something in a property may require a closer inspection.
   2. Examples of red flag issues could include musty odors, ceiling stains, or a crack in the foundation.

3. Red flag issues should be examined by an expert, typically not the licensee, to determine if anything needs to be done if a problem is discovered. For example, an aging water heater could be a problem. While replacing a water heater may be inexpensive compared to other replacement items in the house, if the water heater were to fail, the cost of repair resulting from the damage could be very expensive.
4. The real estate professionals responsibility to inquire about red flag issues varies among states.
5. Some states require real estate professionals to perform a visual inspection of the property and write down any red flags they observe.
6. Real estate professionals may not disclose any information that may result in unlawful discrimination under state law or federal law. They should disclose, for example, that a house is built in an area over which airplanes take off from a nearby airport.
7. In summary, real estate professionals are expected to disclose all material facts. A material fact is one that, if the buyer were made aware, would influence their decision on whether to buy the house.

C. Responding to non-client inquires
1. Real estate professionals working with non-clients or customers may be bound by state license laws to treat all parties honestly and fairly.
2. Real estate professionals also are responsible for disclosing material facts that might influence a customer's decision and to perform with fair-minded skill and care.

IV. Material facts related to property condition or location

A. Land/soil conditions
1. Buyers also should be aware of the existence of radon in soil. Radon is an odorless and tasteless radioactive gas, which can enter a house through cracks in the foundation and cause cancer over a long period of time.
2. Location in a superfund site would be a red flag for the buyer as previously discussed on land use controls and regulations.
3. The buyer should be aware of the existence of a septic tank; an alternative system for waste disposal where there is no sewer system available. Seepage of discharge can permeate the groundwater, resulting in health problems.

B. Accuracy of representation of lot or improvement size, encroachments, or easements affecting use
1. Encroachments could include a fence built by a neighbor on the land you are considering buying. It is possible that the fence was built on your lot and has been there for many years, creating an easement by prescription.
2. Neighbors will sometimes extend their gardens into other people's lots creating encroachments.
3. A survey error may result in a lot being advertised as having 200 feet of lake frontage when the lot actually has 100 feet of lake frontage.
4. A home with a shared driveway could be a red flag to many buyers; the shared driveway is likely to be based on an easement.

C. Pest infestation, toxic mold, and other interior environmental hazards
   1. Pest infestation
      a. Indicators of pest infestation inside a house
         (1) Animal feces can be analyzed to determine which kind of pest is in the house.
         (2) Strange odors can be used to identify type of pest.
         (3) The presence of dead bugs could indicate that that type of bug will be found in the house.
         (4) Partially eaten plants can indicate the presence of outdoor pests.
      b. The previous indicators are but a few of the possible pest infestations that can create the need for further investigation to determine if a bigger problem exists.
   2. Mold and toxic mold were previously discussed in Chapter 4.
   3. Other interior environmental hazards
      a. Lead poisoning—lead is a chemical element that has been used extensively because of its pliability, its ability to impede water flow, and its rust resistance.
         (1) Becomes a health hazard when ingested.
            a. Children under six years of age are most vulnerable to exposure to lead-based paint.
         (2) Sources of lead poisoning—peeling paint and water systems
      b. Owners of residential properties built before 1978, when the use of lead-based paint was banned, must disclose to buyers or renters the presence of lead-based paint hazards, if known to owner (seller) or landlord.
      c. A lead-based paint disclosure statement must be attached as a separate item to all real estate sales and lease contracts on pre-1978 residential properties.
      d. Real estate professionals must distribute to buyers and renters a federal lead hazard pamphlet.
      e. Buyers will have up to 10 days to have a lead-risk assessment performed on the property, if they want one.
      f. Asbestos—material used for many years as insulation on plumbing pipes and heat ducts and as general insulation because it is a poor heat conductor; also used in floor and roofing material.
         (1) Relatively harmless if not disturbed; can become life-threatening during its removal, because of accompanying dust. Cleanup requires encapsulation and abatement.
         (2) Exposure to asbestos dust may exist if
            a. The asbestos ages and starts to disintegrate. This disintegration is referred to as being friable.
            b. Remodeling projects include the removal of asbestos shingles, roof tile, or insulation that can cause the dust to form in the air and expose people in the area to the health hazard.

g. Carbon monoxide—anything using combustion can produce a colorless, tasteless, and odorless gas resulting from incomplete combustion called carbon monoxide (CO). This includes water heaters, fireplaces, or furnaces that burn fuels, such as natural gas, oil, or wood.
   (1) If appliances are not operating properly, may increase concentrations of carbon monoxide, resulting in death, as well as the need for hospital emergency room care.
   (2) Many communities have made carbon monoxide detectors mandatory in residential buildings.

h. Radon gas was previously discussed in Chapter 4.

D. Known alterations or additions
   1. Any alterations or additions made without a building permit may be non-conforming and illegal.
   2. If any alterations or additions were made without proper permits, the code enforcement officials for the municipality have the legal authority to require permits, as well as place penalties on a property owner for non-compliance.
   3. The new owner also could be required to remove the alterations or additions at the owner's cost.
   4. Alterations and additions done without proper permits can pose serious safety problems, such as a previous owner updating the electrical work in the house without complying with the municipal electrical code.

V. Material facts related to public controls, statutes of public utilities

A. Zoning and planning information
   1. Generally administered by a local zoning and building code through a planning department.
   2. Municipality is concerned with compatibility among land uses.
   3. Misrepresentation of zoning or building permits can result in the city issuing a stop work order.
   4. Providing false information to a city also could result in fines or jail time, or even revocation of permits, resulting in the city requiring the structure to be torn down.
   5. If a nonconforming use is purchased, and then damaged, it is possible that based on the percent of damage, (usually 50%) that the city could require that the property be demolished.

B. Local taxes and special assessments, other liens
   1. Real estate taxes and special assessments, if unpaid, can result in the property owner losing ownership.
   2. Other liens, such as unpaid judgments or federal tax liens, if unpaid, can result in the property owner losing his property.
   3. The potential impact of unpaid liens make it imperative that the buyer of a home have a title search performed prior to taking title to the property.

C. External environmental hazards
   1. Real estate licensees must be aware of possible environmental hazards and where to get professional advice.
   2. External hazards include any impact on air quality, noise, or public health and safety.

3. Possible hazards include global warming and its potential impact on coastal sea conditions and flooding, as well as contamination of water from leaking underground storage tanks.
4. Environmental site assessments are one approach to becoming aware of hazards; real estate licensees are generally not responsible for disclosure of environmental hazards unless it can be shown that they should have been aware.

D. Stigmatized/psychologically impacted property, Megan's Law issues
   1. Stigmatized properties are properties perceived negatively by some people because of events that have occurred there (such as a murder) or because the house has a certain reputation (e.g., people think the house is haunted). Disclosure requirements of such stigma are determined by state law.
   2. Megan's Law—properties also can be stigmatized by the presence of convicted sex offenders in the neighborhood. Megan's Law is a federal law that requires states to notify the public about the presence of convicted sex offenders in their communities.

CHAPTER 8 QUIZ

1. Broker Matt is going to contact customer Pierre who would like to see one of Matt's listings. Matt should make his agency disclosure
   1. prior to meeting with Pierre.
   2. prior to discussing Pierre's financial qualification and type of house desired.
   3. prior to actually showing the listed property.
   4. prior to writing an offer to purchase.

2. All of the following would be classified as a latent defect *EXCEPT*
   1. an unknown underground oil tank.
   2. hidden structural damage.
   3. a large crack in the living room ceiling.
   4. a cracked heat exchanger in the furnace.

3. An owner had a grease fire and it spread to the ceiling. The kitchen was remodeled and the charred ceiling joists were sealed with paint. When the seller sells the property, the hidden charred ceiling joists should be disclosed as
   1. nothing, because they were repaired.
   2. discoverable defects.
   3. caveat emptor.
   4. latent defects.

4. If a buyer's agent knows the house her buyer desires to purchase has been stigmatized by a recent murder-suicide, ethically, what should the buyer's agent do?
   1. Remain silent to protect the seller
   2. Remain silent, because the incident didn't harm the structure
   3. Disclose it to the buyer after the purchase agreement is signed
   4. Disclose it to the buyer before the buyer writes an offer

5. All of the following statements describe a "red flag" issue *EXCEPT*
   1. a red flag issue is any indication that a property may have a problem that may require a closer inspection.
   2. red flag issues could include ceiling stains or odors.
   3. an aging water heater would not be a red flag issue, because replacing a water heater is inexpensive compared to other items in the house.
   4. agent responsibility to inquire about red flag issues varies among states.

6. All of the following statements are correct about the property inspection process *EXCEPT*
   1. a licensed home inspector will look for problems, such as structural or electrical issues.
   2. the inspection process can take up to three or four hours.
   3. the buyer should not accompany the inspector and ask questions.
   4. the buyer can use the inspection contingency to reject the offer.

7. All of the following are considered to be a latent defect *EXCEPT*
   1. the roof is sagging.
   2. the electrical system was redone without the required permit.
   3. a leaking vent stack.
   4. the property is served by a joint well.

8. All of the following statements correctly describe a home warranty program *EXCEPT*
   1. the program is generally offered to the seller in the process of listing the home.
   2. the program is often purchased by the seller to provide reassurance to potential buyers regarding the condition.
   3. the program allows the seller to avoid costly repair bills during the selling period.
   4. the program protects buyers for up to two years after the move.

9. A buyer should have a certified inspector check around toilets, showers, sinks, and basement walls to detect what kind of problem?
   1. Radon
   2. Carpenter ants
   3. Methane gas
   4. Mold

MATCHING QUIZ

The column on the right contains brief memory links to important terms in Chapter 8.

Write the letter of the matching term on the appropriate line.

A. Agency disclosure

B. Latent defect

C. Home warranty program

D. Disintegration of asbestos

E. Structural issue

F. A haunted house

G. Septic tank

H. "Red flag" issue

I. Home inspection contingency

J. Seller's property disclosure act

K. Disclosed dual agency

L. Undisclosed dual agency

M. Lead-based paint

N. Lead risk assessment

O. Agent mandatory disclosure of a material fact

1. _______ Illegal form of representation
2. _______ Vital step in buyer determining whether to purchase a home
3. _______ Musty odors
4. _______ An alternative system for waste disposal
5. _______ Informing a potential buyer about the proximity of a landfill
6. _______ Hazardous substance found in housing built prior to 1978
7. _______ Informing sellers and buyers of your working relationship
8. _______ Friable
9. _______ Sagging roof line
10. _______ Stigmatized property
11. _______ Not discoverable by an ordinary inspection
12. _______ Federal law gives the buyer 10 days after offer acceptance to do this
13. _______ Legislation requiring the seller to reveal the property condition
14. _______ Provides reassurance to potential home buyers
15. _______ Legally representing both the seller and buyer in the same transaction

CHAPTER 8 QUIZ ANSWERS

1. **(2)** While this is generally correct, you should consult your state licensing board on the disclosure timing. (105)

2. **(3)** A latent defect would not be discovered by an ordinary inspection. (105)

3. **(4)** Latent defects are hidden structural defects that can't be discovered by ordinary inspection. These defects can potentially threaten the soundness or safety of the property. *Caveat emptor* means "buyer beware," but with seller property disclosure laws, that kind of thinking is unfair and unacceptable. (105)

4. **(4)** The buyer's agent has an ethical duty to tell the buyer everything he or she knows that relates to the decision-making process, unless the disclosure violates the law, such as the racial composition of a neighborhood. (110)

5. **(3)** If the water heater were to fail, the cost of repair resulting from the damage could be very expensive. (107)

6. **(3)** The buyer should, if possible, accompany the inspector and ask questions. (106)

7. **(1)** A buyer would have no way of knowing the answers 2 and 4 without a disclosure by seller or an inspection by a home inspector or plumber. For example, a vent stack (vent pipe) enters through the roof, and even if it is leaking, the damage might not have shown up on the ceiling of the kitchen or bathroom of a house. (105–106)

8. **(4)** The program generally protects buyers for up to one year after they move. (105–106)

9. **(4)** Mold is the end result of a moisture problem. Once mold dries, it can become airborne, and then it poses a health threat to those allergic to the mold spores. (108)

TEST SCORE

PROPERTY DISCLOSURES			
Rating	**Range**	**Your Score**	
Good = 80% to 100%	8–9	Total Number	9
Fair = 70% to 79%	7	Total Wrong	–
Needs improvement = Lower than 70%	6 or less	Total Right	

Passing Requirement: 7 or Better

ANSWER KEY: MATCHING QUIZ

1. **L**
2. **I**
3. **H**
4. **G**
5. **O**
6. **M**
7. **A**
8. **D**
9. **E**
10. **F**
11. **B**
12. **N**
13. **J**
14. **C**
15. **K**

Contracts

OUTLINE OF CONCEPTS

I. General knowledge of contract law

A. Voluntary agreement between legally competent parties to do or refrain from doing some legal act, supported by legal consideration

B. Essential elements for valid contracts

1. Competent parties—must be of legal age (18) and mentally competent.
2. Offer and acceptance (mutual assent)—must have a "meeting of the minds."
   a. Any offer or counteroffer may be withdrawn at any time prior to acceptance by the offeree.
   b. A counteroffer invalidates the original offer.
3. Legality of object—purpose must be legal.
4. Consideration—an act of forbearance, or the promise thereof, given by one party in exchange for something from the other. Forbearance is a promise not to do something that a party is legally entitled to do.
5. Description of real estate—must be accurate.
6. Written and signed—generally required by the statute of frauds for most real estate contracts.

C. Contract Classifications

1. Expressed—parties state terms and show intentions in words; may be either oral or written. Real estate contracts are typically express written agreements.
2. Implied—agreement demonstrated by acts and conduct.
3. Bilateral—both parties promise to do something; one promise is given in exchange for another.
4. Unilateral—only one party makes a promise; if the second party complies, the first party is obligated to keep the promise, such as an option or open listing.
5. Executory—something remains to be done by one or both parties. The period from when the offer is accepted until the contract closes

6. Executed—both parties have fulfilled their promises and thus performed the contract. Also can mean all parties have signed the contract.

D. Legal Effect of a Contract
   1. Valid—complies with all essentials of a contract; binding and enforceable on both parties.
   2. Void—lacks an essential element of a valid contract; has no legal effect.
   3. Voidable—appears to be valid on its surface but may be disaffirmed, because one of the parties signed when a minor, when under duress, or as a result of fraud or misrepresentation.
   4. Unenforceable—appears to be valid, but neither party may sue the other to force performance; for example, an oral agreement to pay a commission.

E. When Contract is Considered Performed/Discharged
   1. Performance—all terms carried out.
   2. Substantial performance—party remains liable, because the contract was not completed exactly as required.
   3. Mutual agreement—parties agree to cancel.
   4. Operation of law—voided by minor or because of fraud or the expiration of the statute of limitations.

F. Assignment and Novation
   1. Assignment—the transfer in writing of rights or interest in a bond, mortgage, lease, or other instrument. Does not release all liability of the original signor.
   2. Novation—acceptance by parties to replace an existing contract with a new contract. Release all liability from the original signor

G. Breach of Contract and Remedies for Breach
   1. Breach of contract—the failure, without legal excuse, of one of the parties to a contract to perform according to the contract.
   2. Remedies for breach if seller defaults
      a. Rescind, or terminate the contract and recover the earnest money.
      b. Sue for specific performance.
      c. Sue the seller for damages.
   3. Remedies for breach if buyer defaults
      a. Declare the contract forfeited.
      b. Rescind the contract and keep all or part of the deposit as liquidated damages.
      c. Sue for specific performance.
      d. Sue for damages.

H. Contract Clauses
   1. Clauses or contingencies are conditions in a contract that require a certain event or events to happen before the contract is complete. Sometimes referred to as "subject to" clauses.
   2. Contingency clauses have three distinguishing features:
      a. Actions needed to satisfy the contingency.
      b. Time frame within which actions must be performed.
      c. Statement identifying (if necessary) who will be responsible for paying any related costs.

3. Examples of contingencies frequently used include:
    a. A financing contingency that makes the contract subject to the buyer obtaining financing with certain terms (interest rate, etc.) within a stated period of time.
    b. An inspection contingency that makes the contract subject to the buyer obtaining satisfactory inspections of the property, such as an inspection by a state-certified home inspector.

II. Listing Contracts—a contract between an owner (as principal) and a licensed real estate brokerage by which the brokerage is employed to list and sell real estate on the owner's terms within a given time, for which service the landowner agrees to pay a commission.

A. General requirements for a valid listing that may vary among states
    1. Be in writing to have an enforceable commission clause
    2. State the rate or exact amount of commission to be earned by the broker
    3. Specify a definite termination date for the agreement
    4. State the price of the real estate and terms of the sale
    5. Include a description specifically identifying the property
    6. Name the broker
    7. Bear the signature of the person who is to pay the broker commission

B. Exclusive listings
    1. Exclusive—right-to-sell listing
        a. One brokerage is given the exclusive right to sell the property.
        b. The seller gives up the right to sell the property without paying the broker's commission.
        c. The brokerage receives the commission regardless of who sells the property.
    2. Exclusive—agency listing
        a. Only one brokerage is authorized to act as the exclusive agent of the principal.
        b. The seller retains the right to sell the property without obligation to the brokerage.
        c. The brokerage receives a commission only if its firm is the procuring cause or caused the sale to happen.

C. Non-exclusive listings—open listing
    1. The seller may employ any number of brokerage firms.
    2. The seller is obligated to pay a commission only to the brokerage who produces a buyer (procuring cause).
    3. If the seller personally sells the property, without the aid of any broker, the seller is not obligated to pay the commission.

D. All listings are contracts between the brokerage firm and the seller, not the salesperson or broker associate. Accordingly, if a salesperson or broker associate leaves his or her brokerage firm, all of their listings remain the property of the brokerage firm.

III. Buyer/tenant representation contracts, including key elements and provisions of buyer and/or tenant agreements

A. Exclusive right contracts—unless agreed that the seller pays the commission, the buyer or tenant must compensate his or her representative whenever purchasing or renting a property of the type described within the period described.

B. Exclusive agency contract—the buyer/tenant is assured of buyer/tenant loyalty relative to any other brokerage firms. The buyer or tenant may, however, purchase or rent property on his or her own without the assistance of the brokerage firm who hold the contract, and thus without any compensation being due to the buyer/tenant's agent.

C. Ways in which buyer or tenant's broker can be compensated
   1. Retainer fee
      a. Gives buyer or tenant incentive to perform contract.
      b. Fee may be refundable or nonrefundable.
   2. Flat or fixed fee
      a. The fee can be paid by the buyer or tenant or as a co-op fee by the seller or landlord.
      b. The hourly fee should reflect the market, as well as what other professionals are receiving.
   3. Percentage fee
      a. Can be a percentage of sales or rental price or MLS co-op fee.
      b. Creates a disincentive for buyer or tenant's broker to get a lower price or rent for buyer/tenant.

IV. Purchase Contracts (offers)

A. General requirements for offers/contracts
   1. Required by the statue of frauds to be in writing to be enforceable.
   2. Sets forth all details of the agreement between the buyer and seller for the purchase and sale of real estate.
   3. When the contract has been prepared and signed by a ready, willing, and able buyer, it is an offer to purchase; the subject of real estate.
   4. All offers must be promptly presented by the broker to the principal when received.
   5. An offer becomes accepted when the sellers sign the offer and the buyer is notified of the acceptance.
   6. When the offer is signed by all parties, it becomes a legally binding executory contract, and the buyer has equitable title. Seller still holds legal title.
   7. Contract sets the requirements for closing, not the deed.

B. Earnest money deposits—not required for a valid contract
   1. Generally give evidence of intention to carry out the terms of contract.
   2. Usually must be held by the broker in a special trust, or escrow, account.
   3. Cannot be commingled, mixed with a broker's operating funds, or converted to a broker's own use.
   4. The amount is generally determined by negotiation between the buyer and seller.

C. Contingencies (previously discussed in contact clauses) and time is of the essence
   1. All contingencies must be met before the property closing takes place, and by the time frames set in the contract.
   2. A "time is of the essence" contract must be performed in the time specified; any party who does not perform on time is guilty of a breach of contract.

V. Counteroffers/Multiple Counteroffers.

A. Counteroffer terminates original offer—a counteroffer is a new offer made in response to an offer received; the original offer is, in effect, rejected and cannot be accepted thereafter unless it is revived by the offeror.

VI. Leases

A. Types of leases, e.g. percentage, gross, net, ground
   1. Lease defined
      a. A lease is a contract between a landlord (the lessor) and a tenant (the lessee) transferring the right to exclusive possession and use of the landlord's real property to the lessee for a stated period of time and for a stated consideration (rent).
      b. Statute of Frauds requires leases for longer than a certain period of time (generally one year) must be in writing to be enforceable.
   2. Percentage lease
      a. Generally used for leases of retail businesses in shopping malls and may take the form of a gross lease or a net lease.
      b. Rent is based on a minimum fixed rental fee plus a percentage of the gross sales.
   3. Gross/Fixed lease
      a. Often residential
      b. Tenant pays fixed rent and the landlord pays all of the operating expenses for the property.
   4. Net lease
      a. Often commercial
      b. Tenant pays rent plus a portion of the operating expenses.
   5. Ground lease
      a. Generally used in the development of commercial property and are for a long term of 50 years or more.
      b. Tenant leases unimproved land from the owner and constructs a building.
      c. Generally net leases in which tenant pays most of operating expenses as well as a rent on the ground.

B. Leases with obligation to purchase or lease with an option to purchase
   1. Lease with right to purchase—lessee enters into a contract to purchase a property at a later date for a predetermined price and agrees to pay rent during the period in which the property is being rented.
   2. Lease with an option to purchase—lessee enters into a contract to rent a property, as well as an option to purchase the property at a later date; the lessee is not obligated to buy the property as in a lease with an obligation to purchase.

VII. Other real estate contracts

A. Options
   1. Unilateral contract by which the optionor (owner) gives the optionee (prospective buyer) the right to buy at a fixed price within a stated period of time.

2. The optionee pays the fee for the option right and assumes no obligation to make any other payment until the optionee decides, within a specified time, to either exercise the option right or allow the option to expire.

B. Right of first refusal—a clause in which the owner gives a tenant an opportunity to buy a property before selling it to another party.

C. Installment Contract/Contract for Deed/Land Contract
   1. Means of financing a purchase: the buyer (vendee) typically gives the seller a nominal down payment and regular periodic payments over a number of years, including interest.
   2. Legal title to real estate remains in the seller's (vendor's) name during the term of contract, and buyer has equitable title.
   3. The buyer takes possession when the contract is executed (finalized).
   4. The buyer will not receive the deed/title to the property until the entire purchase price has been paid.

VIII. Other Real Estate Contractual Concepts

A. Counteroffer—new offer made in response to an offer received; the original offer is, in effect, rejected, and cannot be accepted thereafter unless it is revived by the offeror.

B. Amendments—licensees in many states are required to fill out amendment forms to change the language in either the listing contract or the offer to purchase.

C. Cancellation or termination agreements—forms used to terminate a transaction; used in some states by a broker to get a written release from both the buyer and seller to authorize the refund of earnest money.

D. Leasing contracts—written or oral contracts between the tenant (lessee) and the landlord (lessor); transfers the right to exclusive possession and the use of the landlord's real property to the lessee for a stated consideration (rent) for a specified period of time; the statute of frauds requires that a lease for more than one year be in writing to be enforceable.

E. Addendum—adds further terms and conditions to the approved forms, thus incorporating them into the legal document; may or may not require preparation by an attorney. Examples include: disclosure of controlled business arrangements, and lead-based paint disclosures required to be signed by the seller if the house was built prior to 1978.

F. Net listing—list prices based on the amount of money the seller will receive if the property is sold, plus the commission; net listings are prohibited in most states.

G. Statute of limitations—the law pertaining to the period of time within which certain actions must be brought to court.

H. Broker Protection Clause—states that the property owner will pay the listing broker a commission if, within a specified number of days after the listing expires, the owner transfers the property to someone the broker originally introduced to the owner.

CHAPTER 9 QUIZ

1. A contract in which the intentions of the parties are shown by their actions is
   1. an expressed contract.
   2. an implied contract.
   3. an executory contract.
   4. a bilateral contract.

2. Which of the following is *NOT* an essential element of a contract?
   1. An earnest money deposit
   2. Legality of object
   3. Offer and acceptance (mutual assent)
   4. Competent parties

3. The lessee in a leasing agreement is the
   1. tenant.
   2. property manager.
   3. landlord.
   4. rental agent.

4. A lease that is signed by a person who is 17 years of age (still a minor) is
   1. unilateral.
   2. void.
   3. illegal.
   4. voidable.

5. Contracts for sale of real estate must be in writing to be enforceable, according to the
   1. statute of limitations.
   2. parol evidence rule.
   3. statute of frauds.
   4. real estate commission.

6. A broker lists a home for $80,000. The broker brings an offer to the seller for $78,000, which is rejected by the seller. The broker obtains another offer, for $80,000, for the seller. Before she can deliver the offer, however, the offeror withdraws it by calling the broker at the seller's home. There is
   1. an implied contract.
   2. a unilateral contract.
   3. an executory contract.
   4. no contract.

7. A salesperson entered into an option contract with an optionee who has 30 days to exercise his option. The option is what kind of contract?
   1. Voidable contract
   2. Unilateral contract
   3. Unenforceable contract
   4. Bilateral contract

8. A broker has received several offers for a property he has listed. The broker must present each offer to the seller
   1. promptly on receipt.
   2. individually.
   3. as soon as the seller has decided on any previous offer.
   4. prior to the seller deciding on any previous offer.

9. Without discussing price, you order dinner in a restaurant. You are required to pay for the dinner through what kind of contract?
   1. Bilateral
   2. Express
   3. Voidable
   4. Implied

10. A broker and a seller have signed an open listing contract. This agreement is an example of a(n)
    1. unilateral contract.
    2. executed contract.
    3. bilateral contract.
    4. unenforceable contract.

11. Which of the following correctly describes an open listing?
    1. The seller may employ any number of brokers.
    2. Only one broker is authorized to act as agent for the seller.
    3. The broker is entitled to a commission regardless of who sells the property.
    4. The broker's commission is based on the excess over the sales price stated in the listing.

12. A contract that lacks legal object is considered to be
    1. voidable.
    2. unenforceable.
    3. void.
    4. canceled.

13. All of the following may legally terminate a listing with a broker *EXCEPT*
    1. bankruptcy of the client.
    2. insanity of the broker.
    3. inability of the broker to find a buyer within a reasonable amount of time.
    4. an economic depression.

14. Ayers gave an option on her property for 90 days to Benitez and received a cash consideration of $100. Benitez later assigned the option to Columbus for a valuable consideration. Before expiration of the option, Ayers stated that she no longer wanted to sell the property. Which of the following is correct?
    1. The option is void, because an option cannot be assigned.
    2. The option is not binding on Ayers, for $100 is not sufficient consideration.
    3. Columbus would have a good chance in court to compel Ayers to sell to him, if he exercises the option before its expiration date.
    4. Ayers can refuse to sell, because the consideration paid by Columbus was not in cash.

15. Both the buyer and the seller agree to wait until the broker's exclusive-right-to-sell listing has expired. They then have a third party buy the home. After a short while, the third party conveys ownership to the interested buyer, who was actually introduced to the owner by the listing broker. In this case,
    1. the broker is not entitled to a commission, because the listing expired.
    2. if the listing broker can prove collusion, he or she may collect a full commission.
    3. the broker may sue both the buyer and the seller for the commission.
    4. the broker is entitled to his commission, because he performed the task for which he was hired.

16. Procuring cause would *NOT* be required for a broker to receive a commission in a(n)
    1. open listing.
    2. exclusive-right-to-sell listing.
    3. net listing.
    4. exclusive agency listing.

17. When a broker sold a property, the sales contract contained the following statement: "Buyer to accept property in 'as is' condition." However, both the seller and the broker knew the plumbing was in a major state of disrepair but did not tell the buyer. Would an action for damages against the broker, based on fraud, be successful?
    1. No. The "as is" provision in the contract is evidence of a meeting of the minds.
    2. No. The contract specifically stated that the property was being sold "as is."
    3. Yes. The duty to disclose a material fact cannot be avoided by an "as is" provision.
    4. Yes. "As is" refers only to exterior defects.

18. A broker brings a seller an offer-to-purchase contract for the listed price of $114,500, with an additional stipulation that the seller must furnish a title insurance policy to prove marketable title. The seller refuses the offer. The broker
    1. can collect full commission, because sellers always must provide title insurance.
    2. can collect one-half of the commission.
    3. can collect nothing.
    4. can collect one-half of the first month's mortgage payment.

19. A salesperson for a brokerage listed an owner's home under an exclusive-right-to-sell listing contract. Which of the following statements correctly describes this situation?
    1. The listing belongs to the salesperson.
    2. If the principal sells his own house, he will not have to pay a commission.
    3. The listing belongs to the brokerage.
    4. The listing belongs to both the salesperson and the brokerage.

20. An owner gives an exclusive-right-to-sell listing to a broker for a six-month period. During the exclusive period, the owner also gives an open listing to another broker who produces a buyer. What is the owner's liability for payment of a commission?
    1. Only one commission must be paid, which both brokers share on a 50/50 basis.
    2. The owner is liable only to the first broker for the payment of a commission.
    3. The owner is liable for payment of a commission to both brokers.
    4. The owner is liable only to the second broker for the payment of a commission.

21. A buyer has contracted with a seller to purchase property. The contract was ratified on January 10. The closing was on March 31. What is the status of the contract on April 1?
    1. Void
    2. Anticipatory
    3. Executed
    4. Executory

22. An exclusive-right-to-sell listing contract is a bilateral contract and may be considered
    1. a conveyance.
    2. an employment contract.
    3. an option.
    4. a contingency agreement.

23. A salesperson
    1. may receive a commission directly from a principal.
    2. can carry out activities in his or her own name.
    3. is responsible primarily to the broker under whom she or he is licensed.
    4. may place a blind ad.

24. The buyer's offer requires the seller pay for a licensed termite inspector to inspect a house. If active infestation exists, the buyer can either agree to have the property treated or can decline the offer. This part of an offer is *BEST* known as
    1. a condition.
    2. a contingency.
    3. a chattel.
    4. a cloud.

25. If a buyer offers to purchase a home for $350,000 subject to the sale of the buyer's home, what is the subject to sale called?
    1. Contingency
    2. Condition
    3. Cloud
    4. Cancellation

26. A tenant decided to purchase a farm on an installment land contract for deed with a ten-year balloon. During the ten years, what kind of title does the vendee have in the farm?
    1. Legal
    2. Conditional
    3. Equitable
    4. Substantial

MATCHING QUIZ

The column on the right contains brief memory links to important terms in Chapter 9.

Write the letter of the matching term on the appropriate line.

A. Consideration
B. Earnest money
C. Expressed contract
D. Implied contract
E. Unilateral contract
F. Voidable contract
G. Specific performance
H. Open listing
I. Exclusive right to sell
J. Executory contract
K. Listing contracts
L. Statute of frauds
M. Equitable title
N. Legal title
O. A purchase agreement
P. Acceptance
Q. Optionor
R. Vendee
S. Counteroffer
T. Contingency

1. _______ In a real estate office, these contracts are the property of the broker
2. _______ Prior to acceptance, these are considered offers
3. _______ A type of title also known as an insurable interest
4. _______ Pumping gas prior to paying is an example of this type of contract
5. _______ A type of title that one receives as the deed is delivered
6. _______ Notification and delivery to buyers of their signed offer by the seller
7. _______ Requires contracts of sale, such as purchase agreements to be in writing
8. _______ Type of listing stating, regardless of who procures the buyer, the listing broker gets paid
9. _______ Only the real estate firm who procures the buyer gets paid by the seller
10. _______ A contract with a minor
11. _______ An option is an example of this type of contract
12. _______ A court order requiring a promise made to be carried out
13. _______ Something remains to be done by one of the parties
14. _______ If specified in the contract, this can be used as liquidated damages
15. _______ A legal requirement to create a valid contract that can be good and signed by an offeror or valuable
16. _______ A contract in which the parties state the exact terms
17. _______ This act by the offeree invalidates an original offer
18. _______ A termite inspection is an example of this prerequisite to settlement
19. _______ The person who owns the property and has a signed an option contract with a potential buyer
20. _______ The buyer in a land contract for deed

CHAPTER 9 QUIZ ANSWERS

1. **(2)** An expressed contract would be oral or written. An executory contract is one in which parties to the contract have not fulfilled their contractual obligations. An accepted offer to purchase would be an example of a bilateral contract. (117)

2. **(1)** Earnest money can be used as consideration to create a contract, but it is not essential. A contract to purchase a home may be written with the agreement that a check is to be written at closing for the full amount. To create a contract requires consideration, but the consideration may be a promise to pay the full amount at closing in return for the owner's property. (120)

3. **(1)** The landlord is the lessor. A property manager is considered a general agent because of the broad responsibilities assumed on the property owner's behalf. (121)

4. **(4)** A minor may enter into a contract; however, upon reaching majority age, the minor may either ratify (accept) or disaffirm (reject) the contract. (117)

5. **(3)** The statute of limitations is the period of time within which one may judicially challenge a contract. The real estate commission is a regulatory body that is responsible for enforcing rather than making the laws of a state. The parol evidence rule provides that prior or contemporaneous oral agreements modifying a written contract will not be admitted in a court of law to modify or contradict a written contract. (117)

6. **(4)** An offer can be withdrawn at any time prior to notification of acceptance. (117)

7. **(2)** An option is a unilateral contract until the optionee chooses to exercise the option right to buy, at which time it becomes a bilateral contract. The optionor may not void the contract, which is enforceable by the optionee. (121–122)

8. **(1)** The broker must present all offers simultaneously. The broker does not have the right to withhold offers from the seller. (120)

9. **(4)** The ordering of the dinner is considered an implied contract. An express contract is one where words have been exchanged, whereas in an implied contract, the parties' conduct often demonstrates their willingness to enter into a contract. (117)

10. **(1)** A bilateral contract would require two promises. An open listing would be enforceable but clearly is not an executed contract, as the parties must perform. In a unilateral contract, only one party is required to perform. (117)

11. **(1)** Answer number 4 would be a net listing, while number 2 would be an exclusive agency or exclusive-right-to-sell listing. The seller in an open listing has the right to sell the property herself without paying the listing broker a commission. (119)

12. **(3)** A contract that does not have legal object is void. A voidable contract is valid but may be disaffirmed depending on the parties involved. An enforceable contract is one that meets the test of a valid contract. (118)

13. **(4)** A listing contract may be terminated by acts of the parties or by operation of law. (118)

14. **(3)** The optionor promises to sell and has no right to cancel; the optionee has the choice of exercising the option right. (121–122)

15. **(2)** The broker's rights would be based on the broker protection clause. (122)

16. **(2)** The open and exclusive agency listings allow the sellers to sell the property personally on their own without owing the broker a commission. (119)

17. **(3)** The broker is required to disclose any known material fact that might affect the decision of the buyer. In an "as is" contract, it is always best to define what is "as is." Is the plumbing in the bathroom "as is"? Or is the wiring in the entire house "as is"? Or is the entire property "as is"? (118)

18. **(3)** The contingency is not consistent with the terms of the listing, thus relieving the seller of the obligation to pay a commission to the broker. (118–119)

19. **(3)** The salesperson is not a party to the contract. The exclusive right-to-sell provision prevents the seller from being able to avoid paying a commission. (120)

20. **(3)** The first broker is protected under the exclusive-right-to-sell provision; the second broker is entitled under procuring cause. (119)

21. **(3)** The closing means that the contract is no longer anticipatory or executory. (117–118)

22. **(2)** The exclusive right-to-sell listing contract is a bilateral contract and is also an employment agreement. It is considered a bilateral contract because the seller promises to pay a commission and the broker promises to use diligence to procure a purchaser. Therefore, what legally exists is a promise for a promise, which is the definition of a bilateral contract. (117–119)

23. **(3)** The salesperson works for the broker and may not receive commission from anyone other than the broker for whom he or she works. Blind ads are prohibited. (119)

24. **(2)** A contingency best describes this situation. Although the offer is conditioned upon the inspection, all of the elements of a contingency exist to make it the best answer. (118–119)

25. **(1)** The subject to sale is called a contingency. (118–119)

26. **(3)** Equitable title is sometimes referred to as an insurable interest. Legal title is passed ten years later when the deed is transferred to the vendee by the vendor. (122)

TEST SCORE

CONTRACTS			
Rating	**Range**	**Your Score**	
Good = 80% to 100%	21–26	Total Number	26
Fair = 70% to 79%	18–20	Total Wrong	–
Needs improvement = Lower than 70%	17 or less	Total Right	

Passing Requirement: 18 or Better

ANSWER KEY: MATCHING QUIZ

1. **K**
2. **O**
3. **M**
4. **D**
5. **N**
6. **P**
7. **L**
8. **I**
9. **H**
10. **F**
11. **E**
12. **G**
13. **J**
14. **B**
15. **A**
16. **C**
17. **S**
18. **T**
19. **Q**
20. **R**

CHAPTER 10

Leasing and Property Management

OUTLINE OF CONCEPTS

I. General Principles of Property Management Agreements

A. An owner can manager his own property without a license. In most states, an owner can hire an employee who does not have a real estate license to manage the property of the owner. Review your state laws to determine under what circumstances a person would need a license to manage property for others. A property management agreement is a personal service contract, which means it is terminated upon the death of either party.

B. The owner may also enter into a contract with a brokerage firm to manage property. If the brokerage firm is hired to manage the property, an agent for the brokerage may be the property manager. A written management agreement between the owner and the brokerage stipulates whether payment is to be on a flat-fee basis or a percentage of the gross income.

C. Whichever relationship or method of payment is negotiated, the brokerage firm and property manager have a fiduciary relationship with the owner. The property manager is the general agent of the owner, meaning the manager is involved in an ongoing business relationship and can enter into contracts on behalf of the owner.

D. The property manager has a fiduciary relationship with the owner, which includes the duties of care, obedience, accounting, loyalty, and disclosure.

1. The duty of care means to use care and skill while managing the property, binding the owner to contracts, and being responsible in every way to the owner.
2. The duty of obedience means to carry out, in good faith, the owner's instructions. The property manager should immediately terminate the relationship if asked to do something illegal or unethical.
3. The duty of accounting means to maintain and accurately report to the owner the status of all funds received on behalf of, or from, the property owner.

4. The duty of loyalty means to put the property owner's interests first and act without self-interest in every transaction.
5. The duty of disclosure means to keep the owner informed of all material facts regarding the management of the property.

E. Property managers may specialize in a particular type of property, such as condominium communities, apartment buildings, warehouses, factories, industrial parks, hotels, office buildings, and so on.

II. Basic Provisions/Purpose/Elements of Property Management Agreements

A. There is a difference between a management plan and a management agreement. The property manager will be responsible for creating a management plan that meets the owner's objectives, a budget of projected revenues and expenses, and occupancy and absorption rates.

B. The management agreement is negotiated between the owner and the brokerage/property manager, and it creates an agency relationship with fiduciary duties to the owner.

C. If a brokerage firm is hired to manage property, the broker may hire an agent to manage the property. The agreement is between the brokerage firm and the owner, not the agent and the owner.

D. States may have specific laws regarding such agreements, but generally, the following must be included to establish the scope of the agent's authority:
1. Identification of the parties
2. Identification of the property, which may include a legal description
3. Statement of owner's purpose
4. Duties and responsibilities of the manager
5. Responsibilities of the owner
6. Rate and schedule of compensation
7. Accounting and report requirements
8. Starting date, termination date, and provisions for renewal options
9. Amount and method of determining the minimum security deposit to be collected from the tenants for each unit managed
10. Procedure for returning or retaining the security deposit
11. Provision setting forth the conditions under which the manager is authorized to pay expenses of the property being managed and any other authority given to the manager
12. Copy of the lease that will be used
13. Antitrust provisions
14. Fair housing provisions
15. Signatures of the parties

E. The property manager will develop an operating budget, cash flow report, profit and loss statement, and budget comparison statement.

F. Operating budget
1. An operating budget is based on the anticipated revenues and expenses. When the property manager develops the budget, it must reflect the owner's long-term goals. The budget will allocate money for continuous, fixed expenses, such as employees' salaries, property taxes, and insurance. It will also establish a cash reserve fund for variable expenses, such as repairs and supplies.

G. Cash flow formula

1. Most owners require that the property manager create a monthly report of income and expenses.

Potential gross rental income
+ Additional income (vending equipment, parking garage fees, etc.)
– Vacancy rates and credit losses
Effective gross income

a. The gross income of an apartment complex may be based on the room count of the space, whereas commercial properties may be computed by the square footage of the space.

2. The following also may be used to compute the effective gross income. They are different from the previous steps.

Potential gross income
– Vacancy rates and credit losses
+ Additional income
Effective gross income

Effective gross income
– Operating expenses
Net operating income before debt service (Debt service is the mortgage payment.)

Net operating income before debt service
– Debt service
Cash flow (also called before-tax cash flow)

Cash flow
– Taxes
After-tax cash flow

3. The return on investment (ROI) is one way to measure the profitability of a property. The ROI is the ratio of the property's after-tax cash flow (ATCF) to the money invested (equity [E]) in the property.

a. The formula for computing the return on investment is

$$\text{ROI} = \frac{\text{ATCF}}{\text{E}} \times 100\%$$

b. The ROI also may be computed on a before-tax basis.

c. A property with a $10,000 ATCF in which the owner has $100,000 invested would have an ROI of 10%. When this formula is used to analyze the owner's investment, it is called a cash-on-cash investment, and it may be computed on either a before-tax or an after-tax basis.

H. Profit and loss statement

1. Quarterly, semiannual, or annual profit and loss statements are compiled from the monthly cash flow reports. From this, the

owner can analyze how the property was managed, decide what changes should be made, and make projections for the next year.

2. Only the interest portion of each mortgage payment should be deducted as an expense on the profit and loss statement, whereas on the monthly reports, the entire debt service is used.
   a. The following is an example of a profit and loss statement.

Profit and Loss Statement Period: January 1, XXXX, to December 31, XXXX	
Receipts	$198,948.43
Operating Expenses	– 74,343.89
Operating Income	$124,604.54
Total Mortgage Payment	– 54,567.89
Mortgage Loan Principal Add-Back	+ 6,493.20
Net Profit	$ 76,529.85

3. The profit and loss statement may be compared with the operating budget that was prepared for the year. Such a comparison can measure the performance of the property manager and determine the changes that will need to be made in the future.

I. Budget Comparison Statement
   1. The purpose of the budget comparison is to compare the actual income and expenses with the projected budget.

III. Types of Contracts

A. The tenant may be represented by an attorney when negotiating the lease agreement, or the property manager may act as the owner's agent, the lessee's agent, or a dual agent.

B. Unless the property manager is also an attorney, the property manager may only fill in the blanks of lease agreements; he may not write them. When the lease is negotiated between the owner and the tenant, a bilateral contract is created, and exclusive possession is given to the tenant. It is the owner's responsibility to provide the lease agreement that is to be used by the property manager.

C. Whether leasing residential, commercial, or industrial property, qualifying the tenant is one of the major responsibilities of the property manager. Filling out a lease application that may ask for verification of identity, authorization to secure a credit report, financial statement, special needs of the tenant, and securing rental history is a part of the process.

D. The lease negotiations could include concessions, such as free rent to influence a prospect to become a tenant, rent reductions and rebates, length of the lease period, tenant alterations, expansion options, noncompeting tenant restrictions, and lease buy-out, assumption, and subletting.

E. The provisions of a valid lease are essentially the same as for any valid contract. There must be an offer and acceptance by parties with the legal capacity to contract. The terms of a lease include
   1. names and addresses of the parties,
   2. description of the property,
   3. term of the lease,
   4. security deposit (amount and location of the deposit),
   5. possession and use of the premises,
   6. rights and obligations of the parties,

7. consideration (when and to whom rent payments are made),
8. late payments,
9. payment of utilities and appliances,
10. provisions for assignment and sublease,
11. provisions for maintenance and condition,
12. pets and alterations,
13. loss or damage,
14. default,
15. lead-based paint disclosure,
16. default and termination provisions,
17. warranty of quiet enjoyment,
18. warranty of habitability,
19. surrender, and
20. signatures of the parties.

F. Types of leases
   1. Estate for years or tenancy for years
      a. This is a lease with a definite time period or specified beginning and ending dates.
      b. No notice is needed to terminate the estate.
      c. A tenant who remains in possession after expiration is considered a holdover.
   2. Estate from period to period/estate from year to year/periodic tenancy
      a. This is a lease with an indefinite time period that automatically renews until proper notice to terminate is given.
   3. Estate at will or tenancy at will
      a. This is a lease that gives the tenant the right to possess the property with the consent of the landlord for an uncertain time period. The lease can be terminated at any time by the landlord or by the tenant giving proper notice to the other party.
      b. The death of either party also terminates the lease.
   4. Estate at sufferance or tenancy at sufferance
      a. This is a tenancy created when a tenant remains in possession of the property without the consent of the landlord after the lease expires.
      b. If the landlord gives permission to a tenant to remain on the property after the expiration of a lease, the tenant may be treated as a holdover, and a tenancy at will or periodic tenancy may be created.
   5. Index lease
      a. This allows rent to be increased or decreased periodically, based on an agreed index such as the change in the government cost of living index.
   6. Gross lease
      a. The tenant pays a fixed rent, while the landlord pays all the taxes, insurance, etc.

G. Termination of leases
   1. Abandonment by the tenant
      a. When the tenant abandons the lease, the tenant is still liable for the terms of the lease. In a residential lease, the landlord is responsible for mitigating damages by attempting to find another tenant in a timely manner.

2. Death of one of the parties
    a. Unless the lease agreement specifies that the lease is terminated when the landlord or tenant passes, the lease agreement is still binding and effective. (Mortgages, credit cards, and other contracts the deceased person entered into are also binding. They become a part of the estate settlement.) Exceptions to this rule include the following:
        (1) When the owner of a life estate passes, all lease agreements the life tenant may have entered into are terminated.
        (2) The death of either party will terminate a tenancy at will.
3. Destruction of the premises
    a. The lease agreement should specify the status of the lease when the premises are destroyed. In a residential lease, most state laws will terminate the lease upon the destruction of the premises. Many commercial leases are binding upon the destruction of the premises.
4. Fulfillment of the terms
    a. A lease is terminated when the parties have fulfilled the obligations of the lease.
5. Merger
    a. If the tenant purchases the property, the lease agreement is terminated.
6. Mutual agreement
    a. The landlord and tenant may mutually agree to terminate the lease.
7. Operation of law
    a. Bankruptcy of either party or the process condemnation will terminate a lease agreement. Condemnation can mean the property is found uninhabitable or the government is taking it through eminent domain.
8. Sale of the property
    a. The sale of the property does not terminate a residential lease agreement, and the new owner would need to honor the existing leases. Many commercial leases do terminate upon the sale of the property, and the commercial lease should address that issue. If the new owner has the right to terminate the lease, a sale clause will be found in the lease, which gives the tenant some time before the lease is terminated.

IV. Duties and Obligations of the Parties

A. The property management and lease agreements will stipulate the specific duties and responsibilities of each party. The following is a summary of the primary duties of each party.
    1. Owner's duties
        a. Provide specific goals and objectives to the property manager.
        b. Provide the lease agreement to the property manager.
        c. Keep the property safe and habitable. This includes snow and ice removal, adequate lighting in parking lots and hallways, working sprinkler systems, smoke detectors, and so forth. Comply with health and building codes. Follow federal, state, and local laws.

d. Give reasonable notice to inspect, make repairs for improvements, and to enter the property.
e. If a residential tenant abandons the property before the lease expires, the owner must make reasonable efforts to rent the abandoned space.
f. Set up a trust or escrow account for security deposits. Note that some states prohibit security deposits from being commingled with earnest money deposits.
g. Set up a business account for other monies.
h. Maintain proper insurance on the property.
i. Provide lead-based paint disclosures and reports to tenants.
j. Follow eviction laws.
k. Unless paid by the tenant, the owner must pay property taxes, special assessments, and utilities.
l. Provide the tenant with building rules and other laws that must to be followed. (This will be a part of the lease agreement.)
m. Notify the tenant of the location of the security deposit and the terms for its return. (This will be a part of the lease agreement.)

2. Property manager's duties
   a. Meet the goals and objectives of the owner by generating the highest net operating income while maintaining the property.
   b. Develop a management plan, operating budget, profit and loss statement, cash flow reports, and budget comparison reports.
   c. Analyze rental rates, screen and select qualified tenants, collect the rent, and evict tenants.
   d. Market and advertise the property. Comply with all advertising and fair housing laws.
   e. Maintain good relations with the tenant.
   f. Maintain the property by hiring qualified contractors to make repairs.
   g. Evaluate risk management and make recommendations to the owner.
   h. Comply with federal, state, and local laws, such as providing the lead-based paint disclosures and being in compliance with the Americans with Disabilities Act.
   i. Be aware of environmental issues and comply with laws.
   j. Be accountable for money, employees, and service contracts.
   k. Hire, supervise, and discharge employees and contractors.
   l. Enter into contracts with service providers on behalf of the owner (phone, electricity, water, trash removal, etc.).
3. Tenant duties
   a. Read the lease agreement to ensure compliance and understanding of the terms.
   b. Use the property for legal purposes and keep the property in a habitable condition.
   c. Pay the full rent due in a timely manner.
   d. The tenant may not use the property in any way that interferes with the rights of neighbors or other tenants.
   e. The tenant may not alter the property unless it is allowed within the terms of the lease agreement.

f. The tenant agrees to obey federal, state, and local laws in regards to the use of the property.
g. Notify the owner or property manager of needed repairs.
h. Give proper notice when moving. Proper notice is determined by state law or the terms of the lease. Generally, in a residential lease, proper notice is the time frame when the rent is paid. If rent is paid every 30 days, then 30 days' notice is required. If rent is paid every two weeks, then two weeks' notice is required.

4. Evictions
   a. Rent is paid in advance, usually on the first of the month, and the property manager must know state and local laws regarding eviction procedures as they relate to rent. The lease agreement should specify the day the rent is due, the grace period and the late fee, and when eviction procedures will begin. If a lease agreement does not specify the due date, then rent is due at the end of the leasing period.
   b. A tenant is usually evicted or ejected because of nonpayment of rent, unlawful use of the premises, or noncompliance with health and safety codes.
   c. Rent control is a regulation by the state or local government agencies restricting the amount of rent landlords can charge their tenants. The primary purpose of rent control is to remedy high rents caused by the imbalance between supply and demand in housing.
   d. Actual eviction is when the landlord files a suit for possession because the tenant has breached the lease.
   e. Constructive eviction is when the landlord breaches the lease and the tenant must leave the premises because they have become uninhabitable.

V. Market Analysis and Tenant Acquisition

A. A property manager can choose from a range of advertising media to reach a target audience. This could include placing a sign on the property identifying the management firm and the person to call for further information; this also includes flyers, newspaper advertising, regional magazines and trade journals, radio, television, direct mail and brochures, and internet sites.

B. The first step in the development of a marketing plan is to determine if there is a low or high vacancy rate in the area for the type of property being leased. If there is a high vacancy rate, attracting tenants for immediate occupancy is the primary goal. Concessions, such as free rent or reduced rent through a graduated lease or rebates, may be offered to a tenant. If there is a low-vacancy rate, an ad campaign would promote the many amenities of the property and the owner would analyze if potential tenants are willing to pay a higher rent.

C. A market is created when two or more people meet for the purpose of selling or leasing a commodity. These transactions occur at a national, regional, or local level. A property manager must be able to evaluate market trends to determine the rent that may be charged. This would include supply and demand and local economic conditions, as well as a neighborhood market analysis.

D. Regional market analysis
   1. A regional market analysis should include demographic and economic information in the area where the property is located. This information includes population statistics, income and employment data, a description of transportation facilities, and supply and demand trends.
E. Neighborhood market analysis
   1. Property managers rely on a neighborhood market analysis because much of their business is generated at a local level. The neighborhood market analysis would include boundaries and land usage, transportation and utilities, economy, supply and demand, and neighborhood amenities and facilities. Once the regional and neighborhood market surveys are complete, the property manager analyzes the data to determine the special features of the property and how it fits the needs of potential tenants.
F. Tenant acquisition
   1. The best method of renting property is to secure referrals from satisfied tenants. Many times, an owner will pay cash or rental incentives (concessions) to current tenants for such referrals. Press releases sent to local newspapers and brokers may gain free publicity for the property when leasing new or large developments. The interest also provides a new media for advertising and obtaining tenants.
   2. The property manager also may decide to work with a leasing agent, who is an independent contractor and whose primary function is to show the property, follow up with prospective tenants, and lease the space. Leasing agents may be paid a flat referral fee or a split-commission basis.
   3. Once the prospective tenant's needs have been determined, the next step is to qualify the tenant. The property manager should provide disclosures that are required by state and federal laws, such as agency disclosures, lead-based paint disclosures, and other documents required by state law. Of course, a copy of the lease agreement should be available to the tenant.
   4. While showing the property, the manager describes the benefits of the space, building, and neighborhood as they meet the tenant's needs. If the property is occupied, the current tenant must be notified of the showing.
   5. The occupancy terms to be negotiated include concessions, rent schedules, rebates, length of the leasing period, tenant alterations, expansion options, noncompeting tenant restrictions, and the defraying of moving expenses. The property manager must negotiate these terms to meet the needs of both the owner and the tenant.
   6. Once the lease agreement has been negotiated, the landlord must give exclusive possession of the property to the tenant. The covenant of quiet enjoyment means the landlord must honor the tenant's right of possession. This means the landlord may not enter the property without the tenant's permission to provide services or make repairs, or other unusual circumstances. Landlords may always enter property if there is an emergency.

7. The implied warranty of habitability requires that the landlord keep the property in good condition. This would include maintaining the common areas and equipment, providing utilities, and being in compliance with state and local codes.
8. The property manager should develop (and the owner should approve) a screening process that provides equal professional services to all potential tenants. One of the first areas of qualification of potential tenants must be in meeting a tenant's needs as far as space requirements are concerned. The needs are different for a residential tenant than for a commercial tenant.
9. Other tenant considerations include
   a. motives for moving,
   b. the expiration of the current lease,
   c. projected budget for the new space,
   d. parking and transportation needs, and
   e. any special needs of the tenant.
10. Each prospective tenant should be required to fill out a lease application. For residential tenants, credit references, personal references, and rental history must be secured and checked by the property manager. For commercial property, a profit and loss statement of the company should be reviewed to demonstrate that the company is financially sound. All federal laws, such as fair housing and the Americans with Disabilities Act, must be obeyed when screening applicants.
11. In negotiating a commercial lease, the property manager must be sure that the person being interviewed has the authority to negotiate contracts for the company. This can be accomplished by asking for a copy of the articles of incorporation or partnership agreement.
12. A property manager establishes communication with a prospective tenant during the initial interviewing process. This communication continues and is strengthened during the screening and the negotiation of the lease. Complaints that constitute an emergency are handled immediately, while other complaints should be resolved in compliance with the lease. The property manager and owner should develop a complaint process that is either outlined in the lease or available to the tenant as a separate document.
13. Tenants must know that they cannot use their space in such a way as to infringe on the rights of others and that noncompliance with building rules, violations of the law, or any activities that disrupt other tenants are grounds for eviction.

VI. Accounts and Disbursement

A. The property management agreement should provide the manager with the bank and account number of the business account in which the collected rents are deposited, and the trust account for the security deposits. Laws vary by state, but normally there cannot be a commingling of security deposits into business or personal accounts because the security deposit belongs to the tenant.

B. State laws may stipulate that the tenants be informed of the bank and the account number where their security deposits are located. Furthermore, state laws and the lease agreement regulate the disbursement of security deposits and may specify who receives the interest earned from the security deposits. Some states do not allow security deposits to be placed in an interest-bearing account.

C. The owner may require the property manager to be bonded. The purpose of the surety bond, which is sometimes called a fidelity bond, is to protect the owner if the property manager is dishonest in the reporting or management of monies received on the owner's behalf. The property management agreement usually limits the dollar amount for a check the manager may write without requiring the owner's signature.

VII. Property Maintenance and Improvements

A. A property manager is responsible for building security and handling emergencies. Life safety is the industry term for those responsibilities. The four goals of life safety programs are
   1. preventing emergencies and security breaches by installing smoke detectors, sprinkler systems, paging systems, closed-circuit television, video camera, and security alarms;
   2. detecting a breach as early as possible;
   3. containing or confining the damage or intrusion; and
   4. counteracting the damage by prompt and proper action.

B. This also would include the responsibility of hiring and training a life safety officer to assist in the evacuation of tenants and to enforce safety guidelines. Tenants should be educated so they know what to do in case of a disaster, such as a hurricane, tornado, earthquake, fire, bomb threat, or other accident.

C. Property managers and agents must have a working knowledge of hazardous substances and wastes and the laws regulating owners. A hazardous waste is a byproduct of a manufactured item, while a hazardous substance may include everyday items, such as household cleaning products and paint. The Environmental Protection Agency (EPA) was established to centralize the federal government's environmental responsibilities.

D. Environmental hazards that property managers will most likely encounter are asbestos, radon, contents of underground storage tanks, urea formaldehyde, polychlorinated biphenyls (PCBs), and lead paint.

E. Property managers must be in compliance with the antitrust laws, federal fair housing laws, the Equal Credit Opportunity Act, the Fair Credit Reporting Act, and the Lead-Based Paint Hazard Reduction Act, all of which are discussed in various units in this book. In addition to these laws, the property manager must be in compliance with the Americans with Disabilities Act, Megan's Law, and the Uniform Residential Landlord and Tenant Act (URLTA). Many states have enacted their own landlord-tenant laws, which must be followed.

F. Known lead-based paint and lead hazards must be disclosed to the tenant before the lease takes effect. Any prior lead hazard reports the owner has must be given to the potential tenant, as well as the booklet Protect Your Family From Lead in Your Home. Federal laws require that the disclosure form be kept for three years.

G. The primary goals of a property manager are to generate the highest net operating income while maintaining the property. To preserve the physical condition of the property, the manager must be able to accurately assess the various levels of maintenance operations presented in the following list.
   1. Preventive maintenance
      a. Preserves the physical building and eliminates costly problems before major repairs become necessary (seasonal servicing of equipment).
   2. Corrective maintenance
      a. Fulfills the owner's responsibilities to the tenant by keeping the building's equipment, utilities, and amenities functioning properly (making necessary repairs on equipment).
   3. Routine maintenance
      a. Includes routine housekeeping, such as maintenance of the common areas and grounds, and maintaining the physical cleanliness of the building itself.
   4. New construction maintenance
      a. Occurs to meet the needs of a tenant and could be something as simple as installing new carpeting or as complex as upgrading or remodeling the property to meet the tenant's needs. Tenants many times require a build-out, which involves alterations to the space to meet their needs.

H. Risk management
   1. One of the primary duties of the property manager involves risk management, which is usually done through the purchase of insurance. Risk management involves identifying the risk and deciding to avoid, control, retain, or transfer it. A property manager will monitor risks to determine the action that must take place in the future.
   2. Types of insurance that may be purchased to protect the owner include
      a. fire and hazard insurance to cover losses by fire, tornados, high winds, hail, smoke, et cetera;
      b. flood insurance to cover losses caused by heavy rains or other damages caused by water—managers should check the floodplain map at the Federal Emergency Management Agency (FEMA);
      c. property insurance to cover natural disasters, fires, and vandalism;
      d. general liability insurance to cover contractors and real and personal property;
      e. loss of income insurance to cover loss of rents, profits, and commissions;
      f. replacement cost insurance to cover the cost of a replacing a part of or the entire building;
      g. workers' compensation to cover liability for injury to employees;
      h. commercial automobile liability to cover injury and damage by vehicles; and
      i. machinery and equipment insurance to cover machinery and equipment.

CHAPTER 10 QUIZ

1. The property manager has a fiduciary duty with the owner and is considered
   1. a general agent.
   2. a limited agent.
   3. a special agent.
   4. a universal agent.

2. When a property manager binds a principal/owner to a contract, the manager is directly operating under the fiduciary duty of
   1. accounting.
   2. care and skill.
   3. loyalty.
   4. obedience.

3. A leasing agent's primary responsibility is to
   1. find a qualified tenant.
   2. make property repairs.
   3. hire the owner's employees.
   4. evict complying tenants.

4. A property management agreement is classified as
   1. a unilateral work-for-hire agreement.
   2. a bilateral work-for-hire agreement.
   3. a unilateral personal service contract.
   4. a bilateral personal service contract.

5. If there is a low-vacancy rate, the property manager should probably
   1. raise the rent.
   2. lower the rent.
   3. offer free rent.
   4. offer rebates.

6. Unless the lease agreement stipulates otherwise, the upkeep of the electrical, heating, and plumbing systems is the responsibility of the
   1. owner/lessee.
   2. owner/lessor.
   3. tenant/lessee.
   4. tenant/lessor.

7. When a lease is assigned, the assignee is
   1. the new tenant.
   2. the original tenant.
   3. the owner.
   4. the agent.

8. A school leased a small, commercial shopping strip. When classes started, the other tenants started complaining to the landlord that the students of the school were taking up the majority of the parking spaces and their customers had no place to park. The lease required that the students park in spaces away from the other businesses. The school asked the students to park in the assigned spaces, but most continued to park where it was convenient. The landlord evicted the school. Is this action legal?
   1. No, the landlord cannot evict the school because parking is available to the public.
   2. No, because the school asked the students to park in the assigned spaces, they cannot be evicted.
   3. Yes, the landlord can evict the school, and it is called actual eviction.
   4. Yes, the landlord can evict the school, and it is called constructive eviction.

9. A potential tenant is inspecting a property built in 1970. The potential tenant must be given
   1. 10 days to inspect for lead-based paint.
   2. copies of prior inspections and reports regarding lead-based paint.
   3. the previous tenant's lease agreement.
   4. the owner's home address.

10. The property manager may not commingle funds. This means the property manager should
    1. place a security deposit check into an owner's escrow account.
    2. pay a vendor from the owner's business checking account.
    3. pay herself from the owner's business account.
    4. place a security deposit check into the owner's business account.

11. When the lessee breaches the lease, it gives the lessor the right to proceed with
    1. actual eviction by filing a suit for possession.
    2. actual eviction by filing a suit for specific performance.
    3. constructive eviction by filing a suit for possession.
    4. constructive eviction by filing a suit for specific performance.

12. One of the property manager's responsibilities is to keep the building's equipment in working order. This action would fall under
    1. preventive maintenance.
    2. corrective maintenance.
    3. routine maintenance.
    4. new construction maintenance.

13. Which of the following is the *BEST* method for attracting tenants to a property?
    1. Cooperating with brokers in the area
    2. Developing an advertising campaign
    3. Having press releases published in the local newspapers to create publicity
    4. Securing referrals from satisfied tenants

14. A person entered into a property management agreement with Barron Properties, Inc. The property management agreement *MOST* likely stipulates that he will be paid a percentage of
    1. last year's net income.
    2. this year's potential income.
    3. this year's gross income.
    4. last year's gross income.

15. Which of the following criteria is the *MOST* important for a property manager to use to qualify and screen a potential tenant?
    1. Space requirements and financial history
    2. Projected moving dates and number of children
    3. Special needs of the potential tenant and commission earned
    4. Parking needs of the potential tenant and the number of disabled customers

16. All of the following events would probably terminate a residential lease agreement *EXCEPT*
    1. the property being taken by eminent domain.
    2. when the life tenant, who had leased the property, dies.
    3. when the owner sells the property.
    4. when the lessee buys the land from the lessor.

17. The primary purpose of a profit and loss statement is to analyze
    1. how the property was managed, what changes should be made, and projections for the new year.
    2. how the operating budget was calculated and budget projections for the new year.
    3. the ratio of the operating expenses to the operating income.
    4. the ratio of the rate of return to the debt service.

18. On a profit and loss statement, all of the following are entered *EXCEPT*
    1. mortgage loan principal add-back.
    2. receipts.
    3. operating expenses.
    4. the property manager's compensation.

19. What do asbestos, radon, and urea formaldehyde all have in common?
    1. They are classified as environmental hazards, and a property manager must be aware of them.
    2. They are all classified as hazardous substances, and a property manager must be aware of them.
    3. They are produced as a result of the natural decay of radioactive substances, so they cannot be avoided.
    4. They are produced as a result of the natural decay of organic substances, so they cannot be avoided.

20. All of the following are grounds for constructive eviction *EXCEPT*
    1. the nonpayment of rent by the tenant.
    2. the furnace that has not worked for five days in the middle of winter.
    3. the water that is turned off because the owner did not pay the water bill.
    4. the property that is declared uninhabitable by the local government.

21. All of the following occupancy terms are negotiated between a property manager and a prospective tenant *EXCEPT*
    1. expansion options.
    2. length of the leasing period.
    3. tenant alterations.
    4. the owner's profit.

22. The duties and responsibilities of a property manager are *LEAST* likely to include which of the following?
    1. Investing profits generated by the property for the owner
    2. Supervising the remodeling of the property
    3. Showing the property to prospective tenants
    4. Collecting the rent from current tenants

23. A property manager showed a prospective tenant an available apartment. Which of the following would *NOT* be a consideration in qualifying the potential tenant?
    1. Credit history
    2. Race
    3. Space requirements
    4. Personal references

24. Which of the following does *NOT* normally terminate a lease?
    1. Death of the lessor
    2. Nonpayment of rent
    3. Constructive eviction
    4. Condemnation of the property

25. The owner of an investment property died at 10:00 pm last night. Can the property manager collect the rent checks that are due today?
    1. Yes, it is property manager's duty to collect the rent checks for the estate.
    2. Yes, the property manager should collect the rent checks because it is her job.
    3. No, the property manager should not collect the rent checks because her contract terminated upon the owner's death.
    4. No, the property manager should not collect the rent checks until the executor of his estate gives her permission to do so.

26. A hurricane destroyed several apartment buildings in a community, creating an imbalance between the supply and demand of rental units. If the local government imposes a law that restricts the amount of rent a landlord may charge, it is called
    1. rent control.
    2. rent restriction.
    3. fixed rent.
    4. gross rent.

27. A property manager hired a contractor to build a wheelchair ramp, install Braille markings on the elevators, and make the restrooms in the lobby accessible to people with wheelchairs. The property manager is ensuring that the owner is in compliance with which law?
    1. FFH
    2. ADA
    3. ECOA
    4. CRA

MATCHING QUIZ

The column on the right contains brief memory links to important terms in Chapter 10. *Write the letter of the matching term on the appropriate line.*

A. ROI
B. Rent control
C. Lease
D. Graduated lease
E. Commingle
F. Covenant of quiet enjoyment
G. Fidelity bond
H. Corrective maintenance
I. Risk management
J. Leasing agent
K. Management agreement
L. Operating budget
M. Tenancy for years
N. Periodic tenancy
O. Estate at will
P. Estate at sufferance
Q. Holdover
R. Constructive eviction
S. Routine maintenance
T. Warranty of habitability

1. _______ This lease may be used to entice tenants to rent spaces that are difficult to rent.
2. _______ The landlord's duty to honor the tenant's right of possession.
3. _______ The government's right to set the rent that landlords can charge.
4. _______ Repairing equipment and amenities to keep the building functional for the tenant.
5. _______ The property manager's report of anticipated revenues and expenses.
6. _______ Lease with definite beginning and ending dates.
7. _______ The landlord's duty to keep the property in good repair.
8. _______ The tenant has the right to possess the property with the consent of the landlord, but the lease can be terminated at any time by either party.
9. _______ When a tenant remains in possession after the lease expires, the tenant is given this title.
10. _______ The landlord breaches the lease and the tenant must leave the premises.
11. _______ This estate is created when the tenant remains in possession after the lease has expired.
12. _______ This document is a bilateral contract that gives exclusive possession to the tenant.
13. _______ The owner may require the property manager to purchasc this to protect the owner should the manager mishandle monies.
14. _______ Housekeeping and maintenance of the common areas and grounds.
15. _______ Used to compute the profitability of the investment.
16. _______ A lease that will automatically renew unless proper notice is given.

17. _______ To place funds in the wrong bank account, such as placing the security deposit in a business account.

18. _______ Identifying risk and deciding to avoid, control, retain, or transfer the risk.

19. _______ If a brokerage is hired to rent property, this agreement is negotiated between the brokerage firm and the owner.

20. _______ Responsible for securing a qualified tenant for the owner.

CHAPTER 10 QUIZ ANSWERS

1. **(1)** The property manager is expected to be in an ongoing business relationship and is a general agent of the owner. (131)
2. **(2)** When negotiating contracts that are binding to the owner, the property manager should be aware of her duty of care and skill. (131)
3. **(1)** The leasing agent is only responsible for finding a qualified tenant. (134)
4. **(4)** The property management agreement is classified as a personal service contract that is also bilateral because both the owner and the manager have duties to perform. (131)
5. **(1)** If there is a low-vacancy rate, the property manager should probably raise the rent. (138)
6. **(2)** Unless the lease agreement stipulated otherwise, it is the responsibility of the owner/lessor to maintain the property. (136–137)
7. **(1)** In an assignment, the original tenant is the assignor, and the new tenant receiving the assignment is the assignee. (118, 121)
8. **(3)** The landlord can evict the school, and it is called actual eviction. (138)
9. **(2)** For properties built prior to 1978, tenants must be given copies of prior inspections and reports regarding lead-based paint. (141)
10. **(1)** The word *commingle* means to mix together. Security deposit checks must be placed in a separate escrow or trust account for that purpose. (140–141)
11. **(1)** If the tenant breaches the lease, the lessor may file a suit for possession (actual eviction). (138)
12. **(2)** Making sure the building's equipment is in working order is corrective maintenance. (142)
13. **(4)** All the answers provide methods that a property manager can use to attract tenants. Referrals from satisfied tenants are the best. (139)
14. **(3)** Property managers are usually paid a percentage of the gross income. (132–133)
15. **(1)** When qualifying a potential tenant, a property manager must consider many factors. The space requirements, financial history and projected moving date are the most important criteria. (139)
16. **(3)** When the owner sells the property, the buyer must honor the existing lease. (136)
17. **(1)** The purpose of a profit and loss statement is to analyze how the property was managed, what changes should be made, and projections for the new year. (133–134)
18. **(4)** The property manager's compensation is not entered on a profit and loss statement. (134)
19. **(1)** Asbestos, radon, and urea formaldehyde are all environmental hazards of which a property manager must be aware. (141)
20. **(1)** Constructive eviction occurs when the landlord breaches the lease. If the tenant doesn't pay the rent, the tenant has breached the lease, which is actual eviction. (138)
21. **(4)** The owner's profit is not a term negotiated with a tenant. (134–135)
22. **(1)** The property manager does not invest the owner's profit. (137)
23. **(2)** The race of a potential tenant is not a consideration of the property manager when negotiating a lease. (137–138)
24. **(1)** The death of the lessor does not affect the lease in any way. (136)

25. **(3)** Property management contracts are personal service contracts and terminate upon the death of either party. The executor may hire the same property manager, but the question does not provide that information and it should not be assumed. (136)

26. **(1)** By definition of rent control. (138)

27. **(2)** The Americans with Disabilities Act (ADA) requires that places of public accommodations be accessible by people with disabilities. (141)

TEST SCORE

LEASING AND PROPERTY MANAGEMENT			
Rating	**Range**	**Your Score**	
Good = 80% to 100%	22–27	Total Number	27
Fair = 70% to 79%	19–21	Total Wrong	–
Needs improvement = Lower than 70%	18 or less	Total Right	

Passing Requirement: 19 or Better

ANSWER KEY: MATCHING QUIZ

1. **D**
2. **F**
3. **B**
4. **H**
5. **L**
6. **M**
7. **T**
8. **O**
9. **Q**
10. **R**
11. **P**
12. **C**
13. **G**
14. **S**
15. **A**
16. **N**
17. **E**
18. **I**
19. **K**
20. **J**

CHAPTER 11

Transfer of Title

OUTLINE OF CONCEPTS

I. **Transfering title**
   A. Title Insurance
      1. Protects insured against loss resulting from certain defects in the title, such as a forgery or defect in the public record, other than those exceptions listed in the policy.
      2. Most standard coverage policies will not cover situations arising from questions of survey, defects of which the policy-holder has knowledge, or unrecorded documents.
      3. Extended coverage policies will cover additional risks that may be discovered only by inspection of the property, including unrecorded rights of persons in possession, or by examination of an accurate survey.
      4. It is an indemnity contract.
   B. Title searches, title abstracts, chain of title
      1. Title searches
         a. An inspection of public records to determine if any defects exist in the chain of title
         b. The inspection begins with the present owner and is traced backward for a period of time depending on state statute; the period of time is typically 40 to 60 years.
      2. Title abstracts—a condensed history of all instruments on record affecting the title to the property.
      3. Chain of title—a record of the ownership of a property that connects the present owner back to the earliest recorded owner; a break in the chain of ownership would create a gap or cloud in the chain title.
   C. Cloud on title, suit to quiet title
      1. Cloud on title—a defect in title, such as a recorded mortgage that had been paid in full but for which a satisfaction of mortgage was never recorded.
      2. Suit to quiet title—a court action to cure a cloud or gap in the chain of title.

II. Deeds

A. Purpose of deed, when title passes
   1. Voluntary alienation, either by gift or sale—to transfer title during his or her lifetime, an owner must use some form of written deed or conveyance to transfer title to another.
   2. Purpose of deeds
      a. A written instrument used to convey title to real estate to another party.
      b. The owner conveying title is the grantor, while the recipient is the grantee.
   3. Title passes to the grantee when the executed (signed) deed is delivered and accepted.

B. Types of deeds (general warranty, special warranty, quit claim) and when used.
   1. General warranty deed—contains promises and covenants
      a. Provides the greatest protection for the grantee of any deed.
      b. Includes five covenants, or promises, the grantor makes.
         (1) Covenant of seisin—the grantor has the title and possession and has the right to convey.
         (2) Covenant against encumbrances—the grantor warrants that the property is free from any liens or encumbrances except those specifically stated in the deed.
         (3) Covenant of quiet enjoyment—the grantor guarantees that the title is good against a third party.
         (4) Covenant of further assurance—the grantor promises to obtain and deliver any instrument required to make the title good against third parties.
         (5) Covenant of warranty forever—the grantor guarantees that if the title fails, the grantee will be compensated for the loss sustained.
   2. Special warranty deeds—the grantor warrants only that the property was not encumbered during the time that the grantor held title, except as noted in the deed.
   3. Quitclaim deed—contains no warranties or promises and conveys only such interest, if any, that the grantor may have when the deed is delivered, but conveys that interest completely; often used to cure a defect in title.

C. Essential elements of deeds
   1. Requirements for a valid conveyance deed
      a. Grantor (seller)—must have legal existence, be of legal age, and be legally competent to convey the title.
      b. Grantee (Buyer)—must be named in the deed in such a way that he or she can be identified.
      c. Consideration—something of value that must be acknowledged by the grantor; in most states, consideration must be stated in dollars.
      d. Granting clause—must contain words that state the grantor's intention to convey the property.
      e. Description of real estate—must use a legal description that is understood by all parties.

f. Signature of grantor—must be signed by all grantors named in the deed.
g. Delivery and acceptance—actual delivery of the deed by the grantor and either actual or implied acceptance by the grantee.

2. Other items that may be required
a. Acknowledgment—provides evidence that the signature is voluntary and genuine; not essential to the validity of the deed unless required by state statutes.
b. Habendum clause—follows granting clause when necessary to define the terms of ownership to be enjoyed by grantee.
c. Exceptions and reservations ("subject-to clauses")—should specifically not be encumbrances, reservations, or limitations that affect the title being conveyed, such as liens, easements, and restrictions.

D. Importance of recording
1. Recording of deeds
a. The title passes to the grantee when the executed deed is delivered and accepted.
b. Exceptions:
(1) Torrens property—the title transfers when deed has been examined and accepted for registration.
(2) Closing in escrow—the date of delivery is generally the date that it was deposited with the escrow agent; if the escrow does not close, no title passes.
c. Recording a deed or taking possession of property gives constructive notice to the world that one has rights in the property.
d. An unrecorded deed is valid between the parties to a transaction.

III. Escrow or closing; tax aspects of transferring title to real property

A. Responsibilities of escrow agent
1. An escrow or closing agent is a neutral third party authorized to coordinate the closing activities of a real estate transaction.
2. Responsibilities include:
a. holding financial deposits in trust
b. gathering required legal documents
c. ordering an examination on the property
d. preparing specific closing instructions
e. gathering documents from the buyer's lender
f. ensuring that all terms of the offer to purchase have been completed
g. recording any necessary documents, such as the deed

B. Prorated items
1. Proration involves the sharing of responsibility between the seller and the buyer for items such as property taxes.
2. Other prorated items include:
a. utility bills
b. rents
c. mortgage interest
d. homeowners association dues

3. Certain charges, such as property taxes, are divided between the seller and the buyer (prorated) based on either a 360 or 365 day year.
4. Charges are prorated as of the date of closing in most states with the seller being responsible for the date of closing.

C. Closing Statement
1. Estimating closing costs
   a. The good-faith estimate required by RESPA provides estimates on items such as:
      (1) loan origination fee
      (2) loan application fee
      (3) appraisal fee
      (4) credit report
      (5) property taxes from the day of closing to the end of the tax year
   b. IRS rules require closing agents to report details of closing to the IRS using form 1099S.
2. Property and income taxes
   a. Capital gains
      (1) As of 2018–2025, a married couple may exclude as much as $500,000 from capital gains tax for profits on the sale of a principal residence if they file jointly.
      (2) Homeowners who file as individuals are entitled to a $250,000 exclusion each.
      (3) There is no limit on the number of times homeowners may take advantage of this benefit, as long as the homeowners have occupied the property as their residence for at least 24 months of the past five years.
      (4) A 1998 law lowers the required holding period for a noncorporate taxpayer from 18 to 12 months for long-term capital gain.
3. Home-related expenses that are tax deductible for the owners
   a. Some loan origination fees
   b. Interest paid on mortgages on first and second home (for mortgage balances below $750,000, or $375,000 if married filing separately)
   c. Real estate taxes but not penalties for late payment
   d. Discount points on loans
   e. Prepayment penalties on loans
   f. 1031 tax-deferred exchange
      (1) Under Section 1031 of the IRS Code, real estate investors can defer taxation of capital gains by making a property exchange.
      (2) A property owner may exchange his or her property for another property and have tax liability on the sale only if an additional capital or property is received.
      (3) Tax on exchange is deferred rather than eliminated.
      (4) Properties involved in exchange must be of like kind.
         a. Like kind refers to any real property to be held for income purposes or investment; excludes dealer property or residences.

(5) Additional capital or personal property included in a transaction to even out the exchange is considered boot; the party receiving boot is taxed at the time of the exchange.
(6) Use a qualified intermediary to retain the money in the tax-deferred exchange.

4. Special processes
   a. Foreclosure/short sale and redemption
      (1) Judicial foreclosure
         a. Lender sues the borrower in court; obtains judgment and court order to sell.
         b. Property sold at public sale to the highest bidder.
      (2) Nonjudicial foreclosure
         a. The mortgage generally must include a power-of-sale clause.
         b. A notice of default must be recorded and a public sale advertised in the newspaper.
         c. The property is sold at a public sale to highest bidder.
         d. Power of sale clause is standard in a deed of trust and allows the trustee based upon state law to foreclose and sell the property for the lender/beneficiary.
      (3) Strict foreclosure—the court may award title to the lender.
      (4) Deed in lieu of foreclosure—borrower gives the lender a deed to the property. When borrower is in default under terms of loan. Lender may not accept if there are junior liens.
      (5) Short sale—a procedure to prevent foreclosure that a bank uses in an effort to minimize the financial loss that would be involved in foreclosing. Lenders negotiate with lienholders for a payoff that is less than they are owed, or for the sale of real estate for an amount that is less than the full amount of the debt.
      (6) Redemption—process by which the borrower regains interest in the property.
         a. Equitable redemption
            (i) Occurs prior to public sale.
            (ii) If the borrower pays the back payments dues plus fees and interest prior to the public sale, the mortgage is reinstated.
            (iii) If not redeemed, the property is sold at a public sale to the highest bidder.
         b. Statutory redemption
            (i) Occurs after public sales in some states and continues for a period of time specified by law.
      (7) Deficiency judgment—if the property is sold and the proceeds are insufficient to pay the loan and foreclosure costs, the difference is a deficiency; the lender usually can sue the original borrower for the difference (process of deficiency judgment).

b. Real estate owned (REO)
   (1) Property that has been foreclosed and repossessed by a lender or a bank.
   (2) Once the bank or the lender has conducted a foreclosure action and failed to receive an acceptable bid, the title to the property reverts back to the bank or the lender and becomes classified as a REO.
   (3) Upon receiving the title to the property, the bank or lender makes every effort to sell the REO, including working with REALTORS® to list the property on MLS, as well as placing the property on online websites.
   (4) Neither banks nor lenders are interested in holding title to REOs; they are considered to be non-earning assets.
   (5) Anyone considering the purchase of a REO property should be sure to have an inspection done since REO properties are generally sold "as is."

D. Other Important Concepts
   1. Transfer of title by will—takes effect only after the death of the testator (devisor) and will go through probate to pass title to the devisee (the recipient of the real property).

CHAPTER 11 QUIZ

1. The deed that provides the buyer the greatest protection is the
   1. bargain and sale deed.
   2. general warranty deed.
   3. quitclaim deed.
   4. specialty warranty deed.

2. A warranty deed transfers title to the grantee when it is
   1. acknowledged.
   2. signed by the grantee.
   3. signed by the grantor.
   4. delivered and accepted.

3. Which of the following would be an example of voluntary alienation?
   1. Sale
   2. Eminent domain
   3. Escheat
   4. Adverse possession

4. A grantee has received an executed, notarized deed. The grantee takes possession of the property but does not record the deed. The conveyance is
   1. invalid between the parties and valid as to third parties with constructive notice.
   2. valid as between the parties and valid as to the subsequent recorded interests.
   3. valid as between the parties and invalid as to subsequent recorded interests without notice.
   4. invalid as between the parties.

5. All of the following statements correctly describe a properly executed will *EXCEPT*
   1. it takes effect only after the death of the devisee.
   2. it specifies who will inherit the owner's property.
   3. it must conform to the state statute.
   4. it cannot supersede state laws of dower and curtesy.

6. Generally, title insurance coverage extends to
   1. defects known to the buyer.
   2. liens listed in the policy.
   3. defects listed in the policy.
   4. defects not found in the public record.

7. A deed must be signed by the
   1. grantor.
   2. vendee.
   3. grantee.
   4. vendor.

8. Roberts and Sanchez have entered into a binding offer to purchase. Sanchez will buy Roberts's house. Which of the following statements correctly describes the status of the transaction?
   1. Roberts will have equitable title until closing.
   2. Sanchez will have legal title when the offer to purchase becomes binding on both parties.
   3. Roberts will have legal title until the offer becomes binding, at which time Roberts will hold equitable title.
   4. Roberts will hold legal title until closing, and Sanchez will hold equitable title until closing.

9. All of the following statements correctly describe equitable title *EXCEPT*
   1. upon creation of a binding offer to purchase, buyer holds equitable title.
   2. equitable title converts to legal title upon delivery and acceptance of the deed.
   3. if so specified, it may be conveyed by deed.
   4. it may not be conveyed by will.

10. The need for a loan closing to be prepared on a settlement statement is a requirement of
    1. Truth-in-Lending.
    2. the federal fair housing laws.
    3. Government National Mortgage Association (GNMA, or Ginnie Mae).
    4. RESPA.

11. The requirement that a lender give each loan applicant a copy of *Settlement Costs and You* is created under
    1. Federal Home Loan Mortgage Corporation (FHLMC, or Freddie Mac).
    2. Federal Housing Administration (FHA).
    3. RESPA.
    4. Truth-in-Lending.

12. The person conducting the closing must report details on the closing to the IRS on
    1. IRS form 1099.
    2. IRS form 1099S.
    3. IRS form 1099 MISC.
    4. IRS form 1099 R.

13. Section 1031 of the Internal Revenue Code allows real estate investors to do which of the following when making a property exchange?
    1. Avoid the capital-gains tax only if the exchange is of like kind
    2. Phase out the capital-gains tax
    3. Defer the capital-gains tax
    4. Avoid the capital-gains tax even if the exchange is not of like kind

14. A single person listed a house and accepted an offer from a buyer. Then, before closing, the person married. At closing, the other spouse signed a deed to relinquish an inchoate interest in the property being sold. What kind of deed would be used to convey their inchoate interest without imposing any legal obligations to defend its title?
    1. Quitclaim
    2. Bargain and sale
    3. Special warranty
    4. General warranty

15. When a grantor appears before a notary, the notary attests that the grantor is who he or she says they are, and that their signing is
    1. legal.
    2. deliberate.
    3. voluntary.
    4. insured.

16. RESPA requires that borrowers be provided with a good faith estimate of settlement costs by lenders no later than how many business days after the loan application?
    1. One
    2. Two
    3. Three
    4. Four

17. Brenda and Carl, a married couple, bought a principal residence in 1998 for $300,000. They sold the property in 2019 with a capital gain of $600,000. How much of the profit would be subject to capital gains tax?
    1. $0
    2. $100,000
    3. $600,000
    4. $900,000

18. Which deed would typically be used to cure a defect in title?
    1. Bargain and sale deed
    2. General warranty deed
    3. Quitclaim deed
    4. Special warranty deed

MATCHING QUIZ

The column on the right contains brief memory links to important terms in Chapter 11.
Write the letter of the matching term on the appropriate line.

A. Short sale
B. Redemption
C. Strict foreclosure
D. REO
E. Grantee
F. Grantor
G. Abstract of title
H. Title insurance
I. Judicial foreclosures
J. Covenant of seisen
K. "As Is"
L. Cloud on title
M. Acknowledgement
N. General warranty deed
O. IRS Code 1031
P. Equitable redemption
Q. Deed in lieu of foreclosure
R. RESPA
S. Quit Claim Deed

1. _______ Provides greatest protection of any deed
2. _______ Right to convey
3. _______ Allows mortgagor to avoid foreclosure
4. _______ Settlement costs legislation
5. _______ IRS code that governs tax-deferred exchanges
6. _______ A type of deed that conveys title without imposing any future title liability on the grantor
7. _______ Occurs prior to public sale
8. _______ Procedure used by bank to prevent foreclosure
9. _______ Property that has been foreclosed and repossessed by a lender
10. _______ Court may award title to lender
11. _______ Process by which borrower regains interest in property
12. _______ Property sold at public sale to highest bidder
13. _______ Mortgage satisfaction that was never recorded
14. _______ The person who conveys title to someone else by deed
15. _______ A summary made from the recorded legal history of a property
16. _______ Provides evidence that signature is voluntary and genuine
17. _______ Insurance that protects against loss from title defects
18. _______ The person who receives title by deed
19. _______ Way in which REO properties are generally sold

CHAPTER 11 QUIZ ANSWERS

1. **(2)** The general warranty deed provides the buyer with the greatest protection. The quitclaim deed provides the buyer with the least amount of protection. A special warranty deed protects the buyer against title defects but only during the ownership period of the grantor. (152)

2. **(4)** The title transfers once the deed is delivered and accepted by the grantee. It is signed by the grantor; the grantee's name must appear on the deed, but the deed is not signed by the grantee. The deed is often notarized, and the notary attests the grantor's acknowledgement that the grantor signature is a voluntary act and that they are in fact who they say they are. The notarized signature is an attempt to keep forged documents from being recorded. (152)

3. **(1)** Obviously, a sale is a voluntary alienation; all the other responses are examples of involuntary alienation. Eminent domain is the right of the government to take private property for public use or public benefit if just compensation is paid to the landowner. Escheat applies when a person dies without a will and without heirs capable of inheriting and the government then takes ownership of the abandoned property. Adverse possession is the open and notorious use of another's land under a claim of right or color of title. (152)

4. **(3)** The grantee must give constructive notice that he has an interest in the property. Constructive notice is given by recording the deed in the registrar of deeds office or by occupying the property. (153)

5. **(1)** A devise is a gift of real property by will. The devisor is the donor of the gifted real property, and the devisee is the recipient of the real property. (156)

6. **(4)** Title insurance does not cover liens or defects listed in the policy. (151)

7. **(1)** The vendor is the seller in a land contract; the vendee is the buyer. The grantee must be identified in the deed but does not have to sign it. (122)

8. **(4)** Sanchez will have equitable title until closing, after which Sanchez will have legal title. (122)

9. **(4)** The seller maintains legal title and the buyer has equitable title until the closing takes place and the deed transfers to the buyer. (120)

10. **(4)** Regulation Z requires disclosure of cost in credit transactions. The Federal Fair Housing laws prohibit discrimination against groups of people identified as protected classes. GNMA functions in the secondary mortgage market. (154)

11. **(3)** Freddie Mac buys seller mortgages in the secondary mortgage market. The FHA provides public mortgage insurance for home loans. Regulation Z requires credit cost disclosure and provides for right of rescission in certain types of credit transactions under certain conditions. (154)

12. **(2)** IRS rules require closing agents to report details of closing to the IRS using IRS form 1099S. Use 1099 MISC to report commissions paid to salespeople by brokers. (154)

13. **(3)** Section 1031 of the IRC does not allow real estate investors to either avoid or phase out the capital gains tax; it only allows for the deferring of the tax. (154–155)

14. **(1)** Use a quitclaim deed to convey title without imposing any liability on the grantor to defend its quality. (152)

15. **(3)** The act must be voluntary. By the deed being signed in the presence of a notary, the recorder's office is confident that the grantor's signature has not been forged. (153)

16. **(3)** RESPA allows three (3) business days or 72 hours to receive a good faith estimate from the lender. The purpose of this legislation is to empower the consumer with accurate and timely information about the actual settlement costs they are expected to pay at closing. (154)

17. **(2)** \$600,000 – \$500,000 = \$100,000. A married couple may exclude \$500,000 from capital gains tax for profits on the sale of a principal residence if they file jointly. (154)

18. **(3)** The bargain and sale deed, general warranty deed, and special warranty deed all contain some type of warranty; whereas the quitclaim deed is to be used to "quit" any claim against title, such as the defect caused by a forged signature. The injured party (grantor) would be compensated for damages suffered by his or her forged signature. (152)

TEST SCORE

TRANSFER OF TITLE			
Rating	**Range**	**Your Score**	
Good = 80% to 100%	15–18	Total Number	18
Fair = 70% to 79%	13–14	Total Wrong	–
Needs improvement = Lower than 70%	12 or less	Total Right	

Passing Requirement: 13 or Better

ANSWER KEY: MATCHING QUIZ

1. **N**
2. **J**
3. **Q**
4. **R**
5. **O**
6. **S**
7. **P**
8. **A**
9. **D**
10. **C**
11. **B**
12. **I**
13. **L**
14. **F**
15. **G**
16. **M**
17. **H**
18. **E**
19. **K**

CHAPTER 12

Practice of Real Estate

OUTLINE OF CONCEPTS

I. Trust/escrow accounts (generally, not state specific)

- A. Purpose and definition of trust accounts, including monies held in trust accounts
    1. Most states require a brokerage firm to maintain a trust account for the purpose of holding all funds entrusted to the brokerage in connection with a real estate transaction.
    2. Brokers and salespeople are required to promptly deposit or give to principal broker, any funds received from a client or customer in the trust account.
    3. Most states require that a real estate broker working as a fiduciary deposit any trust funds received within 24 to 72 hours after acceptance of an offer (e.g. when it becomes a contract).
- B. Responsibility for trust monies, including commingling/conversion
    1. The purpose of the trust account is to keep the broker's money separated from the client's money.
    2. Neither the broker nor his or her salespeople may use a client's money in their trust account for their own use; using the client's money would be an example of conversion.
    3. Brokers may not mix their own money with their client's money; mixing their funds with those of their clients would be an example of commingling.
    4. Either conversion or commingling of funds in the broker's trust would result in disciplinary action by the state licensing board.
    5. A broker also is required to keep detailed records regarding deposits and disbursements of entrusted funds.

II. Federal Fair Housing Laws

- A. Protected classes
    1. Covered transactions
    2. Specific laws and their effects
- B. Compliance
    1. Types of violations and enforcements
    2. Exceptions

C. Civil Rights Act of 1866—prohibits racial discrimination in the buying, renting, selling, holding, or conveying of real and personal property.

D. Federal Fair Housing Act of 1968—provides that it is unlawful to discriminate on the basis of race, color, religion, or national origin when selling or leasing residential property.

   1. In 1974, the Housing and Community Development Act added gender to the list of protected classes.

E. In 1988, the federal fair housing law was amended to add handicapped and familial status to the list of protected classes.

F. The 1988 amendment defines familial status as one or more individuals who have not reached the age of 18, being domiciled with a parent or another person who has or is seeking legal custody.

   1. A person who is pregnant also is included in the definition of familial status.
   2. All properties must be made available under the same terms and conditions as available to all other persons unless a property meets the standards for exemption as "housing for older persons."

G. The 1988 amendment defines disability as a physical or mental impairment that substantially limits one or more of a person's major life activities.

   1. A definition of disability does not include the current illegal use of, or addiction to, a controlled substance.
   2. Persons who have AIDS are protected under the handicapped classification.
   3. Persons renting a dwelling are required to permit handicapped persons to make modifications of existing premises at their own expense, if these modifications are necessary to afford full enjoyment of the premises.
   4. In a rental property situation, a landlord may condition the agreement to allow modifications with the stipulation the tenant restores the interior of the premises to the premodification condition. (It is a legitimate landlord action to limit occupancy based on honest square footage limits.)
   5. There are a number of accessibility and usability requirements covering certain types of newly constructed residential buildings that must be met under federal law; access is required for a common-use and public areas of the building, as well as adaptive and accessible design for the interior of the dwelling units.
   6. A licensee may not disclose to a seller or landlord that a prospective buyer or tenant is a member of a protected class.
   7. Alcoholics and drug addicts who have been diagnosed, treated, and are not currently addicted are protected under federal fair housing laws; they are considered to have a disability. However, convicted drug dealers are not covered under any condition.
   8. People diagnosed as mentally ill also are protected under the federal laws.
      a. Mentally ill people do not have to be currently receiving treatment to be protected under the law.

  b. If a mentally ill tenant is behaving inappropriately and reasonable action, such as counseling, has not solved the problem, the tenant may be evicted. In other words, a landlord does not have to tolerate such behavior by a mentally ill tenant.
  c. Landlords must make accommodations for service animals.

H. Types of illegal activity under familial status include
  1. Charging higher security deposits.
  2. Segregating families within buildings.
  3. Maintaining "adults-only" complexes that do not constitute housing for older adults.

I. Types of illegal activity under provisions for the handicapped include
  1. Refusal to permit reasonable modifications that are necessary for the full enjoyment at the renter's expense.
  2. Refusal to make reasonable accommodations in rules, policies, practices, or services.
  3. Failure to design and construct for first occupancy, as of March 1991, an accessible route into and through a dwelling.

J. The 1988 amendments also provide that certain properties may be restricted for occupancy by the elderly.
  1. The amendments provide an exemption from the familial status protection for housing intended for or occupied solely by persons 62 years of age or older, or housing intended for or occupied by at least one person 55 years of age or older per unit.
  2. Properties complying with the "55-or-older" exemption must have at least 80% of the units occupied by at least one individual who is 55 years of age or older.
  3. Exemption properties also must publish policies and procedures that demonstrate the intent to provide housing for these individuals.

K. The 1988 amendments do not require that housing be made available to
  1. Individuals whose tenancy would constitute a direct threat to the health or safety of other individuals or that would result in substantial physical damage to the property of others.
  2. Individuals who have been convicted of the illegal manufacture or distribution of controlled substances.

L. The 1988 amendments also made significant changes to the enforcement mechanisms under the Federal Fair Housing Act of 1968, including
  1. Authorizing administrative law judges to award both economic and noneconomic damages, injunctive relief, and reasonable attorney fees and to impose civil penalties against violators of the act.
  2. Expanding the statute of limitations for initiating administrative proceedings from 180 days to one year after the alleged discriminatory housing practice.
  3. Authorizing administrative law judges within HUD to hold contested case hearings.
  4. Requiring HUD to proceed with cases on behalf of any person alleging that she or he has been the victim of housing discrimination, regardless of whether the alleged victim provides his or her own legal counsel.

M. Remedies under the new amendments include
   1. A civil penalty against the respondent, not exceeding $16,000 for the first offense.
   2. A penalty not exceeding $37,500, if another offense was committed within the past five years.
   3. A penalty not exceeding $65,000, if two or more discriminatory practices have been found in the past seven years.
   4. An order for "appropriate" relief that may include actual damages, injunctive relief, and "other equitable relief."
   5. A recommendation for disciplinary action against a named respondent whose licensure by a governmental agency is related to the complaint (including license suspension or revocation).

N. Other prohibited discriminatory acts include
   1. Refusing to sell, rent, or negotiate with any person as a means of discrimination.
   2. Changing terms for different individuals as a means of discrimination.
   3. Making discriminatory advertising statements.
   4. Representing that a property is unavailable as a means of discrimination.
   5. Blockbusting—making a profit by inducing owners to sell because of the prospective entry of minorities into the neighborhood.
   6. Redlining—discriminatory denial of loans or insurance to people in selected areas, regardless of their qualifications.
   7. Steering—leading prospective homebuyers to specific areas or avoiding specific areas either to maintain or to change the character of an area.
   8. Denying membership in a multiple-listing service (MLS) or related groups as a means of discrimination.

O. Exemptions from the fair housing law but not the Civil Rights Act of 1866, there are no exemptions for discriminating based on race.
   1. Sale or rental of a single-family home if home is owned by a person who does not own more than three such homes at one time and if certain conditions exists.
      a. A broker is not used.
      b. Discriminatory advertising is not used.
      c. If the owner is not currently living in the home or was not the most recent occupant, only one such exempt sale has been made within any two-year period.
   2. Rental rooms or units in an owner-occupied, one-family to four-family dwelling
   3. Dwelling units owned by religious organizations may be restricted to persons of the same religion if membership is not restricted on the basis of race, color, sex (or gender), national origin, disability, or familial status.
   4. Lodgings of a private club may be restricted to members as long as the lodgings are not operated commercially.

III. Equal Housing Poster—the 1974 amendment to the 1968 Federal Fair Housing Act requires that the Equal Housing Opportunity logo poster be posted with the brokerage license.

IV. Federal Equal Credit Opportunity Act—prohibits discrimination against credit applicants on the basis of race, color, religion, national origin, sex, marital status, age (if the applicant is of legal age), or dependency on public assistance; it requires that all rejected credit applicants be informed, in writing, of the reasons for credit denial within 30 days.

V. Americans with Disabilities Act (ADA)

A. This 1990 law affects real estate licensees, because it addresses the rights of individuals with disabilities in employment and public accommodations.

B. The ADA provides for the employment of qualified job applicants regardless of their disabilities.

C. Any employer with 15 or more employees as of July 26, 1994 must adopt nondiscriminatory employment procedures and make reasonable accommodations to enable an individual with a disability to perform in her or his employment.

D. The ADA (Title III) states that individuals with disabilities have the right to full and equal access to businesses and public services; thus, building owners and managers must ensure that obstacles restricting those rights are eliminated.

E. The ADA also provides comprehensive guidance for making public facilities accessible.

F. The law seeks to protect property owners from incurring burdensome expense to extensively retrofit an existing building by recommending reasonable achievable accommodations that will accomplish the purpose of providing access to the facility and services.

G. Because it costs less to incorporate accessible features in the design than to retrofit, new construction, including remodeling, must meet higher standards, being readily accessible and usable.

H. Types of alterations that might be made to public facilities and services include

1. Attaching grab bars to restroom stalls.
2. Providing automatic-entry doors.
3. Adjusting the height of a pay telephone to make it accessible to a person in a wheelchair.
4. Converting information on real estate listings to large-print or audio format.

I. The ADA provides for enforcement by allowing several remedies for a person who is discriminated against, including

1. A temporary or permanent injunction.
2. The court may grant any equitable relief that the court considers appropriate.
3. A civil penalty of up to $50,000 may be assessed for a first violation of the law, and a penalty of up to $100,000 may be assessed for any subsequent violation.

VI. Advertising and technology

A. Incorrect "factual" statements versus "puffing"
   1. Incorrect factual statements (fraud) is a misrepresentation of facts known to be false, made with the intent to deceive and relied on by the injured party to his or her detriment; it also includes intentional or negligent nondisclosure of pertinent facts by silence.
   2. Puffing is an opinion or exaggeration that no one relies on for decision making; for example, "This is the most beautiful view in the county."
   3. Truth in advertising—the Truth-in-Lending Act (TILA) affects lenders, as well as real estate brokers or even property owners advertising their own real estate, when financing terms are included in their advertising.
   4. The broker is generally prohibited from placing blind ads—those that do not identify the broker as the advertiser.

B. Fair housing issues in advertising
   1. HUD advertising guidelines state that advertisements of property for rent or sale are not allowed to include language that indicates a limitation or preference.
   2. HUD's advertising guidelines cover the categories of
      a. Race, color, and national origin
      b. Religion
      c. Sex
      d. Disability
      e. Familial status
      f. Photographs or illustrations of people

C. Fraud, technology issues
   1. Uninformed misrepresentation versus deliberate misrepresentation (fraud)
      a. Uninformed misrepresentation is making a false statement unintentionally.
   2. Deliberate misrepresentation is knowingly making a false statement with intent to deceive; it is fraud.
   3. The deliberate misrepresentation would involve a material fact.

D. A material fact is a fact that, if disclosed, would impact the decision of the person to whom the disclosure is being made.

E. Technology issues in advertising and marketing
   1. Electronic contracting is governed by two federal laws: the Electronic Signatures in Global and National Commerce Act (E-Sign) and the Uniform Electronic Transactions Act (UETA).
      a. E-Sign makes electronic contracts, signatures, and records relating to a transaction legally enforceable even if a state statute requires that the records be in writing.
         (1) A detailed disclosure and consent process is required under E-Sign if the parties wish to substitute electronic documents and signatures for written documents and signatures.
         (2) E-Sign disclosure requires that consumers consent electronically; written consent is not sufficient.

b. UETA establishes basic rules for creating legally enforceable electronic contracts.
    (1) The primary aim for UETA is to establish commonality among states with regard to paper records and the validity of electronic signatures.
    (2) More specifically, UETA states that a contract cannot be denied its legal effect just because an electronic signature, record, or format was used.
c. UETA serves as the electronic transactions law in some states, while E-Sign serves a similar capacity in states that have not enacted UETA.
d. Situations exist where one party wants to complete the real estate transaction using electronic means, while the other party does not have the ability to use electronic means or will not provide the electronic consent.
    (1) Electronic consent is not required from the client if there is an agent-to-agent email delivery of transaction documents.

2. Federal Telemarketing Law
    a. Federal telemarketing law, or the Do Not Call law, limits telephone sales calls.
    b. Under this law, people register with the Federal Trade Commission (FTC) or with their appropriate state agency and are placed on the do-not call lists.
    c. Registration provides brokers access to all telephone numbers on the federal and state lists for verification before making sales calls.
    d. The purpose of the do-not-call lists is to restrict the cold calling of individuals who do not want to be called, and to identify telephone numbers at which they do not want to be called by salespeople.
    e. Real estate licensees are considered telemarketers under this law.
    f. The do-not-call regulations do not apply unless the call is intended to sell real estate, real estate services, or other products or services.
    g. The rules are not intended to interfere with ongoing transactions or to deter calls in the regular course of business; in other words, if the real estate professional in his or her professional opinion, determines that the telephone call is necessary for completion of a given transaction or to render ongoing services to a client or a customer, the agent can make the call. Agents may not call owners who are selling their own house (FSBOs) to offer listing services if the homeowners are on any do-not-call list unless the person has given written permission.
    h. Follow-up calls to previous customers or clients may be made within 18 months of the previous sale involving the client.

3. Internet Advertising
    a. An increasing proportion of real estate advertising is being done online with agents using their own websites.
    b. Agents can use websites as a means to gain maximum exposure to their listings and also to connect with buyers.

c. Agents submit their websites to search engines, such as Yahoo and Google, which attract various types of viewers.
d. Agents may connect with the Internet through the use of computers, tablets, and cell phones.
e. Websites of real estate agencies provide databases that allow viewers to search for listings, as well as other types of real estate information.
f. Internet Listing Display Policy (ILDP) is a primary database used in the marketing of real estate.
   (1) ILDP gives all members of the Multiple Listing Service (MLS) equal rights to display MLS data, and recognizes the rights of property owners and their listing brokers to market a property as they desire.
   (2) A blanket opt-out provision also is provided, which states that those MLS participants interested in keeping their listings off the websites of competitors' websites cannot then display other real estate brokers' listings.
   (3) Brokers who choose to opt out of displaying their listings on competitors' websites can, at the direction of a seller, make an exception and display the seller's property on the MLS website.

VII. Licensee supervision

A. Liability/responsibility for acts of associated licensees and employees
   1. Principal/employing broker, broker associate, or salesperson relationships
      a. The nature of a real estate salesperson's relationship with a principal employing broker is determined by mutual agreement.
      b. The actual form of the employment contract between a brokerage and employed licensees depends on whether the licensee is to operate as the broker's employee or as an employed independent contractor.
      c. Most real estate licensees are affiliated with their brokers as employed independent contractors.
   2. Licensees as employees
      a. Brokerage firms can control working conditions over salespeople who are employees.
      b. Employees can be required to follow rules, such as maintaining assigned working hours, attendance at sales meetings, and comply with dress codes.
      c. The federal government requires a brokerage to deduct income taxes and social security taxes from wages paid to employees.
      d. A principal or employing broker could be held liable for the acts of his or her employees.
   3. Licensees as independent contractors
      a. A principal broker can control what an independent contractor will do but cannot control how they do it.
      b. A principal broker cannot control the working conditions of an independent contractor, such as requiring the maintenance of specific office hours or attending sales meetings.

c. Independent contractors must pay their own social security taxes and income taxes.
d. A principal broker could be held liable for the acts of his or her independent contractor.

B. Responsibility to train and supervise associated licensees and employees
1. Licensees as employees could be required to go through training classes and to become familiar with policy and procedures manuals.
2. Licensees as independent contractors can be invited to attend training classes and to become familiar with policy and procedure manuals, but the broker has no control over what they choose to do.

VIII. Commissions and Fees

A. Procuring cause/protection clause
1. Procuring cause
a. Procuring cause refers to who caused the sale to happen and thus would be entitled to receive the commission.
b. Brokers claiming procuring cause must have started a chain of events that resulted in a sale.
c. When a brokerage is employed by a seller, and finds a buyer who is ready, willing, and able to purchase on the terms and conditions of the listing or on any terms acceptable to the seller, the brokerage is entitled to the commission even if
(1) The sale is not completed because of the principal's default.
(2) The buyer cancels because of the seller's fraud, of which the broker had no knowledge.
2. Protection clause
a. Extends listing protection for the broker.
b. Provides protection of broker's commission for a period of time after expiration of the listing contract for identified parties, such as a buyer who negotiated on the property during the listing period and who buys the property after the listing has expired.

B. Referrals and other finder's fees
1. Referral fee is an amount of money given to a person who provides a buyer or a seller for a transaction.
2. Referral fees and finder's fee are used interchangeably to describe a fee paid for referrals resulting in a sale of real estate.
3. Many states require that referral fees can only be paid to a real estate broker or salesperson who is licensed in the state.
4. If the agreements are legal, they should be in writing and reviewed by an attorney to ensure they are permitted under state law.
5. Salespeople may receive money only from the principal broker and not other licensees.

IX. General ethics

A. Practicing within area of competence
   1. State license laws require real estate licensees to be competent in their practice.
   2. For example, a broker who has sold houses during his entire career in real estate and has no knowledge of farms would have his competency questioned if he were to list a dairy farm.
   3. State license law would generally allow the broker to co-list the dairy farm along with a broker who is knowledgeable about dairy farms

B. Avoiding unauthorized practice of law
   1. Real estate professionals can avoid activities constituting the unauthorized practice of law by following procedures such as:
      a. never telling a client or customer that they don't need legal advice.
      b. never sign a document on behalf of a client or customer (unless acting as a universal agent with a power of attorney).
      c. do not change the terms and conditions of an approved form unless directed by the client.

X. Antitrust laws

A. Antitrust law prohibitions
   1. Allocation of customers or markets—agreement among brokerage firms or real estate professionals to divide their markets and refrain from competing for each other's business; division may take place on geographic basis or on a certain price range of homes.
   2. Price fixing—conspiracy among brokerages to set prices for their services, rather than negotiate such fees
   3. Boycotting—two or more businesses conspire against other businesses to reduce competition
   4. Tie-in agreements—agreements to sell one product only if buyer purchases another product as well
   5. Real estate professionals violating the Sherman Antitrust Act may be found guilty of a felony punishable by a maximum $1 million dollar fine for an individual and ten years in prison.
   6. In a civil suit, a broker found guilty of a violation of the Sherman Antitrust Act is liable for triple damages plus attorney's fees and court costs.
   7. The purpose of antitrust law is to protect competition.

B. Antitrust violations in real estate
   1. If the local board of REALTORS® agrees that every brokerage firm in the city will charge the same rate of commission, this is illegal and would be an example of price fixing.
   2. A real estate professional has a listing for a house that a customer wants to buy and he tells the customer that he will only sell the house to the customer if the customer agrees to list her or his house with the professional; this would be an example of a tie-in agreement.

CHAPTER 12 QUIZ

1. The federal fair housing laws prohibit discrimination on the basis of
   1. sexual orientation.
   2. political beliefs.
   3. marital status.
   4. sex.

2. Persuading someone to sell by telling her or him that minorities are moving into the neighborhood is illegal and is called
   1. redlining
   2. blockbusting.
   3. testing.
   4. steering.

3. Which of the following is exempted from the federal fair housing laws?
   1. Rental of rooms in an owner-occupied five-family dwelling
   2. Rental of an owner-occupied five-family dwelling
   3. Rental of a single-family home when a broker is used
   4. Lodgings of a private club when the lodgings are not operated commercially

4. The practice of channeling potential buyers of one race into one area and potential buyers of another race into another area is known as
   1. canvassing.
   2. blockbusting.
   3. redlining.
   4. steering.

5. A real estate broker may
   1. refuse to rent to a qualified minority person.
   2. solicit listings in a minority neighborhood.
   3. refuse to negotiate with a minority person
   4. change the terms of sale for a minority person

6. The federal fair housing laws prohibit which of the following types of private housing?
   1. A Lutheran organization giving preference to its members in renting
   2. A Norwegian advertising his house for "Norwegians only"
   3. The Elks Club operating a rooming house on a nonprofit basis
   4. A Masonic Lodge operating a rooming house when the lodgings are not operated commercially

7. Which of the following categories is *NOT* protected against discrimination under the federal fair housing laws?
   1. Religion
   2. Familial status
   3. Disabled status
   4. Lawful source of income

8. The denial of a loan by a lender would *NOT* be a violation of federal fair housing laws if it were based on
   1. lack of income.
   2. sex.
   3. age.
   4. marital status.

9. Which of the following laws provides comprehensive guidance for making public facilities accessible?
   1. RESPA
   2. Truth-in-Lending
   3. Federal fair housing laws
   4. Americans with Disabilities Act (ADA)

10. Which of the following activities would be legal under the familial status category of the federal fair housing laws?
    1. Charging higher rents for people with pets
    2. Charging higher security deposits for families with children
    3. Segregating families within buildings
    4. Segregating families in certain buildings

11. Converting information on a real estate listing to large-print or audio format would be a response to
    1. federal fair housing laws.
    2. the Americans with Disabilities Act.
    3. Regulation Z.
    4. RESPA.

12. The Americans with Disabilities Act (ADA) requires all of the following alterations to be made to public facilities and services *EXCEPT*
    1. attaching grab bars to a restroom stall.
    2. providing automatic entry doors.
    3. providing an automatic sprinkler system.
    4. converting real estate listing information to large print or audio format.

13. Which of the following rental practices would be legal under federal fair housing laws?
    1. A property manager discloses to the landlord that a prospective tenant is a minority.
    2. A property manager charges a mother and her six-year-old son a higher security deposit than another woman with no children.
    3. A rental agent refuses to rent an apartment to a person who is convicted drug dealer.
    4. A property manager refuses to rent to a blind man because he has a seeing-eye dog and the property does not allow dogs.

14. The Civil Rights Act of 1866 prohibits discrimination in housing on the basis of
    1. religion.
    2. race.
    3. sex.
    4. handicap.

15. All of the following are considered a protected class under the Federal Equal Credit Opportunity Act *EXCEPT*
    1. marital status.
    2. age.
    3. sexual orientation.
    4. dependency on public assistance.

16. Disclosure of cost in a credit transaction is required by
    1. RESPA.
    2. Truth-in-Lending.
    3. the Federal Equal Credit Opportunity Act.
    4. the 1968 Federal Fair Housing Act.

17. According to the Federal Equal Credit Opportunity Act, a rejected credit applicant must be informed, in writing, of the reason for credit denial within
    1. 3 days.
    2. 10 days.
    3. 30 days.
    4. 90 days.

18. A landlord allowed a tenant confined to a wheelchair to make several minor physical changes to an apartment. These changes are called
    1. disability accommodations.
    2. familial accommodations.
    3. trade fixture modifications.
    4. reasonable accommodations or modifications.

19. Which of the following is a legitimate landlord action under fair housing's familial status?
    1. Charging a higher security deposit for families with children
    2. Segregating families within a building
    3. Segregating families into certain buildings
    4. Limiting occupancy based on local zoning requirements.

20. Most states require real estate licenses to be conspicuously displayed by the brokerage firm. What else is the broker of a real estate office required to conspicuously display?
    1. EHO poster
    2. Listings
    3. Civil Rights act of 1866
    4. ECOA legislation

21. A broker was listing a seller's home for sale when the seller stated that he would be unwilling to sell to an Asian. The broker should
    1. list the property, because the seller has the right to choose who will buy his house.
    2. list the property, but be sure to discreetly urge any Asian buyer to live in a different neighborhood.
    3. list the property, but avoid getting involved in any negotiations between an Asian buyer and the owner.
    4. not accept the listing.

22. The Federal Fair Housing Act of 1968 was amended in 1988 to prohibit
    1. blockbusting.
    2. discrimination against pregnant women.
    3. redlining.
    4. steering.

23. The Federal Telemarketing Law allows follow-up calls to previous customers or clients to be made within
    1. 6 months of the previous sale involving the agent.
    2. 12 months of the previous sale involving the agent.
    3. 18 months of the previous sale involving the agent.
    4. 24 months of the previous sale involving the agent.

24. All of the following statements correctly describe the E-Sign law *EXCEPT*
    1. E-Sign is one of two federal laws governing electronic contracting.
    2. E-Sign allows consumers to provide written consent if they wish to substitute electronic documents for written documents.
    3. E-Sign makes electronic records relating to the transaction legally enforceable even if a state statute requires that the records be in writing,
    4. E-Sign requires a detailed disclosure and consent process if the parties wish to substitute electronic signatures for written signatures.

25. All of the following statements correctly describe the Federal Telemarketing Law *EXCEPT*
    1. people may register with the Federal Trade Commission and are placed on do-not-call lists.
    2. real estate licensees are not considered telemarketers under the law.
    3. the law does not apply unless the call intended to sell real estate.
    4. the rules are not intended to interfere with ongoing transactions.

26. A licensed real estate broker who engages the services of a licensed salesperson on the basis that the broker can direct what the salesperson can do but not how it is done has
    1. engaged an independent contractor.
    2. discriminated illegally.
    3. practiced steering.
    4. established an employer-employee relationship.

MATCHING QUIZ

The column on the right contains brief memory links to important terms in Chapter 12.

Write the letter of the matching term on the appropriate line.

A. Civil Rights Act of 1866
B. HUD
C. AIDS
D. Reasonable accommodation
E. Familial status
F. Title VIII
G. EHO poster
H. 62 years and older
I. Blockbusting
J. Redlining
K. Steering
L. Annual Percentage Rate
M. ECOA
N. ADA
O. Truth-in-Lending
P. Discrimination

1. _______ The Federal Fair Housing Act of 1968
2. _______ Prohibits property discrimination based on race
3. _______ Inducing owners to sell because of entry of minorities into neighborhoods
4. _______ American legislation that gives disabled people accommodations equal employment rights
5. _______ Protected under HUD's disability definition of the Fair Housing Act
6. _______ Protected class that includes persons who are pregnant
7. _______ Segregating families with children to certain buildings or floors within a building
8. _______ Federal fair housing enforcement agency
9. _______ An authorized discrimination age for senior housing exempt from familial status
10. _______ Intentionally not loaning money in neighborhoods
11. _______ Lenders must use this to clearly state for comparative purposes the cost of their loans
12. _______ Legislation that requires disclosure for the cost of credit
13. _______ Showing minorities only targeted neighborhoods rather than the entire market
14. _______ Tenant granted permission to put in bathroom grab bars and raise electrical outlets
15. _______ Legislation protecting against discrimination in lending
16. _______ Required to be conspicuously displayed in real estate, appraising, and lender offices

CHAPTER 12 QUIZ ANSWERS

1. **(4)** Some states and local governments prohibit discrimination on the basis of sexual orientation, political beliefs, and marital status. (164)

2. **(2)** Redlining is denying loans or insurance to people in selected neighborhoods regardless of their qualifications. Testing is done to enforce the law, and steering restricts freedom of choice. (166)

3. **(4)** The exemption applies to up to four units of owner-occupied rental housing. (166)

4. **(4)** Canvassing involves personal solicitation of opinions or sentiments, which is generally legal. Blockbusting and redlining are illegal. (166)

5. **(2)** Discrimination is treating people differently when they are members of a protected class. (166)

6. **(2)** Religious organizations and private clubs may discriminate under certain circumstances. An individual homeowner must comply with certain conditions to be exempt from federal fair housing laws. (166)

7. **(4)** Nevertheless, lawful source of income is a protected class in some states. The Federal Equal Credit Opportunity Act also protects borrowers in a similar manner. (166)

8. **(1)** Lack of income is an acceptable reason for denying a loan, provided all lawful sources of income are considered as previously discussed. (166)

9. **(4)** Regulation Z is the Truth-in-Lending Law. Ginnie Mae functions in the secondary mortgage market. Federal fair housing law does not deal with accessibility to public facilities. (167)

10. **(1)** Since pets are not a protected class, landlords may charge higher rents for renters with pets. (165)

11. **(2)** The 1968 Federal Fair Housing Act includes handicapped as a protected class, but the specific measures are identified in the ADA. Truth-in-Lending requires disclosure of cost in a credit transaction. RESPA is aimed at protecting consumers from abusive lending practices. (167)

12. **(3)** The fire codes would require the providing of an automatic sprinkler system. (167)

13. **(3)** Convicted drug dealers are never protected under federal fair housing laws. (164)

14. **(2)** The Civil rights Act of 1866 makes clear that there is no situation in which racial discrimination may be practiced. (164)

15. **(3)** Sexual orientation is a protected class in a number of states; however, it is not protected under federal housing or lending laws. (167)

16. **(2)** RESPA provides consumer protection with regard to closing procedures and costs. The Federal Equal Credit Opportunity Act prohibits credit providers from discriminating against members of certain protected classes. The 1968 Federal Fair Housing Act prohibits discrimination in the sale or rental of housing. (79)

17. **(3)** The Federal Equal Credit Opportunity Act also states that a borrower is entitled to a copy of the appraisal report, paid for by the borrowers. (167)

18. **(4)** Under federal law, the tenant is allowed (at the tenant's expense) to make reasonable modifications. (167)

19. **(4)** The landlord is allowed to limit the number of people in a unit based on square footage. (164–165)

20. **(1)** The Equal Housing Opportunity poster with the logo of an equal sign inside the outline of a house. (167)

21. **(4)** The Federal Fair Housing Act of 1968 prohibits discrimination on the basis of race or national origin. (164)

22. **(2)** The Federal Fair Housing Act was amended in 1989 to prohibit discrimination on the basis of familial status, which includes pregnant women. Blockbusting, redlining, and steering were prohibited by the Federal Fair Housing Act of 1968. (164)

23. **(3)** The Federal Telemarketing Law allows real estate professionals to make follow-up calls to previous customers or clients within 18 months of the previous sale involving the agent. (169)

24. **(2)** E-Sign requires consumers to provide electronic consent if they wish to substitute electronic documents for written documents. (168–169)

25. **(2)** Real estate licensees are considered telemarketers under the Federal Telemarketing law. (169)

26. **(1)** A broker cannot control salespeople's working conditions as in an employer-employee relationship. An agent is not required to follow illegal instruction, such as discrimination. (170–171)

TEST SCORE

PRACTICE OF REAL ESTATE			
Rating	**Range**	**Your Score**	
Good = 80% to 100%	21–26	Total Number	26
Fair = 70% to 79%	19–25	Total Wrong	–
Needs improvement = Lower than 70%	18 or less	Total Right	

Passing Requirement: 19 or Better

ANSWER KEY: MATCHING QUIZ

1. **F**
2. **A**
3. **I**
4. **N**
5. **C**
6. **E**
7. **P**
8. **B**
9. **H**
10. **J**
11. **L**
12. **O**
13. **K**
14. **D**
15. **M**
16. **G**

CHAPTER 13

Real Estate Calculations

OUTLINE OF CONCEPTS

This review is designed to familiarize you with some basic mathematical formulas that are used most frequently in the computations required on state licensing examinations. These same computations also are important in day-to-day real estate transactions. If you think you need additional help in working these problems, you may want to order a copy of *Mastering Real Estate Mathematics*, 8th edition (Dearborn Real Estate Education, 2012).

A. Basic math concepts

1. Percentages

Most calculators have a key with a % sign on it called the percent key. This key converts percentages into decimals for calculation purposes. For example, if you need to compute a 6% commission on a $200,000 sale, enter $200,000, and then multiply (×) it by 6 and press the % key to compute the commission. $200,000 × 6% = $12,000.

Many real estate computations are based on the calculations of percentages. A percentage expresses a portion of a whole (or total) that is expressed as 100. For example, 50% means 50 parts of the 100 parts constituting the whole. Percentages greater than 100% contain more than one whole unit. Thus, 163% is one whole plus 63 parts of another whole. Remember that a whole is always thought of as equaling 100%.

60% = 0.60   7% = 0.07   175% = 1.75

To express a percentage as a fraction, place the percentage over 100. For example:

$$50\% = \frac{50}{100}$$

These fractions then may be reduced to make working the problem easier. To reduce a fraction, determine the highest number that will divide both the numerator and denominator evenly—that is, with no remainder—then divide each of them by that number. For example:

$^{25}/_{100}$ = ¼ (both numbers are divided by 25)

$^{49}/_{63}$ = $^{7}/_{9}$ (both numbers are divided by 7)

- A broker is to receive a 7% commission on a sale of a $50,000 house. What will the broker's commission be?

0.07 × $50,000 = $3,500 broker's commission

Percentage problems contain three elements: *percentage*, *total*, and *part*. To *determine a specific percentage of a total*, multiply the percentage by the whole. This is illustrated by the following formula:

Percent × total = part

5% × 200 = 10

This formula is used in calculating mortgage loan interest, brokers' commission, loan origination fees, discount points, the amount of earnest money deposits, and income on capital investment.

A variation or inversion on the percentage formula is used to find the total amount when the part and percentage are known. Therefore:

$$\text{total} = \frac{\text{part}}{\text{percentage}}$$

- A broker received a $3,600 commission for the sale of a house. The broker's commission was 6% of the total sales price. What was the total sales price of this house?

$$\text{total sales price} = \frac{\$3,600}{0/06} = \$60,000$$

Simplified, the equation looks like this: $3,600 = 6% of x. To solve this equation, both sides are divided by 6% to cancel the 6% out of the right side of the equation. The result looks like this: $3,600 divided by 6% OR .06 = (6% ÷ 6%) x. So, $3,600 divided by 6% or .06 = $60,000.

Another way of looking at this same problem is to translate the algebraic formula into a simple sentence. **Divide any part of its % of the total and you'll find the total number**.

We know that $3,600 is 6% of the total. Therefore, if that number ($3,600) is divided by 6% or .06, then the resulting number must be the total. The solution is figured like this: $3,600 ÷ 6% or .06 = $60,000.

Let's try another example. Statistically, a move-up buyer's next home is (on the average) 52% higher than his or her current home. If a seller is asking $200,000, what is the estimated value of a potential buyer's current home?

What do we know? We know that $200,000 represents both the value of the buyer's current home and 52% more. Therefore, the

$200,000 listed property is 152% of the unknown total. Accordingly, the part ($200,000) divided by its percentage of total 152% or 1.52) will result in the total. $200,000 ÷ 152% = $131,579. Thus, for target marketing purposes, the listing agent should target market in a $132,000 neighborhood in order to find prospective move-up buyers.

FIGURE 13.1

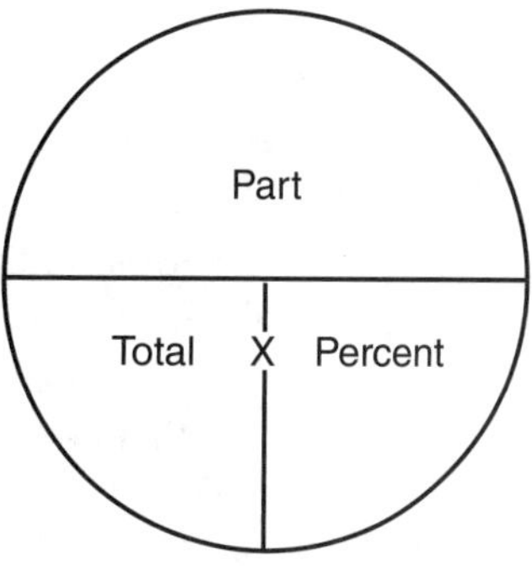

This formula is used in computing the total mortgage loan principal still due if the monthly payment and interest rate are known. It also is used to calculate (1) the total sales price when the amount and percentage of commission or earnest money deposit is known, (2) the interest due if the monthly payment and interest rate are known, and (3) the market value of property if the assessed value and the ratio (percentage) of assessed value to market value are known.

To determine the percent when the amounts of the part and the total are known:

$$\text{percent} = \frac{\text{part}}{\text{total}}$$

This formula may be used to determine the tax rate when the taxes and assessed value are known or the commission rate if the sales price and commission amount are known.

An easy way to remember the *formula* (or part, percent, and total) is with the diagram in Figure 13.1. First, draw the circle and divide it in half; then divide the bottom half in half. Put the term *part* in the top half of the circle and the other two terms in the two bottom portions.

Next, substitute the known amounts for the words that represent those amounts. The word that remains represents the element for which you are solving. If the terms for which you have figures are below the line that divides the entire circle in half, multiply them to find the third element; if one figure is above the other, divide the top term by the bottom one.

2. Rates

Property taxes, transfer taxes, and insurance premiums usually are expressed as rates. A rate is expressed as cost per unit; for example, in a certain county, tax is computed at the rate of $50 per $1,000 or assessed value. The formula for *computing rates* follows:

$$\frac{\text{value}}{\text{unit}} \times \text{rate per total} = \text{total}$$

- A house assessed at $50,000 is taxed at an annual rate of $25 per $1,000 assessed valuation. What is the yearly tax?

Step 1: $50,000 ÷ 1,000 = 50

Step 2: $50 × $25 =$1,250 total annual tax

3. Area

People in the real estate profession must know how to compute the area of a parcel of land or to figure the amount of living area in a house. *To compute the area of a square or rectangular parcel,* use this formula:

Area = length × width (A = l × w)

What is the area of a rectangular lot 200 feet long by 100 feet wide?

200' × 100' = 20,000 square feet

Area is always expressed in square units.

To compute the width of a rectangular parcel, use this formula:

$$\text{width} = \frac{\text{area}}{\text{length}}$$

What is the length of a rectangular lot that measures 40 feet wide and has an area of 3,600 square feet?

$$\frac{3{,}600 \text{ sq. ft.}}{40 \text{ ft.}} = 90 \text{ feet}$$

To compute the amount of surface in a triangular-shaped area, use one of these formulas:

area = ½ (base × height) [A = ½ (b × h)]

or

area = (½ base) × height [A = (½b) × h)]

The part of an equation enclosed in parentheses always is computed before any other part of the equation. The base of a triangle is the bottom, the side on which the triangle rests. The height is an imaginary line extending from the point (or vertex) of the uppermost angle straight down (perpendicular) to the base (see Figure 13.2).

FIGURE 13.2

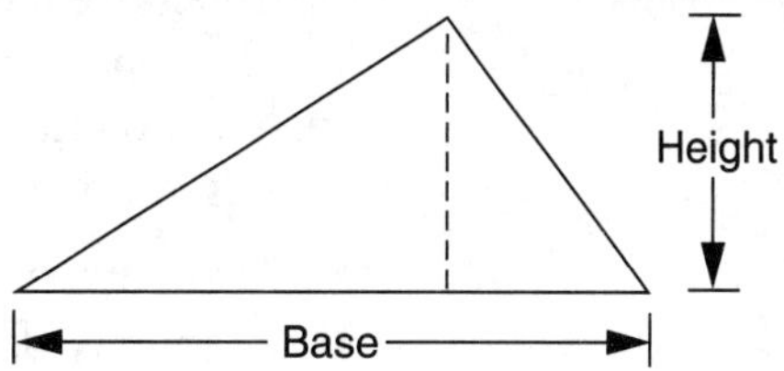

A triangle has a base of 50 feet and a height of 30 feet. What is the area?

$$\tfrac{1}{2}(50' \times 30') = \text{area in square feet}$$

$$\tfrac{1}{2}(1{,}500) = 750 \text{ square feet}$$

Or

$$50 \div 2 = 25 \times 30 = 750 \text{ square feet}$$

To compute the area of an irregular room or parcel of land, divide the shape into regular rectangles, squares, or triangles. Next, compute the area of each regular figure and add the areas together to obtain the total area.

Compute the area in the hallway in Figure 13.3:

FIGURE 13.3

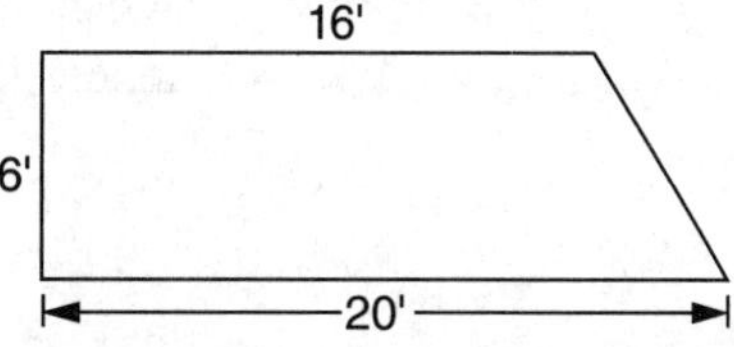

First, make a rectangle and a triangle by drawing a single line through the figure as shown in Figure 13.4.

FIGURE 13.4

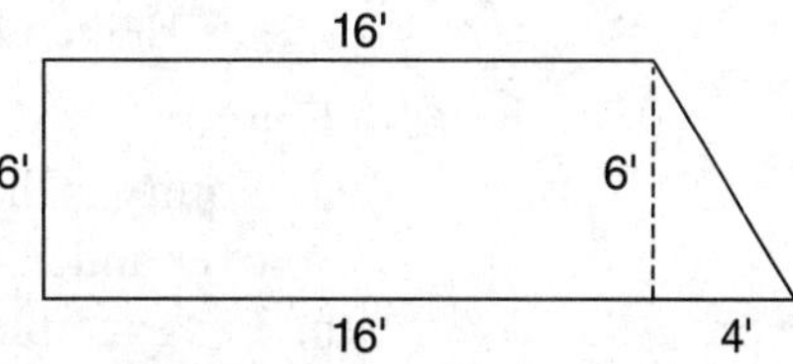

Compute the area of the rectangle:

$$\text{area} = \text{length} \times \text{width} \qquad 16' \times 6' = 96 \text{ square feet}$$

Compute the area of the triangle:

$$\text{area} = \tfrac{1}{2}(\text{base} \times \text{height}) = \tfrac{1}{2}(4' \times 6')\text{—}\tfrac{1}{2}(24) = 12 \text{ square feet}$$

Add the two areas:

$$96 + 12 = 108 \text{ square feet total area}$$

4. Loan-to-value ratios (LTV)
   a. Lenders use the LTV ratio to express the relationship between the amount of the mortgage loan and the appraised value of the real estate being pledged as collateral.

b. The LTV ratio is one of the important risk factors considered by lenders when qualifying borrowers for a mortgage.
c. Calculate the LTV ratio by dividing the amount of the loan by the appraised value of the property.
d. For example, if a man is buying a home worth $200,000 and his mortgage is for $160,000, the LTV ratio is 80%;

amount of loan	$160,000
appraised value of home	$200,000 = 80%

5. Discount points
   a. Discount points are an added loan fee charged by a lender to increase the yield on a lower-than-market-value loan competitive with higher-interest loans.
   b. Point—a unit of measurement used for various loan charges; one point equals 1% of the amount of the loan.
   c. In general, each discount point paid to the lender will increase the lender's return by 1/8 of 1% (.00125); to estimate the lender's real return (and cost to the borrower) from the loan, add 1/8% to the stated mortgage interest rate.
   d. To calculate the actual dollar cost added by discount points, multiply the loan amount by the percent of discount (1 point = 1%)

Example:

Assume that you need to find the amount of yield to a lender if 3 discount points are charged for an FHA loan showing a contract interest rate of 4%.

Convert discount point to percent of increase

(1 point = 1/8 of 1% increase)

(3 points = 3/8% increase)

4% + 3/8 % = 4 3/8% (approximate yield to lender)

Remember that 1 discount point = 1% of the loan amount.

6. Equity
   a. Equity is the value or interest that an owner has in the property over and above any mortgage indebtedness.
   b. For example, if a homeowner has a home with an appraised value of $280,000 and a first mortgage of $140,000 and a second mortgage of $20,000, the owner has an equity of $120,000.
7. Down payment/amount to be financed
   a. Mortgage financial package
      (1) A mortgage financial package includes:
         a. the down payment
         b. Conventional, FHA
         c. the impact of any discount points
         d. taxes on the mortgage if any are charged
         e. the full monthly payment, which will include principal, interest, taxes and insurance (PITI).

b. The required down payment varies based on the financing alternatives available, such as conventional, FHA, or VA.
c. Alternative mortgage loan down payments
   (1) Conventional mortgage down payments vary from 20% to 3% on a loan that is backed by private mortgage insurance.
   (2) VA mortgage loans previously discussed can require no down payment for eligible veterans depending on the amount of the loan, as well as other factors.
   (3) FHA mortgage loans allow for a home to be purchased with a down payment of 3.5%.
   (4) Discount points, if any are charged, vary with the state of the mortgage market and the terms of financing.
   (5) Amount to be financed
      a. The amount of the loan generally includes the PITI (principle, interest on the loan, real estate taxes, and insurance, if insurance is required).

B. Calculations for transactions, including mortgage calculations.
   1. Prorations (utilities, rent, property taxes, insurance, etc.)

PRORATIONS

When closing a real estate transaction, it generally is necessary to divide the financial responsibility between the buyer and seller for items such as taxes, loan interest, fuel bills, and rents. Prorations provide for an equitable distribution of income and expenses between the seller and the buyer. Accrued items, such as real estate taxes, are owed by the seller but will be paid later by the buyer. The seller pays for accrued items by giving the buyer a credit at closing. A prepaid item—such as fuel oil that has not been used—requires a credit to the seller at closing.

Proration may be done through the day prior to closing or through the day of closing. The sales contract (offer to purchase) or custom of the area generally determines whether the buyer or seller will pay for the actual day of closing. For example, if real estate taxes are prorated through the day of closing, the seller will pay the taxes for the day of closing per tradition in the state. On the license exam, prorations should be done based upon the information in the question.

Prorations may be calculated on either a 360-day year (12 months of 30 days each) or a 365-day year. The 365-day year requires determination of the daily charge multiplied by the actual number of days in the proration period. Compute all prorations by carrying the division to four decimal places. The third and fourth decimal places should not be rounded off to cents until the final proration figure has been determined.

The first step in the proration process is to determine the time period involved in the proration process (the number of days charged to or through the closing date).

The second step is to calculate the dollar amount per day.

The third step is to determine the proration by multiplying the time period by the dollar amount per day.

For testing purposes, proration problems will state the number of days in a month you are expected to use.

a. General guidelines for prorations
   (1) Because property taxes are paid in arrears, the taxes are typically prorated through the day of closing. The prorated tax will be credited to the buyer and debited (charged) to the seller.
   (2) If a buyer assumes a seller's existing loan, the balance of the loan will be credited to the buyer and debited to the seller. Because interest on the loan is paid in arrears, the amount of interest owed from the day of the last payment through the day of closing will be debited to the seller.
   (3) If a water bill is prepaid, the prepaid time must be computed. The amount of the prepaid item will be debited to the buyer and credited to the seller.
   (4) The broker's commission is normally debited to the seller.
   (5) Items credited to the seller and debited to the buyer generally include
      a. The sales price
      b. Any tax and insurance reserve in the case of a buyer assuming the seller's loan
      c. Prepaid real estate taxes
      d. Any fuel oil remaining in the storage tank on the day of closing
   (6) Items credited to the buyer and debited to the seller include
      a. Unpaid utility bills
      b. The buyer's earnest money
      c. The unearned portion of rent collected in advance

C. Property tax calculations

Example

Using a 365-day year, prorate the taxes for a December 14 closing, if the annual tax bill is $1,224 and is prorated through the day of closing.

Solution

First, determine the time period during which taxes have accrued

Jan—31 days	May—31 days	Sept—30 days
Feb—28 days	June—30 days	Oct—31 days
Mar—31 days	July—31 days	Nov—30 days
Apr—30 days	Aug—31 days	Dec—14 days
		Total = 348 days

Second, divide the annual tax by the days in the year to determine the amount per day.

$1,224 ÷ 365 days = $3.3534 per day

Finally, multiply the time period by the amount per day.

$3.3534 × 348 = $1,166.99 debit to the seller and credit to the buyer (rounded)

D. Prorations

1. Rent

a. Rent collected in advance belongs to the buyer from the day of closing, if the buyer is in title for that day, to the end of the month.

b. The total rent for the rental period is divided by the number of days in the period of rent and then allocated on a daily basis.

Example

Assume that a property rents for $800 per month. The closing date is on the 14th day of a 30-day month. The proration would be as follows:

$800 ÷ 30 days = $26.66666 per day

$26.66666 × 17 days = 453.33333 or rent = $453.33 due buyer from seller

Because the seller has already collected the rent, the seller will owe the buyer $453.33.

E. Commission and Commission Splits

1. Real estate brokerage firms may share a commission only with their own sales people or with other licensed brokers.
2. Commission splits with the broker's salespeople or broker associates are generally based on the independent contractor agreement.
3. The majority of homes in most states are listed in a Multiple Listing Service (MLS), which allows member brokers to market and sell another broker's listing.
4. When a broker's listing is sold by a member broker of MLS, it is called a co-broke or co-operative sale.
5. If a broker lists a property that is sold by one of her salespeople, the commission will be split between the listing broker and the listing broker's salesperson.
6. If broker A lists a property that is sold by another MLS (broker B), the commission will be split between broker A and broker B. If a salesperson of A listed the property, and a salesperson of B sold the property, a commission split would occur between
   a. Broker A and the listing salesperson
   b. Broker B and the selling salesperson
   c. Broker A and broker B
7. Let's look at some commission problems
   a. Broker K listed and sold a house for $220,000. If broker K received a 6% commission on the sale, how much did K receive?

      Total × percent = Part

      $220,000 × .06 = $13,200

      $\frac{\text{part}}{\text{percent whole}}$

   b. Broker J sold a house for which she was paid a commission of 5%. J was paid a commission of $12,000. What was the selling price of the property?

      Part ÷ percent = Total

      $12,000 ÷ .05 = $240,000

F. Seller's proceeds of sale
 1. The net amount that seller receives at closing after accounting for all proration as well as other debits and credits
 2. The calculations are shown on the closing statement, which is not a state-approved form.
 3. The seller also needs to consider any income taxes due on any profit resulting from the sale of the home.
 4. As previously stated, a married couple may exclude as much as $500,000 from capital gains tax for profit on the sale of a principal residence if they file jointly.
 5. Homeowners who file as individuals are entitled to a $250,000 exclusion each.
 6. Most states also allow for the similar capital gains tax deduction to be taken by a seller.

G. Transfer tax/conveyance tax/revenue stamps
 1. One-time only charges on some portion of a transaction involving real property.
 2. Taxes are charged on a portion of a value of the transaction, which in many states and municipalities is often the sales price.
 3. Some states require a transfer tax to be paid on the sales price at a rate per $100 of the value of the property or fraction thereof; the seller generally is required to pay the transfer tax to the register of deeds at the time the deed is recorded.

    For example, Wisconsin imposes a real estate transfer fee on most conveyances of $0.30 per $100 of the value of the property or fraction thereof.
 4. Some states and municipalities require that a conveyance fee be paid on the transfer of real property; the fee often is based on the value of the real estate sold or transferred from one person to another.

    For example, in Ohio the fee includes 1 mill of the property value, and counties also may impose an additional transfer tax of up to three mills.
 5. Revenue stamp taxes are required to be paid on the sales price by some states and municipalities. The stamps must be paid before the transfer of title can be legally recorded.

    For example, in New Hampshire, the tax is based on the actual price agreed to by the parties; the tax is imposed on both the buyer and the seller at the rate of $.75 per $100 of the price. The buyer and seller buy stamps from the register of deeds in the county where the property is located. The register affixes the stamp to the deed and the deed is recorded, which provides evidence publicly that the tax was paid on the transfer and the amount paid.

    Example: A state has a real estate transfer fee of $0.60 per $100 of the value of the property or fraction thereof. What would the transfer fee be for a property that sold for $100,000?

$$\$100{,}000 \div 100 = 1{,}000 \times .60 = \$600$$

If the transfer tax is paid by the seller, the seller would have to pay $600 to the state.

H. Amortization

The majority of mortgage and deed-of-trust loans are amortized loans. Regular payments are made for up to 30 years, with each payment being applied first to interest owed and the balance deducted from the principal. The amount of interest due on a specific payment date is determined by calculating the total year's interest based on the unpaid loan balance and dividing that figure by the number of payments for each year. For example, if the current outstanding loan balance is $100,000 with interest at a rate of 8% per year and constant payments of $769, the interest and principal due on the next payment would be calculated as shown.

$$\$100{,}000 \times .08 = \$8{,}000$$

$$\$8{,}000 \div 12 = \$666.666 \text{ (round to \$666.67)}$$

$769.00	monthly payment
–666.67	month's interest
$102.33	month's principal

All interest due, and the full amount of principal due, will be paid at the end of the term.

Lenders generally use the fully amortized loan plan in which the borrower pays a constant amount, which usually is monthly. Each payment is credited first to the interest due, with the balance of the payment being applied to the principal amount of the loan. A prepared mortgage payment book or a mortgage factor chart is used to determine the amount of the constant payment. The mortgage factor chart indicates the amount of monthly payment per $1,000 of loan depending on the term and interest rate.

The factor is multiplied by the number of thousands (and fractions thereof) of the amount being borrowed. The following chart shows the monthly payment (mortgage).

MONTHLY PAYMENT FACTORS (PER $1,000)		
Rate	15 Years	30 Years
7.00%	$8.99	$6.65
7.25%	9.13	6.82
7.50%	9.27	6.99
7.75%	9.41	7.16
8.00%	9.56	7.34
8.25%	9.70	7.51
8.50%	9.85	7.69
8.75%	10.00	7.87
9.00%	10.15	8.05
9.25%	10.30	8.23
9.50%	10.45	8.41
9.75%	10.60	8.60
10.00%	10.75	8.78
10.25%	10.90	8.97
10.50%	11.06	9.15
10.75%	11.21	9.34
11.00%	11.37	9.53
11.25%	11.53	9.72
11.50%	11.69	9.91
11.75%	11.85	10.10
12.00%	12.01	10.29
12.25%	12.17	10.48
12.50%	12.33	10.68
12.75%	12.49	10.87
13.00%	12.66	11.07

Example

What is the monthly payment on a $60,000 loan at 9 percent for 30 years?

Solution

Refer to the monthly payment factors chart above. Move down the Rate column to 9%. Then move to the right to the column headed 30 years to find the payment on a $1,000 loan ($8.05). To find the monthly payment on the $60,000 loan:

$$\text{monthly payment} = \frac{\text{amount of mortgage}}{\$1{,}000} \times \begin{array}{c}\text{payment for \$1,000 loan}\\ \text{(from monthly payment}\\ \text{factors chart)}\end{array}$$

$$\frac{\$60{,}000}{\$1{,}000} \times \$8.05 = 60 \quad \$8.05 = \$483.00$$

The $483 monthly payment is for the principal and interest only. The lender might add an amount for homeowner insurance premiums and for real estate taxes.

If you know how much a borrower has available to spend on a monthly payment, you can use the mortgage factor chart to determine the amount of the loan that the borrower can afford.

Assume that a prospective buyer can afford $800 per month for principal and interest, and the lender will make a loan for 30 years at 8%. To find the amount of the loan, move down column 1, Rate, to find the interest rate, then move to the right to find where the rate and the 30-year column meet. You will find 7.34. Every $7.34 of monthly payment will support a loan of $1,000.

Amount borrower has available to spend each month for amount of loan = Principal and interest = $800 ÷ $7.34 monthly payment per $1,000

108.9918 thousands or $108,992

The mortgage factor chart also can be used to determine how much interest will be paid over the life of the loan.

Using the $800 monthly payment figure, what is the total interest paid during the life of this loan?

$800 (monthly payment) × 360 months = $288,000

$288,000	(total principal and interest)
–108,991	(amount of principal)
$179,009	(total interest paid over life of loan)

1. Buyer qualification ratios
   a. Lenders have traditionally used two ratios to determine how much a buyer can afford to pay for a home:
      (1) Front-end ratio, which identifies the payment that a buyer can afford for a monthly payment.
         a. The front end ratio for a FHA loan is 31%, as opposed to a conventional loan, which is 33%.
         b. Thus, if your monthly gross income is $5,000, the lender would state that your monthly payment for principal, interest, taxes and insurance cannot exceed $1,650 for a conventional loan (5,000 × .33).
      (2) Back-end ratio, which identifies how much a buyer can afford for a mortgage payment as well as recurring debt.
         a. The back-end ratio for a FHA loan is 43% of a buyer's gross monthly income, as opposed to a conventional loan, which is 45%.
         b. Thus, if your monthly gross income is $6,000 and you have a monthly car payment of $200 and monthly credit card payments of $200, a total monthly debt for a conventional loan would be

6,000 × .45 = 2,700 – recurring debts of $400 = $2,300 for a monthly payment of 38.3% of your monthly gross income.

Thus, you would qualify for a conventional loan.

(3) As of January, 2014, the Dodd-Frank Wall Street Reform and Consumer Protection Act requires that all residential mortgages meet an Ability to Repay (ATR) standard.
   a. Lenders must use a debt to income ratio of 43% including PITI, debt, and other obligations.
   b. The 43% cap is waived for up to seven years for loans satisfying underwriting requirements of Fannie Mae, Freddie Mac, FHA, VA or Rural Housing.

I. Calculations for valuation
   1. Competitive/comparative market analysis (CMA)
      a. Unlike the sales comparison approach used by an appraiser, real estate professionals doing a CMA do not generally make adjustments between the comparables and the property being considered for sale or purchase.
      b. The professionals simply group comparable properties to establish a range of values as a basis for negotiating with a seller or buyer in order to establish a preferred listing or purchase price.
      c. Real estate professionals input the criteria from the subject property into a search program, such as the MLS, to identify comparables including:
         (1) Three to four currently listed properties
         (2) Three to four comparables, which have sold preferably within the last 3–4 months.
         (3) Three to four expired comparable listings in order to provide information on the price at which properties are not selling.
      d. Real estate professionals usually emphasize sold comparables, which have sold within the last 3–4 months.
      e. Location and square footage generally rank among the most important criteria for choosing comparables.

      Consider the following sample problem.

Summary

You find five comparable homes currently listed.

	List Price	Days on the Market (DOM)
Comp 1	$450,000	426
2	450,000	617
3	565,000	249
4	570,000	251
5	625,000	179

Average of 5 properties: $532,000

Currently Listed Properties
Average of 5 properties $532,000
Minimum: $450,000
Maximum: $625,000
Median: $565,000
Average DOM: 668

You find seven comparable homes that were sold.

	List	Sale	DOM
Comp 1	$399,900	$390,000	140
2	499,500	460,000	109
3	525,000	477,000	619
4	575,000	550,000	337
5	599,000	575,000	22
6	624,900	615,000	199
7	649,900	625,000	222

Average of 7 properties: $527,429
Minimum: $390,000
Maximum: $625,000
Median: $550,000
Average DOM: 235

You find four properties that did not sell.

	List	DOM
Comp 1	$550,000	111
2	575,000	183
3	599,900	182
4	619,000	714

Average: $585,975
Minimum: $550,000
Maximum: $619,000
Median: $587,450
Average DOM: 297

No comparables are currently under contract.

LISTING SUMMARY STATISTICS						
Status	**Homes**	**Average**	**Low**	**High**	**Median**	**DOM**
Active	5	$532,000	$450,000	$625,000	$565,000	668
Pending	0	$0	$0	$0	$00	
Sold	7	$527,429	$390,000	$625,000	$550,000	235
Expired	4	$585,975	$550,000	$619,000	$587,450	297
Total	16	$554,819	$399,900	$649,900	$572,500	

Average Sold Price	Lowest Sold Price	Highest Sold Price
$527,429	$390,000	$625,000
235 days on market	22 days on market	619 days on market

Comp 3 of the sold properties was listed for $525,000 and sold for $477,000 but it took 619 days to sell

The seller's home is considered to be similar to, but more appealing to buyers than Comparables 3 in what is considered an upscale market in your city.

A list price of $550,000 to $575,000 would be a suggestible recommendation to the seller.

2. Net operating income
   a. Used to measure the value of an income-producing property
   b. Calculated by subtracting operating expenses from effective gross income produced by a property

Example

Effective gross income	= $320,000
Operating expenses	= $270,000
Net operating income	= $ 50,000

3. Depreciation
   a. Loss in value to a property from any cause that could be internal, such as an outdated floor plan, or external, such as a depressed economy causing a loss of jobs resulting in a lessened demand for houses.
   b. Can be expressed in a dollar amount or a percent.

> *Example*
>
> A house has an effective age of 15 years and an annual depreciation rate of 2%. The reproduction cost (new) of the house is $150,000. What is the current amount of depreciation?
>
> 15 × 2% = 30% × $150,000 = $45,000
>
> or
>
> depreciation of 30%

4. Capitalization rate
   a. Used to estimate value in the income capitalization approach
   b. Value of property is estimated by dividing net operating income into the value of the property.

> *Example*
>
> An investor paid $400,000 for a commercial building that earns a net income of $60,000 per year. What is the capitalization rate of the investment?
>
> $$\frac{\text{income}}{\text{value}} = \text{capitalization rate}$$
>
> $$\frac{\$60{,}000}{400{,}000} = 15\%$$

5. Gross rent and gross income multipliers (GRM, GIM)
   a. Gross rent multiplier is used as a substitute for the income approach where the property being appraised is a single-family residence, and where the only source of income is rent.

> *Example*
>
> It is estimated that based on comparable homes sold that were rented at the time of their sale, that the property being appraised would have a GRM of 120; the subject property (property being appraised) is currently renting for $1,500 a month.
>
> GRM = monthly rent × GRM = 120 × $1,500 = $180,000

   b. Gross income multiplier

> Example: An apartment building sold two weeks ago for $500,000; the building had an annual gross income of $50,000.
>
> $$\text{GIM} = \frac{\text{selling price}}{\text{annual gross income}} = \frac{\$500{,}000}{50{,}000} = 10$$

CHAPTER 13 QUIZ

1. A broker sold a home for $62,000. The broker charged the seller a 7% commission and will pay 25% of that amount to the listing salesperson and 30% to the selling salesperson. What amount of commission will the listing salesperson receive from the sale of the home?
   1. $1,085
   2. $1,302
   3. $4,340
   4. None of these

2. A man signed an agreement to purchase a home. The contract stipulated that the seller replace the damaged bedroom carpet. The carpet the buyer has chosen costs $14.95 per square yard, plus $3.50 per square yard for installation. If the bedroom dimensions are as illustrated in the below figure, how much will the seller have to pay for the job?
   1. $164.45
   2. $173.62
   3. $222.50
   4. $256.27

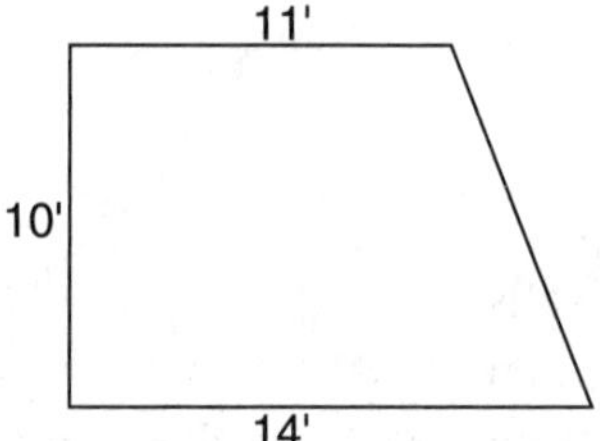

3. Three investors decided to pool their savings and purchase some commercial real estate for $150,000. If one invested $40,000, and the second contributed $20,000, what percentage of ownership was left for the third investor, if ownership interests were allocated on the basis of capital investment?
   1. 60%
   2. 40%
   3. 26%
   4. 13%

4. A father is curious to know how much money his son and daughter-in-law still owe on their mortgage loan. The father knows that the interest portion of their last monthly payment was $582.84. If they are paying interest at the rate of 12%, what was the approximate outstanding balance of their loan before the last payment was made?
   1. $48,520
   2. $58,284
   3. $63,583
   4. $69,941

5. You bought a house one year ago for $102,900. Property in your neighborhood is said to be increasing in value at a rate of 4% annually. If this is true, what is the current market value of your real estate?
   1. $171,600
   2. $170,160
   3. $107,188
   4. $107,016

6. You own a home valued at $75,000. Property in your area is assessed at 80% of its value, and the local tax rate is $32.50 per $1,000. What is the amount of your monthly taxes?
   1. $1,950.00
   2. $243.75
   3. $195.00
   4. $162.50

7. If a home owner has a home with an appraised value of $320,000 and a first mortgage of $210,000, and a second mortgage of $30,000, how much equity does the owner have in her or his home?
   1. $60,000
   2. $120,000
   3. $100,000
   4. $80,000

8. You receive a monthly salary of $500 plus 3% commission on all of your listings that sell, and 2.5% on all of your sales. None of the listings you took sold last month, but you received $7,350 in salary and commission. What was the value of the property you sold?
   1. $245,000
   2. $247,000
   3. $274,000
   4. $294,000

9. A residence has proved difficult to sell. The salesperson suggests that it might sell faster if the owners enclosed a portion of the backyard with a privacy fence. If the area to be enclosed is as illustrated in the below figure, how much would the fence cost at $7.25 per linear foot?
   1. $1,051.25
   2. $1,232.50
   3. $1,486.25
   4. $1,667.50

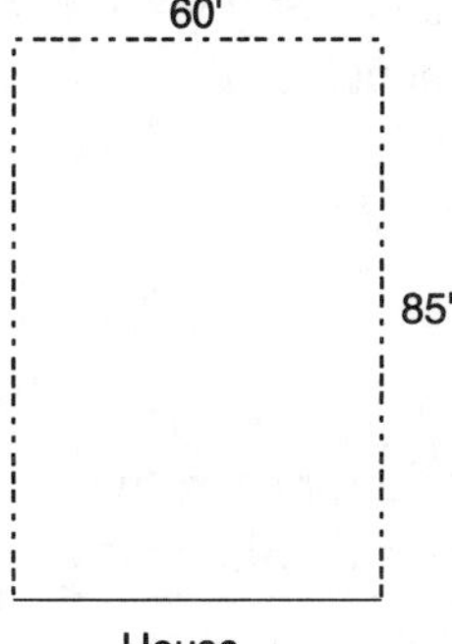

10. An owner leases the 24 apartments in his building for a total monthly rental of $6,000. If this figure represents a 9% annual return on the owner's investment, what was the original cost of the property?
    1. $800,000
    2. $720,000
    3. $666,667
    4. None of these

For the following questions regarding closing statement prorations, base your calculations on a 30-day month. Carry all computations to three decimal places and round off after all computations have been made.

11. A sale is to be closed on April 15. Real estate taxes for the current year are $1,860 and have not been paid. What amount of the real estate tax proration will be credited to the buyer?
    1. $434
    2. $542.51
    3. $1,317.49
    4. $1,860

12. You sell your house to a married couple. They are assuming your 11% interest rate loan, which has a $65,400 mortgage balance. Your house payment is paid in arrears each month, and you made your last payment on September 1. You expect to close on September 14. What amount of prorated interest will be debited against you at closing? (Use a 360-day year.)
    1. $279.77
    2. $319.74
    3. $419.74
    4. $599.50

13. Your brother sells a home on October 10. At the closing, the buyer assumes a three-year prepaid waste disposal contract, which is due to expire at the end of May of the next year. The original cost of the contract was $740. What proration amount will be charged to the buyer at closing? (Use a 360-day year.)
    1. $144.76
    2. $158.28
    3. $255.49
    4. None of these

14. In a sale of residential property, real estate taxes for the current year amounted to $1,630 and already have been paid by the seller. The sale is to be closed on November 4. What is the settlement sheet entry for the tax proration?
    1. $237.19 debit to seller; $237.19 credit to buyer
    2. $253.56 credit to seller; $253.56 debit to buyer
    3. $1,476.05 debit to seller; $153.95 credit to buyer
    4. $253.56 credit to seller only

15. You are buying a house and assuming the seller's mortgage. The unpaid balance after the most recent payment (August 1, the first of the month) was $64,750. Interest is paid in arrears each month at an annual rate of 12%. The sale is to be closed on August 18. What is the amount of the mortgage interest proration to be credited to you at the closing?
    1. $140.72
    2. $388.49
    3. $539.19
    4. None of these

16. A 200-acre farm is divided into house lots. The streets require one-eighth of the whole farm, and there are 220 lots. How many square feet are there in each lot?
    1. 34,650 square feet
    2. 39,784 square feet
    3. 43,916 square feet
    4. None of these

17. The taxes of $2,140 have been paid for the entire calendar year. The seller sells on November 1. What is the amount of the remaining prepaid proration through the day prior to closing?
    1. $1,961.67
    2. $1,783.30
    3. $356.67
    4. $178.33

18. A broker received a $28,000 commission check for the sale of a house. The broker's commission was 6% of the total sale price. What was the total sale price of the house?
    1. $560,000
    2. $466,667
    3. $297,872
    4. $168,000

19. A seller wants to sell his house and realize $80,000 from the sale. If his only cost of selling is a 7% commission, what is the minimum amount for which he could sell his house and realize his desired net?
    1. $85,600
    2. $86,022
    3. $87,400
    4. None of these

20. You have been making constant payments of $623 per month on your mortgage. The balance after your last payment was $59,200. The interest rate on your mortgage is 7%. What will be the balance of your mortgage after your next payment?
    1. $55,056
    2. $58,577
    3. $58,922.33
    4. None of these

21. Using the mortgage factor chart, what is the monthly payment for a $150,000 loan at 11.5% for 30 years?
    1. $1,429.50
    2. $1,486.50
    3. $1,525.50
    4. $1,543.50

22. Using the numbers in question 21, what is the total interest paid over the life of the loan?
    1. $150,000
    2. $385,140
    3. $533,653
    4. None of these

23. A young couple want to purchase a home and feel that they can afford to pay $990 PI per month on a loan. They have saved enough to make a $14,000 down payment and pay closing costs. If lenders are offering 30-year loans at 8.25% interest, what is the maximum amount this couple can pay for a home using the loan factor of $7.51 per thousand?
    1. $131,800
    2. $141,300
    3. $145,824
    4. $155,400

24. An appraiser has estimated the replacement cost of an office building at $300,000. The building is 18 years old and has an estimated useful life of 50 years. What is the current total depreciation of the property?
    1. $96,000
    2. $102,000
    3. $108,000
    4. $114,000

25. What is the value of an apartment building that is expected to produce a net annual income of $40,000, if the owner estimates that she should receive a return of 9% on her investment?
    1. $444,444
    2. $500,000
    3. $571,428
    4. $666,666

26. If the current interest rate of 7% is bought down to 6½%, how much more money can someone who can afford a $1,500 PI payment borrow? (Use the amortization rate of $6.65 per thousand for 7% amortized over 30 years, and $6.32 per thousand for 6½% amortized over 30 years; and then round to the nearest dollar.)
    1. $11,778
    2. $225,564
    3. $237,342
    4. None of these

27. How much is the PI payment on a 6%, $200,000 mortgage, amortized over 30 years using the amortization factor of 6.00?
    1. $1,200
    2. $1,800
    3. $3,333
    4. None of these

28. On a 30-year amortized loan of $200,000, what is the principal portion of the first payment, if the interest rate is 6% and the PI payment is $1,200?
    1. $150
    2. $200
    3. $600
    4. $1,000

29. A homeowner makes a monthly PI payment of $900. Property taxes, homeowner's insurance, and private mortgage insurance add another $380 per month. What percentage of the PI payment does it take to cover the additional $380? (Round to 0.1%.)
    1. 32.2%
    2. 42.2%
    3. 52.2%
    4. 58.2%

30. A borrower makes $5,000 a month and has $750 in monthly recurring debt. If the borrower is allowed to use 36% of the monthly income minus the recurring debt, how much money is available for a house payment?
    1. $1,050
    2. $1,500
    3. $1,800
    4. $2,550

31. If a person qualifies to make a PI payment of $700, how much can he afford to borrow at 7% amortized over 30 years using a per thousand factor of 6.65? (Round to the closest dollar.)
    1. $66,500
    2. $70,000
    3. $105,263
    4. $205,263

32. A house payment is referred to as principal, interest, taxes, and
    1. recurring debt.
    2. life insurance.
    3. maintenance reserves.
    4. homeowner's insurance.

33. If a person is allowed to use 75% of an $1,800 PITI payment for PI, how much can be spent on PI?
    1. $1,350
    2. $1,400
    3. $1,500
    4. $1,700

34. How much total interest is paid on a $100,000 loan amortized over 30 years at 7% interest, using a factor of $6.65 per thousand?
    1. $66,500
    2. $100,000
    3. $139,400
    4. $239,400

35. How much total interest is paid on a $100,000 loan amortized over 15 years at 7% interest, using a factor of $8.98 per thousand?
    1. $61,640
    2. $89,800
    3. $161,640
    4. $171,640

36. A buyer finds a house and needs $200,000 in order to afford the transaction. If the buyer qualifies for a $1,300 PI payment, and the current interest rate is 7% amortized over 30 years ($6.65 factor), how much money is the buyer eligible to borrow? (Round to the nearest dollar.)
    1. $66,500
    2. $133,000
    3. $195,489
    4. $200,000

37. A buyer asks a seller to pay some discount points in order to lower the existing 7% interest rate to 6.75%. If the buyer can afford a $1,300 PI payment, using a factor of $6.49 (6.75% amortized over 30 years), how much money is the buyer eligible to borrow? (Round to the nearest dollar.)
    1. $87,750
    2. $133,000
    3. $200,308
    4. None of these

38. A buyer made a 10% down payment of $15,000. The buyer was then required to purchase private mortgage insurance and pay an annual premium of 0.52% of the loan. What was the buyer's monthly PMI payment?
    1. $58.50
    2. $150
    3. $702
    4. $880

39. If the VA charges a 2% financed funding fee on a $200,000 VA guaranteed loan, how much is the funding fee?
    1. $200
    2. $400
    3. $2,000
    4. $4,000

40. FHA charges an upfront insurance premium of 1.75%, which is financed into the loan. On a $135,000 FHA-insured loan, how much is the upfront insurance premium?
    1. $1,500
    2. $1,350
    3. $2,030
    4. $2,362.50

MATCHING QUIZ

The column on the right contains brief memory links to important terms in Chapter 13.
Write the letter of the matching term on the appropriate line.

A. $= \pi (3.14) \times R^2$

B. $A = L \times W$

C. $A = ½(B \times H)$

D. $A = \frac{(B1 + B2) \times H}{2}$

E. diameter × π(3.14)

F. L × W × H

G. part divided by total

H. part divided by percent

I. total × percent

J. Amount charged for real estate services

K. Millage

L. $\frac{\text{replacement cost}}{\text{years of useful life}}$

M. (net) income/rate

N. (net) income/value

O. (cap) rate × value

P. loan divided by 1,000 × amortization factor

Q. $\frac{\text{numerator}}{\text{denominator}}$

1. _______ Circumference of a circle
2. _______ Volume of a cube
3. _______ Area of a circle
4. _______ Area of a rectangle
5. _______ Commission
6. _______ Area of a triangle
7. _______ A word that is equated with tax rate
8. _______ Formula to find monthly PI
9. _______ Area of a trapezoid
10. _______ A fraction
11. _______ Formula to find part
12. _______ Formula used to arrive at net operating income
13. _______ Formula used to find total
14. _______ Formula used to find %
15. _______ Straight-line depreciation formula
16. _______ Formula used to arrive at value
17. _______ Formula used to find cap rate

CHAPTER 13 QUIZ ANSWERS

1. $62,000 sales price × 7% commission = $62,000 × 0.07 = $4,340, broker's commission

   $4,340 × 25% = $4,340 × 0.25 = $1,085

   Correct answer: **1**

2. 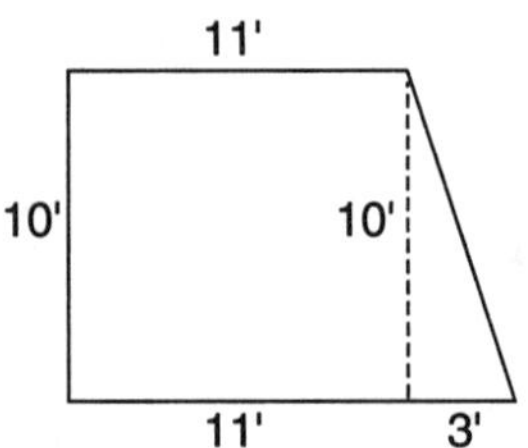

   11' × 10' = 110 square feet, area of rectangle

   ½(3' × 10') = ½(30') = 15 square feet, area of triangle

   110 + 15 = 125 square feet, total area

   Divide by 9 to convert square feet to square yards.

   125 ÷ 9 = 13.89 square yards

   $14.95 + $3.50 installation = $18.45, cost per square yard

   $18.45 × 13.89 square yards = $256.27

   Correct answer: **4**

3. $40,000 first investor + $20,000 second investor = $60,000

   $150,000 – $60,000 = $90,000 third investor's contribution

   $\frac{\text{part}}{\text{total}} = \text{percent}$

   $90,000 ÷ $150,000 = 0.60, or 60%

   Correct answer: **1**

4. $582.84 × 12 = $6,994.08 annual interest

   $\frac{\text{part}}{\text{total}} = \text{total}$

   $6,994.08 ÷ 12% = $6,994.08 ÷ 0.12 = $58,284

   Correct answer: **2**

5. $102,900 × 4% = $102,900 × 0.04 = $4,116, annual increase in value.

   $102,900 + $4,116 = $107,016, current market value

   Correct answer: **4**

   Read your calculator carefully. Answer choices with the same number combinations can be misleading.

6. $75,000 × 80% OR $75,000 × 0.80 = $60,000 in taxable value

   Divide by 1,000 because tax rate is stated per $1,000.

   $60,000 ÷ 1,000 = $60

   $60 × 32.50 = $1,950, annual taxes

   Divide by 12 to get monthly taxes.

   $1,950 ÷ 12 = $162.50

   Correct answer: **4**

7. **(2)** $320,000 – (210,000 + $30,000) =

   $320,000 – $240,000= $80,000

   Correct answer: **4**

8. $7,350 – $500 salary = $6,850 commission on sales

   $6,850 ÷ 2.5% = $6,850 ÷ 0.025 = $274,000, value of property sold

   Correct answer: **3**

9.

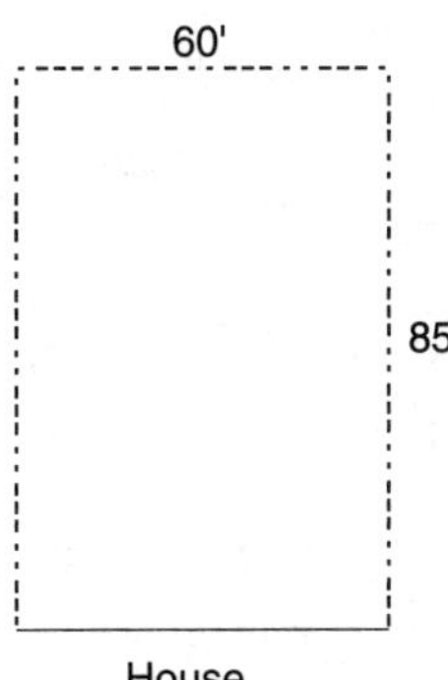

Two sides of 85' plus one side of 60'

85' × 2 = 170 feet

170 + 60 = 230 linear feet

230 × $7.25 = $1,667.50

Correct answer: **4**

10. $6,000 × 12 = $72,000 annual return

$72,000 ÷ 9% = $72,000 ÷ 0.09 = $800,000, original cost of property

Correct answer: **1**

11. $1,860 ÷ 12 months = $155 per month

$155 ÷ 30 days = $5.167 per day

$155 × 3 months = $465

$5.167 × 15 days = $77.505

$465 + $77.505 = $542.505, rounds to $542.51

Correct answer: **2**

12. $65,400 × 11% OR $65,400 × 0.11 = $7,194

$7,194 ÷ 360 days = $19.9833 per diem cost

September 1 through 14 = 14 days

14 days × $19.9833 = 279.7662, rounds to $279.77

Correct answer: **1**

13. $740 ÷ 3 years = $246.667 per year

$246.667 ÷ 12 = $20.556 per month

$20.556 ÷ 30 days = $.685 per day

$20.556 × 7 months = $143.892

$.685 × 20 days = $13.70

$143.892 + $13.70 = $157.592, rounds to $157.59

Correct answer: **4**

14. $1,630 ÷ 12 months = $135.833 per month

$135.833 ÷ 30 days = $4.528 per day

$4.528 × 26 days = $117.728

$135.833 + $117.728 = $253.561, rounds to $253.56

Correct answer: **2**

The taxes have been paid. The seller is entitled to a refund for 1 month and 26 days. He therefore will receive a credit and the buyer will be charged (debited) for the same amount.

15. $64,750 × 12% = $64,750 × 0.12 = $7,770

$7,770 ÷ 12 months = $647.50

$647.50 ÷ 30 days = $21.583 per day

$21.583 × 18 days = $388.494, rounds to $388.49

Correct answer: **2**

16. 43,560 square feet/acre × 200 acres = 8,712,000, total square feet

8,712,000 square feet × 1/8 = 8,712,000 × 0.125 = 1,089,000 square feet for streets

8,712,000 – 1,089,000 = 7,623,000 square feet for lots

7,623,000 square feet ÷ 220 lots = 34,650 square feet per lot

Correct answer: **1**

17. Time period: 2 months (November/December)

$2,140 per year ÷ 12 = $178.33 per month

$178.33 × 2 = $356.67

Correct answer: **3**

18. Part = $28,000, Percent = 6%

part ÷ percent = total

$28,000 ÷ .06 = $466,667

Correct answer: **2**

19. part ÷ percent = total

$80,000 ÷ 0.93 = $86,021.5, rounds to $86,022

Correct answer: **2**

20. $59,200 × .07 = $4,144.00 annual interest

$4,144 ÷ 12 = $345.33 interest for one month

$623.00 (P&I) – 345.33 = $277.67 principal payoff

$59,200 – $277.67 = $58,922.33 balance after next payment

Correct answer: **3**

21. $1,486.50 (150,000 × 9.91)

Correct answer: **2**

22. $1,486.50 × 360 months = $535,140 (total P&I) – $150,000 (P) = $385,140

Correct answer: **2**

23. The payment chart indicates 8.25 percent loans are 7.51 per $1,000.

$990 affordable monthly payment ÷ 7.51 = 131,824.23

$131.82423 × 1,000 = $131,824.33 maximum loan amount

$131,824.33 plus down payment = $145,824.33 maximum selling price of house.

Correct answer: **3**

24. $300,000 ÷ 50 years = $6,000 annual depreciation charge

$6,000 × 18 years = $108,000 current total depreciation

Correct answer: **3**

25. I ÷ R = V

$40,000 ÷ 9% (0.09) = $444,444

Correct answer: **1**

26. Divide $1,500 by the 7% factor of 6.65.

1,500 divided by 6.65 = 225.56 × 1,000 = 225,564

Next divide $1,500 by the 6½% factor of 6.32.

1,500 ÷ 6.32 = 237.34 × 1,000 = 237,342.

The difference is 237,342 – 225,564 = $11,778.

Correct answer: **1**

27. 200 (thousands) × 6.00 = $1,200

Correct answer: **1**

28. $200,000 × 6% = $12,000 divided by 12 months = $1,000. The difference then is $1,200 (PI) – $1,000 (I) = $200 (P)

Correct answer: **2**

29. $380 divided by $900 = .422 or 42.2%.

Correct answer: **2**

30. $5,000 × 36% = $1,800. $1,800 – 750 = $1,050.

Correct answer: **1**

31. $700 divided by 6.65 = $105.26 × 1,000 = $105,263

Correct answer: **3**

32. Together these items are referred to as PITI.

Correct answer: **4**

33. This elementary process is utilized every day in the real estate business. $1,800 (PITI) × 75% = $1,350 (PI)

Correct answer: **1**

34. The payment is 100 (thousands) × 6.65 or $665. This amount then is multiplied by 360 months to discover the total amount spent on PI payments. $665 × 360 = $239,400. Next, subtract the amount borrowed ($100,000) to find the solution of $139,400.

Correct answer: **3**

35. The payment is 100 (thousands) × 8.98 or $898. This amount then is multiplied by 180 months to discover the total amount spent on PI payments. $898 × 180 = $161,640 – $100,000 (original loan) = $61,640

Correct answer: **1**

36. $1,300 divided by 6.65 = $195.49 × 1,000 = $195,489

Correct answer: **3**

37. $1,300 divided by 6.49 = $200.31 × 1,000 = $200,308

Correct answer: **3**

38. First find the loan amount. $15,000 divided by 10% = $150,000

Then subtract the down payment of $15,000 to arrive at the loan amount of $135,000.

$135,000 × .52% = $702 divided by 12 months = $58.50 each month for PMI.

Correct answer: **1**

39. $200,000 × 2% = $4,000. Buyer's closing costs on a VA loan include an origination fee, the financed funding fee, and actuals. The VA waives the funding fee for disabled veterans.

Correct answer: **4**

40. $135,000 × 1.75% = $2,362.50. A portion of this amount is refunded if the property is resold within seven years.

Correct answer: **4**

TEST SCORE

REAL ESTATE CALCULATIONS			
Rating	**Range**	**Your Score**	
Good = 80% to 100%	32–40	Total Number	40
Fair = 70% to 79%	28–31	Total Wrong	–
Needs improvement = Lower than 70%	27 or less	Total Right	

Passing Requirement: 28 or Better

ANSWER KEY: MATCHING QUIZ

1. **E**
2. **F**
3. **A**
4. **B**
5. **J**
6. **C**
7. **K**
8. **P**
9. **D**
10. **Q**
11. **I**
12. **O**
13. **H**
14. **G**
15. **L**
16. **M**
17. **N**

CHAPTER 14

Salesperson Examinations

The sample examinations that follow evaluate your general real estate knowledge and test-taking ability. Simulate as closely as possible the actual test conditions (see Chapter 1, "Use of the Manual"), avoid distractions, and use only those tools permitted by your state. Like the national portion of the PSI exam, these sample exams contain 80 questions each. Circle your answer for each question. Remember that the PSI exam includes an additional 40- to 50-question portion that tests your knowledge of your state's real estate laws and specific real estate practices.

After completing and grading the sample exams, carefully analyze your results. Did you complete all the questions in the allotted time? Did you answer a minimum of 65 or 81 questions correctly? It will be useful to mark in the answer key all the questions you missed. The answers and explanations are keyed to pages in the concepts-to-understand outlines for each part. The pattern of your errors should immediately suggest which areas require additional study.

As a final check, you may wish to review all the exam questions in the *Guide* that relate to a specific topic. Feel free to test and retest yourself. The greater your familiarity with the scope and style of the PSI exam, the better you are likely to perform.

SALESPERSON EXAMINATION I

1. All of the following would be considered real property *EXCEPT*
   1. mineral rights.
   2. a leasehold estate.
   3. fixtures.
   4. air.

2. The servient estate in an easement appurtenant is the property
   1. owned by the landlord.
   2. on which the easement is placed.
   3. owned by the tenant.
   4. that benefits from the easement.

3. Which of the following statements concerning encumbrances is *NOT* true?
   1. All encumbrances are liens.
   2. All liens are encumbrances.
   3. Restrictions beneficial to the grantee are encumbrances.
   4. An easement is a physical encumbrance.

4. Which of the following is *NOT* a specific lien?
   1. Mortgage lien
   2. State inheritance taxes
   3. Real estate taxes
   4. Mechanic's lien

5. You have entered into a lease that requires you to pay 20% of the owner's expenses. Your lease would be an example of a
   1. variable lease.
   2. net lease.
   3. percentage lease.
   4. gross lease.

6. If a husband and wife own an apartment building and the husband owns an undivided three-fourths interest and the wife owns a one-fourth interest, what type of tenancy exists?
   1. Leasehold estate
   2. Joint tenancy
   3. Tenancy in common
   4. Tenancy by the entirety

7. The highest form of ownership interest a person may hold in real estate is
   1. life estate.
   2. fee simple.
   3. legal life estate.
   4. base fee.

8. Two unrelated people own a three-unit apartment building as tenants in common. One wants to sell but the other does not. Which of the following statements describes the legal rights of the party who wants to sell?
   1. The party may request a court to partition the building.
   2. The party may require the co-owner to sell.
   3. The party may record a lis pendens on the property.
   4. The party may refinance the mortgage in her or his own name, thus eliminating the co-owner's interest in the property.

9. Your aunt died intestate and you inherited her house. The way in which you acquired the title to her house is by
   1. curtesy.
   2. descent.
   3. escheat.
   4. laches.

10. All of the following statements correctly describe a legal life estate *EXCEPT*
    1. during his or her life estate, the life tenant is generally answerable to the holder of the future interest.
    2. the life tenant may not commit any acts that would permanently injure the property.
    3. there may be a reversionary interest.
    4. there may be a remainder interest.

11. All of the following are examples of a leasehold estate *EXCEPT*
    1. an estate for years.
    2. periodic estate.
    3. time-share estate.
    4. estate from year to year.

12. A state wants to build a publicly owned convention center to attract private development in its largest city. Can the state use eminent domain to acquire the land?
    1. No, because private investments would not be allowed.
    2. Yes, if just compensation is paid to the owners of the land.
    3. No, because eminent domain can only be used for highway expansion.
    4. Yes, if the owners hold fee-simple interest in the land.

13. The city in which you live has a zoning ordinance. The basis for the city to have such an ordinance is
    1. eminent domain.
    2. escheat.
    3. police power.
    4. riparian right.

14. Which of the following terms are *NOT* related?
    1. Freehold estate–fee simple
    2. Grantor–person conveying title
    3. Leasehold estate–personal property
    4. Police power–deed restriction

15. Strict liability under Superfund means that
    1. each of the individual owners is personally responsible for the damages in whole.
    2. the owner is responsible to the injured party without excuse.
    3. the liability is not limited to the person who currently owns the property but also includes people who have owned the site in the past.
    4. the owner is not responsible to the injured party unless it can be proved that the owner was aware of the problem.

16. All of the following correctly describes how real estate licensees should handle the possibility of hazardous substances on a property being sold *EXCEPT*
    1. clients should be asked about the possibility of hazardous substances on the property.
    2. licensees should consider the consequences of potential liability.
    3. licensees should be scrupulous in considering environmental issues.
    4. licensees should not disclose the problem, because it might harm the seller.

17. Sources of groundwater contamination do *NOT* include
    1. waste disposal sites.
    2. underground storage tanks.
    3. use of pesticides in farming communities.
    4. radon.

18. Your neighbor has given you revocable permission to go hunting on his farm. You have a(n)
    1. leasehold estate.
    2. easement appurtenant.
    3. license.
    4. defeasible fee estate.

19. A claim based on adverse possession of property must *NOT* be
    1. notorious.
    2. open.
    3. hostile.
    4. secretive.

20. A person who receives real property by will is called a
    1. trustee.
    2. devisee.
    3. testator.
    4. hypothecator.

21. Riparian rights would exist in a
    1. condominium on a bay.
    2. house on a bay.
    3. hotel whose land abuts a large lake.
    4. cooperative on a river.

22. A developer was able to buy two adjoining single-family lots for $20,000 each. He combined the lots into one parcel with a value of $90,000. The developer's action reflects the process of
    1. accession.
    2. attachment.
    3. exchange.
    4. plottage.

23. A restaurant opened in a neighborhood and was enjoying substantial profits. Within a year, another restaurant was built across the street and resulted in the first restaurant losing, in the next year, 30% of its profits. This is an example of the principle of
    1. competition.
    2. conformity.
    3. highest and best use.
    4. progression.

24. A meatpacking plant has just been built one block from your house. The strong odors are lowering property values in your neighborhood. The loss in value would be classified as
    1. functional obsolescence.
    2. physical deterioration.
    3. the principle of change.
    4. external obsolescence.

25. In the appraisal of a public building, an appraiser would use the
    1. cost approach.
    2. income capitalization approach.
    3. sales comparison approach.
    4. gross rent multiplier.

26. A four-bedroom house with one bathroom would be an example of
    1. physical deterioration.
    2. functional obsolescence.
    3. economic obsolescence.
    4. environmental obsolescence.

27. Which of the following is *NOT* a stage in the appraisal process?
    1. State the problem.
    2. Analyze the tax consequences of the property owner.
    3. Reconcile the data for the final value estimate.
    4. Analyze and interpret the data.

28. An appraiser uses the cost approach in appraising a home. The appraiser should *NOT* use which of the following types of information?
    1. Physical deterioration
    2. Cost of replacement of house
    3. Depreciation of land
    4. Economic obsolescence

29. A house that is the least expensive in its neighborhood has nevertheless grown significantly in value over the years because of an increasing number of larger, more expensive houses being built nearby. This growth in value is an example of the principle of
    1. regression.
    2. competition.
    3. progression.
    4. highest and best use.

30. You are preparing a competitive market analysis on a house that you hope to list for sale. Which of the following approaches to value will be used in the development of the estimated value?
    1. Cost approach
    2. Gross rent multiplier
    3. Income approach
    4. Sales comparison approach

31. A competitive market analysis reflects the use of the
    1. cost approach.
    2. income approach.
    3. sales-comparison approach.
    4. gross-rent-multiplier method.

32. First Bank holds a lien on a home on which Second Bank already had a lien. The lenders subsequently entered into an agreement in which First Bank moved into a first lien position. This is an example of a
    1. hypothecation agreement.
    2. disintermediation agreement.
    3. reverse annuity mortgage.
    4. subordination agreement.

33. If the Federal Reserve Board raises its discount rate, which of the following is likely to occur?
    1. Mortgage money will become more available.
    2. Interest rates will stay the same.
    3. Mortgage money will become less available.
    4. Interest rates will decline.

34. You have a mortgage in which you make the same payment each month for principal and interest, with the principal payment increasing and the interest payment decreasing from month-to-month. This is called a(n)
    1. amortized mortgage.
    2. term mortgage.
    3. reverse annuity mortgage.
    4. partially amortized mortgage.

35. Which agency is involved in purchasing government-related loans?
    1. Fannie Mae
    2. Ginnie Mae
    3. Freddie Mac
    4. The "Fed"

36. All of the following agencies are included in the secondary mortgage market *EXCEPT*
    1. FHA.
    2. FNMA.
    3. GNMA.
    4. FHLMC.

37. All loans subject to the Real Estate Settlement Procedures Act (RESPA) require lenders to
    1. charge the seller for all loan discount points.
    2. document any reason for declining credit to a loan applicant.
    3. deliver a settlement statement form to both buyer and seller.
    4. allow the buyer to rescind the contract any time prior to the first payment due date.

38. You mortgaged your property and just made the final payment. Recording which of the following documents will provide notice that the mortgage lien has been removed?
    1. Reconveyance deed
    2. Satisfaction of mortgage
    3. Alienation of the mortgage instrument
    4. Reversion of the deed

39. Salesperson Alvarez for broker Brooks has listed a home. Salesperson Cooke for broker Davidson is acting as a buyer's agent and is trying to sell the same home to his buyer. Salesperson Cooke is primarily responsible to
    1. his own buyer.
    2. salesperson Alvarez.
    3. broker Brooks.
    4. broker Davidson.

40. In *MOST* states, the listing broker has a fiduciary duty with
    1. the customer.
    2. the listing salesperson.
    3. the principal.
    4. the buyer.

41. A broker was employed by an owner, as an agent, to sell her home. All of the following statements correctly describe the broker's relationship to the owner *EXCEPT*
    1. the broker has become the seller's agent.
    2. the broker owes fiduciary duty to the seller.
    3. the broker is a special agent.
    4. the broker is a general agent.

42. You listed a home that was subsequently shown by six cooperating outside brokers. How many seller-agency relationships are involved in this transaction?
    1. One
    2. Six
    3. Seven
    4. None of these

43. A salesperson listed a home for sale and transferred to another brokerage firm two weeks later. Which of the following statements describes the status of the listing?
    1. The listing is terminated.
    2. The listing is transferred to the new brokerage.
    3. The two brokerage firms will negotiate to decide who will hold the listing.
    4. The listing will stay with the former brokerage firm of the salesperson.

44. A salesperson presented an offer that was accepted and received an earnest money payment for $2,000. The salesperson should
    1. hold the payment until the buyer has received a financing commitment.
    2. give the earnest money to his broker.
    3. open up a trust account and deposit the payment in it.
    4. deposit the payment in the seller's checking account.

45. You are working as a buyer's broker for a client. All of the following would describe your role as a buyer's broker *EXCEPT*
    1. you should show the buyer properties only in which your commission is protected.
    2. you should counsel the buyer about developing accurate objectives.
    3. you should search for the best properties for your buyer to inspect, widening the marketplace to include homes for sale by owners (FSBOs).
    4. you should help the buyer prepare the strongest offer.

46. According to the law of agency, a real estate broker owes the principal all of the following duties *EXCEPT*
    1. exercising reasonable care.
    2. acting in good faith.
    3. conforming with the principal's legal instructions.
    4. offering legal advice.

47. A broker acting as the agent of a seller
    1. can agree to a change in the listing price without the principal's approval.
    2. may share her commission with the salesperson of another broker.
    3. must report all offers to the principal unless instructed otherwise.
    4. must maintain as confidential all information the principal says not to disclose.

48. A broker listed a residential property under a valid written listing agreement. After the sale was completed, the owner refused to pay the broker's fee. Which of the following can the broker do?
    1. She can take the seller to court and sue for the commission.
    2. She is entitled to a lien on the seller's property for the amount of the commission.
    3. She can go to court and stop the transaction until she is paid.
    4. She can collect the commission from the buyer.

49. Commissions and fees paid by the seller to a listing agency are determined by
    1. standards promulgated by the local board of REALTORS®.
    2. negotiations between the seller and the listing licensee.
    3. applying the prevailing customary fees charged in that area.
    4. an industry index computed monthly from multiple-listing service data.

50. A listing broker is considered to have earned a commission from a principal when which of the following events occur?
    1. An offer to purchase has been presented to the client.
    2. Title has been transferred to the buyer.
    3. The seller accepts and signs an offer to purchase.
    4. A "ready, willing, and able buyer" signs a noncontingent or cash offer that meets the terms of the listing contract.

51. A broker listed an owner's home and later received an offer from another licensee that met all of the listing terms and conditions. After considering the offer, the owner informed the broker that the owner no longer wished to sell and asked to be immediately released from the listing agreement. Which of the following statements *BEST* describes the broker's position in this situation?
    1. The broker must release the owner without obligation.
    2. The broker must tell the owner that the offeror may sue for specific performance.
    3. The broker may succeed in collecting an earned commission from the owner.
    4. The broker may keep the earnest money that accompanied the offer as liquidated damages.

52. On July 1 an owner and a salesperson entered into a six-month exclusive-right-to-sell agreement for a residential property. On July 15, the owner rejected a low offer and fired the listing agent. On August 1, there was a house fire that required extensive kitchen repairs. On September 12, the owner entered into another exclusive-right-to-sell agreement with a salesperson from a different agency. On January 1, the property was still unsold. On which date was the first listing agreement MOST likely to terminate and why?
    1. July 15, because the salesperson was dismissed
    2. August 1, because the listed property suffered material damage
    3. September 12, because the owner breached the first listing agreement by signing a second
    4. January 1, because the first listing agreement ended at midnight on December 31

53. An option, prior to being exercised, is an example of
    1. an assignable contract.
    2. a unilateral contract.
    3. a bilateral contract.
    4. an executed contract.

54. Which of the following is a similarity between an exclusive-right-to-sell listing and an exclusive-agency listing?
    1. Under both, the seller avoids paying the brokerage a commission if the seller sells the property without the help of the brokerage.
    2. Both give the responsibility of representing the seller to just one brokerage firm.
    3. Both are net listings.
    4. Under both, the seller authorizes one specific salesperson to show the property.

55. A buyer has entered into an agency agreement with more than one buyer's agent but only owes compensation to the one who puts an actual transaction together. This arrangement is known as a(n)
   1. multiple-listing agreement.
   2. exclusive right agreement.
   3. exclusive agency agreement.
   4. nonexclusive agency agreement.

56. Which of the following types of clauses governs the right of a listing broker to collect a commission from an owner who waits until the listing period expires and then personally contracts to sell the property to a party the broker had shown the property to during the listing period?
   1. Alienation
   2. Protection
   3. Defeasance
   4. Habendum

57. You wrote an offer on a house for $214,000. The seller gave you a counteroffer for $218,000. The seller may withdraw the counteroffer any time
   1. within 72 hours after acceptance.
   2. prior to the buyer's acceptance.
   3. prior to removal of all contingencies in the offer.
   4. prior to closing.

58. You signed a lease for one year and took possession of an apartment. When the lease expired, you continued to live in the apartment without the owner's consent. Your tenancy would be considered to be a(n)
   1. estate for years.
   2. estate from year to year.
   3. tenancy at will.
   4. tenancy at sufferance.

59. A commercial lease that allows rent to be increased or decreased periodically based on changes in economic indicators is a(n)
   1. graduated lease.
   2. gross lease.
   3. percentage lease.
   4. index lease.

60. In theory, which of the following types of deeds gives a property buyer the *MOST* protection against problems that may arise with the title?
   1. Quitclaim
   2. Bargain and sale
   3. Special warranty
   4. General warranty

61. You have entered into an installment land contract for the sale of your home. Which of the following statements is *FALSE*?
   1. The buyer is the vendee.
   2. The buyer will take possession when the contract is signed by both parties, if the contract so provides.
   3. The buyer will hold legal title during the term of the contract.
   4. The buyer will hold equitable title during the term of the contract.

62. Personal property is generally conveyed by a
   1. bill of sale.
   2. certificate of title.
   3. quitclaim deed.
   4. trust deed.

63. The movement of land caused by an earthquake would be an example of
   1. accretion.
   2. avulsion.
   3. erosion.
   4. hypothecation.

64. When property transfers from one party to another, recording the deed provides what is called
   1. validation of the agreement between the parties.
   2. a writ of attachment.
   3. certificate of title.
   4. constructive notice.

65. A salesperson desires to advertise a property without including the brokerage name. This situation is allowed when
   1. the salesperson is the listing agent.
   2. the salesperson includes his or her name in the ad.
   3. the salesperson is the actual owner and advertising as a for sale by owner.
   4. the salesperson is willing to pay for the ad.

66. Brokers who violate the Sherman Antitrust Act may be punished by a maximum fine of
    1. $10,000.
    2. $25,000.
    3. $50,000.
    4. $1 million.

67. The Civil Rights Act of 1866 prohibits discrimination based on
    1. handicap.
    2. familial status.
    3. race.
    4. sex.

68. Broker Xavier is showing buyer Yang, an Asian, homes only in Asian neighborhoods. The broker may be guilty of
    1. arbitrage.
    2. blockbusting.
    3. redlining.
    4. steering.

69. Which of the following is *NOT* a category protected by federal fair housing laws against discrimination in housing?
    1. Race
    2. National origin
    3. Sexual orientation
    4. Familial status

70. You sign an agreement to purchase a home. The contract requires that the seller replace the damaged living room carpet. The carpet you have chosen costs $16.95 per square yard, plus $4.50 per square yard for installation. If the living room dimensions are as illustrated in the below figure, how much will the seller have to pay for the job?
    1. $357.50
    2. $314.60
    3. $353.93
    4. None of these

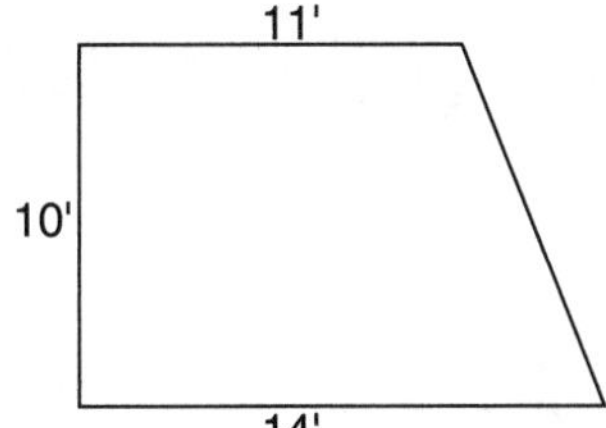

71. Licensed or certified appraisers performing federally related transactions must comply with the Uniform Standards of Professional Appraisal Practice (USPAP). A federally related transaction is any transaction with a value greater than
    1. $100,000.
    2. $150,000.
    3. $200,000.
    4. $250,000.

72. A sale is to close on June 23. Real estate taxes of $2,640 for the current year have *NOT* been paid. What is the amount of the real estate tax proration to be credited to the buyer? (Use a 30-day month for calculation.)
    1. $168.67
    2. $868.67
    3. $1,268.66
    4. None of these

73. A home is valued at $92,000. Property in this city is assessed at 70% of its value, and the local tax rate is $3.40 per $100. What is the amount of the owner's monthly taxes?
    1. $182.47
    2. $260.67
    3. $2,189.60
    4. None of these

74. A mother wants to know how much money her son owes on his mortgage loan. The mother knows that the interest part of the last monthly payment was $473.26. If her son is paying interest at the rate of 9%, what was the outstanding balance of the loan before the last payment was made?
    1. $52,584.44
    2. $55,921.03
    3. $63,101.33
    4. None of these

75. You are selling your house and a buyer is assuming your outstanding mortgage, which has an unpaid balance of $58,700 after the last payment on August 1. If the annual interest rate is 9% and interest is paid in arrears each month, what is the amount of mortgage interest to be debited against you at closing, using a closing date of August 18?
   1. $161.43
   2. $176.10
   3. $190.78
   4. $264.15

76. Using $9.91 as a mortgage factor, what is the monthly payment for a $150,000 loan at 11.5% for 30 years?
   1. $1,429.50
   2. $1,486.50
   3. $1,525.50
   4. $1,581.00

77. Using the information in question 76, what is the total interest paid over the life of the loan?
   1. $297,300
   2. $371,625
   3. $535,140
   4. None of these

78. A broker sold a home for $146,000. The broker charged the owner 6% commission and will pay 25% of that amount to the listing salesperson and 30% to the selling salesperson. What amount of commission will the listing salesperson receive from the sale?
   1. $2,058
   2. $2,190
   3. $2,628
   4. None of these

79. You receive a monthly salary of $600 plus 3.5% commission on all of your listings that sell, and 2.5% on all of your sales. None of the listings that you took sold last month, but you receive $8,460 in salary and commission. What was the value of the property you sold?
   1. $131,000
   2. $224,571
   3. $314,400
   4. None of these

80. You bought a home one year ago for $83,500. Property in your neighborhood is said to be increasing in value at a rate of 6% annually. If this is true, what is the current value of your real estate?
   1. $86,840
   2. $87,675
   3. $88,510
   4. None of these

ANSWER KEY: SALESPERSON EXAMINATION I

NOTE: The number in parentheses at the end of each explanation refers to the page number where this material is discussed.

1. **(2)** A leasehold estate is a non-freehold estate involving the tenant's right to occupy the real estate during the term of the lease. (21)

2. **(2)** A servient estate also is referred to as a servient tenement. The property that benefits from the easement is known as the dominant tenement. (24)

3. **(1)** Encumbrances may be liens, which affect the title, or physical encumbrances, which affect the condition of the land. However, an easement is an example of an encumbrance that is not a lien. Therefore, not all encumbrances are liens, but it is true that all liens are encumbrances. (23–24)

4. **(2)** State inheritance taxes are a general lien and affect all the debtor's property. (24)

5. **(2)** A tenant in a net lease pays rent plus all or part of the property charges. A tenant in a gross lease pays a fixed rent, while the landlord pays all his or her own expenses. (121)

6. **(3)** Tenancy in common allows for percentage differences in ownership. A leasehold estate is a personal property interest. Joint tenancy and tenancy by the entirety require equal percentages of interests in most states. (26–27)

7. **(2)** A fee simple is the highest form of interest. A base fee is subject to certain limitations imposed by the owner. A life estate is limited to the life of an owner or some other person. Legal life estates are created by state law. (25)

8. **(1)** Tenants in common may partition the property by agreement and, if no agreement, by judicial determination. (26–27)

9. **(2)** When a person dies intestate, the decedent's real estate and personal property pass to his or her heirs according to the statutes. (26)

10. **(1)** The life tenant generally is not answerable to the holder of the future interest. (26)

11. **(3)** A time-share estate may include a fee-simple interest in condominium ownership. (29)

12. **(2)** The government has the right to acquire private property for public use while paying just compensation to the owner. The convention center would attract private development of hotels and retail establishments. The type of estate held by owners would not prevent the state from acquiring the land. (42)

13. **(3)** Police power is the power of the state to establish legislation to protect public health and safety and promote general welfare. (42)

14. **(4)** Police power is a public-land-use control; a deed restriction is a private-land-use control. (42, 49–50)

15. **(2)** Joint and several liability means that each owner is personally responsible for the damages in whole; if only one owner is financially able to handle the total damage, that individual owner will have to pay all and attempt to collect from the other owners their proportionate shares. Retroactive liability means that liability also extends to people who have owned the site in the past. (44)

16. **(4)** The first three answers describe how licensees should handle that type of transaction. (46)

17. **(4)** Radon is an odorless radioactive gas released from rocks under the earth's surface that finds its way to the surface; it usually is released into the atmosphere. (46)

18. **(3)** License is permission to enter the land of another for a specific purpose, and the owner of the property may revoke it at any time. (25)

19. **(4)** A claim based on adverse possession must be notorious, open, and hostile. (26)

20. **(2)** A testator is a person who makes a will. Devise refers to a transfer of real property under a will. (156)

21. **(4)** Riparian rights are water rights granted to owners along a river or stream. (23)

22. **(4)** Accession refers to acquiring title to real property through the annexation of a fixture. Attachment is the act of placing a lien upon a person's property by a court. An exchange is a transaction in which part or all of the consideration is the transfer of like-kind property. (64)

23. **(1)** The principle of competition states that excess profits create ruinous competition. (59)

24. **(4)** Functional obsolescence and physical deterioration refer to a loss of value within the property, while external obsolescence refers to a loss of value outside the property. (61)

25. **(1)** The cost approach is considered most reliable in the appraisal of special-purpose buildings, such as churches and schools. (61)

26. **(2)** Functional obsolescence is a loss in the value of a property resulting from a deficiency in the floor plan of a house. One bathroom would be inadequate for a four-bedroom house. (61)

27. **(2)** Tax consequences would be analyzed in a feasibility study exploring the potential for profitability in a proposed project. (61)

28. **(3)** Depreciation generally is applied to a wasting asset, such as a building. Land is not considered a wasting asset. (61)

29. **(3)** The answer is progression. The principle of regression states that the value of the most expensive home in a neighborhood will be lessened by the presence of less expensive homes being built nearby. The principle of competition states that excess profits create ruinous competition. Highest and best use states that each parcel of land should be developed to its most profitable use subject to legal constraints, such as zoning. (59)

30. **(4)** The cost approach is most applicable to the appraisal of special-purpose properties, such as a church. The gross rent multiplier is used as a substitute for the income approach in the valuation of a single-family home. The income approach is, of course, used in the appraisal of an income-producing property. (60–61)

31. **(3)** The sales-comparison approach relies on comparable sales, as well as sales that involve willing buyers and sellers, with neither under abnormal pressure. (63)

32. **(4)** Hypothecation refers to the pledging of property as security for a loan in which the borrower retains possession of the property pledged as security. Disintermediation results in less availability of mortgage money for lenders. A reverse annuity mortgage allows the borrower to receive periodic payments from the lender on the equity in the home. (82)

33. **(3)** Raising the discount rate would increase the interest rates and make mortgage money less available because of the increased cost of borrowing. (75)

34. **(1)** A term mortgage allows for payment of interest only with a lump-sum balloon payment at maturity. A partially amortized loan also involves a lump-sum or balloon payment at maturity. (74)

35. **(2)** Ginnie Mae purchases FHA-insured, VA-guaranteed, and Rural Development loans on the secondary mortgage market. (76)

36. **(1)** The FHA insures mortgages made in the primary mortgage market. FNMA, GNMA, and FHLMC are major warehousing agencies in the secondary mortgage market. (76)

37. **(3)** RESPA provides for use of a settlement statement. (80)

38. **(2)** An alienation clause states that if the borrower sells the property, the lender has the choice of either declaring the entire debt due and payable or allowing the buyer to assume the loan. A reconveyance clause is used to release the lien created by a trust deed. A reversion clause could be used in a deed and stipulates that if not complied with, the property reverts to the owner. (83)

39. **(4)** Salesperson Cooke is primarily responsible to his broker Davidson. As an exclusive buyer's agent, a vicarious agency relationship would exist between the broker and the buyer, because all exclusive buyer-agency agreements are the property of the broker. (93)

40. **(3)** The fiduciary relationship of trust and confidence exists between the agent and the principal (client). The listing broker does not automatically have a fiduciary duty to the buyer or customer. (91)

41. **(4)** A real estate broker is a special agent authorized to represent the principal in one specific transaction. (92)

42. **(1)** In the absence of state law, the six cooperating brokers are not agents of the seller. In 1996, the National Association of REALTORS® eliminated the offering of subagency between cooperating brokers. Cooperating brokers may extend compensation and cooperation to outside brokers, but the offering of subagency is not sanctioned by the NAR. (91)

43. **(4)** The salesperson's listing of the home created an agency relationship between the seller and the salesperson's brokerage. The listing belongs to the brokerage. (119)

44. **(2)** Earnest money must be placed in the brokerage firm's trust account. (163)

45. **(1)** The buyer's broker has a fiduciary relationship with the buyer. (94–95)

46. **(4)** The broker may not offer legal advice—only a licensed attorney may do so. (96)

47. **(3)** Unless instructed otherwise, the broker is responsible for submitting all offers to his or her principal. (94–95)

48. **(1)** In most states, the broker has no lien on a property for a commission due on negotiating the sale of that property. Accordingly, the broker may not go to court to stop the transaction. The broker cannot collect the commission from the buyer, because the buyer is not in the agency relationship between the seller and broker. In some states, a broker may place a lien on property if in compliance with the statute. (96)

49. **(2)** The broker is not required to charge a commission; the commission is negotiable. (92)

50. **(4)** The broker generally earns the commission when he or she produces a "ready, willing, and able" buyer. (119)

51. **(3)** The owner has the power to terminate the listing contract but not necessarily the right; the broker may be able to sue the owner for damages. The offeror would not be able to sue for specific performance, because the offer was not accepted; the owner is not obligated to accept the offer. The broker would not be entitled to the earnest money, because the offer was never accepted; the earnest money would have to be returned to the offeror. Finally, the point at which a commission is earned is no longer an absolute in all jurisdictions. (96)

52. **(3)** Dismissal of the salesperson does not affect the listing, because the broker, not the salesperson, is a party to the contract. Material damage is not destruction. Signing a second listing while the first listing is in effect is a clear breach of contract. (Note, though, that the first listing broker may have some recourse against the seller for expenses). Expiration of the listing was too late, in light of the second listing having been signed. (119)

53. **(2)** An option is an example of a unilateral contract. An option is a promise to keep open for a specified period an offer to sell or purchase property. When the optionee exercises an option, it becomes a bilateral contract. (121–122)

54. **(2)** The exclusive-agency listing allows the seller to sell his or her own house without paying the broker a commission. The broker, under an exclusive-right-to-sell listing, receives a commission regardless of who sells the property. Either type is given to only one broker. (119)

55. **(4)** The buyer–nonexclusive agency agreement is similar to an open listing–seller agreement. (119)

56. **(2)** Standard listings contain a clause that stipulates that if the property is sold to someone who was introduced to the property by the broker, even after the listing has expired, the broker is entitled to a commission. Usually, there is a time period written into the clause. This is called the protection clause. Alienation and defeasance are related to mortgages; the habendum clause is found in a deed. (122)

57. **(2)** Any offer or counteroffer may be withdrawn at any time prior to acceptance by the offeree. (117)

58. **(4)** A tenant at sufferance continues to hold possession without consent of the landlord. (135)

59. **(4)** An index lease is adjusted periodically based on changes in an agreed cost-of-living index. (135)

60. **(4)** A general warranty deed with title insurance provides the grantee with the most protection. A special warranty deed only promises to warrant against title defects during the grantor's time of ownership. However, with title insurance, this is a good deed. The quitclaim deed is the least protective, because it makes no expressed or implied warranties. (152)

61. **(3)** The buyer (vendee) will not receive the deed to the property until the entire land contract has been paid in full. (122)

62. **(1)** Real property is conveyed by deed. (152)

63. **(2)** Erosion is the wearing away of land by natural forces, such as wind; avulsion is the sudden removal of soil by an act of nature. (30)

64. **(4)** Deeds are recorded to establish priority and provide protection against third parties. (152)

65. **(3)** A broker is prohibited by most state laws from advertising listed property without using the name of the brokerage in the ad. Agents likewise are prohibited from running blind ads whether they are the listing agent or willing to pay for the ad. The only exception is if the agent desires to advertise the sale of her own property. Normally these sales don't involve the brokerage; they resemble for-sale-by-owner transactions. (96)

66. **(4)** In addition to the maximum fine, the broker may have to serve up to 10 years in prison. (172)

67. **(3)** As part of the Fair Housing Act of 1968, sex became a protected class in 1974; familial status and disability became protected classes in 1988. (164)

68. **(4)** Blockbusting, racial steering, and redlining are violations of the Federal Fair Housing Act of 1968, which was discussed. Arbitrage refers to an increase in return created by the difference between interest rates charged in financing arrangements. (166)

69. **(3)** The federal fair housing laws do not include age, marital status, or sexual orientation in their protected arrangements. (164–165)

70. **(4)** See the below figure.

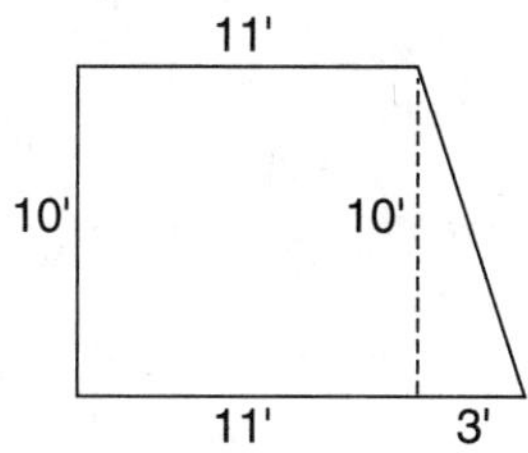

11' × 10' = 110 square feet, area of rectangle

½(3' × 10') = ½(30') = 15 square feet, area of triangle

110 + 15 = 125 square feet

To convert square feet to square yards, divide by 9.

125 ÷ 9 = 13.888 square yards

$16.95 + $4.50 installation = $21.45, cost per square yard

$21.45 × 13.888 square yards = $297.92 (185)

71. **(4)** Appraisal ethics are discussed in Chapter 5. (57)

72. **(3)** $2,640 ÷ 12 months = $220 per month

$220 ÷ 30 days = $7.333 per day

$220 × 5 months = $1,100

$7.333 × 23 days = $168.66

$1,100 + $168 = $1,268.66 (188)

73. **(1)** $92,000 × 70% (0.70) = $64,400 assessed value

Divide by 100, because the tax rate is stated per $100

$64,400 ÷ 100 = $644

$644 × $3.40 = $2,189.60, annual taxes

Divide by 12 to get the monthly taxes

$2,189.60 ÷ 12 = $182.47 (188)

74. **(3)** $473.26 × 12 = $5,679.12 annual interest

part ÷ percent = total

$5,679.12 ÷ 9% (0.09) = $63,101.33 (191)

75. **(4)** $58,700 × 9% (0.09) = $5,283

$5,283 ÷ 12 months = $440.25 per month

$440.25 ÷30 days = $14.675 per day

18 days × $14.675 = $264.15 (191)

76. **(2)** $150,000 ÷ 1,000 = $150 × 9.91 = $1,486.50 (191)

77. **(4)** $1,486.50 × 360 months =

$535,140 (total principal and interest) – $150,000 amount of loan =

$385,140, total interest paid over the life of the loan (191)

78. **(2)** $146,000 sales price × 6% commission

$146,000 × 0.06 = $8,760 × 0.25 = $2,190 (181)

79. **(3)** $8,460 – $600 = $7,860, commission on sales

$7,860 ÷ 2.5% (0.025) = $314,400, value of property sold (187–188)

80. **(3)** $83,500 × 6% (0.06) = $5,010, annual increase in value

$83,500 + $5,010 = $88,510, current market value (183)

SALESPERSON EXAMINATION II

1. A grantor wishes to convey title to a grantee in a deed that creates the least protection for the grantee. The grantor should give the grantee a
   1. bargain and sale deed.
   2. quitclaim deed.
   3. general warranty deed.
   4. special warranty deed.

2. Of the following liens, which generally would be given the highest priority?
   1. A judgment issued last year
   2. A mortgage recorded four years ago
   3. A special assessment
   4. A mechanic's lien for work begun two months ago

3. You are showing a property described as being in the "nicest neighborhood in town" when, in fact, other neighborhoods are arguably as nice. A statement such as this is *MOST* likely to be categorized as
   1. fraud.
   2. puffing.
   3. misrepresentation.
   4. professional negligence.

4. You are chairperson of the Democratic party in your state, and you also own an eight-unit apartment building you currently rent out. You are taking a rental application from a prospective tenant when she informs you that she works for the Republican party of your state. You inform her that all the apartments have been rented even though you know they have not been rented. Which of the following statements correctly describes this unethical situation?
   1. You have violated Truth-in-Lending.
   2. You have violated the federal fair housing law.
   3. You have exercised your rights as an owner of private property to discriminate.
   4. You have violated RESPA.

5. When a listing agreement includes a broker protection clause, the clause
   1. protects the broker against any lawsuits filed by the client.
   2. allows the broker to buy the listed property if the broker is unable to sell it.
   3. automatically extends the listing for six months if the broker is unable to see the property.
   4. states that the owner will pay a commission to the listing broker if the property is sold to a buyer with whom the broker negotiated during the listing term within a specific time after the listing expires.

6. Which of the following would *NOT* be considered to be real property?
   1. Trees
   2. Buildings
   3. Trade fixtures
   4. Water rights

7. A sale is to be closed on June 23. Real estate taxes of $3,760 for the current year have not been paid. What is the amount of real estate tax proration to be credited to the buyer? (Use a 30-day month for calculation.)
   1. $1,566.65
   2. $1,806.86
   3. $1,879.98
   4. None of these

8. The giver of an option is called the
   1. vendor.
   2. optionor.
   3. vendee.
   4. optionee.

9. Which of the following types of depreciation is generally incurable?
   1. Physical deterioration
   2. Economic or external obsolescence
   3. Functional obsolescence
   4. Physical depreciation

10. Three investors decided to pool their savings and buy a motel for $330,000. If one invested $90,000 and the second contributed $50,000, what percentage of ownership was left for the third investor?
    1. 14.1
    2. 27.3
    3. 57.6
    4. None of these

11. Which of the following clauses gives a lender the right to declare the entire debt due and payable if the mortgaged property is either assumed without lender approval or sold with a contract for deed without lender approval?
    1. Acceleration clause
    2. Equitable redemption
    3. Defeasance clause
    4. Alienation clause

12. A woman owns a tract of land that also is a servient tenement. The easement over, through, or under the tract is a(n)
    1. lien.
    2. encumbrance.
    3. license.
    4. encroachment.

13. In an exclusive-right-to-sell listing agreement, how many brokers are involved?
    1. Two
    2. One
    3. As many as the owner/lister chooses
    4. As many salespeople as the broker has in his or her office

14. The broker has listed an owner's home. This agreement will be terminated by all of the following *EXCEPT*
    1. death of the listing salesperson.
    2. death of the owner.
    3. death of the broker.
    4. bankruptcy of the broker.

15. A drunken man signed an offer to purchase. The contract that he signed is
    1. valid.
    2. void.
    3. voidable.
    4. unenforceable.

16. You sign an agreement to purchase a home. The contract requires that the seller replace the damaged living room carpet. The carpet you have chosen costs $18.95 per square yard plus $5.50 per square yard for installation. If the living room dimensions are as illustrated below, how much will the seller have to pay for the job?
    1. $315.82
    2. $407.48
    3. $490.81
    4. None of these

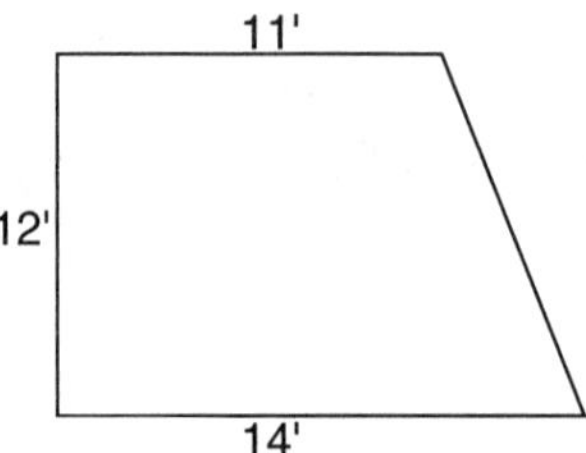

17. All of the following agency relationships could be used to describe a cooperating broker in a real estate transaction *EXCEPT*
    1. a subagent.
    2. an exclusive buyer's broker.
    3. a selling broker.
    4. a non-exclusive buyer's broker.

18. An appraiser is trying to determine the value of an income property by capitalizing the income stream. Which of the following factors will the appraiser use?
    1. Mortgage interest
    2. Net income
    3. Replacement cost
    4. Income taxes

19. A partial release clause generally is found in a
    1. construction mortgage.
    2. package mortgage.
    3. blanket mortgage.
    4. wraparound mortgage.

20. All of the following scenarios would be considered discriminatory under federal fair housing laws *EXCEPT*
    1. a man owns and lives in his four-unit apartment building, and he refuses to rent to families with children.
    2. a landlord charges higher security deposits to tenants with children.
    3. a landlord places all families in selected buildings in his apartment complex.
    4. a landlord refuses to rent to a pregnant woman.

21. Which of the following is a requirement for a valid deed?
    1. The grantee must sign the deed.
    2. The consideration must be in dollars.
    3. It must contain a subordination clause.
    4. It must contain a granting clause.

22. You bought a home one year ago for $115,900. Property in your neighborhood is said to be increasing in value at a rate of 8% annually. If this is true, what is the current value of your real estate?
    1. $125,172
    2. $134,444
    3. $144,063
    4. None of these

23. An enforceable contract may contain any of the following as consideration *EXCEPT*
    1. money.
    2. love.
    3. affection.
    4. duress.

24. You have just given an option to buy your restaurant to a friend. Which of the following statements is *NOT* correct?
    1. Your friend is the optionee.
    2. You are the optionor.
    3. Your friend is obligated to buy your restaurant.
    4. Your friend may pay a fee of some kind for the option right.

25. A broker listed a home under the condition that the owner receive $210,000 from the sale, with the broker being able to sell the property for as much as possible and keep the difference as the commission. This unethical, if not illegal, agreement is an example of
    1. an exclusive-agency listing.
    2. an exclusive-right-to-sell listing.
    3. a net listing.
    4. an option listing.

26. A broker was offered a listing by homeowners who stated that they would not sell to a minority. The broker should
    1. accept the listing and allow the owners the right to choose the buyer.
    2. file a complaint with the local board of REALTORS®.
    3. accept the listing and ensure that no minorities are shown the property.
    4. refuse to accept the listing based on this condition.

27. All of the following would be public land use controls *EXCEPT*
    1. zoning.
    2. environmental protection laws.
    3. subdivision regulations.
    4. deed restrictions.

28. A home is valued at $103,000. Property in this city is assessed at 80% of its value, and the local tax rate is $3.60 per $100. What is the amount of the owner's monthly taxes?
    1. $247.20
    2. $824
    3. $2,966.40
    4. None of these

29. Which person would *NOT* be protected under the familial status definition according to the federal fair housing law?
    1. A 19-year-old girl living with her mother
    2. A 17-year-old boy living with his father
    3. A 14-year-old girl living with a person who is seeking legal custody of her
    4. A 21-year old woman who is pregnant

30. You are working as a salesperson for a broker and have just sold a home. You will receive your share of the commission on the sale from
    1. the cooperating broker.
    2. the seller.
    3. your broker.
    4. the buyer.

31. You have been given oral permission to park in a friend's driveway while attending a football game. Their permission is a(n)
    1. easement appurtenant.
    2. encroachment.
    3. license.
    4. littoral right.

32. Charging a rate of interest in excess of the maximum rate allowed by law is
    1. novation.
    2. subordination.
    3. laches.
    4. usury.

33. Which of the following categories represents the first one to be protected by federal law against discrimination in housing?
    1. Familial status
    2. Sex
    3. Race
    4. Sexual orientation

34. Using a mortgage factor of $7.69, what is the monthly payment for a $170,000 loan at 8.5% for 30 years?
    1. $1,247.80
    2. $1,276.70
    3. $1,307.30
    4. $1,337.90

35. Using the information in question 34 above, what is the total interest paid over the life of the loan?
    1. $279,208
    2. $300,628
    3. $311,644
    4. None of these

36. The requirement that a lender use the settlement statement form for certain government-related loans is a requirement of
    1. IRS regulations.
    2. RESPA.
    3. Truth-in-Lending.
    4. Federal Housing Administration (FHA) regulations.

37. All of the following would be considered a lien except a(n)
    1. encroachment.
    2. judgment.
    3. mechanic's lien.
    4. mortgage.

38. The borrower under a note secured by a mortgage is the
    1. mortgagor.
    2. trustee.
    3. mortgagee.
    4. vendee.

39. Which of the following licensees is *MOST* likely to act as a general agent for a client?
    1. Broker
    2. Property manager
    3. Cooperative broker
    4. Listing salesperson

40. The relationship of trust and confidence that a broker has with a principal is called a(n)
    1. fiduciary relationship.
    2. hypothecation.
    3. escrow.
    4. trustor relationship.

41. You received a real estate loan from a bank in which the lender was privately insured against loss in the event of default and foreclosure. The loan would have been which of the following?
    1. Conventional insured
    2. Federal Housing Authority (FHA)
    3. Veterans Administration (VA)
    4. Rural development

42. A 500-acre farm is divided into house lots. The streets require one-eighth of the whole farm, and there are 300 lots. How many square feet are in each lot?
 1. 48,636
 2. 55,584
 3. 63,525
 4. 72,600

43. Which of the following real estate loans is guaranteed against loss by the government?
 1. Conventional
 2. Veterans Administration (VA)
 3. Federal Housing Authority (FHA)
 4. Seller carries back in excess of $100,000

44. The agency that serves as the nation's banker and fiscal manager is the
 1. United States Treasury.
 2. Federal Reserve System.
 3. Federal National Mortgage Association (FNMA), or Fannie Mae.
 4. Federal Home Loan Mortgage Corporation (FHLMC), or Freddie Mac.

45. You receive a monthly salary of $1,200 plus a 3% commission on all of your listings that sell and 2.5% on all of your sales. None of the listings that you took sold last month, but you receive $6,300 in salary and commission. What is the value of the property that sold?
 1. $170,000
 2. $204,000
 3. $252,000
 4. None of these

46. All of the following describe a loan in which private mortgage insurance is required *EXCEPT*
 1. the buyer may obtain a conventional loan for up to 95% of the property's appraised value.
 2. the lender is protected against loss on the upper 20 to 25% portion of the loan.
 3. PMI insurance premiums are made a part of the borrower's monthly payments.
 4. insurance must generally be held for two years.

47. Andrew, who works for broker Christopher on a 50-50 basis, sold a house listed by broker Elisa for $193,950. The seller agreed to pay a 6% commission but stipulated in the listing that 60% was to go to the selling broker. How much commission (to the nearest dollar) will Andrew make on this sale?
 1. $2,327.40
 2. $2,909.25
 3. $3,491.10
 4. $4,189.32

48. You removed an old furnace and installed a new furnace with central air conditioning in your home. This newly installed personal property becomes a
 1. trade fixture.
 2. chattel fixture.
 3. fixture.
 4. physical trade fixture.

49. An easement would generally be used in which of the following?
 1. Accession
 2. Novation
 3. Partition
 4. Right of way

50. You had an exclusive-right-to-sell listing with a seller, and you showed the property to a prospective buyer during the listing term. The seller openly negotiated with this prospective buyer and asked him to wait until the listing had expired to buy the property so there would be a commission savings on the transaction. You found out that the property was sold to the prospective buyer within a month of the time the listing expired. Are you entitled to a commission? Why or why not?
 1. No; because the entire transaction occurred after the listing expired.
 2. No; because exclusive right-to-sell listings allow the seller to sell the property themselves without owing a commission.
 3. Yes; because you were the procuring cause of the sale.
 4. Yes; because you are entitled to a commission if the property is sold by anyone within a year of the listing period.

51. All of the following would be an example of economic or external obsolescence *EXCEPT*
    1. changing land uses in a neighborhood.
    2. the major employer in the city going out of business.
    3. a poor floor plan.
    4. a nearby landfill contaminating the ground waste.

52. A lender that refuses to provide loans on properties located in a minority neighborhood regardless of the ethnicity of the applicant would be engaged in a discriminatory practice known as
    1. steering.
    2. redlining.
    3. blockbusting.
    4. hypothecating.

53. A house located next to an airport would be an example of
    1. functional obsolescence.
    2. economic or external obsolescence.
    3. physical deterioration.
    4. physical depreciation.

54. An odorless radioactive gas produced by the decay of other radioactive materials in rocks under the earth's surface is which of the following?
    1. Asbestos
    2. UFFI
    3. Lead
    4. Radon

55. Within the field of real estate finance, to what does the secondary mortgage market refer?
    1. Placing of junior liens
    2. Transferability of mortgages among mortgagees
    3. Transferability of mortgages among mortgagors
    4. None of these

56. Which of the following types of depreciation contains elements that are incurable only?
    1. Physical deterioration
    2. Economic or external obsolescence
    3. Functional obsolescence
    4. Physical depreciation

57. A woman wants to know how much money she owes on her mortgage loan. She knows that the interest part of the last monthly payment was $647.91. If she was paying an interest rate of 9%, what was the outstanding balance of her loan before the last payment was made?
    1. $64,791.10
    2. $77,749.20
    3. $86,388
    4. $97,186.50

58. Which of the following factors would *NOT* be considered by an appraiser in conducting a neighborhood analysis?
    1. Relation to the rest of the community
    2. Rent levels
    3. Racial characteristics of the residents
    4. Zoning

59. A contract in which the intentions of the parties are shown by their conduct is
    1. an express contract.
    2. an implied contract.
    3. a bilateral contract.
    4. an executory contract.

60. All of the following would be considered an agent *EXCEPT*
    1. a broker who has listed an owner's home for sale.
    2. a property manager who manages property for others for a fee.
    3. a salesperson employed by a broker.
    4. a nonlicensed personal assistant of an agent.

61. A swollen, rushing river sweeps away an outcropping of land with several trees on it. The term that *MOST* accurately identifies this kind of property loss is
    1. erosion.
    2. avulsion.
    3. accretion.
    4. disenfranchisement.

62. You have purchased three lots and combined them into one large parcel to build an apartment building. This is an example of
    1. the principle of progression.
    2. assemblage.
    3. the principle of substitution.
    4. plottage value.

63. A summary of all the recorded instruments affecting the title to a property is called a(n):
    1. abstract of title.
    2. certificate of title.
    3. escrow.
    4. title insurance policy.

64. A contract in which one party promises to do something if the other party performs a specific act is a(n)
    1. unenforceable contract.
    2. unilateral contract.
    3. void contract.
    4. bilateral contract.

65. Federal fair housing laws prohibit housing discrimination against all of the following groups of people *EXCEPT*
    1. women.
    2. college students.
    3. ethnic minorities.
    4. families with minor children.

66. The form of listing that provides the *MOST* protection to the broker is the
    1. exclusive agency.
    2. exclusive-right-to-sell.
    3. net listing.
    4. open listing.

67. All of the following represent environmental hazards that may affect the marketability of a residential property *EXCEPT*
    1. xenon.
    2. radon gas.
    3. lead-based paint.
    4. underground storage tanks.

68. Brokers who violate the Sherman Antitrust Act may be punished by a maximum prison term of
    1. one year.
    2. two years.
    3. ten years.
    4. five years.

69. Martinez, a real estate broker, was renting Paulson's apartments as Paulson's property manager. Martinez showed the remaining vacant apartment to Smith, an African-American woman. Martinez checked Smith's job, credit, and housing references and was about to inform Smith that she would be able to sign a lease when Paulson called and inquired about Smith's color. Martinez should
    1. tell Paulson, because Martinez has a fiduciary responsibility of loyalty to Paulson.
    2. tell Paulson only on the condition that Paulson keeps the information in confidence.
    3. not tell Paulson, because it is not a material fact.
    4. not tell Paulson, because Smith is a member of a protected class.

70. An appraiser has estimated the replacement cost of an office building at $300,000. The building is 22 years old and has an estimated useful life of 60 years. What is the current total depreciation of the building?
    1. $90,000
    2. $110,000
    3. $130,000
    4. None of these

71. What is the value of an apartment building that is expected to produce a net annual income of $20,000 if the owner estimates that she should receive a return of 8% on her investment?
    1. $120,000
    2. $160,000
    3. $200,000
    4. $250,000

72. Andrew and Bethany, a married couple, sold their principal residence in 1999 and made a profit on the sale of $600,000. Andrew and Bethany had lived in that property since 1987. Andrew and Bethany will have to pay capital gains tax on
   1. $100,000.
   2. $250,000.
   3. $500,000.
   4. $600,000.

73. A portion of Joseph's land is protected from judgment for unsecured debts. Joseph's protection is based on
   1. riparian rights.
   2. dower rights.
   3. littoral rights.
   4. homestead rights.

74. Sam has given Carlos permission to park in Sam's driveway during the month of July. Carlos has
   1. an easement appurtenant.
   2. a life estate.
   3. a license.
   4. an easement by prescription.

75. Which of the following types of loans would be considered conventional?
   1. A privately insured loan
   2. An FHA loan
   3. A Freddie Mac loan
   4. A VA loan

76. Which of the following is *NOT* an agency that purchases loans on the secondary mortgage market?
   1. FDIC
   2. FNMA
   3. FHLMC
   4. GNMA

77. If a woman is buying a home worth $300,000, and her mortgage is for $240,000, her loan to value ratio would be
   1. 20%
   2. 40%
   3. 60%
   4. 80%

78. Which of the following statements would *NOT* be a material fact to be disclosed by a seller's agent?
   1. Presentation of all offers
   2. A relationship that the agent has with the buyer
   3. Buyer's ability to make a lower offer
   4. Discussion of disadvantages of an offer

79. Under capital gains tax law, a single person may take up to $250,000 in capital gains tax-free on the sale of a home if that person has lived in the house for at least
   1. the past year.
   2. two of the past five years.
   3. one of the past three years.
   4. two of the last four years.

80. Lois gave Mark a deed with no express or implied warranty. The deed was *MOST* likely a
   1. general warranty deed.
   2. special warranty deed.
   3. bargain and sale deed.
   4. quitclaim deed.

ANSWER KEY: SALESPERSON EXAMINATION II

NOTE: The number in parentheses at the end of each explanation refers to the page number where this material is discussed.

1. **(2)** The general warranty and special warranty deed contain express warranties. A bargain and sale deed has an implied warranty. A quitclaim deed contains no warranty. (152)

2. **(3)** Special assessments and real estate taxes take priority over all other liens, regardless of the date of recording. (24)

3. **(2)** Your opinion would be an example of puffing. (168)

4. **(3)** Political belief is not a protected class under the federal fair housing laws. (164)

5. **(4)** The broker protection clause refers to the broker's commission. The broker protection clause does not exist in Connecticut. In addition, the automatic extension of listing agreements is against the law in most states. (122)

6. **(3)** Trade fixtures are items installed by a tenant for conducting a business. (30)

7. **(2)** \$3,760 ÷ 12 months = \$313.33 per month

   \$313.33 ÷ 30 days = \$10.444 per day

   \$313.33 × 5 months = \$1,566.65

   \$10.444 × 23 = \$240.21

   \$1,566.65 + \$240.21 = \$1,806.86 (187)

8. **(2)** The giver of an option is the optionor; the buyer is the optionee. The vendor is a seller of realty; the vendee is the purchaser of realty. (121–122)

9. **(2)** Functional obsolescence and physical deterioration and depreciation may be incurable. Economic obsolescence generally is incurable. (61)

10. **(3)** \$90,000 (first investor) + \$50,000 (second investor) = \$140,000

    \$330,000 – \$140,000 = \$190,000, third investor's contribution

    part ÷ total = percent

    \$190,000 ÷ \$330,000 = 0.5757 or 57.6% (182)

11. **(4)** An acceleration clause states that if the borrower defaults, the lender has the right to declare the entire debt due and payable. The defeasance clause requires the lender to execute a satisfaction of mortgage when the note is fully paid. Equitable redemption refers to the right of borrowers to redeem this interest in their property prior to a public foreclosure sale. (83)

12. **(2)** The tract of land over which an easement appurtenant runs is the servient tenement; an easement appurtenant is an encumbrance, as are the lien, license, and encroachment. (23–24)

13. **(2)** In an exclusive-right-to-sell listing, there is only one broker. Regardless of who procures a buyer, the exclusive-right-to-sell broker receives a commission, which is then often split with the co-op broker who brought the buyer. (119)

14. **(1)** The listing salesperson is a subagent whose death will not affect the listing contract. (119)

15. **(3)** A voidable contract may be disaffirmed, because one of the parties signed when under duress. (118)

16. **(2)** See the below figure.

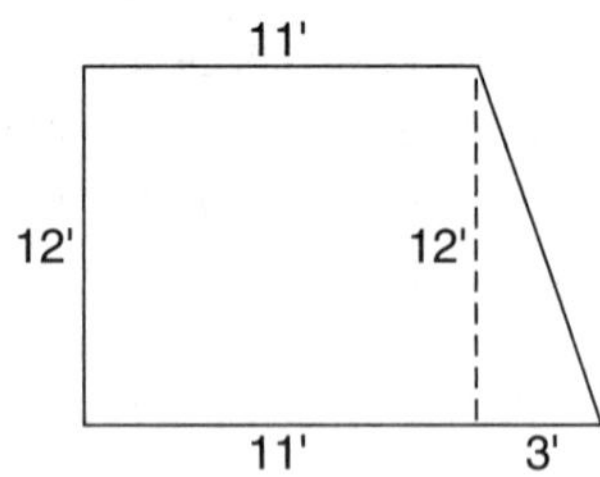

11' × 12' = 132' = 132 square feet, area of rectangle 3'

½(3' × 12') = ½(36') = 18 square feet, area of triangle

132 + 18 = 150 square feet

To convert square feet to square yards, divide number of square feet by 9.

150 ÷ 9 = 16.666 square yards

$18.95 + $5.50 = $24.45, cost per square yard

$24.45 × 16.666 square yards = $407.48 (184)

17. **(1)** The listing broker would be the only agent of the seller, and none of the cooperating brokers could legally represent the seller, because the offering of subagency to outside brokers is against public policy. (119)

18. **(2)** The net income in an operating statement does not reflect interest and taxes. (61)

19. **(3)** A blanket mortgage covers more than one property or lot; it is typically used to finance the development of a subdivision. (83)

20. **(1)** Rentals of rooms in an owner-occupied one to four-family dwelling are exempt from federal fair housing laws. (166)

21. **(4)** The grantor must sign the deed. Consideration can be monetary or nonmonetary. Subordination clauses are used in mortgages. (152)

22. **(1)** $115,900 × 8% (0.08) = $9,272 annual increase in value

$115,900 + $9,272 = $125,172 current market value (182)

23. **(4)** A valid contract must be based on good and valuable consideration. If duress is involved, however, there would not be a meeting of the minds; the contract would thus not be valid. (117)

24. **(3)** The optionee (prospective buyer) pays for the option right but assumes no obligation to make any other payments until she decides whether or not to exercise her option right. (121–122)

25. **(3)** The other listings would include a commission agreed on in advance in terms of a percentage dollar amount. (122)

26. **(4)** Federal fair housing laws provide that it is unlawful to discriminate on the basis of race when selling residential property. The broker must refuse to accept the listing based on this condition. (164)

27. **(4)** Zoning, environmental protection laws, and subdivision regulations are public land-use controls. (49–50)

28. **(1)** $103,000 × 80% (0.80) = $82,400 assessed value

Divide by 100, because the tax rate is stated per $100.

$82,400 ÷ 100 = $824.00

$824 × $3.60 = $2,966.40, annual tax

$2,966.40 ÷ 12 = $247.20 (184)

29. **(1)** Under certain circumstances, the familial status category protects individuals who have not reached the age of 18. (164)

30. **(3)** A salesperson can only receive compensation from the broker for whom she works. (171)

31. **(3)** A license provides permission to enter the land of another for a specific purpose. Littoral rights involve water rights. An encroachment is an illegal extension of the building beyond the land of its owner. An easement appurtenant requires two tracts of land. (25)

32. **(4)** Charging a rate of interest in excess of the maximum rate allowed by law is known as usury. Novation refers to an agreement in which a new debtor is accepted in place of an old one. Laches is a court doctrine used to bar a legal claim because of undue delay in asserting the claim. Subordination refers to an agreement that changes the order of priority of liens between two creditors. (82)

33. **(3)** Race became a protected class in 1968; sex in 1974. Sexual orientation is not a protected class under federal fair housing laws. (164)

34. **(3)** $170,000 ÷ 1,000 = 170 × 7.69 = $1,307.30 (191)

35. **(2)** $1,307.30 × 360 months = $470,628

    Total principal and interest –170,000. Amount of loan $300,628

    Total interest paid over life of the loan (191)

36. **(2)** The other choices do not deal with a closing form. (154)

37. **(1)** An encroachment is an encumbrance. (24–25)

38. **(1)** The borrower under a note secured by a mortgage is a mortgagor. The lender is a mortgagee. The trustee holds the real estate as a security for the loan under a trust deed. The vendee is the buyer in a real estate contract. (78)

39. **(2)** Often, a property manager has multiple duties to perform for the principal. The broker is considered a special agent, because the broker's task is often singular (procure a buyer or find a property). (92)

40. **(1)** Hypothecation is the pledging of property as security for a loan without losing possession of it. Escrow is a third-party agreement; the trustor is the borrower in a trust deed. (91)

41. **(1)** Privately insured loans are conventional loans. All non-FHA and non-VA loans are conventional loans. (73)

42. **(3)** 43,560 sq. ft. per acre × 500 acres

    21,780,000 × (0.125) = 2,772,500 sq. ft. for streets

    21,780,000 – 2,722,500 = 19,057,500 sq. ft. for lots

    19,057,500 sq. ft. ÷ 300 lots = 63,525 sq. ft. per lot (22)

43. **(2)** The Department of Veterans Affairs (VA) loan provides a guarantee to the lender. There is no insurance premium for a guaranteed loan. However, an FHA loan is insured by the federal government, and an insurance premium is charged. (77)

44. **(1)** The U.S. Treasury is responsible for supervising the daily fiscal operations of the federal government. FHLMC and FNMA are warehousing agencies in the secondary mortgage market. The Federal Reserve regulates the flow of money through member banks. (75)

45. **(2)** \$6,300 – \$1,200 = \$5,100, commission on sales

    \$5,100 ÷ 2.5% (0.025) = \$204,000, value of property sold (182)

46. **(1)** The buyer may obtain a conventional loan for up to 97% of the property's appraised value. (73)

47. **(3)** \$193,950 sales price × 6% (0.06) commission = \$11,637, broker commission

    \$11,637 × 60% (0.60) = \$6,982.20 × 0.50 = \$3,491.10, selling salesperson's commission (182)

48. **(3)** A trade fixture is attached to real property for the purpose of carrying on a business. A chattel fixture is an item of personal property. (21)

49. **(4)** An easement gives the dominant tenant a right-of-way. (24)

50. **(3)** The broker's commission would be protected by the broker protection clause in the listing contract. (119)

51. **(3)** A poor floor plan is considered functional obsolescence. Economic or external obsolescence is a loss in value due to factors outside the property. (63)

52. **(2)** Redlining refers to discriminatory denial of loans to people in selected areas, regardless of their qualifications. (166)

53. **(2)** Economic or external obsolescence is a loss in value resulting from an environmental factor outside of the property's boundaries, such as being located next to an airport. (61)

54. **(4)** Asbestos is a material used for many years as insulation on heating pipes and ducts. Prior to 1978, UFFI was used to insulate buildings; because of its toxic outgassing, it was removed from the market. Lead is a material used to impede water flow. (46)

55. **(2)** The secondary mortgage market deals only with the first mortgages of mortgagors (borrowers) transferred among mortgagees (lenders). (76)

56. **(2)** Economic obsolescence occurs outside the property. (61)

57. **(3)** \$647.91 × 12 = \$7,774.92

    \$7,774.92 ÷ 9% (0.09) = \$86,388 (187)

58. **(3)** Appraisers are not allowed to discuss racial characteristics in an appraisal report. (164)

59. **(2)** A contract in which the parties show their intentions by conduct is an implied contract; intention is shown by words in an expressed contract. Promises are exchanged in a bilateral contract. Something remains to be performed in an executory contract. (117)

60. **(4)** A nonlicensed personal assistant working for an agent would not be considered an agent. The personal assistant could act either as an employee or independent contractor for the licensed agent. (96)

61. **(2)** Avulsion is the sudden tearing away of land by action of nature, while erosion is the gradual wearing away of land by natural forces of water and wind. (30)

62. **(2)** Plottage is the value increment resulting from assemblage. (64)

63. **(1)** A buyer's attorney examines the abstract for flaws and prepares a written opinion of the condition of ownership. (151)

64. **(2)** An unenforceable contract appears to be valid, but neither party may sue the other to force performance. A void contract lacks an essential element of a valid contract and thus has no legal effect. A bilateral contract is a contract in which both parties promise to do something. (118)

65. **(2)** Sex, race, and familial status are protected classes under federal fair housing laws. (164)

66. **(2)** Under an exclusive-right-to-sell listing, the broker receives the commission regardless of who sells the property. (119)

67. **(1)** Xenon is an inert gas and trace element in air. (45)

68. **(3)** The Sherman Antitrust Act also provides for a maximum $1 million fine. (172)

69. **(4)** A licensee may not disclose that a prospective tenant is a member of a protected class. (164)

70. **(2)** $300,000 ÷ 60 = $5,000, annual depreciation charge

    $5,000 × 22 = $110,000, current total depreciation (61)

71. **(4)** I ÷ R = V

    $20,000 ÷ .08 = $250,000, estimated value (61)

72. **(1)** Andrew and Bethany would be entitled to an exclusion of $500,000. (154)

73. **(4)** Riparian and littoral rights are water rights, while dower rights are a legal life estate. (23)

74. **(3)** An easement appurtenant requires a dominant tenement, while an easement by prescription requires use without the owner's approval. A life estate is limited to the lifetime of the owner of the life estate or the lifetime of another (pur autre vie). (24–25)

75. **(1)** A conventional loan is neither insured nor guaranteed by the government agency. (74)

76. **(1)** FDIC is insurance paid by lenders to protect their customer's deposits up to $250,000. The others are members of the secondary mortgage market. (76)

77. **(4)** $$\frac{\text{Amount of loan}}{\text{Appraised value of home}} = \frac{\$240{,}000}{\$300{,}000} = 80\%$$

    (182)

78. **(3)** A seller's agent would disclose, in most states, that the buyer was able to make a higher offer. (107)

79. **(2)** A single person may take up to $250,000, and a married couple may take up to $500,000 in capital gains tax-free, provided that the principal residence is occupied for at least two out of the last five years. (154)

80. **(4)** Warranty deeds contain promises or covenants; the quitclaim deed provides no promises or covenants of warranty. In a quitclaim deed, the grantor is only releasing or quitting an interest possessed; no warranty is provided to the grantee. (152)

SALESPERSON EXAMINATION III

1. Which of the following terms would include the interests, benefits, and rights inherent in the ownership of real estate?
   1. Chattel
   2. Personal property
   3. Real property
   4. Trade fixtures

2. Which of the following is a physical characteristic of land?
   1. Scarcity
   2. Situs
   3. Permanence of investment
   4. Immobility

3. Pam and Marco held title as joint tenants. Which of the following statements would *NOT* correctly describe the requirements for them to own as joint tenants?
   1. Pam and Marco have the right of survivorship.
   2. Pam and Marco must have equal interests.
   3. Pam and Marco must be married.
   4. Pam and Marco may partition the land.

4. All of the following would correctly describe easements *EXCEPT*
   1. an easement is an encumbrance.
   2. an easement appurtenant must have a dominant tenement and a servient tenement.
   3. an easement in gross must have a dominant tenement.
   4. an easement constitutes an interest in land.

5. David has a property that is a servient tenement in an easement appurtenant. David is considering selling his property to Franco. All of the following statements would correctly describe their potential transaction *EXCEPT*
   1. the easement is an encumbrance.
   2. the easement may have a negative effect on the value of the property.
   3. the easement is very likely to prevent David from selling his property to Franco.
   4. the easement may have an impact on Franco's use of the property.

6. Contractor Ricardo replaced the roof on Tom's house. If Tom refuses to pay Ricardo for the work, Ricardo has the right to
   1. remove the roof.
   2. take Tom's personal property and hold it as compensation should the lien be unpaid.
   3. file a mechanic's lien.
   4. record a judgment.

7. The local utility company holds an easement to install power lines on a vacant lot. This is an easement
   1. appurtenant.
   2. in gross.
   3. by necessity.
   4. by prescription.

8. A wife and husband may hold title to their home in all of the following situations *EXCEPT*
   1. tenants by the entirety.
   2. tenants at will.
   3. tenants in common.
   4. joint tenants.

9. Luke, Mario, and Paula are joint tenants. If Luke dies,
   1. Luke's interest will go to his surviving spouse.
   2. Luke's interest will go to Mario or Paula depending on the terms of Luke's will.
   3. Luke's interest will escheat to the state.
   4. Luke's interest will go to Mario and Paula.

10. The SE ¼ of the SW ¼ of the NE ¼ of Section 23 contains
    1. 10 acres.
    2. 40 acres.
    3. 160 acres.
    4. 320 acres.

11. Valerie has been informed that her land is being taken by the state for the development of a new highway. The state will pay Valerie for her land. This process illustrates the right of
    1. escheat.
    2. police power.
    3. taxation.
    4. eminent domain.

12. All of the following would be a governmental restriction on land *EXCEPT*
    1. police power.
    2. deed restriction.
    3. eminent domain.
    4. taxation.

13. Kevin builds an office building on commercially zoned land that is subsequently rezoned by the city to residential. Kevin will
    1. have to close his office building.
    2. have to get his land rezoned by the city to continue operating his building.
    3. need a conditional use permit to continue operating his property.
    4. be able to continue with his office building, which is now a nonconforming use.

14. Tina wants to build a medical clinic in a neighborhood that is zoned residential. Tina will need to obtain a
    1. nonconforming use.
    2. downzoning.
    3. variance.
    4. conditional use permit.

15. Electromagnetic fields (EMFs) are created by
    1. peeling paint.
    2. the movement of electrical currents.
    3. contaminated groundwater.
    4. the decay of radioactive materials in rocks under the earth's surface.

16. Which of the following hazardous substances typically enters a house through the basement floor of a house?
    1. Asbestos
    2. Radon
    3. Lead
    4. Urea-formaldehyde foam insulation

17. The water rights of a landowner adjacent to a stream are known as
    1. equitable rights.
    2. littoral rights.
    3. riparian rights.
    4. prior appropriation rights.

18. A Holiday Inn was developed just outside a city and within six months was operating at 95% occupancy. One year later, a Marriott was built across the street. This would be an example of the principle of
    1. competition.
    2. contribution.
    3. progression.
    4. increasing and decreasing returns.

19. A four-bedroom house with only one bathroom is an example of
    1. physical deterioration.
    2. functional obsolescence.
    3. environmental obsolescence.
    4. locational obsolescence.

20. The *MOST* reliable approach for appraising a single-family home would be the
    1. cost approach.
    2. income approach.
    3. sales comparison approach.
    4. gross income multiplier.

21. Which of the following statements correctly describes how effective gross income is calculated in the operating statement?
    1. Annual potential gross income minus annual operating expenses
    2. Annual potential gross income minus vacancy and rent loss
    3. Annual potential gross income ÷ the capitalization rate
    4. Annual potential gross income ÷ annual operating expenses

22. An example of a governmental action to consider in a neighborhood analysis would be
    1. the street pattern.
    2. new construction.
    3. population density.
    4. special assessments.

23. All of the following would be a characteristic of value *EXCEPT*
    1. effective demand.
    2. utility.
    3. plottage.
    4. scarcity.

24. Deposits in commercial banks are insured by
    1. FDIC.
    2. SAIF.
    3. FNMA.
    4. GNMA.

25. All of the following statements correctly describe the secondary mortgage market *EXCEPT*
    1. FNMA buys conventional, FHA, and VA loans.
    2. GNMA works with FNMA in the tandem plan.
    3. FHLMC administers special assistance programs.
    4. FNMA sells government guaranteed bonds.

26. Deposits in commercial banks are insured for up to
    1. $50,000.
    2. $100,000.
    3. $200,000.
    4. $250,000.

27. All of the following provide its own money for loans on real estate *EXCEPT*
    1. commercial banks.
    2. mortgage brokers.
    3. savings and loan associations.
    4. life insurance companies.

28. A trust deed generally is released by a(n)
    1. satisfaction document.
    2. release document.
    3. reconveyance deed.
    4. acceleration document.

29. Using the mortgage factor of 10.45, what is the monthly payment for a $200,000 loan at 9.5% for 15 years?
    1. $1,682
    2. $2,060
    3. $2,090
    4. $2,120

30. Using the information in question 29, what is the total interest paid over the life of the loan?
    1. $176,200
    2. $181,600
    3. $463,200
    4. $552,400

31. Which of the following mortgages includes real and personal property?
    1. Blanket mortgage
    2. Package mortgage
    3. Wraparound mortgage
    4. Participation mortgage

32. Which of the following laws would use an advertising "trigger"?
    1. Statute of limitations
    2. Truth-in-Lending
    3. RESPA
    4. Statute of frauds

33. Reserve requirements for banks are controlled by the
    1. BIF.
    2. FDIC.
    3. FED.
    4. U.S. Treasury.

34. The agency relationship between the listing broker and his or her seller-client is
    1. universal.
    2. general.
    3. specific.
    4. special.

35. Broker Phil listed Susana's house. Phil has the authority to
    1. modify the listing price.
    2. accept an offer for Susana.
    3. encourage prospective buyers to make an offer at less than list price.
    4. market the property.

36. Broker Hernandez listed Wilson's house, which was sold by a broker from another company, Young. Which of the following would *NOT* describe Young's role in the transaction?
    1. Young was the buyer's agent.
    2. Young was a cooperating broker.
    3. Young was expecting some compensation.
    4. Young was a subagent of the seller.

37. You listed a home for $200,000 and agreed to a 7% commission on the selling price. You and the seller subsequently amended the list price to $190,000 with a commission of 6% of the selling price. The house sold two weeks later for $180,000. Your commission was
    1. $10,800.
    2. $11,400.
    3. $12,600.
    4. $14,000.

38. Broker Mike listed the home of owner Vince who indicated that she was very anxious to sell her house. Mike may
    1. disclose to prospective buyers that the seller will take less than the list price.
    2. not disclose the seller's motivation unless he has the owner's permission to do so, in writing.
    3. not disclose the seller's motivation under any condition.
    4. disclose the seller's motivation only if he is showing Vince's house to a buyer with whom he has a buyer-agency agreement.

39. All of the following would be a violation of the antitrust law *EXCEPT*
    1. two brokers agreeing to boycott by not sharing listings with a third broker.
    2. a broker in a listing presentation informs a prospective client that she would have to receive a 7% commission, because it was the local board rate.
    3. a broker refuses to sell his listed house to a customer unless the customer lists her present home with the broker.
    4. a broker refuses to give another broker the same MLS commission as she offered to the rest of the brokers on MLS.

40. Tom, who works for broker Yvonne on a 50-50 basis, sold a house listed by broker S for $206,000. The seller agreed to pay a 7% commission but stipulated in the listing that 55% was to go to the selling broker. How much commission (to the nearest dollar) will Tom make on this sale?
    1. $3,966
    2. $7,931
    3. $14,420
    4. None of these

41. All of the following would be classified as a latent defect *EXCEPT*
    1. nonconforming use of property.
    2. inadequate electrical outlets.
    3. exposed floor joists charred from a kitchen fire.
    4. an inadequate furnace.

42. Which of the following statements correctly describes the status of dual agency?
    1. Dual agency is always allowed as long as the broker tells the parties.
    2. Dual agency is legal in every state.
    3. Disclosure of dual agency should be made subsequent to completing an offer to purchase.
    4. Dual agency is not allowed unless all parties agree to it.

43. Assuming single agency, which of the following statements *BEST* describes a material fact to be disclosed by a seller's agent back to the seller?
    1. Presentation of lower offers
    2. The buyer's ability to make a higher offer
    3. Disclosure of the property's deficiencies
    4. Disclosure of how long the property has been listed

44. Phillip signed an offer to purchase in a state of obvious drunkenness. The next morning, he realized what he had done and told the broker that he did not want to be bound by the terms of the contract. This would be an example of a(n)
    1. valid contract.
    2. void contract.
    3. voidable contract.
    4. unenforceable contract.

45. All of the following would terminate a listing contract *EXCEPT*
    1. the listing broker dies.
    2. the salesperson dies.
    3. the listed property is destroyed.
    4. bankruptcy of the owner of the listed property.

46. Greg and Jerry entered into a contract to purchase that is subject only to Greg's getting financing. The contract would *BEST* be described as
    1. a voidable contract.
    2. an executed contract.
    3. a unilateral contract.
    4. an executory contract.

47. Buyer Selena and seller Robert have entered into a binding offer to purchase. Which of the following would correctly describe the rights of the parties at this point in the transaction?
    1. Robert holds equitable title.
    2. Selena is entitled to immediate possession.
    3. Selena holds equitable title.
    4. Robert may terminate the contract.

48. Which of the following require certain real estate contracts to be in writing in order to be enforceable?
    1. Statute of descent and distribution
    2. Statute of frauds
    3. Statute of limitations
    4. Uniform Commercial Code

49. Raul gave Julia an option to buy her home for $225,000. Julia has 30 days to inform Raul as to whether he will exercise his option. At this point in the transaction, the option contract is considered to be a(n)
    1. bilateral contract.
    2. unenforceable contract.
    3. unilateral contract.
    4. anticipatory contract.

50. Mario and Cindy wish to change the closing date on their binding purchase contract . They should generally use which of the following forms to modify the language?
    1. An amendment or contractual modification
    2. A counteroffer
    3. An addendum
    4. A multiple counteroffer

51. A man forged his wife's name on a deed and sold their home. The wife subsequently was able to have the title insurance company give her a check for one-half the market value of the home. Which type of deed would the wife usually give to the title company upon receipt of the check?
    1. A warranty deed
    2. A bargain and sale deed
    3. A special warranty deed
    4. A quitclaim deed

52. One of the covenants in a general warranty deed promises that the grantor has title and the right to convey. This is the covenant of
    1. further assurance.
    2. quiet enjoyment.
    3. seisin.
    4. warranty forever.

53. Which of the following parties must sign the deed in order for it to be a valid conveyance?
    1. The listing broker
    2. The director of the public record office
    3. The grantor
    4. The grantee

54. Which of the following requires the recorded summary of a property to be updated and an attorney to render a report about the quality of title?
    1. Abstract and opinion
    2. Torrens system
    3. Certificate of title
    4. Title insurance

55. A married couple sold their primary residence for $400,000 in 2004 after living in it for 10 years. They purchased their property in 1992 for $190,000. The balance of their mortgage when they sold was $30,000. The capital gains tax on their profit will be
   1. $42,000.
   2. $52,500.
   3. $0.
   4. $160,000.

56. Which of the following laws prohibits the payment of referral fees by lenders when no services are actually rendered?
   1. Truth-in-Lending
   2. RESPA
   3. Statute of frauds
   4. Statute of limitations

57. Brian had been diagnosed as mentally ill when his rental application was rejected by a landlord based on his mental health problems. Which of the following statements correctly describes Brian's status under the Federal Fair Housing Act?
   1. Brian's illness does not provide him with protected class status.
   2. Once Brian has signed a lease, he may not be evicted because he is a member of a protected class.
   3. Brian is protected under the law but must file a complaint within one year after the alleged discriminatory housing practice.
   4. Brian is not protected unless he is currently receiving treatment for his illness.

58. All of the following would be a protected class under the Federal Equal Credit Opportunity Act *EXCEPT*
   1. sex.
   2. marital status.
   3. dependency on public assistance.
   4. sexual orientation.

59. All of the following would be protected under the Federal Fair Housing Act *EXCEPT*
   1. a person diagnosed as mentally ill.
   2. a convicted drug dealer.
   3. an alcoholic who has been diagnosed and treated and is not currently addicted.
   4. a drug addict who has been diagnosed and treated and is not currently addicted.

60. Which of the following laws regulate the advertising of credit terms by lenders?
   1. Truth-in-Lending
   2. RESPA
   3. Federal Equal Credit Opportunity Act
   4. Statute of frauds

61. Which of the following properties would *NOT* be exempt from the Federal Fair Housing Act?
   1. The rental of an owner-occupied one-family home
   2. The Elks Club renting only to members on a nonprofit basis
   3. The Lutheran Church renting its own dwelling units on the condition that they be occupied by only Lutherans
   4. The rental of an owner-occupied five-family apartment building

62. Which of the following laws utilizes "trigger terms"?
   1. Federal Equal Credit Opportunity Act
   2. RESPA
   3. Truth-in-Lending
   4. Statute of frauds

63. A broker sold a home for $154,000. The broker charged the seller a 6% commission and will pay 30% of that amount to the listing salesperson and 35% to the selling salesperson. What amount of commission will the listing salesperson receive from the sale of the home?
   1. $2,310
   2. $2,772
   3. $3,234
   4. None of these

64. Buyer Alicia bought a house for $200,000. She was required to pay her bank a discount fee of $9,600 for points on her $160,000 loan. How many points did Alicia pay for the loan?
   1. 4
   2. 5
   3. 6
   4. 7

65. You want to know how much money you owe on your mortgage loan. You know that the interest portion of your last monthly payment was $619.73. If you are paying interest at the rate of 9%, what was the outstanding balance of your loan before the last payment was made (to the nearest dollar)?
    1. $82,631
    2. $92,960
    3. $106,239
    4. None of these

66. You own a home valued at $146,000. Property in your area is assessed at 70% of its value, and the local tax rate is $2.84 per $100. What is the amount of your semiannual taxes?
    1. $241.87
    2. $1,451.24
    3. $2,902.48
    4. None of these

67. You bought a house one year ago for $172,900. Property in your neighborhood is said to be increasing at a rate of 5% annually. If this is true, what is the current market value of your real estate?
    1. $179,816
    2. $181,545
    3. $183,279
    4. None of these

68. You receive a monthly salary of $600 plus 2% commission on all of your listings that sell and 3% on all of your sales. None of the listings you took sold last month, but you received $7,940 in salary and commission. What was the value of the property you sold?
    1. $146,800
    2. $244,667
    3. $367,000
    4. None of these

69. An owner leases the 16 apartments in his building for a total monthly rental of $12,800. If this figure represents an 8% annual return on the owner's investment, what was the original cost of the property?
    1. $153,600
    2. $1,706,667
    3. $1,920,000
    4. $2,194,286

For the next two questions regarding closing statement prorations, base your calculations on a 30-day month. Carry all computations to three decimal places and round off after all computations have been made.

70. A sale is to be closed on March 14. Real estate taxes for the current year are $3,170 and have not been paid. What amount of the real estate tax proration will be credited to the buyer?
    1. $651.62
    2. $660.42
    3. $642.81
    4. None of these

71. In a sale of residential property, real estate taxes for the current year amounted to $2,840 and already have been paid by the seller. The sale is to be closed on December 3. What is the settlement sheet entry for the tax proration?
    1. $220.87 debit to seller; $220.87 credit to buyer
    2. $212.98 credit to seller; $212.98 debit to buyer
    3. $2,627.02 debit to seller; $205.09 credit to buyer
    4. $212.98 credit to seller only

72. Rita purchased a fee-simple interest in one of 40 units in a property development. Rita also received a 2% share of the ownership in all of the grounds and facilities outside the units. Rita owns which of the following types of property?
    1. Partnership
    2. Time-share
    3. Cooperative
    4. Condominium

73. Jessica borrowed from several banks to get into an investment she could not have financed on her own. This is an example of
   1. appreciation.
   2. leverage.
   3. equity buildup.
   4. pyramiding.

74. What is the actual value of your property if the annual taxes are $2,880 and real estate is assessed at 30% of actual value? (Figure a levy of 4.8%, or 48 mills, or $4.80 per 100.)
   1. $86,400
   2. $120,000
   3. $200,000
   4. None of these

75. Three investors decided to pool their savings and buy some commercial real estate for $180,000. If one invested $60,000 and the second invested $40,000, what percentage of ownership was left for the third investor, if the percentage is based on capital investment rather than services rendered?
   1. 22.2%
   2. 33%
   3. 44.4%
   4. None of these

76. Susan and Joe, a married couple, bought a principal residence in 1991 for $200,000. They sold the property in 1999 with a capital gain of $150,000. Capital gains tax on their profit will be
   1. nothing.
   2. $50,000.
   3. $150,000.
   4. $200,000.

77. If a buyer puts 20% down and borrows $200,000, what is the purchase price of her new home?
   1. $210,000
   2. $220,000
   3. $240,000
   4. $250,000

78. All of the following home-related expenses would generally be tax-deductible for a homeowner *EXCEPT*
   1. interest paid on a second mortgage.
   2. penalties for late payment of real estate taxes.
   3. prepayment penalties on loans.
   4. real estate taxes.

79. A 300-acre farm is divided into house lots. The streets require one-eighth of the whole farm, and there are 280 lots. How many square feet are in each lot?
   1. 38,115
   2. 40,838
   3. 46,671
   4. None of these

80. The process of reviewing the various approaches to value in order to arrive at a final estimate of market value is called
   1. assemblage.
   2. capitalization.
   3. balance.
   4. reconciliation.

ANSWER KEY: SALESPERSON EXAMINATION III

NOTE: The number in parentheses at the end of each explanation refers to the page number where this material is discussed.

1. **(3)** Chattels and trade fixtures are personal property. (21)

2. **(4)** Scarcity, situs, and performance of investment are economic characteristics. (21)

3. **(3)** Joint tenants do not have to be married. (27)

4. **(3)** An easement in gross does not have a dominant tenement; it has a servient tenement only. (24)

5. **(3)** An easement would have to be disclosed to a potential buyer but is unlikely to affect the transfer of title to the property. (24)

6. **(3)** Ricardo would have to give notice of the lien and then file a court suit within the time required by state law. (24)

7. **(2)** The easement held by the utility company is a commercial easement in gross. (24)

8. **(2)** In the leasehold estate known as a tenancy at will, a person continues occupancy of the real estate with the owner's permission. (28)

9. **(4)** Luke's interest will automatically go to Mario and Paula under the right of survivorship. (27)

10. **(1)** $4 \times 4 \times 4 = 64$

    640 acres ÷ 64 = 10 acres (22)

11. **(4)** Escheat is a state law that provides for ownership to transfer to the state when an owner dies intestate (without a will) leaving no heirs and no will. Police power is used to enact laws, such as zoning ordinances and building codes. Taxation on real estate is used to raise funds to meet the needs of the government. (25)

12. **(2)** A deed restriction is a private land-use control. In the event of a conflict between a zoning ordinance and a deed restriction, the more restrictive of the two takes precedence. (49–50)

13. **(4)** Zoning ordinances are not retroactive; Kevin's property was appropriately zoned when he developed it, thus he can continue to operate his building. (42)

14. **(4)** A conditional-use permit allows for a use specifically permitted. Here, a commercial use is desired in a residential zone, which is not permitted. (42)

15. **(2)** EMFs are suspected of causing cancer and related diseases. (48)

16. **(2)** Asbestos is used in insulation. Lead was used as an ingredient in oil-based paint. Urea-formaldehyde was used primarily in building insulation. (46–47)

17. **(3)** Water rights are discussed in Chapter 4. Littoral rights are granted to owners along a large lake or ocean. (23)

18. **(1)** The principle of competition states that excess profits create ruinous competition. (59)

19. **(2)** Functional obsolescence is a loss in value due to a deficiency in the floor plan or design of a house. One bathroom in a four-bedroom home is inadequate and, therefore, functionally obsolescent. (63)

20. **(3)** The cost approach is the most applicable to the appraisal of a special-purpose property, such as a school. The income approach is most reliable for income-producing property. The gross income multiplier also is used in appraising income property. (60–61)

21. **(2)** Annual net operating income is calculated by subtracting annual operating expenses from effective gross income. Annual net operating income is then capitalized to arrive at an estimate. (61)

22. **(4)** Zoning also could be a governmental factor. (62)

23. **(3)** Plottage is the additional value created by assembling parcels of land to create a higher and better use. (64)

24. **(1)** Deposits in commercial banks are insured by the FDIC. (75)

25. **(3)** Special assistance programs are administered by GNMA. (76)

26. **(4)** The Federal Deposit Insurance Corporation provides insurance for up to $250,000 per depositor. (75)

27. **(2)** Mortgage brokers generally originate loans for other lenders; they do not use their own money. (75)

28. **(3)** Mortgages are released by a satisfaction or release of mortgage documents; an acceleration clause is used in a mortgage to deal with default on the part of the borrower. (78)

29. **(3)** $200,000 ÷ 1,000 = 200 × 10.45 = $2,090 (191)

30. **(1)** $2,090 × 180 months = $376,200 – $200,000 = $176,200, total interest paid on the life of the loan (191)

31. **(2)** A package mortgage includes both real and personal property, such as a loan to purchase a motel. (83)

32. **(2)** Truth-in-Lending regulates real estate ads relating to mortgage financing terms. Specific credit terms, such as down payment, are referred to as "trigger" terms and may not be advertised unless the ad includes five categories of information, including cash price and required down payment. (79)

33. **(3)** The Federal Reserve controls reserve requirements of member banks as part of its monetary policy authority. (75)

34. **(4)** The relationship is known as special agency. (92)

35. **(4)** Phil is a special agent responsible for finding a buyer for the seller's property. (92)

36. **(4)** Young represents the buyer as an agent. According to the National Association of REALTORS®, Young cannot represent the seller if he works for a different real estate company. The reason is because the offering of subagency to an outside firm places a menacing contingent liability on the cooperating broker. (92)

37. **(1)** $180,000 × .06 = $10,800 (182)

38. **(2)** The listing broker has a fiduciary relationship with the seller, including loyalty. A buyer-agency relationship would not affect the listing broker's loyalty to the seller. (91)

39. **(4)** An individual broker can react negatively to another broker; this is not a violation of the antitrust law. (172)

40. **(1)** $206,000 sales price × 7% (0.07) commission = $14,420 broker commission

$14,420 × 55% (0.55) = $7,931

$7,931 × 0.50 = $3,966. (182)

41. **(1)** A latent defect is a structural defect that may not be discovered by an ordinary inspection. (105)

42. **(4)** The risks of dual agency have resulted in the practice being illegal in some states. Disclosure alerts the parties that they may have to assume greater responsibility for protecting their interests than would be the case if they had agents representing only their own interests. (92–93)

43. **(2)** Material facts refer to relevant information that the seller's agent knows or should be aware of and communicated to the seller. Obviously, the seller's agent has a fiduciary duty to present all offers. The buyer's agent is concerned about disclosing the property's deficiencies and how long it has been on the market. (94–95)

44. **(3)** Phillip did not have the mental capacity to be bound by the terms of a binding contract; thus, he may disaffirm it if he wishes. Phillip has a voidable contract. (118)

45. **(2)** The salesperson is not a party to the listing contract. (119)

46. **(4)** In an executory contract, something remains to be done by one or both parties. (117)

47. **(3)** Selena receives equitable title and will receive legal title at closing. (120)

48. **(2)** According to the statute of frauds, certain contracts must be in writing to be enforceable by the courts. (120)

49. **(3)** The option becomes a bilateral contract if the optionee chooses to exercise the option right. (121–122)

50. **(1)** The addendum adds additional language to offers. The counteroffer and multiple counteroffer can only modify language prior to the offer becoming a binding contract on all parties. (122)

51. **(4)** A quitclaim deed contains no warranties; the grantor simply quits or releases any claim she has against the property. (152)

52. **(3)** The covenant of seisin also promises that the grantor has possession. (152)

53. **(3)** The grantee has to be identified but does not have to sign the deed for it to be valid. (153)

54. **(1)** In abstract states, the abstract is brought up to date, and an attorney renders an opinion to the buyer about the quality of the seller's title. In title insurance states, the title company does an internal search. (151)

55. **(3)** A married couple may exclude up to $500,000 from capital gains on the sale of their principal residence if they file jointly. The couple must have occupied the property as their residence for at least two of the past five years. (154)

56. **(2)** Referral fee would take the form of anything of value for services, such as mortgage loans or title insurance. (80)

57. **(3)** Mentally ill people do not have to be currently receiving treatment to be protected under the law. However, they would have to file their complaint within the one-year period to be protected under the law. (164–165)

58. **(4)** Sexual orientation is not a protected class under the Federal Fair Housing Act. (164–165)

59. **(2)** Convicted drug dealers are not protected under the federal fair housing laws under any condition. (164)

60. **(1)** Truth-in-Lending requires full disclosure of the true cost of financing, including the annual percentage rate (APR) before the completion of a transaction. (79–80)

61. **(4)** The rental of an owner-occupied apartment building of four units or less is exempt from the Federal Fair Housing Act. (166)

62. **(3)** The statute of frauds is a law that requires certain contracts to be in writing in order to be enforceable. (79)

63. **(2)** $154,000 × 6% (0.06) commission = $9,240 broker's commission

    $9,240 × 30% (0.30) = $2,772 (182)

64. **(3)** $9,600 ÷ $160,000 = .06 or 6%

    1 point equals 1% of the loan amount

    6% = 6 points (186)

65. **(1)** $619.73 × 12 = $7,436.76 annual interest

    $\frac{\text{part}}{\text{percent}} = \text{total}$

    $7,436.76 ÷ 9% (0.09) = $82,630.67, rounds to $82,631 (191)

66. **(2)** $146,000 × 70% (0.70) = $102,200 assessed value

    Divide by 100, because tax rate is stated per $100

    $102,200 ÷ 100 = $1,022

    $1,022 × $2.84 = $2,902.48 annual taxes

    Divide by 2 to get semiannual taxes

    $2,902.48 ÷ 2 = $1,451.24 (183)

67. **(2)** $172,900 × 5% (0.05) = $8,645 annual increase in value

    $172,900 + $8,645 = $181,545 current market value (182)

68. **(2)** $7,940 – $600 salary = $7,340 commission sales

    $7,340 ÷ 3% (0.03) = $244,667 value of property sold (182)

69. **(3)** $12,800 × 12 = $153,600 annual return

    $153,600 ÷ 8% (0.08) = $1,920,000 original cost of property (181)

70. **(1)** $3,170 ÷ 12 months = $264.166 per month

    $264.166 ÷ 30 days = $8.806 per day

    $264.166 × 2 months = $528.332

    $8.806 × 14 days = $123.284

    $528.332 + 123.284 = $651.616, rounds to $651.62 (187)

71. **(2)** $2,840 ÷ 12 months = $236.666 per month

    $236.666 ÷ 30 days = $7.888 per day

    $7.888 × 27 days = $212.976, rounds to $212.98

    The taxes have been paid. The seller is entitled to a refund for 27 days. He, therefore, will receive a credit, and the buyer will be charged (debited) for the same amount. (187)

72. **(4)** An owner of a condominium unit holds fee-simple title to the unit and a specified share (as a tenant in common) in the common elements. (28)

73. **(2)** Leverage is using borrowed money to finance an investment. The amount of leverage used by an investor is in direct proportion to the risk. (83)

74. **(3)** $2,880 ÷ 0.048 = $60,000, assessed value

    $60,000 ÷ 30% (0.30) = $200,000, market value (181)

75. **(3)** \$60,000 first investor + \$40,000 second investor = \$100,000

\$180,000 – \$100,000 = \$80,000, third investor's contribution

part ÷ total = percent

\$80,000 ÷ \$180,000 = 44.4% (181)

76. **(1)** A married couple may exclude \$500,000 from capital gains tax for profits on the sale of a principal residence if they file jointly. (154)

77. **(4)** 200,000 divided by 80% = \$250,000 (181)

78. **(2)** Real estate taxes, but not penalties for late payments of taxes, are deductible. (154)

79. **(2)** 43,560 square feet per acre × 300 acres = 13,068,000 square feet

13,068,000 square feet × (0.125) = 1,633,500 square feet for streets

13,068,000 – 1,633,500 = 11,434,400 sq. ft. for lots

11,434,500 square feet ÷ 280 lots = 40,838 square feet per lot (181)

80. **(4)** Reconciliation is the next-to-last step in the appraisal process. (62)

CHAPTER 15

Broker Examinations

The PSI broker examination, like the salesperson exam, consists of two parts: (1) a national exam, and (2) a state exam.

The national portion of the broker examination contains questions that closely resemble the national salesperson exam in that both exams cover the same categories. The differences between the two exams involve slight variations in weighing of categories, math, and brokerage management. The subject area and number of questions in each area varies from state to state.

The two sample broker examinations that follow evaluate your general real estate knowledge and your test taking ability.

BROKER EXAMINATION I

1. Which of the following would be considered real property?
   1. A leasehold estate
   2. Fixtures
   3. Chattels
   4. Trade fixtures

2. Your uncle died without a will, and you inherited his real estate. The way in which you would acquire his estate is by
   1. accession.
   2. the statute of descent and distribution.
   3. escheat.
   4. novation.

3. A man receives possession of property under a deed that states that he will own the property as long as the present building standing on the property is not torn down. The type of estate the man holds is which of the following?
   1. Life estate
   2. Nondestructible estate
   3. Fee-simple estate
   4. Determinable fee estate

4. You would like to hire more than one broker to sell your house and be able to sell the house yourself without paying a commission to a broker. Which of the following listing agreements should you choose?
   1. Net
   2. Open
   3. Exclusive agency
   4. Exclusive-right-to-sell

5. Which of the following is responsible for investigating and prosecuting violations of federal fair housing laws?
   1. National Association of REALTORS® (NAR)
   2. Equal Employment Opportunity Commission (EEOC)
   3. Department of Housing and Urban Development (HUD)
   4. Association of Real Estate License Law Officials (ARELLO)

6. You have been making constant payments of $653.00 per month on your mortgage. The balance after your last payment was $80,300. The interest rate on your mortgage is 8%. What will the balance of your mortgage be after your next payment?
   1. $79,647.00
   2. $80,067.32
   3. $80,182.33
   4. $80,300.00

7. Using the mortgage factor of 6.65, what is the monthly payment for $121,000 at 7% for 30 years?
   1. $733.19
   2. $804.65
   3. $816.75
   4. $847.00

8. Using the numbers in the previous question, what is the total interest paid over the life of the loan?
   1. $166,709.23
   2. $167,514.74
   3. $168,319.46
   4. $168,674.00

9. Which of the following statements correctly identifies a defining characteristic of conventional mortgages?
   1. They are assumable.
   2. There is no down payment.
   3. They are guaranteed by the federal government.
   4. Their interest rates are set by the lender.

10. A home valued at $92,000 is assessed at 70% of its value and is taxed at a rate of $3.40 per $100. What are the semiannual taxes on this property?
    1. $1,094.80
    2. $1,564.80
    3. $2,189.60
    4. None of these

11. A broker has been showing homes to some prospects. The prospects have learned of a home for sale by its owner, which they are interested in visiting. The broker calls the owner to arrange a showing, although the owner will not list with the broker. The broker shows the home and writes the offer to purchase, which is accepted by the owner. Which of the following statements correctly describes this situation?
    1. The owner is legally bound to pay the broker a commission.
    2. The prospects are responsible for paying a commission to the broker.
    3. The owner and the prospects are legally bound to pay a commission to the broker.
    4. Neither the owner nor the prospects are legally bound to pay a commission to the broker.

12. A veteran wishes to receive a loan for $70,000 to buy a home. The home has been appraised by the VA at $68,000. Which of the following statements *MOST* accurately describes the veteran's situation?
    1. The veteran may buy the home with a VA loan only if he is able to lower the price to $68,000.
    2. The veteran may buy the home with a VA loan if the seller agrees to hold a second mortgage of $2,000.
    3. The veteran may buy the home with a VA loan if he makes a down payment of $2,000.
    4. The veteran may not buy the home.

13. You are paying interest only on a $75,000 mortgage for three years after which the entire loan is due. This is called a(n)
    1. amortized mortgage.
    2. graduated payment mortgage.
    3. purchase-money mortgage.
    4. term mortgage.

14. A farmer is unable to pay the county taxes on his farm. The delinquent taxes would be considered
    1. a lien.
    2. an attachment.
    3. an easement.
    4. an appurtenance.

15. A licensee's relative asks the licensee for information about one of the licensee's listings. After reviewing it, the relative arranges to see the property with the licensee. Two weeks later, the relative submitted an offer through another agency on the licensee's listing. Which of the following statements about this situation is correct?
    1. The listing licensee should disclose the family relationship with the buyer to the seller.
    2. The selling licensee should refuse to continue with the transaction if the buyer mentions the listing licensee's family status.
    3. The buyer has breached an express agency relationship with the listing licensee and must resubmit the offer using the listing licensee.
    4. The listing licensee is entitled to a portion of the selling licensee's compensation for having introduced the buyer to the property.

16. A retired woman owns her home free and clear and is looking for a mortgage that would provide her with monthly payments until she dies. This type of mortgage is called a
    1. guaranteed payment mortgage.
    2. blanket mortgage.
    3. participation mortgage.
    4. reverse mortgage.

17. A man leased a store with the agreement that he would pay a fixed rent and the landlord would pay all operating expenses. This is an example of a
    1. gross lease.
    2. graduated lease.
    3. net lease.
    4. percentage lease.

18. You have entered into a land contract for the sale of your home. All of the following statements are true *EXCEPT*
    1. the seller is the vendor.
    2. the buyer is the vendee.
    3. the seller will hold legal title during the term of the contract.
    4. the seller will retain possession during the term of the contract.

19. Which of the following terms identifies the practice of charging loan interest rates in excess of the maximum allowed by law?
    1. Usury
    2. Leverage
    3. Arbitrage
    4. Novation

20. Which of the following statements correctly describes the way in which a listing broker should represent her client?
    1. The listing broker can tell a prospective buyer the lowest price her client will accept.
    2. The listing broker may choose which offers to present to her client.
    3. The listing broker with two offers may hold back on presenting the second offer until her client has responded to the first offer.
    4. The listing broker must present all offers to her client promptly when received.

21. Which of the following is true as it relates to an easement appurtenant?
    1. This easement may be acquired by prescription only.
    2. The easement right cannot be terminated.
    3. The dominant tenement owner pays taxes only on the dominant estate.
    4. The easement right reverts to the owner of the servient estate on the death of the owner of the dominant estate.

22. Andy died and left a will that transferred one-half of his 36-unit apartment building to his wife, one-fourth to his son, and one-fourth to his daughter. The devisees will be holding title as
    1. tenants in common.
    2. tenants by the entirety.
    3. joint tenants.
    4. tenants at will.

23. A licensee has entered into a written buyer-broker agreement with a client whereby the licensee will be compensated if the client buys a property of the type described in the agreement within the agreement period, regardless of whether the licensee located the property for the buyer. This type of agreement is known as
    1. dual agency.
    2. open-buyer agency.
    3. exclusive-buyer agency.
    4. exclusive-agency buyer agency.

24. A mortgage is all of the following *EXCEPT*
    1. an encumbrance.
    2. a lien on real property.
    3. a recordable legal document.
    4. an example of involuntary alienation.

25. Three investors decided to pool their savings and buy an office building for $200,000. If one invested $70,000 and the second contributed $40,000, what percentage of ownership was left for the third investor?
    1. 20%
    2. 35%
    3. 45%
    4. None of these

26. A broker is selling a home for $85,900. The owner tells the broker that the roof needs repair, the basement leaks, and the house is a nonconforming use and that she will accept an offer well below $85,900. The broker now is negotiating with a prospect for the sale of the home. The broker should *NOT* tell the prospect that the
    1. roof needs repair.
    2. basement leaks.
    3. house is a nonconforming use.
    4. seller will accept an offer well below $85,900.

27. You listed a home for sale under an exclusive-right-to-sell agreement and showed the property to a person who wrote an offer with an earnest money check that was subsequently rejected by the owner. What should happen to the earnest money check?
    1. It should be deposited into the broker's trust account.
    2. It should just be returned to the buyer.
    3. It should be returned to the buyer only after the seller signs a release form.
    4. It should be given to the seller.

28. An investor finds that the cost of installing an air-conditioning system in an office building is greater than is justified by the rental increase that might result from the improvement of the property. However, the investor installs the air-conditioning to avoid having tenants move to comparable office space nearby that is air-conditioned. The investor's decision is *MOST* reflective of the principle of
    1. anticipation.
    2. competition.
    3. contribution.
    4. highest and best use.

29. Aubrey loaned money to her sister, and in return, took a mortgage as security for the debt. She immediately recorded the mortgage. Thereafter, Benjamin loaned money to the same sister, took a mortgage, and recorded it. The sister later defaulted, and a court determined that Benjamin's interest had priority over Aubrey's interest. Under these circumstances, chances are that
    1. Aubrey knew Benjamin was going to make a loan before Aubrey made her own loan.
    2. Benjamin's loan was larger than Aubrey's loan.
    3. Aubrey had signed a subordination agreement in favor of Benjamin.
    4. Benjamin had signed a satisfaction.

30. A sale closed on July 29. Real estate taxes of $2,380 for the current year have not been paid. What is the settlement sheet entry for the proration of real estate taxes?
    1. Credit seller $1,381.70; debit buyer $1,381.70
    2. Debit seller $998.30; credit buyer $1,381.70
    3. Debit seller $1,381.70; credit buyer $1,381.70
    4. Debit buyer $00.00; credit seller $2,380.00

31. You receive a monthly salary of $600 plus 3% commission on all your listings that sell and 3.5% on all of your sales. None of the listings that you took sold last month, but you received $4,100 in salary and commission. What was the value of the property you sold?
    1. $100,000
    2. $116,666
    3. $117,142
    4. None of these

32. A broker has been asked to serve as an agent of a friend who wishes to sell his home. Prior to listing the friend's home, the broker is asked by another friend to serve as her agent in finding a home. Relatives of the two friends also have asked the broker to serve as their agent in helping them find homes. Which of the following statements is correct?
    1. The broker is not allowed to work with the relatives, because he would have a conflict of interest.
    2. The broker may not serve as agent to the various parties unless he gets permission from all of the parties.
    3. The broker may serve only as an agent of the seller.
    4. The broker may serve as agent for any of the buyers and sellers.

33. Which of the following types of depreciation is incurable?
    1. A leaky roof
    2. A worn-out water heater
    3. A zoning variance of the neighbor's property for commercial use
    4. Warped doors

34. You have listed a property. The seller told you that he must net at least $14,000 after all fees and expenses are paid. You estimate the seller's closing cost to be $3,500, and he must pay off an existing loan of $108,750. In addition, you are going to charge 7% commission on the sale. What is the *LEAST* amount that the property can sell for to return the seller's desired net?
    1. $126,250
    2. $134,310
    3. $135,088
    4. $135,752.69

35. Which approach to value is an appraiser *MOST* likely to emphasize in the appraisal of a single-family home?
    1. Cost approach
    2. Gross income multiplier approach
    3. Income capitalization approach
    4. Sales comparison approach

36. All of the following statements correctly describe joint tenancy *EXCEPT*
    1. it is a form of co-ownership.
    2. owners have the right of survivorship.
    3. owners must be husband and wife.
    4. owners may partition the property.

37. All of the following statements correctly describe radon gas *EXCEPT*
    1. as radon is released from the rocks, it finds its way to the surface and usually is released into the atmosphere.
    2. radon enters a house through the roof vents.
    3. radon can become concentrated in the crawlspace.
    4. long-term exposure to radon gas is said to cause lung cancer.

38. Strict liability under Superfund means that
    1. each individual owner is personally responsible for the damages in whole.
    2. the owner is responsible to the injured party without excuse.
    3. the liability is not limited to the person who currently owns the property but also includes people who have owned the site in the past.
    4. anyone who has been involved in the transaction will be liable for damages.

39. Which of the following may *NOT* be governed by deed restrictions?
    1. Height of a building
    2. Ethnicity of tenants
    3. Use of a residence as a business
    4. Types of pets that can be housed within the subdivision

40. All of the following would be a protected class under the Federal Equal Credit Opportunity Act *EXCEPT*
    1. race.
    2. marital status.
    3. sexual orientation.
    4. dependence on public assistance.

41. The rent on a house is $400 a month, or $4,800 a year, and the house recently sold for $52,000. The gross rent multiplier on the house was
    1. 10.8.
    2. 108.
    3. 130.
    4. 130.8.

42. The rate of return an investor will require to invest in real estate is called a(n)
    1. gross rent multiplier.
    2. gross income multiplier.
    3. capitalization rate.
    4. assemblage.

43. The principle of combining contiguous property, and, by doing so, increasing the value of the new property, is called the principle of
    1. highest and best use.
    2. substitution.
    3. contribution.
    4. plottage.

44. All of the following statements correctly describe the independent-contractor relationship *EXCEPT*
   1. the salesperson contracts with a broker to produce specific outcomes, such as commission.
   2. the broker may not tell salespeople how to sell real estate.
   3. the broker must provide a pension plan.
   4. the salesperson must pay his or her board dues.

45. A salesperson works for a broker. The salesperson may
   1. work for the broker as an independent contractor.
   2. place an ad without identifying the broker.
   3. receive a commission directly from a seller.
   4. receive a commission directly from another broker.

46. A broker has listed a home. The broker is generally considered to have earned her commission when
   1. she submits an offer to purchase to the seller.
   2. the seller indicates that he thinks an offer to purchase is acceptable.
   3. she finds a "buyer ready, willing, and able" to buy on the terms of the listing.
   4. the closing takes place.

47. A Hispanic buyer has asked a broker to show her homes in a white neighborhood. The broker's response to the buyer should be
   1. "I think you would be happier in a neighborhood with people of similar background."
   2. "I don't think you would be comfortable with the people in that neighborhood, because they do not welcome outsiders."
   3. "I'll be happy to show you homes in that neighborhood, but I think you could do better than that."
   4. "I'll be happy to show you homes in that neighborhood or any other neighborhood."

48. During a listing presentation, the seller tells the broker that she will not sell to Caucasians. Should the broker follow the seller's instructions?
   1. Yes. The owner has a right to choose prospective buyers.
   2. Yes. The broker is the seller's agent and must honor his fiduciary responsibility.
   3. No. The broker might lose any commission by limiting potential buyers.
   4. No. The broker should not accept the listing.

49. You are preparing a competitive market analysis (CMA) on a two-story, three-bedroom house with one bathroom on the first floor and all of the bedrooms on the second floor. The appraisal term that *BEST* identifies how this affects the list price is
   1. physical deterioration.
   2. deferred maintenance.
   3. functional obsolescence.
   4. economic obsolescence.

50. All of the following are examples of real property *EXCEPT*
   1. a neighbor's strawberry bush.
   2. percolating water.
   3. unexcavated clay.
   4. the clay bricks that you will use to build your patio wall.

51. A listing broker acting as a single agent in the course of selling the property would be in violation of the broker's fiduciary duties to the seller by
   1. telling a prospective buyer the lowest price the seller will accept below the list price.
   2. paying for a property appraisal during the course of helping the owner set the list price.
   3. accepting a commission that is lower than usual for marketing similar properties in the area.
   4. allowing prospective buyers to prepare and submit offers through buyer-brokers instead of subagents of the seller.

52. A correct statement about a competitive market analysis (CMA) is that it
    1. must be performed by a licensed appraiser.
    2. must be reviewed by an employing broker in order to be valid.
    3. is based on the sales comparison (market data) approach to value.
    4. will develop a final assessment of value by averaging three bank appraisals.

53. A man wants to know how much money he owes on his mortgage loan. He knows that the interest part of the last monthly payment was $608.52. If he was paying interest at the rate of 10%, what was the outstanding balance of his loan before that last payment was made?
    1. $60,852.20
    2. $66,937.20
    3. $73,022.40
    4. $77,942.26

54. Your aunt bought her house one year ago for $62,400. Property in her neighborhood is said to be increasing at a rate of 7% annually. If this is true, what is the current market value of your aunt's real estate?
    1. $65,520
    2. $66,144
    3. $66,768
    4. $66,971

55. Your home is valued at $104,000. Property in your city is assessed at 70% of its value, and the local tax rate is $3.35 per $100. What is the amount of your monthly taxes?
    1. $192.86
    2. $203.23
    3. $290.33
    4. $331.64

56. In the cost approach, an appraiser makes use of which of the following?
    1. Sales prices of similar properties
    2. The owner's original cost of construction
    3. An estimate of the building's replacement cost
    4. Multiplying the net income by the capitalization rate

57. An appraisal of a church probably would be based on the
    1. sales comparison approach.
    2. cost approach.
    3. income approach.
    4. capitalization approach.

58. With an FHA loan, the buyer will be required to do all of the following *EXCEPT*
    1. pay a 20% down payment.
    2. find an approved lender willing to make the loan.
    3. buy a house that meets minimum FHA safety standards.
    4. buy mortgage insurance to protect the lender.

59. Which of the following statements regarding points is *TRUE*?
    1. Points must be charged to the seller.
    2. One point equals 1% of the loan.
    3. Points must be charged to the buyer.
    4. One point equals .25% of the loan.

60. Smith, who works for broker Romero on a 50-50 basis, sold a house listed by broker Xiang for $167,750. The seller agreed to pay a 7% commission, but stipulated in the listing that 65% was to go to the selling broker. How much commission will Smith make on the sale (to the nearest dollar)?
    1. $2,054
    2. $3,816
    3. $4,110
    4. $7,633

61. Which of the following terms could be found in a lease or a mortgage?
    1. Escalation clause
    2. Alienation clause
    3. Subjugation clause
    4. Redemption clause

62. The discriminatory practice of guiding ethnic minorities toward available housing in neighborhoods made up of residents of the same ethnic group is referred to as
    1. puffing.
    2. steering.
    3. redlining.
    4. blockbusting.

63. All of the following statements apply to both purchase money mortgages and land contracts *EXCEPT*
    1. the seller is financing the transaction.
    2. the buyer takes possession when the contract is executed.
    3. the buyer gives the seller a down payment.
    4. the buyer has equitable title during the life of the contract.

64. Which of the following is covered by Truth-in-Lending?
    1. A personal property credit transaction for $20,000
    2. A loan with three installments
    3. A real estate purchase agreement
    4. An agricultural loan for $29,000

65. Which of the following is exempted from the Federal Fair Housing Act?
    1. The rental of rooms in an owner-occupied, four-family dwelling
    2. The rental of rooms in an owner-occupied, five-family dwelling
    3. The rental of a single-family home when a broker is used
    4. The lodgings of a private club when the lodgings are operated commercially

66. You purchased a residence and neither took possession nor recorded the deed. Which of the following statements *BEST* describes the status of your property ownership?
    1. You have given actual notice of ownership.
    2. You do not have a valid deed from the previous owner.
    3. You have not provided constructive notice of ownership.
    4. You will have to go to court to assert your ownership rights prior to reselling the property.

67. The relationship of the listing broker to the seller who hired him or her is that of a(n)
    1. attorney-in-fact.
    2. strawman.
    3. trustee.
    4. fiduciary.

68. Which of the following would *NOT* be deposited in your trust account?
    1. The commission you earn on a transaction
    2. Earnest money received on a transaction
    3. The down payment for a land contract transaction
    4. An amount sufficient to cover the bank service charges on the account

69. In order to represent legally all parties in the same real estate transaction, a licensee must
    1. hold a securities license.
    2. agree to receive compensation from only one of the principals.
    3. ensure that all documents that the licensee signs are notarized.
    4. obtain the informed consent to dual agency from all principals.

70. You are working as an agent for a prospective buyer. The buyer buys a house listed on the multiple-listing service (MLS) of which you are a member. All of the following statements correctly describe the situation *EXCEPT*
    1. you acted as a disclosed dual agent.
    2. you will be entitled to a commission from the buyer.
    3. you could be paid by the seller if the parties agree.
    4. the listing broker is an agent of the seller.

71. Tenancy in common is distinguished by which of the following characteristics?
    1. The co-owners have right of survivorship.
    2. Ownership interests must be equal.
    3. A co-owner cannot will his or her interest in a property.
    4. Each co-owner's interest may be conveyed separately.

72. A plumbing company installed a new furnace and filed a lien for nonpayment immediately on completion. This was *MOST* likely a
    1. voluntary lien.
    2. general lien.
    3. novation.
    4. specific lien.

73. All of the following are examples of functional obsolescence *EXCEPT*
   1. a five-bedroom house with one bathroom.
   2. outdated plumbing fixtures.
   3. a roof that leaks.
   4. a poor floor plan.

74. A broker listed and sold a seller's home. The broker *MOST* likely earned her commission when
   1. the transaction was closed.
   2. she found a buyer "ready, willing, and able" to buy on the terms of the listing.
   3. the buyer's financing contingency was removed from the offer to purchase.
   4. the buyer's check cleared the bank after closing.

75. A salesperson has taken a four-month exclusive-right-to-sell listing on a house. Prior to the expiration of the listing, the salesperson leaves the state and inactivates her license. Which of the following correctly describes the status of the listing?
   1. The listing automatically terminates when the salesperson leaves the state and inactivates her license.
   2. The seller may terminate the listing once the salesperson has left the state.
   3. The broker will have to negotiate with the seller to retain the listing.
   4. The listing will continue as a valid contract between the seller and the broker.

76. A parcel of property that measures 1/8 mile by 1/8 mile is equal to
   1. 10 acres.
   2. 40 acres.
   3. 160 acres.
   4. 320 acres.

77. All of the following are advantages of an FHA-insured loan *EXCEPT*
   1. low down payment.
   2. buyer protection with FHA insurance.
   3. enables cash-short buyers to enter real estate market.
   4. protects lender with FHA insurance.

78. Which of the following is *NOT* a legal requirement of an option?
   1. A purchase price and how it will be determined
   2. Consideration
   3. The date on which the option will expire
   4. The exercise of the option by the optionee

79. A man hauls his heavy equipment across the land of a neighbor each day for 20 years without the permission of the neighbor.
   1. He has encroached on his neighbor's land.
   2. He has a license.
   3. He has an easement appurtenant.
   4. He has an easement in gross.
   5. He has an easement by necessity.

80. An estate in real property often described as being a potentially perpetual estate is
   1. a fee simple estate.
   2. a base fee estate.
   3. a freehold estate.
   4. a fee simple defeasible.

ANSWER KEY: BROKER EXAMINATION I

NOTE: The number in parentheses at the end of each explanation refers to the page number where this material is discussed.

1. **(2)** A leasehold estate, chattels, and trade fixtures are classified as personal property. (21)

2. **(2)** When persons die intestate, their real estate and personal property pass on to their heirs according to statute. (30)

3. **(4)** The words *as long as* are key to the creation of a determinable fee, sometimes referred to as a qualified fee, conditional fee, or base-fee estate. (25)

4. **(2)** Under an open listing, if the seller personally sells the property without the aid of any broker, the seller is not obligated to pay the commission. (119)

5. **(3)** NAR is the REALTOR® trade association. EEOC deals with discrimination in employment, while ARELLO works with license law issues. (164)

6. **(3)** \$80,300 × .08 = \$6,424 annual interest

   \$6,424 ÷ 12 = \$535.33 interest for one month

   \$653.00 P&I – \$535.33 = \$117.67 principal payoff

   \$80,300 – \$117.67 = \$80,182.33 balance after next payment (191–192)

7. **(2)** \$804.65 (\$121,000 × 6.65) (191–192)

8. **(4)** \$804.65 × 360 months = \$289,674

   \$289,674 total P&I
   –121,000 loan
   \$168,674 total interest (191–192)

9. **(4)** A conventional mortgage is neither insured nor guaranteed by the government. A down payment generally is higher than with insured and guaranteed loans. (74)

10. **(1)** \$92,000 × 70% (0.70) = \$64,400, assessed value ÷ 100 = \$644

    \$644 × \$3.40 = \$2,189.60 annual tax

    Divide by 2 to get the semiannual tax

    \$2,189.60 ÷ 2 = \$1,094.80 (183–184)

11. **(4)** The broker is not entitled to a commission, because he had no contractual agreement with the buyer or the seller. (91)

12. **(3)** The loan amount cannot exceed the VA appraisal on a VA loan. The veteran must pay the difference between the appraised value and the purchase price in cash. (77)

13. **(4)** Payments on an amortized mortgage include principal and interest. A purchase-money mortgage involves seller financing. A graduated payment mortgage has low initial payments that increase over time. (74)

14. **(1)** Attachment refers to the act of taking a person's property into legal custody or placing a lien thereon by court or judicial order to hold it available for application to that person's debt to a creditor. An easement is the right to use the land of another for a specific purpose. An appurtenance is a right, privilege, or improvement that belongs to, and passes with, the transfer of the property but is not necessarily a part of the real property. (23)

15. **(1)** The relationship of the buyer to the listing licensee is of no concern to the selling licensee. Showing a property to

a customer does not create an express agency. Introducing the property to the buyer does not necessarily entitle the listing licensee to a portion of the selling licensee's compensation. (93)

16. **(4)** A reverse mortgage becomes due on a specific date, the sale of the property, or the death of the borrower. (74)

17. **(1)** A graduated lease provides for rent increase at set future dates, while a percentage lease provides for minimum fixed rent plus a percentage of the business income. Under a net lease, the tenant pays rent plus all or part of the property charges. (135)

18. **(4)** The vendee (buyer) takes possession when the contract is executed. (122)

19. **(1)** Leverage is using other people's money to finance an investment. Arbitrage refers to buying and selling credit instruments to profit from differences in prices. Novation occurs when a new obligation is substituted for an old one. (80)

20. **(4)** The listing broker is required to prepare, as well as submit, all offers unless otherwise instructed. The broker does not have the authority to accept or reject those offers for the seller. (94–95)

21. **(3)** The dominant tenement owner may terminate the easement right but does not pay the real estate taxes on the servient tenement. The dominant tenement owner may acquire his or her rights under an easement appurtenant by means other than by prescription. (24)

22. **(1)** Tenants by the entirety must be husband and wife. Joint tenancy requires the interest to be equal. (26)

23. **(3)** For a review of buyer brokerage agreements, see Chapter 7. (119–120)

24. **(4)** A mortgage is a voluntary act, not involuntary. (24)

25. **(3)** \$70,000 (first investor) + \$40,000 (second investor) = \$110,000

    \$200,000 × \$110,000 = \$90,000, third investor's contribution

    $$\frac{\text{part}}{\text{total}} = \text{total}$$

    \$90,000 ÷ \$200,000 = 0.45, or 45% (182)

26. **(4)** The broker is responsible for disclosing physical defects in the house, but to disclose that the seller would take less than the list price would be a violation of the broker's fiduciary responsibilities to the seller. (94–95)

27. **(2)** The offer was not accepted and therefore not ratified. The earnest money was returned before it was even deposited into the broker's trust account. (94)

28. **(2)** If the air-conditioning system is installed because of saleability, it would be contribution. In this case, the installation was due to the market availability of air-conditioned space. (59)

29. **(3)** Neither Aubrey's knowledge of Benjamin's making a loan nor the size of such a loan would affect the priority of claims. The court could not rule in favor of Benjamin if Benjamin had signed a satisfaction. A subordination clause is a clause in which the mortgagee (Aubrey) permits a subsequent mortgage (Benjamin's loan) to take priority. (82)

30. **(3)** \$2,380 ÷ 12 months = \$198.333 per month. 2,380/ 360 = 6.611

    \$198.33 ÷ 30 days = \$6.611 per day

    \$198.33 × 6 months = \$1,189.98

    \$6.611 × 29 days = \$197.719

    \$1,189.88 + \$191.719 = \$1,381.699 or \$1,381.70

The taxes for the year have not been paid, and when they are, the buyer will be in possession and have to pay the bill. The seller, therefore, must pay (be debited) for the portion of the year that he occupied the property. The buyer receives a credit for the same amount. (187–189)

31. **(1)** $4,100 – $600 salary = $3,500, commission sales

$3,500 ÷ 3.5% (0.035) = $100,000 value of property sold (181)

32. **(4)** The broker may serve as an agent of the seller or any of the buyers. The broker could even represent a buyer and a seller in the same transaction, provided that he or she had the knowledge and consent of all parties involved. (95–96)

33. **(3)** A zoning variance for commercial use is economic or locational obsolescence, which would be incurable. (61)

34. **(4)** Start by adding the desired net $14,000 plus existing loan payoff of $108,750 and closing costs of $3,500 = $126,250, which is the minimum that the seller must receive. If the selling price is 100%, the commission is 7% and the net to the seller is 93%.

$126,250 is 93% of the selling price.

Therefore, $126,250 ÷ 93% (0.93) = selling price of $135,752.69. (181)

35. **(4)** The sales comparison approach is considered the most reliable of the three approaches in appraising residential property. (61)

36. **(3)** The owners must be husband and wife in tenancy by the entirety. (27)

37. **(2)** Radon generally enters the house through the basement foundation as well as through the crawlspace. (46)

38. **(2)** Liability under the Superfund is also considered to be retroactive, meaning that the liability is not limited to the current owner but includes previous owners of the site. (44)

39. **(2)** Deed restrictions (private land-use controls) may not be used to discriminate against members of protected classes; they may be terminated by a quitclaim deed executed by the necessary parties. (49–50)

40. **(3)** The Federal Equal Credit Opportunity Act does not protect people on the basis of sexual orientation. (167)

41. **(3)** The gross rent multiplier (GRM) relates to *monthly* income, not annual.

$52,000 sale price ÷ $400 monthly rent = 130 gross multiplier (62)

42. **(3)** The gross rent and gross income multipliers are used as substitutes for the income approach. Assemblage is the joining of two or more properties. (62)

43. **(4)** The actual process of combining these properties into one is called assemblage. (64)

44. **(3)** The broker may not provide fringe benefits, such as health insurance. In addition, the broker may not withhold federal and state income taxes, Social Security taxes, or state unemployment insurance from commissions. (170–171)

45. **(1)** A salesperson cannot place blind ads. The salesperson may not receive monetary compensation for a real estate transaction from anyone other than the broker for whom he or she is working. (170–171)

46. **(3)** It is important to distinguish between earning and receiving a commission. (120)

47. **(4)** The broker must not restrict the buyer's freedom of choice. (164–165)

48. **(4)** It is illegal under federal fair housing laws to accept a listing that involves discrimination, such as refusing to sell to members of a protected class. (164–165)

49. **(3)** Functional obsolescence is a loss in value due to a deficiency in the floor plan or design of the house. (61)

50. **(4)** Real property refers to physical land and appurtenances, including easements, water rights, mineral rights, and fixtures. Strawberry bushes are perennial plants and would be considered real property. Percolating water and unexcavated clay would also be considered real property. Personal property refers to anything that can be moved. (21)

51. **(1)** Disclosing the lowest price that the seller will accept is a violation of the fiduciary relationship. (94–95)

52. **(3)** A competitive market analysis is based on the sales comparison approach to value. (63)

53. **(3)** $608.52 × 12 = $7,302.24

    $7,302.24 ÷ 10% (0.10) = $73,022.40 (191–192)

54. **(3)** $62,400 × 7% (0.07) = $4,368

    $62,400 + $4,368 = $66,768, or

    $62,400 × 107% (1.07) = $66,768 (181–182)

55. **(2)** $104,000 × 70% (0.70) = $72,800 assessed value

    Divide by 100, because the tax rate is stated per $100

    $72,800 ÷ 100 = $728

    $728 × $3.35 = $2,438.80 annual taxes

    Divide by 12 to get monthly payments

    $2,438.80 ÷ 12 = $203.23 (181–182)

56. **(3)** Sales prices of similar properties are used in the sales comparison approach. The net income and capitalization rate are used in the income approach. The owner's original cost of construction would be irrelevant, in any approach to value. (61)

57. **(2)** The sales comparison approach is considered most reliable when appraising a single-family home. The income approach and capitalization approach are stressed in appraising commercial and industrial properties. (61)

58. **(1)** The buyer's down payment on an FHA loan is 3.5% plus closing costs. (77)

59. **(2)** One point equals 1% of the loan. (73)

60. **(2)** $167,750 sales price × 7% (0.07) = $11,742.50 broker's commission

    $11,742.50 × 65% = $7,632.63 × 0.50 = $3,816 selling salesperson's commission (189)

61. **(1)** An escalation clause is found in an index lease that will allow the lease payment to adjust. It is also found in an adjustable-rate mortgage to allow the interest rate to adjust. (83)

62. **(2)** Puffing is sales psychology. Redlining is selecting specific areas and choosing not to make loans in that area; the areas generally are composed of members of protected classes. Blockbusting is panic peddling. (166)

63. **(4)** The vendee in a land contract holds equitable title until the land contract is paid in full, while the mortgagor receives legal title at closing. (74, 122)

64. **(1)** Loans with five or more installments would be covered. An agricultural loan for less than $25,000 also would be covered. (79)

65. **(1)** Rental of rooms in an owner-occupied dwelling of five units or more is not exempted. (166)

66. **(3)** An unrecorded deed is valid between the parties, but constructive notice must be given to protect against subsequent buyers of the property. (153)

67. **(4)** An attorney-in-fact is a competent, disinterested person authorized by another person to act in his or her place. A strawman is one who buys property for someone else to conceal the identity of the real buyer. A trustee holds property in trust for another to secure the performance of an obligation. (91)

68. **(1)** A broker may not commingle his or her personal funds with those of clients in a trust account. (120)

69. **(4)** Brokers generally are prohibited from representing and collecting compensations from both parties to a transaction unless both parties receive prior knowledge and give mutual consent. (95)

70. **(1)** In this situation, you are the agent of the buyer and the listing broker is the agent of the seller. (93)

71. **(4)** Answers 1, 2, and 3 are all characteristics of joint tenancy. (26–27)

72. **(4)** A voluntary lien is a mortgage lien, such as a lien created by an owner who obtains a mortgage loan. A general lien usually affects all the property of a debtor, both real and personal. A specific lien usually is secured by a specific property. (24)

73. **(3)** A roof that leaks would be an example of physical deterioration. (61)

74. **(2)** The broker is entitled to a commission when she is employed by the seller and finds a "ready, willing, and able" buyer. (120)

75. **(4)** The salesperson is an agent of the broker. When the salesperson no longer is employed by the broker, the broker retains any unsold or unexpired listings. The status of the listings remains unchanged. (119)

76. **(1)** $8 \times 8 = 64$

    640 acres ÷ 64 = 10 acres (22)

77. **(2)** FHA insurance is provided as protection for the lender. (77)

78. **(4)** When an option is given, the optionee gives the optionor consideration, the price is determined, and the time is set. The optionee does not have to exercise the option. (121–122)

79. **(3)** An easement appurtenant gives the easement beneficiary the right to use another's property. An encroachment arises when a building illegally extends beyond the land of the owner. A license may be canceled by the licensor. An easement in gross is the right to use the land of another. (24)

80. **(1)** A fee simple estate continues for an indefinite period and is inheritable by heirs of the owner. (25)

BROKER EXAMINATION II

1. You have hauled your heavy farm equipment across some vacant land of your neighbor's for years with your neighbor's knowledge, but not permission. Now, your neighbor wants to make improvements on the property and tells you to stop using it. Assuming you meet the required statutory period for having used the property, you may be able to get the courts to grant you the right to continue using the land, even if it means your neighbor's plans have to be abandoned. Which of the following terms *BEST* identifies the right described above?
   1. License
   2. Adverse possession
   3. An easement appurtenant
   4. An easement by prescription

2. The basic reason for choosing among a general warranty, a special warranty, or a quitclaim deed is to
   1. avoid the need for a habendum clause.
   2. verify the kind of estate the grantee will receive.
   3. explain any restrictions or limitations on the title.
   4. define the covenants by which the grantor is bound.

3. Under their mother's will, a woman and her brother inherited title to a house as tenants in common. The woman married and had title to her share put in joint tenancy with her husband. Her brother is now
   1. a joint tenant with his sister and her husband.
   2. sole owner of the property.
   3. a tenant in common, owning an undivided 1/3 interest.
   4. a tenant in common, owning an undivided 1/2 interest.

4. With permission, a tenant is going to place new carpeting in a rented space. In order to purchase the right size carpeting, the tenant must compute the square feet of a room that is 90' × 60'. What is the square feet of this room?
   1. 5,400
   2. 9,600
   3. 21,600
   4. 10,800

5. You are taking a listing on a property and notice that a neighboring building appears to have a roof overhang encroaching on the property line. The seller has never noticed this, even though the building has been there for several decades. Which of the following statements *BEST* identifies this situation?
   1. The seller must record a party wall easement prior to transferring title.
   2. The seller must perform a title search to discover if this represents a cloud on the title.
   3. The neighbor may be entitled to a prescription easement guaranteeing the right to leave the building as is.
   4. The neighbor may claim ownership of the property under the roof under the doctrine of prior appropriation.

6. Broker Cortez is renting apartments for landlord Marcou. Cortez shows an apartment to an African-American couple. Prior to informing the couple that they may have the apartment, he receives a call from the landlord who asks about the race of the prospective tenants. Which of the following statements correctly describes how Cortez should respond to Marcou's question concerning the race of the prospective tenants?
   1. Cortez should tell the owner that the prospective tenants are African-American.
   2. Cortez should tell the landlord that he cannot answer that question.
   3. Cortez should state that he will answer the question only if the owner promises to keep the information confidential.
   4. Cortez should provide the race of the prospects only if he tells the landlord it is illegal, but he must respond because he owes loyalty to the landlord.

7. The state needs your farm to build a highway. You have rejected their offer. The state may obtain your property by exercising its right of
   1. adverse possession.
   2. eminent domain.
   3. escheat.
   4. police power.

8. Keeping which of the following types of funds in a broker's trust account is *MOST* likely to be illegal?
   1. Rents on an apartment building you are managing
   2. Earnest money deposits
   3. Commission earned on previous sales
   4. Security deposits on properties you are managing

9. Alfonso owns a life estate, and Anita holds the future interest in the life estate. When Alfonso dies,
   1. Alfonso's wife will become the owner under her dower interest.
   2. Alfonso's life estate will pass to his heirs according to the terms of his will.
   3. Alfonso and Anita will hold title as tenants in common.
   4. Anita will hold title to the property.

10. Steve has had an offer to purchase accepted by Emily. Prior to closing, Steve will hold
    1. fee-simple title.
    2. defeasible title.
    3. legal title.
    4. equitable title.

11. A zoning ordinance would *NOT* regulate
    1. land use.
    2. height of the building.
    3. use of the building.
    4. construction standards.

12. When the owner of a property (that is sold for back taxes or mortgage default) is granted a period of time after the sale to buy the property back, this is referred to as the owner's
    1. lien priority.
    2. homestead rights.
    3. statutory right of redemption.
    4. deed in lieu of foreclosure.

13. You have pledged your home as security for a mortgage without giving up possession. This is called
    1. hypothecation.
    2. abstract.
    3. subordination.
    4. release of mortgage.

14. All of the following statements correctly describe the relationship of a salesperson working for a broker as an employee *EXCEPT*
    1. the broker may choose to provide fringe benefits.
    2. the broker may not tell salespeople how to list property.
    3. the broker may require attendance at sales meetings.
    4. the broker is required to withhold federal and state income taxes from commissions.

15. A broker has been found guilty of discrimination under the Federal Fair Housing Act for the third time in the past seven years. The broker will be subject to a civil penalty *NOT* exceeding
    1. $10,000.
    2. $25,000.
    3. $50,000.
    4. $100,000.

16. An earthquake tore away some of the land on a farm. This is an example of
    1. accession.
    2. accretion.
    3. avulsion.
    4. erosion.

17. All of the following practices constitute a discriminatory act under the Federal Fair Housing Act *EXCEPT*
    1. the owner-occupant of a duplex refuses to rent to a family with children.
    2. a lender uses one type of application for whites and another for African-Americans.
    3. a Hispanic broker refers Caucasian prospects only to Caucasian brokers.
    4. a property manager requires a higher security deposit for African-Americans than whites.

18. In the sales comparison approach to value, if a feature in the comparable property is inferior to that of the subject property, a
    1. plus adjustment must be made to the price of the subject.
    2. minus adjustment must be made to the price of the comparable.
    3. plus adjustment must be made to the price of the comparable.
    4. minus adjustment must be made to the price of the subject.

19. If you give your land to your brother for the balance of his life, and at his death the land is to go to your sister, his interest or estate is called a
    1. reversion.
    2. curtesy.
    3. base fee.
    4. life estate.

20. Buyer Smith purchased a home for $148,000 with the help of a mortgage for 90% of the selling price. Four years later, the balance of the mortgage was $129,000. An appraisal of the house at that same time estimated the value of Smith's home at $163,000. Smith's equity in the home is
    1. $14,800.
    2. $19,000.
    3. $34,000.
    4. None of these.

21. A property manager renting units for an apartment owner is an example of a
    1. special agent.
    2. general agent.
    3. subagent.
    4. dual agent.

22. The relationship of trust and confidence that a broker has with a principle is a(n)
    1. escrow relationship.
    2. subordination agreement.
    3. fiduciary relationship.
    4. trustee relationship.

23. A salesperson may legally accept a cash bonus directly from
    1. a seller for whom she did an excellent job.
    2. an appreciative buyer.
    3. a grateful title company.
    4. a broker/employer.

24. A broker knowingly misled a potential buyer on the boundary lines of a property. The buyer discovered the problem after buying the property. Is the broker guilty of fraudulent misrepresentation?
    1. Yes, because the broker should have had the property surveyed before commenting on the property boundary lines.
    2. Yes, because the broker intentionally misled the buyer.
    3. No, because the broker is not a surveyor.
    4. No, because the broker did not provide any misrepresentation in writing.

25. You own a defeasible fee estate and sell it on a land contract. Until the land contract has been paid in full, the buyer will hold a(n)
    1. leasehold estate.
    2. life estate.
    3. equitable title.
    4. fee-simple title.

26. A broker sold a home for $183,000. The broker charged the owner a 7% commission and will pay 30% of that amount to the listing salesperson and 25% to the selling salesperson. What amount of commission will the listing salesperson receive from the sale?
    1. $3,202.50
    2. $3,843
    3. $4,483.50
    4. $12,810

27. A seller asks a listing licensee to drop the price of a property to $105,000 from $120,000 in order to spur a quick sale. The licensee then prepares a new competitive market analysis (CMA), which indicates the property may be worth $115,000. In this situation, the licensee's *BEST* course as a fiduciary for the seller is to
   1. offer to buy the property for $105,000.
   2. follow instructions and drop the price immediately.
   3. encourage the seller to hold the price up for negotiation room.
   4. disclose to the seller that the home is worth $115,000 before proceeding with a list-price change.

28. You have just been given an option to sell your house to your friend. All of the following statements correctly describe your agreement *EXCEPT*
   1. your friend is the optionee.
   2. your friend is not obligated to buy your house.
   3. you are the optionor.
   4. you will have to return the fee for the option right to your friend if he chooses not to buy your house.

29. All of the following facts would need to be disclosed by a broker *EXCEPT*
   1. there is water in the basement.
   2. there is an underground storage tank in the backyard.
   3. there is asbestos wrap on the heating pipes.
   4. the seller has AIDS.

30. A broker has entered into a listing contract with a client in which the broker will receive a commission regardless of who sells the property during the term of the listing contract. The broker's listing is a(n)
   1. exclusive-right-to-sell listing.
   2. net listing.
   3. open listing.
   4. exclusive-agency listing.

31. Three investors decided to pool their savings and buy an office building for $250,000. If one invested $80,000 and the second investor contributed $50,000, what percentage of ownership was left for the third investor?
   1. 20%
   2. 32%
   3. 48%
   4. None of these

32. You own an apartment building that provides you with a gross income of $50,000 a year. Your annual expenses are $12,000. The value of your real estate if you receive a 14% return on your investment is
   1. $85,714.
   2. $170,928.
   3. $271,429.
   4. $325,143.

33. In order to permanently buy down a buyer's interest rate, an owner agrees to pay two points amounting to $3,500. How much money did the buyer borrow?
   1. $175,000
   2. $350,000
   3. $700,000
   4. None of these

34. Brandon owns his home in fee simple. This means that he has
   1. a legal life estate.
   2. a personal property interest.
   3. a tenancy by the entirety.
   4. the highest type of interest in real estate.

35. Your home is valued at $143,000. Property in your city is assessed at 80% of its value, and the local tax rate is $3.65 per $100. What is the amount of your monthly taxes?
   1. $319.37
   2. $347.96
   3. $352.73
   4. $357.50

36. Which of the following represents the *MOST* likely recourse for a lender who has foreclosed on a property and does not recover enough from the sale to cover the outstanding loan amount due?
    1. Sue the borrower for a deficiency judgment
    2. Apply to the appropriate federal agency for the difference
    3. Seek compensation from the borrower's title insurance company
    4. Initiate proceedings to recover the difference from homestead exemption funds

37. You own a home on a block that is zoned residential; however, there is a retail store on the lot next door to you. The retail store
    1. is an example of downzoning.
    2. is a nonconforming use.
    3. will have to close if you file a complaint with the planning commission.
    4. is a buffer zone.

38. Which of the following statements is correct about an exclusive agency listing?
    1. It authorizes the listing agent to sign offers on behalf of the seller.
    2. It authorizes the listing agent to be the only licensee to show the property.
    3. It authorizes the seller to find a buyer and not be obligated to pay a sales commission.
    4. It authorizes the seller to demand that the listing firm purchase the property if it remains unsold at the end of the listing period.

39. A doctor built a $400,000 home in a neighborhood of $200,000 homes. This situation reflects the principle of
    1. competition.
    2. conformity.
    3. progression.
    4. regression.

40. You purchased a home with an FHA-insured loan. At closing, the seller was charged the five discount points for the loan. This money will be paid to
    1. the broker.
    2. the lending institution.
    3. the FHA.
    4. you.

41. What is the major difference between an assignment and a sublease?
    1. When a lease has been assigned, the landlord expects payment from the assignor, but when the property has been sublet, the landlord expects payment from the sublessee.
    2. Only tenants of residential properties can assign leases, and only tenants of commercial properties can sublease properties.
    3. A tenant who transfers all the leasehold interest assigns the lease, while a tenant who subleases transfers less than the leasehold interests in the property.
    4. An assignment is used for long-term leases, but a sublease is used for short-term leases.

42. You have listed a property. The seller told you that she must net at least $18,000 after all fees and expenses are paid. You estimate the seller's closing costs to be $5,200, and she must pay off an existing loan of $104,600. In addition, you are going to charge a 6% commission on the sale. What is the *LEAST* amount for which the property can sell to return the seller's desired net?
    1. $111,277
    2. $130,425
    3. $137,419
    4. None of these

43. Six months after a real estate transaction closes, one of the parties discovers information about the transaction that raises the possibility that he was the victim of fraud. Which of the following terms *BEST* identifies the legal principle governing whether the aggrieved party can still bring a lawsuit this long after closing?
    1. Laches
    2. Equity of redemption
    3. Statute of frauds
    4. Statute of limitations

44. Legislation that has helped resurrect once deserted, defunct, and derelict toxic industrial sites is known as
    1. DNR.
    2. waste field.
    3. due diligences.
    4. Brownfields.

45. A commercial real estate agent needs to determine the number of acres in a vacant parcel of land that measures 800' × 1,200'. How many acres are in this area?
    1. 22.04
    2. 62.04
    3. 2,000
    4. 960,000

46. All of the following responsibilities would be considered part of the licensee's fiduciary duties to a client *EXCEPT*
    1. procuring a buyer for a seller-client.
    2. presenting all offers promptly to the client.
    3. advising a buyer-client how to take title to the property.
    4. ensuring that earnest monies are placed in a trust account.

47. All of the following statements describe the impact of traditional common agency law on real estate agents *EXCEPT*
    1. the real estate agent is often referred to as a fiduciary in common law.
    2. historically, real estate agents represented only the sellers of real estate.
    3. under traditional common law, all duties would have been owed to the seller.
    4. under common law, the agent did not owe a customer the duty to be honest and fair in dealing with his or her customer.

48. Which of the following governs the disclosures required when advertising financing terms for real estate?
    1. Truth-in-Lending
    2. Sherman Antitrust Act
    3. Equal Credit Opportunity Act (ECOA)
    4. Real Estate Settlement Procedures Act (RESPA)

49. Title of the land and building in a cooperative is held by a
    1. corporation.
    2. general partnership.
    3. homeowners association.
    4. syndicate.

50. Which of the following would be required for a deed to be valid?
    1. The grantee must sign the deed.
    2. The deed must be recorded by the grantor.
    3. The grantor must sign the deed.
    4. The deed must be recorded by the grantee.

51. A broker has an accepted purchase contract for a property and would like to change the language to reflect the desire of the buyer and seller to revise the contract. The broker will accomplish this by means of a(n)
    1. addendum.
    2. amendment.
    3. counteroffer.
    4. rescission.

52. The major employer in your city has decided to relocate to another state, resulting in a substantial decline in housing prices. This would be an example of
    1. the principle of regression.
    2. functional obsolescence.
    3. physical deterioration.
    4. economic obsolescence.

53. Which of the following is a physical characteristic of land?
    1. Scarcity
    2. Situs
    3. Immobility
    4. Improvements

54. If an owner listed a property for $300,000 but accepted an offer for $275,000, what was the percentage of change between the asking price and the actual selling price?
    1. 2.75%
    2. 3.00%
    3. 5.50%
    4. 8.33%

55. A correct statement about an easement in gross is that it
    1. benefits the dominant tenement.
    2. has only a dominant tenement.
    3. has only a servient tenement.
    4. has both a dominant and a servient tenement.

56. All of the following statements correctly describe the role of an earnest money deposit in a real estate transaction *EXCEPT*
    1. the deposit must usually be held by the broker in a special trust, or escrow, account.
    2. the amount is generally determined by negotiation between the buyer and seller.
    3. the deposit generally gives evidence of intention to carry out the terms of contract.
    4. a deposit is legally required to create a valid contract.

57. Using the mortgage factor of $7.34, what is the monthly payment for $129,000 at 8% for 30 years?
    1. $923.64
    2. $946.86
    3. $968.79
    4. $99.01

58. Using the numbers in question 61, what is the total interest paid over the life of the loan?
    1. $209,975.88
    2. $210,922.74
    3. $211,869.60
    4. $212,816.46

59. You and your brother have purchased an apartment building as joint tenants. All of the following statements correctly describe your situation *EXCEPT*
    1. you and your brother hold the right of survivorship.
    2. owners must be related in order to own joint tenancy.
    3. the unities of title, time, interest, and possession are required to create a valid joint tenancy.
    4. either you or your brother may partition the land.

60. You and your husband live in a community property state. Which of the following assets owned by you would be considered community property?
    1. A car given to you after your marriage.
    2. A duplex that you and your husband purchased after your marriage.
    3. Stock inherited by your husband after your marriage.
    4. A house that you owned before you were married.

61. An investor paid $500,000 for a commercial building that earns a net income of $75,000 per year. What is the capitalization rate of the investment?
    1. 10%
    2. 15%
    3. 20%
    4. 25%

62. You have listed a property. The seller told you that he must net at least $26,000 after all fees and expenses are paid. You estimate the seller's closing cost to be $5,000 and he must pay off an existing loan of $119,600. In addition, you are going to charge 6% commission on the sale. What is the *LEAST* amount for which the property can sell to return the seller's desired net (to the nearest dollar)?
    1. $127,234
    2. $154,893
    3. $169,825
    4. $160,213

63. The use of lead-based paint in residential properties was banned for health reasons in which year?
    1. 1972
    2. 1978
    3. 1977
    4. 1991

64. A father wants to know how much money his daughter owes on her mortgage loan. The father knows that the interest part of the last monthly payment was $526.49. If his daughter is paying interest at 8%, what was the outstanding balance of the loan before the last payment was made?
    1. $70,198.67
    2. $78,973.50
    3. $90,255.42
    4. None of these

65. A difference between an individual's ownership interest in a cooperative and a condominium is that in a cooperative, the owner
    1. is not subject to real estate taxes.
    2. holds fee-simple title, whereas a condominium owner holds a proprietary lease.
    3. is not responsible for unpaid real estate taxes of other owners, whereas a condominium owner is.
    4. holds a personal property interest, whereas a condominium owner holds a real property interest.

66. A correct statement about agency relationships when a salesperson lists a property is that
    1. the licensee becomes a principal.
    2. the licensee's broker becomes the agent of the seller.
    3. the seller is entitled to subagency from all licensees who show the property.
    4. the seller must sign a dual-agency relationship agreement with all prospective buyers.

67. The denial of a loan by a lender is a violation of the Federal Fair Housing Act if such denial is based on
    1. lack of income.
    2. familial status.
    3. public beliefs.
    4. sexual preference.

68. Which of the following does *NOT* represent a pair of individuals in which the first person has fiduciary responsibilities to the second?
    1. Listing broker to seller
    2. Buyer-broker to buyer
    3. Mortgagor to mortgagee
    4. Appraiser to client

69. A married couple owned their home as tenants by the entirety. They then separated, and the husband continued to live in the house. If the husband decides to sell the home, can he do so without the wife's consent?
    1. Yes, because the wife relinquished her interest when she moved out of the house.
    2. Yes, because under tenancy by the entirety, either party may sell the house without the consent of the other party.
    3. No, because the wife holds a dower interest that will not be extinguished upon the sale of the house.
    4. No, because under tenancy by the entirety, title may be conveyed only by a deed signed by both parties.

70. A salesperson working as an independent contractor
    1. is required to attend sales meetings.
    2. may not be required to follow any set work schedule.
    3. is not responsible for transportation expenses.
    4. may receive fringe benefits if the broker agrees.

71. A broker has met with a customer and declined to work with the person in finding a home. It is legal for the broker to decline the opportunity if the decision is based on the customer's
    1. familial status.
    2. income.
    3. race.
    4. religion.

72. A borrower's three-day right of rescission for a residential real estate loan transaction is based on the provisions of
    1. Truth-in-Lending.
    2. the Federal Fair Housing Act.
    3. the Equal Credit Opportunity Act (ECOA).
    4. the Real Estate Settlement Procedures Act (RESPA).

73. You have listed your house with only one licensed broker but reserved the right to sell the property yourself without owing a commission. This relationship is called a(n)
    1. net listing.
    2. open listing.
    3. exclusive-agency listing.
    4. exclusive-right-to-sell listing.

74. A woman owns a four-unit apartment building but does not live there. She is currently advertising for Lutheran tenants only. Is her advertising policy legal?
    1. Yes, because the property contains four units.
    2. Yes, because no real estate agent is involved in the marketing of the property.
    3. No, because four-unit properties are not exempted from the Federal Fair Housing Act.
    4. No, because she is not living in the apartment building.

75. The civil penalty for a first violation of the Americans with Disabilities Act (ADA) is up to
    1. $10,000.
    2. $25,000.
    3. $50,000.
    4. $100,000.

76. The Americans with Disabilities Act (ADA) requires that an employer with a minimum of how many employees must comply with the ADA requirements?
    1. 3
    2. 5
    3. 10
    4. 15

77. You have just listed a property, and the owner has informed you that the roof leaks and the fourth bedroom was added without a building permit being issued. Which of the following *BEST* describes the type of disclosure you should make to potential buyers?
    1. You should disclose that the roof leaks.
    2. You do not have to disclose that the bedroom was added without a permit, because the project has already been completed.
    3. You do not have to disclose either, unless you are instructed to do so by the seller.
    4. You must disclose both the roof leak and the lack of a building permit.

78. You lease the 36 apartments in your building for a total monthly rental of $8,000. If this figure represents an 8% annual return on your investment, what was the original cost of the property?
    1. $100,000
    2. $236,000
    3. $1,200,000
    4. $2,360,000

79. Alex bought a house for $160,000 five years ago. His mortgage was for $128,000. Today Alex's house is valued at $200,000, and his mortgage balance is $123,000. What is Alex's equity in the property?
    1. $32,000
    2. $37,000
    3. $72,000
    4. $77,000

80. The county zoo holds title to the land that includes a condition that the zoo will hold title so long as it does not charge an admission fee. This is an example of a
    1. fee-simple estate.
    2. defeasible-fee estate.
    3. conventional life estate.
    4. tenancy at will.

ANSWER KEY: BROKER EXAMINATION II

1. **(4)** A license may be canceled by the licensor. Adverse possession would result in a change of ownership. An easement appurtenant requires a dominant tenement. (24)

2. **(4)** The habendum clause follows the granting clause when it is necessary to define the ownership to be enjoyed by the grantee. Any type of deed should explain any restrictions and limitations on the title. (153)

3. **(4)** The sister and her husband jointly own an undivided one-half interest as tenants in common with the brother. (26)

4. **(1)** Square feet is computed by multiplying 90' × 60' = 5,400 sq. ft. (184)

5. **(3)** A title search would not reveal the existence of an encroachment. Prior appropriation relates to water rights. A party wall easement would be appropriate if that were the case and could be negotiated with the neighbor. (24)

6. **(2)** A broker may not disclose that a prospective tenant is a member of a protected class. (164)

7. **(2)** Eminent domain is the right of the government to acquire private property for public use while paying just compensation to the owner. (25)

8. **(3)** A broker may not commingle his funds with those of his clients in his trust account. (120)

9. **(4)** When the life tenant dies, the life estate is terminated. On the death of the life estate owner, full ownership passes to the owner of the future interest. (26)

10. **(4)** After both the buyer and the seller have executed the offer to purchase contract, the buyer acquires equitable title. (120)

11. **(4)** Construction standards are regulated by building codes. (41)

12. **(3)** Lien priority and homestead rights refer to the rights of creditors. A deed in lieu of foreclosure is an alternative to a process of foreclosure. (155)

13. **(1)** Hypothecation is pledging of property as security for a loan without losing possession of it. Arbitrage, subordination, and release of mortgage were previously discussed. (83)

14. **(2)** The broker may guide activities and maintain standards of conduct for a salesperson working as an employee. (170–171)

15. **(3)** Specific penalties under the Federal Fair Housing Act are discussed in Chapter 11. (166)

16. **(3)** Erosion is the gradual wearing away of land by the action of natural forces. Accession and accretion were previously discussed. (30)

17. **(1)** Treating people differently because they are members of a protected class is a violation of the Federal Fair Housing Act. There is, however, an exemption covering rentals if the rooms or units are in an owner-occupied, one-family to four-family dwelling. (166)

18. **(3)** You should use the three steps for making adjustments in the value comparison approach to value:

    1. Always work from the price of the comparable to the subject property.

    2. C.B.S.—comparable better subtract.

    3. S.B.A.—subject better add. (68)

19. **(4)** Your brother's interest is a life estate, because it is limited to your brother's life. A reversion exists only if the land reverted to you. A base fee may be inherited. Curtesy refers to the life estate of a husband. (26)

20. **(3)** \$163,000 (current appraised value) – \$129,000 (current mortgage balance) = \$34,000, which is Smith's equity in the home. (186)

21. **(2)** A broker employed to sell an owner's home would be a special agent. Cooperating brokers under a multiple-listing service (MLS) would be subagents. Dual agency occurs when a broker represents both the seller and the buyer in a transaction. (92)

22. **(3)** An escrow relationship refers to a third-party agreement, such as an escrow agent who does a closing for the buyer and seller. A subordination agreement changes the order of lien priority between the two creditors. A trustee acts as an agent and is generally responsible for handling money or holding title to land. (91)

23. **(4)** A salesperson may accept financial compensation for completing a real estate transaction only from her employing broker. (171)

24. **(2)** This is clearly a case of intentional misrepresentation, which is considered fraudulent. (105)

25. **(3)** The fact that you own a defeasible fee estate does not affect the vendee's interest of equitable title in the estate. (25)

26. **(2)** \$183,000 sales price × 7% (0.07) = \$12,810 × 0.30 = \$3,843 (189)

27. **(4)** The broker has a fiduciary responsibility to the seller, which requires that she disclose her fair opinion of value to the principal. (94–95)

28. **(4)** The fee for the option right belongs to the owner (optionor) regardless of the outcome of the transaction. (121–122)

29. **(4)** Persons who have AIDS are protected under the Federal Fair Housing Act. (164)

30. **(1)** In an exclusive-agency or open listing, the sellers have the right to sell their property on their own without having to pay the broker a commission. A net listing is based on the net price the seller receives if the property is sold; the broker receives any amount received above the net price. The net listing is prohibited or discouraged in most states. (119)

31. **(3)** \$80,000 (first investor) + \$50,000 (second investor) = \$130,000

$\frac{\text{part}}{\text{percent}}$ \$250,000 – \$130,000 = \$120,000 third investor's contribution

= total

\$120,000 ÷ \$250,000 = 0.48, or 48% (181–1682)

32. **(3)** \$50,000 gross income – \$12,000 expenses = \$38,000 net annual income

\$38,000 net annual income ÷ 14% (0.14) = \$271,429 value of real estate (61)

33. **(1)** Divide the discount points by 2%. \$3,500 divided by 2% = \$175,000 (181)

34. **(4)** A fee simple is a real property interest, while a legal life estate is a spouse's estate in all the inheritable real estate of the deceased spouse. Tenancy by the entirety is a unit form of ownership in which the owners must be husband and wife. (25)

35. **(2)** $143,000 × 80% (0.80) = $114,400 assessed value

    Divide by 100, because the tax rate is stated per $100

    $1,144 × $3.65 = $4,175.60 annual taxes

    Divide by 12 to get monthly taxes

    $4,175.60 ÷ 12 = $347.96 (188)

36. **(1)** Deficiency judgments may be obtained for any deficiency. (118)

37. **(2)** Downzoning refers to a situation where the zoning for a parcel of land is changed from a dense to a less-dense usage. The planning commission cannot close the retail store. A nonconforming use generally is removed if it suffers 50% or more damage and is not rebuilt within one year. A buffer zone is a land area that separates one land use from another. (42)

38. **(3)** Only one broker is authorized to act as an exclusive agent of the seller, but the sellers may sell the property themselves. Brokers generally enter into exclusive-right-to-sell listings. (119)

39. **(4)** The principle of regression states that the value of the better property is affected adversely by the presence of the lesser-quality properties. (59)

40. **(2)** Discount points usually are charged by, and paid to, the lender when the FHA interest rate is less than the conventional, or market, rate of interest. (77)

41. **(3)** In an assignment, a tenant transfers all the leasehold interest. In a sublease, a tenant transfers less than the leasehold interest in the property. (30)

42. **(4)** Add the desired net, $18,000, plus the existing loan payoff, $104,600, and the closing costs, $5,200. $127,800 is the minimum that the seller must receive. The correct answer is $127,800 ÷ 0.94 (100% – 6%) = $135,957. (182)

43. **(4)** Laches is a doctrine whereby one is unable to assert a legal right because of waiting too long to enforce it. Equity of redemption refers to the time period for foreclosure during which the buyer may redeem his property. The statute of frauds requires certain contracts to be in writing in order to be enforceable. (122)

44. **(4)** Brownfields legislation promotes the cleanup and reuse of thousands of defunct, derelict, and abandoned industrial sites. Often clustered near prime real estate areas, these once contaminated sites can easily be converted into tax revenue sites. (45)

45. **(1)** The problem is solved by multiplying 800 × 1,200 = 960,000, divided by 43,560 (square feet in an acre) = 22.04. (22)

46. **(3)** A broker may not offer legal advice; only a licensed attorney may do so. (96)

47. **(4)** Under traditional common law, the agent did owe a customer the duty to be honest and fair in his or her dealings with the customer, as well as any duties prescribed in state law, such as confidentiality. (95)

48. **(1)** Truth-in-Lending required disclosure of cost in a credit transaction, as well as the advertising of financing terms. The Sherman Antitrust Act deals with antitrust violations, such as boycotting. ECOA prohibits discrimination against protected classes with regard to loan applications. (79)

49. **(1)** Each buyer in the cooperative becomes a shareholder and receives a proprietary lease. (28)

50. **(3)** The grantee must be identified in the deed. Unrecorded deeds are valid between the parties. However, the deed should be recorded in order to provide constructive notice. (152)

51. **(2)** An amendment changes the language of a contract; an addendum adds additional terms to an offer. (122)

52. **(4)** Functional obsolescence and physical deterioration are losses in value that occur within the property, while economic obsolescence occurs outside the property. The principle of regression was previously discussed. (61)

53. **(3)** Scarcity, situs, and improvements are economic characteristics of land. (21)

54. **(4)** The solution is found by subtracting the difference and then dividing the difference by 300,000. Next, convert the solution from a decimal to a percent. 300,000 – 275,000 = 25,000 divided by 300,000 = 0.833, or 8.33% (182)

55. **(3)** An easement in gross does not have a dominant tenement. (24)

56. **(4)** An earnest money deposit is not legally required to create a valid contract. An earnest money deposit does provide a show of good faith by the buyer and could possibly be retained by the seller if the buyer defaults, which depends on the nature of the default. (120)

57. **(2)** 946.86 ($129,000 × 7.34) (192)

58. **(3)** $946.86 ÷ 360 months = $340,869.60

$340,869.60	total P & I
– $129,000.00	loan
$211,869.60	total interest

(192)

59. **(2)** Owners in joint tenancy do not have to be related. (27)

60. **(2)** Community property includes real and personal property acquired by either spouse during the marriage. Separate property (real or personal) is that owned individually by either spouse before the marriage. Separate property also includes any property acquired by inheritance or gift during the marriage or purchased with separate funds during the marriage. (27)

61. **(2)**

$$\frac{\text{income}}{\text{value}} = \text{capitalization rate}$$

$$\frac{\$75{,}000}{\$500{,}000} = .15 \text{ or } 15\%$$

(61)

62. **(4)** Add the desired net, $26,000, plus the existing loan payoff, $119,600, and the closing cost, $5,000. $150,600 is the minimum that the seller must receive.

If the selling price is 100% and the commission is 6%, the net to seller is 94%.

$150,600 is 94% of the selling price. Therefore, $150,600 ÷ 94% (0.94) = selling price of $160,212.76, rounds to $160,213. (181–182)

63. **(2)** Licensees involved in the sales, financing, appraisal, or management of properties built prior to 1978 face potential liability for any personal injury suffered by occupants resulting from exposure to lead-based paint. (45–46)

64. **(2)** $526.49 × 12 = $6,317.88 annual interest

part ÷ percent = total

$6,317.88 ÷ 8% (0.08) = $78,973.50 (192)

65. **(4)** Each buyer receives a proprietary lease and becomes a stockholder. However, a cooperative is converted to a real estate interest in those states that have adopted the Common Interest Ownership Act. (28)

66. **(2)** The broker is the agent of the seller. The salesperson is the agent of the broker and possible subagent of the seller. (91–92)

67. **(2)** Familial status was added in 1988. (164)

68. **(3)** Mortgagees have a fiduciary relationship with investors who place money in their lending institutions. (91–92)

69. **(4)** Tenancy by the entirety is a unit ownership of the property. (27)

70. **(2)** Independent contractors work under limited supervision from the broker. (170–171)

71. **(2)** Familial status, race, and religion are protected classes under the Federal Fair Housing Act. (164)

72. **(1)** The three-day right of rescission covers a home equity loan or the refinancing of a home mortgage. It does not cover owner-occupied residential purchase-money as first mortgage or deed of trust loans. (79)

73. **(3)** A net listing is based on the amount of money the seller receives if the property is sold. In the open listing, the seller retains the right to employ any number of brokers to act as his or her agents. In an exclusive-right-to-sell listing, the seller gives up the right to sell the property himself or herself, and thus avoids paying the broker's commission. (120–122)

74. **(4)** The Federal Fair Housing Act exempts the rental of units in an owner-occupied, one-family to four-family dwelling. (166)

75. **(3)** A penalty of up to $100,000 may be assessed for any subsequent violation of ADA. (167)

76. **(4)** ADA requires that any employer with 15 or more employees adopt nondiscriminatory employment procedures and make reasonable accommodations to enable an individual with a disability to perform in his or her employment. (167)

77. **(4)** The broker is obligated to disclose to the buyer the material facts relating to property. (105)

78. **(3)** $8,000 × 12 = $96,000 annual return

$96,000 ÷ 8% (0.08) = $1,200,000 original cost of property (181–182)

79. **(4)** $200,000 current value – $123,000 current mortgage = $77,000 equity (181–182)

80. **(2)** A defeasible-fee estate continues for an indefinite period. The period of ownership may be based on either a certain or uncertain event. The words *so long as* indicate that the estate will be extinguished on the occurrence of the designated event; for example, the charging of admission to the zoo. (25)

GLOSSARY

1031 tax deferred exchange Under Section 1031 of the IRS Code, some or all of the realized gain from the exchange of one property for a like kind property may be deferred. It is not a tax-free event; however, in order to accumulate wealth, the payment is deferred.

abandonment The voluntary and permanent cessation of use or enjoyment with no intention to resume or reclaim one's possession or interest. May pertain to an easement of a property.

abstract of title A condensed version of the history of a title to a particular parcel of real estate as recorded in the county clerk's records; consists of a summary of the original grant and all subsequent conveyances and encumbrances affecting the property.

abutting The joining, reaching, or touching of adjoining land. Abutting parcels of land have a common boundary.

accelerated depreciation A method of calculating for tax purposes the depreciation of income property at a faster rate than would be achieved using the straight-line method. Note that any depreciation taken in excess of what would be claimed using the straight-line rate is subject to recapture as ordinary income to the extent of the gain resulting from the sale. *See also* straight-line method.

acceleration clause A provision in a written mortgage, note, bond, or conditional sales contract that in the event of default, the whole amount of the principal and the interest may be declared due and payable at once.

accession Title to improvements or additions to real property is acquired as a result of the accretion of alluvial deposits along the banks of streams or as a result of the annexation of fixtures.

accretion An increase or addition to land by the deposit of sand or soil washed up naturally from a river, lake, or sea.

accrued depreciation The actual depreciation that has occurred to a property at any given date; the difference between the cost of replacement new (as of the date of the appraisal) and the present appraised value.

acknowledgment A declaration made by a person to a notary public or other public official authorized to take acknowledgments that an instrument was executed by him or her as a free and voluntary act.

actual eviction The result of legal action originated by a lessor, by which a defaulted tenant is physically ousted from the rented property pursuant to a court order. *See also* constructive eviction.

actual notice Express information or fact; that which is known; actual knowledge.

administrator The party appointed by the county court to settle the estate of a deceased person who died without leaving a will.

ad valorem tax A tax levied according to value; generally used to refer to real estate tax. Also called *general tax.*

adverse possession The actual, visible, hostile, notorious, exclusive, and continuous possession of another's land under a claim to title. Possession for a statutory period may be a means of acquiring title.

affidavit A written statement signed and sworn to before a person authorized to administer an oath.

agent One who represents or has the power to act for another person (called the principal). The authorization may be express, implied, or apparent. A fiduciary relationship is created under the law of agency when a property owner, as the principal, executes a listing agreement or management contract authorizing a licensed real estate broker to be her or his agent.

agreement of sale A written agreement by which the purchaser agrees to buy certain real estate and the seller agrees to sell, on the terms and conditions set forth in the agreement.

air lot A designated airspace over a piece of land. Air lots, like surface property, may be transferred.

air rights The right to use the open space above one's property. It can be sold to build a skywalk or for a utility company to erect power lines.

alienation The act of transferring property to another. Alienation may be voluntary, such as by sale, or involuntary, such as through eminent domain.

alienation clause (due-on-sale clause) Clause in a mortgage instrument that does not allow the borrower to sell (without lender approval) on assumption or contract-for-deed. If an attempt is made to do so without prior approval, all of the mortgaged balance becomes due on the sale of the property. Also known as the *due-on-sale clause*.

alluvion The actual soil increase resulting from accretion.

amendments Changes to previously approved and adopted written agreements are amendments. For example, in a condominium association, an original policy may allow the renting of units and later amend the rule requiring unit owners to live in their units for at least one year before leasing.

amenities Neighborhood facilities and services that enhance a property's value. They are always outside of the property. Swimming pools, three-car garages, decks, etc., that are on the property are called *features*.

Americans with Disabilities Act (ADA) A federal law, effective in 1992, designed to eliminate discrimination against individuals with disabilities.

amortization The liquidation of a financial burden by installment payments, which include principal and interest.

amortized loan A loan in which the principal and interest are payable in monthly or other periodic installments over the term of the loan.

anticipation An appraising principle created by the expectation of certain future events causing values to either increase or decrease.

antitrust laws The laws designed to preserve the free enterprise of the open marketplace by making illegal certain private conspiracies and combinations formed to minimize competition. Violation of antitrust laws in the real estate business generally involves either price fixing (brokers conspiring to set fixed compensation rates) or allocation of customers or markets (brokers agreeing to limit their trades or dealings to certain areas or properties).

appraisal An estimate of the quantity, quality, or value of something. The process through which conclusions about property value are obtained; also refers to the report that sets forth the process of estimation and conclusion of value.

appraised value An estimate of a property's present worth.

appreciation An increase in the worth or value of a property, due to economic or related causes, which may prove to be either temporary or permanent; opposite of *depreciation*.

appurtenant Belonging to; incident to; annexed to. For example, a garage is appurtenant to a house, and the common interest in the common elements of a condominium is appurtenant to each apartment. Appurtenances pass with the land when the property is transferred.

arbitrage The simultaneous purchase and sale of a security with the purpose of obtaining a higher yield from the differential between its acquisition and selling price.

arbitration A means of settling a controversy between two parties through the medium of an impartial third party whose decision on the controversy (if agreed upon) will be final and binding.

assessment The imposition of a tax, charge, or levy, usually according to established rates.

assignment The transfer in writing of rights or interest in a bond, mortgage, lease, or other instrument.

assumed name statute (fictitious name statute) The law, in effect in most states, that stipulates that no person shall conduct a business under any name other than his or her own individual name, unless such person files the desired name with the county clerk in each county where the business is conducted. In the case of brokers and salespeople, statement of such filing should be submitted to the state's real estate commission.

assumption of mortgage The transfer of title to property to a grantee, by which the grantee assumes liability for payment of an existing note secured by a mortgage against the property. Should the mortgage be foreclosed and the property sold for a lesser amount than that due, the grantee/purchaser who has assumed and agreed to pay the debt secured by the mortgage is personally liable for the deficiency. Before a seller may be relieved of liability under the existing mortgage, the lender must accept the transfer of liability for payment of the note.

attorney-in-fact The holder of a power of attorney.

attorney's opinion of title An instrument written and signed by the attorney who examines the title, stating her or his opinion as to whether a seller may convey good title.

avulsion A sudden tearing away of land by the action of natural forces.

balloon payment The final payment of a mortgage loan that is considerably larger than the required periodic payments, because the loan amount was not fully amortized.

bargain and sale deed A deed that carries with it no warranties against liens or other encumbrances but that does imply the grantor has the right to convey title. Note that the grantor may add warranties to the deed at his or her discretion.

base fee A determinable fee estate that may be inherited.

base line One of a set of imaginary lines running east and west and crossing a principal meridian at a definite point. Base lines are used by surveyors for reference in locating and describing land under the rectangular survey system (or government survey method) of property description.

benchmark A permanent reference mark or point established for use by surveyors when measuring differences in elevation.

beneficiary 1. The person for whom a trust operates or in whose behalf the income from a trust estate is drawn. 2. A lender who lends money on real estate and takes back a note and deed of trust from the borrower.

bequest A provision in a will providing for the distribution of personal property.

bilateral contract A contract in which each party promises to perform an act in exchange for the other party's promise to perform.

bill of sale A written instrument given to pass title to personal property.

binder An agreement that may accompany an earnest money deposit for the purchase of real property as evidence of the purchaser's good faith and intent to complete the transaction.

blanket mortgage A mortgage that covers more than one parcel of real estate and provides for each parcel's partial release from the mortgage lien on repayment of a definite portion of the debt.

blockbusting The illegal practice of inducing homeowners to sell their properties by making representations regarding the entry, or prospective entry, of minority persons into the neighborhood. Sometimes referred to as *panic peddling.*

blue-sky laws The common name for state and federal laws that regulate the registration and sale of investment securities.

boycotting Two or more businesses conspire against other businesses to reduce competition.

branch office A secondary place of business apart from the principal or main office from which real estate business is conducted. A branch office generally must be run by a licensed real estate broker, broker salesperson, or associate broker working on behalf of the broker operating the principal office.

breach of contract The failure, without legal excuse, of one of the parties to a contract to perform according to the contract.

bridge loan A loan that bridges the sale of property. For example, a homeowner borrows from the bank the equity from her current home to use as a down payment on a new home. Then, when her current home sells, she uses her equity to repay a bridge loan.

broker One who buys and sells for another for a commission. *See also* real estate broker.

brokerage The business of buying and selling for another for a commission.

broker/salesperson A person who has passed the broker's licensing examination but is licensed to work only on behalf of a licensed broker and who may be allowed to manage an office. In many states, known as (and licensed as) associate broker or broker/associate.

brownfields Deserted, defunct, and derelict toxic industrial sites in need of renewal. Federal legislation has diminished the innocent landowner's liability exposure and provided the landowner the opportunity to expense cleanup costs rather than capitalize them.

budget loan A loan in which the monthly payments made by the borrower cover not only interest and a payment on the principal, but also $\frac{1}{12}$ of such expenses as taxes, insurance, assessments, private mortgage insurance premiums, and similar charges.

buffer zone A strip of land that separates one land use from another.

building code An ordinance specifying minimum standards of construction of buildings for the protection of public safety and health.

building line A line fixed at a certain distance from the front and/or sides of a lot beyond which no structure can project; a setback line used to ensure a degree of uniformity in the appearance of buildings and unobstructed light, air, and view.

building restrictions The limitations on the size or type of property improvements established by zoning acts or by deed or lease restrictions. Building restrictions are considered encumbrances, and violations render the title unmarketable.

bundle of legal rights The theory that land ownership involves ownership of all legal rights to the land, such as possession, control within the law, and enjoyment, rather than ownership of the land itself.

business plan A three- to five-year blueprint for an organizational or individual real estate practitioner.

buydown A payment made, often by the seller, to help the buyer qualify for the loan.

canvassing The practice of making telephone calls or visiting from door to door to seek prospective buyers or sellers; in the real estate business, generally associated with acquired listings in a given area.

capacity of parties The legal ability of persons to enter into a valid contract. Most persons have full capacity to contract and are said to be competent parties.

capital gain Profit earned from the sale of an asset.

capital investment The initial capital and the long-term expenditures made to establish and maintain a business or investment property.

capitalization The process of converting into present value (or obtaining the present worth of) a series of anticipated future periodic installments of net income. In real estate appraisal, it usually takes the form of discounting. The formula is expressed as

$$\frac{\text{income}}{\text{rate}} = \text{value}$$

capitalization rate The rate of return a property will produce on the owner's investment.

cash flow The net spendable income from an investment, determined by deducting all operating and fixed expenses from the gross income. If expenses exceed income, a negative cash flow is the result.

casualty insurance A type of insurance policy that protects a property owner or other person from loss or injury sustained as a result of theft, vandalism, or similar occurrences.

caveat emptor A Latin phrase meaning, "Let the buyer beware."

certificate of sale The document generally given to a purchaser at a tax foreclosure sale. A certificate of sale does not convey title; generally, it is an instrument certifying that the holder may receive title to the property after the redemption period has passed and that the holder paid the property taxes for that interim period.

certificate of title The statement of opinion on the status of the title to a parcel of real property, based on an examination of specified public records.

chain of title The succession of conveyances from some accepted starting point by which the present holder of real property derives her or his title.

charrettes Community planning tool that welcomes and improves public participation in discussions about a community's future growth and development.

chattels Personal property.

check Tracts of land located repetitively every 24 miles from a principal meridian and 24 miles from a defined base line. Guide meridians and correction lines define a check's boundaries, consisting of 16 townships. A correction line "corrects" for the curvature of the earth, and guide meridians slant to compensate for North Pole directional movement.

city planning commission A local governmental organization designed to direct and control the development of land within a municipality.

claim of right Used as a factor in determining adverse possession claims. Adversely occupying another's real estate for a statutory period of time may create a claim of right.

cloud on title A claim or encumbrance that may affect the title to land.

CLUE An insurance company repository for reported claim activity and previous property damage. CLUE is an acronym for Comprehensive Loss Underwriting Exchange. Insurers use the report to ascertain patterns of possible future claims and adjust their insurance premiums according to risk.

codicil A testamentary disposition subsequent to a will that alters, explains, adds to, or confirms the will, but does not revoke it.

coinsurance clause A clause in insurance policies covering real property that requires the policyholder to maintain fire insurance coverage that is generally equal to at least 80% of the property's actual replacement cost.

collateral Something of value given or pledged to a lender as a security for a debt or obligation.

color of title Used as a factor in an adverse possession claim when the occupying party actually received title but by a defective or incorrect deed (color of title).

commercial property A classification of real estate that includes income-producing property, such as office buildings, restaurants, shopping centers, hotels, and stores.

commingled property Property of a married couple that is so mixed or commingled that it is difficult to determine whether it is separate or community property. Commingled property becomes community property.

commingling The illegal act of a real estate broker who mixes the money of other people with that of his or her own; brokers are required by law to maintain a separate trust account for other parties' funds held temporarily by the broker.

commission The payment made to a broker for services rendered, such as in the sale or purchase of real property; this is usually a percentage of the selling price of the property.

common elements The parts of a property that are necessary or convenient to the existence, maintenance, and safety of a condominium, or that are normally in common use by all of the condominium residents. All condominium owners have an undivided ownership interest in the common elements.

common law A body of law based on custom, usage, and court decisions.

community property A system of property ownership based on the theory that each spouse has an equal interest in the property acquired by the efforts of either spouse during marriage.

comparables The sold properties, listed in an appraisal report, which are substantially equivalent to the subject property.

competent parties Persons who are recognized by law as being able to contract with others; usually those of legal age and sound mind. *See also* capacity of parties.

composite depreciation A method of determining the depreciation of a multibuilding property using the average rate at which all the buildings are depreciating.

Comprehensive Environmental Response, Compensation, and Liability Act (CERCLA) Federal legislation passed in 1980 requiring owners of contaminated properties to bear the cleanup costs. Also known as the Superfund legislation.

condemnation A judicial or administrative proceeding or process to exercise the power of eminent domain.

condominium The absolute ownership of an apartment or a unit, generally in a multiunit building, based on a legal description of the airspace the unit actually occupies, plus an undivided interest in the ownership of the common elements, which are owned together with the other condominium unit owners. The entire tract of real estate included in a condominium development is called a *parcel* or *development parcel*. One apartment or space in a condominium or a part of a property intended for independent use and having lawful access to the public way is called a *unit*. Ownership of one unit also includes a definite undivided interest in the common elements.

conforming mortgages Securitized mortgages sold on the secondary market that meet certain requirements established by Fannie Mae and Freddie Mac.

conformity *See* principle of conformity.

consideration Something of value that induces one to enter into a contract. Consideration may be "valuable" (money or commodity) or "good" (love and affection). Also, an act of forbearance, or the promise thereof, given by one party in exchange for something from the other. Forbearance is a promise *not* to do something.

constructive eviction 1. Acts by the landlord that so materially disturb or impair the tenant's enjoyment of the leased premises that the tenant is effectively forced to move out and terminate the lease without liability for any further rent. 2. A purchaser's inability to obtain clear title.

constructive notice Notice given to the world by recorded documents. All persons are charged with knowledge of such documents and their contents, whether or not they have actually examined them. Possession of property also is considered constructive notice that the person in possession has an interest in the property.

contingencies A provision or condition in the purchase of real estate requiring a certain act to be done or an event to happen before the contract becomes binding.

contract An agreement entered into by two or more legally competent parties by the terms of which one or more of the parties, for a consideration, undertakes to do or to refrain from doing some legal act or acts. A contract may be either *unilateral*, where only one party is bound to act, or *bilateral*, where all parties to the instrument are legally bound to act as prescribed.

contract for deed A contract for the sale of real estate under which the sale price is paid in periodic installments by the purchaser, who is in possession and holds equitable title, although actual title is retained by the seller until final payment. Also called an *installment contract* or *land contract*.

contract for exchange of real estate A contract for sale of real estate in which the consideration is paid wholly or partly in property.

contributory value An appraising principle where the value of a property's component parts are measured by their effect on the selling price of the whole. Appraisers use sold properties as "paired sales" to isolate component parts and to identify their monetary contribution to the whole.

conventional loan A loan that is not insured or guaranteed by a government agency.

conveyance A written instrument that evidences transfer of some interest in real property from one person to another.

cooperative A residential multiunit building whose title is held by a trust or corporation that is owned by, and operated for, the benefit of persons living within the building. These persons are the beneficial owners of the trust or the shareholders of the corporation, each having a proprietary lease.

corporation An entity or organization created by operation of law whose rights of doing business are essentially the same as those of an individual. The entity has continuous existence until dissolved according to legal procedures.

correction lines The horizontal provisions in the rectangular survey system (government survey method) made to compensate for the curvature of the earth's surface. Every fourth township line (at 24-mile intervals) is used as a correction line on which the intervals between the north and south range lines are remeasured and corrected to a full six miles.

cost approach The process of estimating the value of a property by adding the appraiser's estimate of the reproduction or replacement cost of the building, less depreciation, to the estimated land value.

counseling The business of providing people with expert advice on a subject, based on the counselor's extensive, expert knowledge of the subject.

counteroffer A new offer made as a reply to an offer received, having the effect of rejecting the original offer. The original offer cannot be accepted thereafter unless revived by the offeror repeating it.

Covenants, Conditions, and Restrictions (CC&Rs) Condominium documents that serve as the operational procedures describing the rights and prohibitions of the co-owners in a condominium association.

credit scoring A three-digit score that assesses a borrower's credit risk and the probability of default based on his or her past pay performances, outstanding credit balances, credit mix, time on file, and number of search inquiries.

cul-de-sac A dead-end street that widens sufficiently at the end to permit an automobile to make a U-turn.

curtesy A life estate, usually a fractional interest, given by some states to the surviving husband in real estate owned by his deceased wife. Most states have abolished curtesy.

cycle A recurring sequence of events that regularly follow one another, generally within a fixed interval of time.

datum A horizontal plane from which heights and depths are measured.

defeasible fee estate A qualified estate in which the grantee could lose his or her interest upon the occurrence or non-occurrence of a specified event. There are two types of defeasible fee estates: (1) those known as a condition subsequent where the possibility of re-entry takes place, and (2) a qualified limitation, where the grantee's ownership automatically ends with the possibility of reverter (otherwise known as a fee simple determinable). The words as *long as, while, or during* are key to creating a qualified limitation defeasible fee estate.

dba Doing business as.

debenture A note or bond given as evidence of debt and issued without security.

debt Something owed to another; an obligation to pay or return something.

declining balance method An accounting method of calculating depreciation for tax purposes designed to provide large deductions in the early years of ownership. *See also* accelerated depreciation.

decreasing returns *See* diminishing returns.

deed A written instrument that when executed and delivered conveys title to, or an interest in, real estate.

deed in lieu of foreclosure A process by which the mortgagor can avoid foreclosure. Mortgagor gives a deed to mortgagee when mortgagor is in default according to terms of mortgage.

deed of reconveyance The instrument used to reconvey title to a trustor under a deed of trust once the debt has been satisfied; also called a *reconveyance deed.*

deed of trust An instrument used to create a lien by which the mortgagor conveys her or his title to a trustee, who holds it as security for the benefit of the noteholder (the lender); also called a *trust deed.*

deed restrictions The clauses in a deed limiting the future uses of the property. Deed restrictions may impose a variety of limitations and conditions, such as limiting the density of buildings, dictating the types of structures that can be erected, and preventing buildings from being used for specific purposes or from being used at all.

default The nonperformance of a duty, whether arising under a contract or otherwise; failure to meet an obligation when due.

defeasance clause A clause used in leases or mortgages that cancels a specified right on the occurrence of a certain condition, such as cancellation of a mortgage on repayment of the mortgage loan.

deficiency judgment A personal judgment levied against the mortgagor when a foreclosure sale does not produce sufficient funds to pay the mortgage debt in full.

delinquent taxes Unpaid taxes that are past due.

delivery The legal act of transferring ownership. Documents such as deeds and purchase agreements must be delivered and accepted to be valid.

delivery in escrow Delivery of a deed to a third person until the performance of some act or condition by one of the parties.

demand The willingness of persons to buy available goods at a given price; often coupled with *supply.*

density zoning The zoning ordinances that restrict the average maximum number of houses per acre that may be built within a particular area, generally a subdivision.

depreciation 1. In appraisal, a loss of value in property due to all causes, including physical deterioration, functional obsolescence, and economic obsolescence. 2. In real estate investment, an expense deduction for tax purposes taken over the period of ownership of the income property.

descent The hereditary succession of an heir to the property of a relative who dies intestate.

designated agency An agency relationship where a client designates a broker to appoint an office agent to singularly represent his or her interest to the exclusion of all of the other agents in the broker's office.

determinable fee estate A fee-simple estate in which the property automatically reverts to the grantor on the occurrence of a specified event or condition.

devise A transfer of real estate by will or last testament. The donor is the devisor and the recipient is the devisee.

diminishing returns The principle that applies when a given parcel of land reaches its maximum percentage return on investment, and further expenditures for improving the property yield a decreasing return.

discount points An added loan fee charged by a lender to make the yield on a lower-than-market-value loan competitive with higher-interest loans. *See also* point.

discount rate The rate of interest a commercial bank must pay when it borrows from its federal reserve bank. Consequently, the discount rate is the rate of interest the banking system carries within its own framework. Member banks may take certain promissory notes that they have received from customers and sell them to their district federal reserve bank for less than face value. With the funds received, the banks can make further loans. Changes in the discount rate may cause banks and other lenders to reexamine credit policies and conditions.

dispossess To oust from land by legal process.

dominant tenement A property that includes in its ownership the appurtenant right to use an easement over another's property for a specific purpose.

dower The legal right or interest recognized in some states that a wife acquires in the property her husband held or acquired during their marriage. During the lifetime of the husband, the right is only a possibility of an interest; on his death it can become an interest in land.

due-on-sale clause *See* alienation clause.

duress The use of unlawful constraint that forces action or inaction against a person's will.

DVA loan A mortgage loan on approved property made to a qualified veteran by an authorized lender and guaranteed by the Department of Veterans Affairs to limit possible loss by the lender. Also called a *GI-guaranteed mortgage*.

earnest money deposit An amount of money deposited by a buyer under the terms of a contract. In the event that the buyer, for no valid or legal reason, backs out of the transaction, earnest money is sometimes used as liquidated damages.

easement A right to use the land of another for a specific purpose, such as for a right-of-way or utilities; an incorporeal interest in land. An easement appurtenant passes with the land when conveyed.

easement by necessity An easement allowed by law as necessary for the full enjoyment of a parcel of real estate; for example, a right of ingress and egress over a grantor's land.

easement by prescription An easement acquired by continuous, open, uninterrupted, exclusive, and adverse use of the property for the period of time prescribed by state law.

easement in gross An easement that is not created for the benefit of any land owned by the owner of the easement but that attaches personally to the easement owner. For example, the right to an easement granted by *A* to *B* to use a portion of *A*'s property for the rest of *B*'s life would be an easement in gross.

economic life The period of time over which an improved property will earn an income adequate to justify its continued existence.

economic obsolescence The impairment of desirability or useful life arising from factors external to the property, such as economic forces or environmental changes, that affect supply-demand relationships in the market. Loss in the use and value of a property arising from the factors of economic obsolescence is to be distinguished from loss in value from physical deterioration and functional obsolescence, both of which are inherent in the property. Also referred to as *locational obsolescence* or *environmental obsolescence*.

emblements Growing crops that are produced annually through the tenant's own care and labor and that she or he is entitled to take away after the tenancy is ended. Emblements are regarded as personal property even prior to harvest, so if the landlord terminates the lease, the tenant still may reenter the land and remove such crops. If the tenant terminates the tenancy voluntarily, however, he or she generally is not entitled to the emblements.

eminent domain The right of a government or municipal quasi-public body to acquire property for public use through a court action called *condemnation*, in which the court determines that the use is a public use and determines the price or compensation to be paid to the owner.

employee status The status of one who works as a direct employee of an employer. An employer is obligated to withhold income taxes and Social Security taxes from the compensation of his or her employees. *See also* independent contractor.

employment contract A document evidencing formal employment between the employer and the employee or between the principal and the agent. In the real estate business, this generally takes the form of a listing or management agreement.

encroachment A fixture or structure, such as a wall or fence, that invades a portion of a property belonging to another.

encumbrance Any lien that may diminish the value of the property, such as a mortgage, tax, or judgment lien; easement; restriction on the use of the land; or an outstanding dower right.

endorsement The act of writing one's name, either with or without additional words, on a negotiable instrument or on a paper attached to such instrument.

Equal Credit Opportunity Act (ECOA) Federal legislation requiring lenders to make credit equally available without discrimination based on race, sex, color, religion, marital status, age, national origin, or receipt of income from public assistance.

equalization The raising or lowering of assessed values for tax purposes in a particular county or taxing district to make them equal to assessments in other counties or districts.

equitable title The interest held by a vendee under a contract for deed or an installment contract; the equitable right to obtain absolute ownership to property when legal title is held in another's name. (Insurable interest)

equity The interest or value that an owner has in a property over and above any mortgage indebtedness.

erosion The gradual wearing away of land by water, wind, and general weather conditions; the diminishing of property caused by the elements.

errors and omissions insurance Insurance coverage for real estate agents against claims for innocent and negligent misrepresentation.

escheat The reversion of property to the state in the event that its owner dies without leaving a will and has no heirs to whom the property may pass by lawful descent.

escrow The closing of a transaction through a third party called an escrow agent, or *escrowee*, who receives certain funds and documents to be delivered on the performance of certain conditions in the escrow agreement.

estate for years An interest for a certain, exact period of time in property leased for a specified consideration.

estate in land The degree, quantity, nature, and extent of interest that a person has in real property.

estate in severalty An estate owned by one person.

estoppel certificate A legal instrument executed by a mortgagor showing the amount of the unpaid balance due on a mortgage and stating that the mortgagor has no defenses or offsets against the mortgagee at the time of execution of the certificate. Also called a *certificate of no defense.*

estovers Legally allowed necessities, such as the right of a tenant to use timber on leased property to support a minimum need for fuel or repairs.

ethical Conduct conforming to professional standards.

et al Latin, meaning "and others."

et ux The Latin abbreviation for *et uxor*, meaning "and wife."

et vir Latin, meaning "and husband."

eviction A legal process to oust a person from possession of real estate.

evidence of title A proof of ownership of property, which is commonly a certificate of title, a title insurance policy, an abstract of title with lawyer's opinion, or a Torrens registration certificate. *See also* Torrens system.

exchange A transaction in which all or part of the consideration for the purchase of real property is the transfer of like-kind property (that is, real estate for real estate).

exclusive-agency listing A listing contract under which the owner appoints a real estate broker as his or her exclusive agent for a designated period of time to sell the property on the owner's stated terms for a commission. The owner, however, reserves the right to sell without paying anyone a commission by selling to a prospect who has not been introduced or claimed by the broker.

exclusive-right-to-sell listing A listing contract under which the owner appoints a real estate broker as his or her exclusive agent for a designated period of time to sell the property on the owner's stated terms and agrees to pay the broker a commission when the property is sold, whether by the broker, the owner, or another broker.

executed contract A contract in which all parties have fulfilled their promises and thus performed the contract.

execution The signing and delivery of an instrument. Also, a legal order directing an official to enforce a judgment against the property of a debtor.

executor The person designated in a will to handle the state of the deceased. The probate court must approve any sale of property by the executor.

executory contract A contract under which something remains to be done by one or more of the parties.

expenses The short-term costs that are deducted from an investment property's income, such as minor repairs, regular maintenance, and renting costs.

expressed contract An oral or written contract in which the parties state their terms and express their intentions in words.

Fair Housing Act of 1968 The term for Title VIII of the Civil Rights Act of 1968 as amended, which prohibits discrimination based on race, color, sex, religion, national origin, handicaps, and familial status in the sale and rental of residential property.

Federal Home Loan Mortgage Corporation (FHLMC) A federally chartered corporation created to provide a secondary mortgage market for conventional loans (Freddie Mac).

Federal Housing Administration (FHA) A federal administrative body created by the National Housing Act in 1934 to encourage improvement in housing standards and conditions, to provide an adequate home-financing system through the insurance of housing mortgages and credit, and to exert a stabilizing influence on the mortgage market.

federal income tax An annual tax based on income, including monies derived from the lease, use, or operation of real estate.

Federal National Mortgage Association (FNMA) "Fannie Mae" is the popular name for this federally chartered corporation, which creates a secondary market for existing mortgages. FNMA does not loan money directly, but rather buys DVA, FHA, and conventional loans.

fee-simple estate The maximum possible estate or right of ownership of real property continuing forever. Sometimes called a *fee* or *fee-simple absolute*.

FHA appraisal An FHA evaluation of a property as security for a loan. Includes the study of the physical characteristics of the property and surroundings, and the location of the property.

FHA loan A loan insured by the FHA and made by an approved lender in accordance with FHA regulations.

fiduciary relationship A relationship of trust and confidence, as between trustee and beneficiary, attorney and client, principal and agent.

financing statement *See* Uniform Commercial Code.

first mortgage A mortgage that creates a superior voluntary lien on the property mortgaged relative to other charges or encumbrances against the property.

fiscal policy The government's policy in regard to taxation and spending programs. The balance between these two areas determines the amount of money the government will withdraw or feed into the economy in an attempt to counter economic peaks and slumps.

fixture An article that was once personal property but has been so affixed to real estate that it has become real property.

forcible entry and detainer A summary proceeding for restoring to possession of land one who is wrongfully kept out or has been wrongfully deprived of the possession.

foreclosure A legal procedure by which property used as security for a debt is sold to satisfy the debt in the event of default in payment of the mortgage note or default of other terms in the mortgage document. The foreclosure procedure brings the rights of all parties to a conclusion and passes the title in the mortgaged property either to the holder of the mortgage or to a third party who may purchase the realty at the foreclosure sale, free of all encumbrances affecting the property subsequent to the mortgage.

foreign acknowledgment An acknowledgment taken outside of the state in which the land lies.

franchise A private contractual agreement to run a business using a designated trade name and operating procedures.

fraud A misstatement of a material fact made with intent to deceive or made with reckless disregard of the truth and that actually does deceive.

freehold estate An estate in land in which ownership is for an indeterminate length of time, in contrast to a leasehold estate.

functional obsolescence The impairment of functional capacity or efficiency; the inability of a structure to perform adequately the function for which it currently is employed. Functional obsolescence reflects the loss in value brought about by factors that affect the property, such as overcapacity, inadequacy, or changes in the art.

funding fee A fee required by the Department of Veterans Affairs for making a VA guaranteed loan. The funding fee is added in with the loan and then forwarded to the VA to guarantee a veteran's loan.

future interest A person's present right to an interest in real property that will not result in possession or enjoyment until sometime in the future, such as a reversion or right of reentry.

gap A defect in the chain of title of a particular parcel of real estate; a missing document or conveyance that raises doubt as to the present ownership of the land.

general contractor A construction specialist who enters into a formal construction contract with a landowner or master lessee to construct a real estate building or project. The general contractor often contracts with several subcontractors specializing in various aspects of the building process to perform individual jobs.

general lien A lien on all real and personal property owned by a debtor.

general partnership *See* partnership.

general tax *See* ad valorem tax.

general warranty deed A deed that states that the title conveyed therein is good from the sovereignty of the soil to the grantee therein and that no one else can successfully claim the property. This type of deed contains several specific warranties sometimes referred to as the English Covenants of Title.

GI-guaranteed mortgage *See* DVA loan.

government lots Fractional sections in the rectangular survey system (government survey method) that are less than one full quarter-section in area.

Government National Mortgage Association (GNMA) "Ginnie Mae," a federal agency and division of HUD that operates special assistance aspects of federally aided housing programs and participates in the secondary market through its mortgage-backed securities pools.

graduated lease Lease that provides for rent increases at set future dates.

graduated payment mortgage A mortgage loan for which the initial payments are low but increase over the life of the loan.

grant The act of conveying or transferring title to real property.

grant deed A type of deed that includes three basic warranties: (1) the owner warrants that she or he has the right to convey the property, (2) the owner warrants that the property is not encumbered other than with those encumbrances listed in the deed, and (3) the owner promises to convey any after-acquired title to the property. Grant deeds are popular in states that rely heavily on title insurance.

grantee A person to whom real estate is conveyed; the buyer.

grantor A person who conveys real estate by deed; the seller.

gross lease A lease or property under which a landlord pays all property charges regularly incurred through ownership, such as repairs, taxes, insurance, and operating expenses. Most residential leases are gross leases.

gross national product (GNP) The total value of all goods and services produced in the United States in a year.

gross rent multiplier (GRM) A figure used as a multiplier of the gross monthly rental income of a property to produce an estimate of the property's value.

ground lease A lease of land only, on which the tenant usually owns a building or is required to build her or his own building as specified in the lease. Such leases are usually long-term net leases; a tenant's rights and obligations continue until the lease expires or is terminated through default.

guaranteed sale plan An agreement between the broker and the seller that if the seller's real property is not sold before a certain date, the broker will purchase it for a specified price.

guardian One who guards or cares for another person's rights and properties. A guardian has legal custody of the affairs of a minor or a person incapable of taking care of his or her own interests, called a *ward*.

habendum clause The deed clause beginning "to have and to hold," which defines or limits the extent of ownership in the estate granted by the deed.

heir One who might inherit or succeed to an interest in land under the state law of descent when the owner dies without leaving a valid will.

hereditaments Every kind of inheritable property, including personal, real corporeal, and incorporeal.

highest and best use The possible use of land that will produce the greatest net income and thus develop the highest land value.

holdover tenancy A tenancy by which a lessee retains possession of leased property after her or his lease has expired and the landlord, by continuing to accept rent from the tenant, agrees to the tenant's continued occupancy as defined by state law.

holographic will A will that is written, dated, and signed in the handwriting of the maker.

homeowner's insurance policy A standardized package insurance policy that covers a residential real estate owner against financial loss from fire, theft, public liability, and other common risks.

homeowner's warranty program An insurance program offered to buyers by some brokerages, warranting the property against certain defects for a specified period of time.

homestead protection The land and the improvements thereon designated by the owner as his or her homestead and, therefore, protected by state law, either in whole or in part, from forced sale by certain creditors of the owner.

HUD The Department of Housing and Urban Development; regulates FHA and GNMA.

hypothecation The pledge of property as security of a loan in which the borrower maintains possession of the property while it is pledged as security.

implied contract A contract under which the agreement of the parties is demonstrated by their acts and conduct.

implied grant A method of creating an easement. One party may be using another's property for the benefit of both parties—for example, a sewer on a property that serves two or more properties. Sometimes referred to as an *easement by implication*.

improvement 1. Improvements *on* land: any structure, usually privately owned, erected on a site to enhance the value of the property; for example, buildings, fences, and driveways. 2. Improvements *to* land: usually a publicly owned structure; for example, curbs, sidewalks, and sewers.

inchoate right Incomplete right, such as a wife's dower interest in her husband's property during his life.

income approach The process of estimating the value of an income-producing property by capitalization of the annual net income expected to be produced by the property during its remaining useful life.

incorporeal right A nonpossessory right in real estate; for example, an easement or right-of-way.

increasing returns The principle that applies when increased expenditures for improvements to a given parcel of land yield an increasing percentage return on investment.

independent contractor One who is retained to perform a certain act but who is subject to the control and direction of another only as to the end result, and not as to how he or she performs the act. Unlike an employee, an independent contractor pays all of his or her expenses, pays his or her income and Social Security taxes, and receives no employee benefits. Many real estate salespeople are independent contractors.

index lease Lease that allows the rent to be increased or decreased periodically, based on changes in a selected economic index, such as the Consumer Price Index.

industrial property All land and buildings used or suited for use in the production, storage, or distribution of tangible goods.

installment contract *See* contract for deed.

installment sale A method of reporting gain received from the sale of real estate when the sale price is paid in two or more installments over two or more years. If the sale meets certain requirements, a taxpayer can spread recognition of the reportable gain over more than one year, which may result in tax savings.

insurable title A title to land that a title company will insure.

insurance The indemnification against loss from a specific hazard or peril through a contract (called a policy) and for a consideration (called a premium).

interest A charge made by a lender for the use of money.

interim financing A short-term loan usually made during the construction phase of a building project, often referred to as a *construction loan.*

intestate The condition of a property owner who dies without leaving a will. Title to such property passes to his or her heirs as provided in the state law of descent.

invalid Having no force or effect.

invalidate To render null and void.

investment Money directed toward the purchase, improvement, and development of an asset in expectation of income or profits. A good financial investment has the following characteristics: safety, regularity of yield, marketability, acceptable denominations, valuable collateral, acceptable duration, required attention, and potential appreciation.

joint tenancy The ownership of real estate by two or more parties who have been named in one conveyance as joint tenants. On the death of a joint tenant, her or his interest passes to the surviving joint tenant or tenants by the right of survivorship.

joint venture The joining of two or more people to conduct a specific business enterprise. A joint venture is similar to a partnership in that it must be created by agreement between the parties to share in the losses and profits of the venture. It is unlike a partnership in that the venture is for one specific project only, rather than for a continuing business relationship.

judgment The official and authentic decision of a court on the respective rights and claims of the parties to an action or suit. When a judgment is entered and recorded with the county recorder, it usually becomes a general lien on the property of the defendant for a ten-year period.

judgment clause A provision that may be included in notes, leases, and contracts by which the debtor, lessee, or obligor authorizes any attorney to go into court to confess a judgment against him or her for a default in payment. Also called a *cognovit.*

laches An equitable doctrine used by the courts to bar a legal claim or prevent the assertion of a right because of undue delay, negligence, or failure to assert the claim or right. *See also* statute of limitations.

land The earth's surface extending downward to the center of the earth and upward infinitely into space.

land contract *See* contract for deed.

law of agency *See* agent.

lawyer's opinion of title *See* attorney's opinion of title.

lease A contract between a landlord (the lessor) and a tenant (the lessee) transferring the right to exclusive possession and use of the landlord's real property to the lessee for a specified period of time and for a stated consideration (rent). By state law, leases for longer than a certain period of time (generally one year) must be in writing to be enforceable.

leasehold estate A tenant's right to occupy real estate during the term of a lease, generally considered to be a personal property interest.

legacy A disposition of money or personal property by will.

legal description A description of a specific parcel of real estate sufficient for an independent surveyor to locate and identify it. The most common forms of legal description are *rectangular survey, metes and bounds,* and *subdivision lot and block (plat).*

legality of object An element that must be present in a valid contract. If a contract has for its object an act that violates the laws of the United States or the laws of a state to which the parties are subject, it is illegal, invalid, and not recognized by the courts.

lessee The tenant who leases a property.

lessor One who leases property to a tenant.

leverage The use of borrowed money to finance the bulk of an investment.

levy To assess, seize, or collect. To levy a tax is to assess a property and set the rate of taxation. To levy an execution is to seize officially the property of a person to satisfy an obligation.

license 1. A privilege or right granted to a person by a state to operate as a real estate broker or salesperson. 2. The revocable permission for a temporary use of land—a personal right that cannot be sold.

lien A right given by law to certain creditors to have their debt paid out of the property of a defaulting debtor, usually by means of a court sale.

life estate An interest in real or personal property that is limited in duration to the lifetime of its owner or some other designated person.

life tenant A person in possession of a life estate.

liquidated damages Liquidated damages occur when, by contractual agreement, defaulted earnest money becomes the personal property of the seller.

liquidity The ability to sell an asset and convert it into cash at a price close to its true value.

lis pendens A public notice that a lawsuit affecting title to or possession, use, and enjoyment of a parcel of real estate has been filed in either a state or federal court.

listing agreement A contract between a landowner (as principal) and a licensed real estate broker (as agent) by which the broker is employed as agent to list and sell real estate on the owner's terms within a given time, for which service the landowner agrees to pay a commission.

listing broker The broker in a multiple-listing situation from whose office a listing agreement is initiated, as opposed to the selling broker, from whose office negotiations leading to a sale are initiated. The listing broker and the selling broker may, of course, be the same person. *See also* multiple listing.

littoral rights 1. A landowner's claim to use water in large lakes and oceans adjacent to her or his property. 2. The ownership rights to land bordering these bodies of water up to the high-water mark.

lot and block description A description of real property that identifies a parcel of land by reference to lot and block numbers within a subdivision, as identified on a subdivided *plat* duly recorded in the county recorder's office.

management agreement A contract between the owner of income property and a management firm or individual property manager outlining the scope of the manager's authority.

marginal lease A lease agreement that barely covers the costs of operation for the property.

marginal real estate Land that barely covers the costs of operation.

marketable title A good or clear salable title reasonably free from risk of litigation over possible defects; also called a *merchantable title.*

market/data approach A method of appraising or evaluating real property based on the proposition that an informed purchaser would pay no more for a property than the cost to him or her of acquiring an existing property with the same utility. This approach is applicable when an active market provides sufficient quantities of reliable data that can be verified from authoritative sources. The approach is relatively unreliable in an inactive market or in estimating the value of properties for which no real comparable sales data are available. It also is questionable when sales data cannot be verified with principals to the transaction. Also referred to as the *market comparison* or *direct sales comparison approach.*

market price The actual selling price of a property.

market value The most profitable price a property will bring in a competitive and open market under all conditions requisite to a fair sale. The price at which a buyer would buy and a seller would sell, each acting prudently and knowledgeably, and assuming the price is not affected by undue stimulus.

mechanic's lien A statutory lien created in favor of contractors, laborers, and materialmen or material suppliers who have performed work or furnished materials in improving real property.

metes-and-bounds description A legal description of a parcel of land that begins at a well-marked point and follows the boundaries, using direction and distances around the tract, back to the *point of beginning.*

mill A tax rate used by municipalities to compute property tax. For example, 50 mills = 5% of the taxable value, or it can be computed by thinking of millage as $50 per $1,000 of taxable value.

A. 200,000 taxable value × 5% = $10,000

B. 200,000/1,000 = 200 × $50 = $10,000

millage rate A property tax rate obtained by dividing the total assessed value of all the property in the tax district into the total amount of revenue needed by the taxing district. This millage rate then is applied to the taxable value of each property in the district to determine individual taxes.

misrepresentation To represent falsely; to give an untrue idea of a property. May be accomplished by omission or concealment of a material fact.

monetary policy The government regulation of the amount of money in circulation through such institutions as the Federal Reserve Board.

money judgment A court judgment ordering payment of money rather than specific performance of a certain action. *See also* judgment.

money market Those institutions, such as banks, savings-and-loan associations, and life insurance companies, who supply money and credit to borrowers.

month-to-month tenancy A periodic tenancy—the tenant rents for one period at a time. In the absence of a rental agreement (oral or written), a tenancy generally is considered to be from month to month.

monument Fixed natural or artificial objects, used in metes-and-bounds description, to establish the boundaries; located at the corners.

mortgage A conditional transfer or pledge of real estate as security for a loan. Also, the document creating a mortgage lien.

mortgage lien A lien or charge on a mortgagor's property that secures the underlying debt obligations.

mortgagor One who, having all or part of title to property, pledges that property as security for a debt; the borrower.

multiple listing An exclusive listing (generally, an exclusive right to sell) with the additional authority and obligation on the part of the listing broker to distribute the listing to other brokers in the multiple-listing organization.

municipal ordinances The laws, regulations, and codes enacted by the governing body of a municipality.

mutual rescission The act of putting an end to a contract by mutual agreement of the parties.

negligence Carelessness and inattentiveness resulting in violation of trust. Failure to do what is required.

net operating income The gross income of the property minus vacancy, collection losses, and operating expenses (not including debt service).

net lease A lease requiring the tenant to pay not only rent but also costs incurred in maintaining the property, including taxes, insurance, utilities, and repairs. If the tenant pays for everything, it is referred to as a triple net lease.

nonconforming use A use of property that is permitted to continue after a zoning ordinance prohibiting it has been established for the area.

nonhomogeneity A lack of uniformity; dissimilarity. Because no two parcels of land are geographically alike, real estate is said to be nonhomogeneous, or heterogeneous.

notarize To certify or attest to a document, as by a *notary public.*

notary public A public official authorized to certify and attest to documents, take affidavits, take acknowledgments, administer oaths, and perform other such acts.

note An instrument of credit given to attest a debt.

novation Acceptance by parties to an agreement to replace an old debtor with a new one. A novation releases liability.

offer and notification of acceptance The two components of a valid contract; a "meeting of the minds."

officer's deed A deed by sheriffs, trustees, guardians, etc.

one hundred percent commission plan A salesperson compensation plan by which the salesperson pays his or her broker a monthly service charge to cover the costs of office expenses and receives 100% of the commissions from the sales that he or she negotiates.

open-end mortgage A mortgage loan expandable by increments up to a maximum dollar amount, all of which is secured by the same original mortgage.

open listing A listing contract under which the broker's commission is contingent on the broker producing a "ready, willing, and able" buyer before the property is sold by the seller or another broker; the principal (owner) reserves the right to list the property with other brokers.

option The right to purchase property within a definite time at a specified price. No obligation to purchase exists, but the seller is obligated to sell if the option holder exercises the right to purchase.

optionee The party that receives and holds an option.

optionor The party that grants or gives an option.

ownership The exclusive right to hold, possess or control, and dispose of a tangible or intangible thing. Ownerships may be held by a person, corporation, or governmental entity.

package mortgage A method of financing in which the purchase of the land also finances the purchase of certain personal property items. Take, for example, the purchase of a motel, in which washers, dryers, refrigerators, beds, and linen are packaged together.

parol evidence rule A law that states that no prior or contemporary oral or extraneously written agreement can change the terms of a contract.

partial eviction A case in which the landlord's negligence deprives the tenant of the use of all or part of the premises.

participation financing A mortgage in which the lender participates in the income of the mortgaged venture beyond a fixed return, or receives a yield on the loan in addition to the straight interest rate.

partition The division of cotenants' interests in real property when the parties do not all voluntarily agree to terminate the co-ownership; takes place through court procedures.

partnership An association of two or more individuals who carry on a continuing business for profit as co-owners. Under the law, a partnership is regarded as a group of individuals rather than as a single entity. A general partnership is a typical form of joint venture in which each general partner shares in the administration, profits, and losses of the operation. A limited partnership is a business arrangement by which the operation is administered by one or more general partners and funded by limited or silent partners, who are by law responsible for losses only to the extent of their investment.

party wall easement A wall that is located on or at a boundary line between two adjoining parcels for the use of the owners of both properties.

payee The party that receives payment.

payor The party that makes payment to another.

percentage lease A lease commonly used for retail property in which the rental is based on the tenant's gross sales at the premises; often stipulates a base monthly rental plus a percentage of any gross sales above a certain amount.

performance bond A binding agreement, often accompanied by surety and usually posted by one who is to perform work for another, that assures that a project or undertaking will be completed as per the agreement or contract.

periodic estate An interest in leased property that continues from period to period—week to week, month to month, or year to year.

permanent reference marker Referred to as a PRM, it is a fixed object that leads the surveyor to the point of beginning (POB). In most surveys, two different PRMs are used to locate the POB.

personal assistant An individual working for a broker or salesperson who handles non–sales-related aspects of real estate transactions. However, if the personal assistant is licensed, then he or she can also handle the sales-related aspects of the transaction.

personal property Items, called *chattels*, that do not fit into the definition of real property; movable objects.

physical deterioration A reduction in utility resulting from an impairment of physical condition. For purposes of appraisal analysis, it is most common and convenient to divide physical deterioration into curable and incurable components.

plat A map of a town, section, or subdivision indicating the location and boundaries of individual properties.

plat book A book containing recorded subdivisions of land.

point A unit of measurement used for various loan charges; one point equals one percent of the amount of the loan. *See also* discount points.

point of beginning The starting point of the survey situated in one corner of the parcel in a *metes-and-bounds description*. All metes-and-bounds descriptions must follow the boundaries of the parcel back to the point of beginning.

police power The government's right to impose laws, statutes, and ordinances to protect the public health, safety, and welfare, including zoning ordinances and building codes.

power of attorney A written instrument authorizing a person (the attorney-in-fact) to act on behalf of the maker to the extent indicated in the instrument.

premises The specific section of a deed that states the names of the parties, recital of consideration, operative words of conveyance, legal property description, and appurtenance provisions.

prepayment clause In a mortgage, the statement of the terms on which the mortgagor may pay the entire or stated amount of the mortgage principal at some time prior to the due date.

prepayment penalty A charge imposed on a borrower by a lender for early payment of the loan principal to compensate the lender for interest and other charges that would otherwise be lost.

price fixing *See* antitrust laws.

primary mortgage market *See* secondary mortgage market.

principal 1. A sum lent or employed as a fund or investment, as distinguished from its income or profits. 2. The original amount (as in a loan) of the total due and payable at a certain date. 3. A main party to a transaction—the person for whom the agent works.

principal meridian One of 35 north and south survey lines established and defined as part of the rectangular survey system (government survey method).

principle of conformity The appraisal theory stating that buildings that are similar in design, construction, and age to other buildings in the area have a higher value than they would have in a neighborhood of dissimilar buildings.

priority The order of position or time. The priority of liens generally is determined by the chronological order in which the lien documents are recorded; tax liens (like special assessments), however, have priority, even over previously recorded liens.

probate The formal judicial proceeding to prove or confirm the validity of a will or proof of heirship and to settle the affairs of the deceased.

procuring cause The effort that brings about the desired result. Under an open listing, the broker who is the procuring cause of the sale receives the commission.

property disclosure acts State mandated seller's property disclosure reports. These reports place the burden of defect disclosure on the seller. Agents are not required to discover property defects but are required to disclose them if they are known.

property management The operation of the property of another for compensation. Includes marketing space; advertising and rental activities; collecting, recording, and remitting rents; maintaining the property; tenant relations; hiring employees; keeping proper accounts; and rendering periodic reports to the owner.

property tax Taxes levied by the government against either real or personal property. The right to tax real property in the United States rests exclusively with the states, not with the federal government.

proration The proportional division or distribution of expenses of property ownership between two or more parties. Closing statement prorations generally include taxes, rents, insurance, interest charges, and assessments.

prospectus A printed advertisement, usually in pamphlet form, presenting a new development, subdivision, business venture, or stock issue.

public utility easement A right granted by a property owner to a public utility company to erect and maintain poles, wires, and conduits on, across, or under her or his land for telephone, electric power, gas, water, or sewer installation.

pur autre vie A Latin term meaning "for the life of another." A life estate pur autre vie is a life estate measured by the life of a person other than the grantee. Also spelled *per autrie vie.*

purchase-money mortgage A note secured by a mortgage or deed of trust given by a buyer, as a mortgagor, to a seller, as a mortgagee, as part of the purchase price of the real estate.

qualifying The act of determining a prospect's motivation, then matching his or her needs with the available inventory.

quitclaim deed A conveyance by which the grantor transfers whatever interest he or she has in the real estate without warranties or obligations.

range A six-mile strip of land measured east and west from the meridian lines.

"ready, willing, and able" buyer One who is prepared to buy property on the seller's terms and is ready to take positive steps to consummate the transaction.

real estate Land; a portion of the earth's surface extending downward to the center of the earth and upward infinitely into space, including all things permanently attached thereto, whether by nature or by man.

real estate broker Any person, partnership, association, or corporation that sells (or offers to sell), buys (or offers to buy), or negotiates the purchase, sale, or exchange of real estate, or that leases (or offers to lease) or rents (or offers to rent) any real estate or the improvements thereon for others and for a compensation or valuable consideration. A real estate broker may not conduct business without a real estate broker's license.

Real Estate Investment Trust (REIT) Ownership of real estate by a group of individual investors who purchase certificates of ownership in a trust. The trust invests in real property and distributes the profits back to the investors free of corporate income tax.

Real Estate Settlement Procedures Act (RESPA) The federal law ensuring that the buyer and seller in a real estate transaction have knowledge of all the settlement costs when the purchase of a one to four-family residential dwelling is financed by a federally related mortgage loan. Prohibits kickbacks.

reality of consent An element of all valid contracts. Offer and acceptance in a contract usually are taken to mean that reality of consent also is present. This is not the case, however, if any of the following are present: mistake, misrepresentation, fraud, undue influence, or duress.

real property Real property consists of land, anything affixed to it so as to be regarded as a permanent part of the land, that which is appurtenant to the land, and that which is immovable by law, including all rights and interests.

REALTOR® A registered trademark term reserved for the sole use of active members of local REALTORS® boards affiliated with the National Association of REALTORS®.

recapture In the year of sale, all depreciation or cost recovery taken on depreciable property in excess of the amount allowed by the straight-line method is subject to recapture provisions as established by the IRS, which has the effect of taxing the excess at ordinary income rates. Recapture is designed to prevent a taxpayer from taking advantage of both accelerated depreciation and capital gain treatment.

receiver The court-appointed custodian of property involved in litigation, pending final disposition of the matter before the court.

reconciliation 1. The final step in the appraisal process in which the appraiser reconciles the estimates of value received from the market/data, cost, and income approaches to arrive at a final estimate of market value for the subject property. 2. An accounting procedure that balances a trust account by comparing the general ledger with the combined total of the account's individual ledger balances.

recording The act of entering or recording documents affecting or conveying interests in real estate in the recorder's office established in each county. Until recorded, a deed or mortgage generally is not effective against subsequent purchases or mortgage liens.

recovery fund A fund established in some states from real estate license funds to cover claims of aggrieved parties who have suffered monetary damage through the actions of a real estate licensee. To protect the public, some states mandate *errors and omissions* insurance as a requirement for licensure.

rectangular survey system A system established in 1785 by the federal government that provides for surveying and describing land by reference to principal meridians and base lines.

redemption period A period of time established by state law during which a property owner has the right to redeem her or his real estate from a foreclosure or tax sale by paying the sales price, interest, and costs. Many states do not have mortgage redemption laws.

redlining The illegal practice of denying loans or restricting their number for certain areas of a community.

Regulation Z A regulation of the Federal Reserve Board designed to ensure that borrowers and customers in need of consumer credit are given meaningful information with respect to the cost of credit.

release To relinquish an interest in or claim to a parcel of property.

relocation service An organization that aids a person in selling a property in one area and buying another property in another area.

remainder The remnant of an estate that has been conveyed to take effect and be enjoyed after the termination of a prior estate, such as when an owner conveys a life estate to one party and the remainder to another.

renegotiable rate mortgage A mortgage loan that is granted for a term of 3 to 5 years and secured by a long-term mortgage of up to 30 years with the interest rate being renegotiated or adjusted each period.

rent A fixed, periodic payment made by a tenant of a property to the owner for possession and use, usually by prior agreement of the parties.

rent schedule A statement of proposed rental rates, determined by the owner or the property manager or both, based on a building's estimated expenses, market supply and demand, and the owner's long-range goals for the property.

replacement cost The cost of construction at current prices of a building having utility equivalent to the building being appraised but built with modern materials and according to current standards, designs, and layout.

reproduction cost The cost of construction at current prices of an exact duplicate or replica using the same materials, construction standards, design, layout, and quality of workmanship and embodying all the deficiencies, superadequacies, and obsolescences of the subject building.

rescission The termination of a contract by mutual agreement of the parties.

reservation in a deed The creation by a deed to property of a new right in favor of the grantor. Usually involves an easement, a life estate, or a mineral interest.

restriction A limitation on the use of real property, generally originated by the owner or subdivider in a deed.

reverse annuity mortgage A mortgage loan that allows the owner to receive periodic payments based on the equity in the home.

reversion The remnant of an estate that the grantor holds after he or she has granted a life estate to another person; the estate will return or revert to the grantor. Also called a *reverter*.

reversionary right An owner's right to regain possession of leased property on termination of the lease agreement.

rezoning The process involved in changing the existing zoning of a property or area.

right of first refusal A person's right to have the first opportunity to either lease or purchase real property.

right of survivorship *See* joint tenancy.

riparian rights An owner's rights in land that borders flowing water, such as a stream or river. These rights include access to and use of the water.

Rural Development A federal agency of the U.S. Department of Agriculture that channels credit to farmers and rural residents and communities; formerly known as the Farm Service Agency and Farmer's Home Administration (FmHA).

sale and leaseback A transaction in which an owner sells her or his improved property and, as part of the same transaction, signs a long-term lease to remain in possession of the premises.

sales contract A contract containing the complete terms of the agreement between buyer and seller for the sale of a particular parcel or parcels of real estate.

salesperson A person who performs real estate activities while employed by or associated with a licensed real estate broker.

satisfaction A document acknowledging the payment of a debt. Once filed, the collateral pledged (mortgage) is returned to the mortgagor for a "mortgage burning party."

secondary mortgage market A market for the purchase and sale of existing mortgages, designed to provide greater liquidity for mortgages; also called the secondary money market. Mortgages are originated in the primary mortgage market.

section A portion of a township under the rectangular survey system (government survey method). A township is divided into 36 sections numbered 1 to 36. A section is a square with mile-long sides and an area of one square mile, or 640 acres.

self-proving will A will in which the witnesses give their testimony at the time of signing. This testimony is preserved in a notarized affidavit to eliminate the problem of finding the witnesses at the maker's death and to assist in the probating procedure.

selling broker *See* listing broker.

separate property The real property owned by a husband or wife prior to their marriage.

servient tenement The land on which an easement exists in favor of an adjacent property; also called a *servient estate.*

setback The amount of space local zoning regulations require between a lot line and a building line.

severalty The ownership of real property by one person only; also called *sole ownership.*

short sale A sale of secured property that produces less money than is owed to the lender, but in order to expedite the sale and avoid foreclosure expense, the lender releases its interest so the property can be sold.

situs The personal preference of people for one area of land over another, not necessarily based on objective facts and knowledge.

sole ownership *See* severalty.

sovereignty of the soil The beginning of the record of ownership of land by conveyance from the sovereign or the state. Historically, this is known also as a *patent.*

special assessment A tax or levy customarily imposed against only those specific parcels of real estate that will benefit from a proposed public improvement, such as a street or sewer.

special warranty deed A deed in which the grantor warrants or guarantees the title only against defects arising during the period of his or her tenure and ownership of the property and not against defects existing before that time, generally using the language "by, through, or under the grantor but not otherwise."

specific lien A lien affecting or attaching only to a certain, specific parcel of land or piece of property.

specific performance suit A legal action brought in a court of equity in special cases to compel a party to carry out the terms of a contract. The basis for an equity court's jurisdiction in breach of a real estate contract is that land is unique, and mere legal damages would not adequately compensate the buyer for the seller's breach.

sponsoring broker A duly licensed real estate broker who employs a salesperson. Under law, the broker is responsible for the acts of her or his salespeople.

squatter's rights Those rights acquired through adverse possession. By "squatting" on land for a certain statutory period under prescribed conditions, one may acquire title by limitations. If an easement only is acquired, instead of the title to the land itself, one has title by prescription, or easement by prescription.

statute of frauds The part of a state law that requires certain instruments, such as deeds, real estate sales contracts, and certain leases to be in writing to be legally enforceable.

statute of limitations That law pertaining to the period of time within which certain actions must be brought to court.

statutory lien A lien imposed on property by statute, for example, a tax lien; in contrast to a voluntary lien, which an owner places on his or her own real estate, for example, a mortgage lien.

steering The illegal practice of channeling home seekers to particular areas or avoiding specific areas, either to maintain or to change the character of an area, or to create a speculative situation.

stigmatized property A property regarded by some as undesirable because of events that have occurred on the property, like murder or suicide, or present paranormal activities. Sometimes, proximity to undesirable property causes a property to become stigmatized, too.

straight-line method A method of calculating depreciation for tax purposes computed by dividing the adjusted basis of a property less its estimated salvage value by the estimated number of years of remaining useful life.

subcontractor *See* general contractor.

subagency An agent appoints a subagent to help the agent in a specified transaction and to act on the principal's behalf.

subdivision A tract of land divided by the owner, known as the subdivider, into blocks, building lots, and streets according to a recorded subdivision plat that must comply with local ordinances and regulations.

subletting The leasing of premises by a lessee to a third party for part of the lessee's remaining term. *See also* assignment.

subordination A relegation to a lesser position, usually in respect to a right or security.

subordination agreement An agreement that changes the order of priority of liens between two creditors.

subrogation The substitution of one creditor for another, with the substituted person succeeding to the legal rights and claims of the original claimant. Subrogation is used by title insurers to acquire the right to sue from the injured party to recover any claims they have paid.

substitution An appraisal principle stating that the maximum value of a property tends to be set by the cost of purchasing an equally desirable and valuable substitute property, assuming that no costly delay is encountered in making the substitution.

suit for possession A court suit initiated by a landlord to evict a tenant from leased premises after the tenant has breached one of the terms of the lease or has held possession of the property after the lease's expiration.

suit for specific performance A legal action brought by either a buyer or a seller to enforce performance of the terms of a contract.

suit (bill) to quiet title A legal action intended to establish or settle the title to a particular property, especially when there is a cloud on the title.

summation appraisal An approach under which value equals estimated land value plus reproduction costs of any improvements after depreciation has been subtracted.

supply The amount of goods available in the market to be sold at a given price. The term often is coupled with *demand*.

surety bond An agreement by an insurance or bonding company to be responsible for certain possible defaults, debts, or obligations contracted for by an insured party; in essence, a policy insuring one's personal and/or financial integrity. In the real estate business, a surety bond generally is used to ensure that a particular project will be completed at a certain date or that a contract will be performed as stated.

survey The process by which boundaries are measured and land areas are determined; the on-site measurement of lot lines, dimensions, and positions of buildings on a lot, including the determination of any existing encroachments or easements.

syndicate A combination of two or more persons or firms to accomplish a joint venture of mutual interest. Syndicates dissolve when the specific purpose for which they were created has been accomplished.

taxation The process by which a government or municipal quasi-public body raises monies to fund its operation.

tax lien A charge against property created by the operation of law. Tax liens and assessments take priority over all other liens.

tax rate The rate at which real property is taxed in a tax district or county. For example, in a certain county, a home is taxed at a rate of 50 mills, or $50 per 1,000, or 5.0% of the taxable value.

tax sale A court-ordered sale of real property to raise money to cover delinquent taxes.

tenancy at sufferance The tenancy of a lessee who lawfully comes into possession of a landlord's real estate but who continues to occupy the premises improperly after her or his lease rights have expired.

tenancy at will An estate that gives the lessee the right to possession until the estate is terminated by either party; the term of this estate is indefinite.

tenancy by the entirety The joint ownership, recognized in some states, of property acquired by husband and wife during marriage. On the death of one spouse, the survivor becomes the owner of the property.

tenancy in common A form of co-ownership by which each owner holds an undivided interest in real property as if he or she were the sole owner. Each individual has the right to partition. Unlike a joint tenancy, there is no right of survivorship between tenants in common, and owners may have unequal interests.

tenant One who holds or possesses lands or tenements by any kind of right of title.

tenement Everything that may be occupied under a lease by a tenant.

termination (lease) The cancellation of a lease by the action of either party. A lease may be terminated by expiration of the term, surrender and acceptance, constructive eviction by lessor, or option, when provided in the lease for breach of covenants.

termination (listing) The cancellation of a broker-principal employment contract. A listing may be terminated by death or insanity of either party, expiration of listing period, mutual agreement, sufficient written notice, or the completion of performance under the agreement.

testate Having made and left a valid will.

testator A will maker.

"time is of the essence" A phrase in a contract that requires the performance of a certain act within a stated period of time.

title insurance Insurance designed to indemnify the holder for loss sustained by reason of defects in a title, up to and including the policy limits.

Torrens system A method of evidencing title by registration with the proper public authority, generally called the registrar. Named for its founder, Sir Robert Torrens.

township The principal unit of the rectangular survey system (government survey method). A township is a square with six-mile sides and an area of 36 square miles.

township lines The horizontal lines running at six-mile intervals parallel to the base lines in the rectangular survey system (government survey method).

trade fixtures The articles installed by a tenant under the terms of a lease and removable by the tenant before the lease expires.

trust A fiduciary arrangement by which property is conveyed to a person or institution, called a trustee, and held and administered on behalf of another person, called a beneficiary.

trust deed An instrument used to create a lien by which the trustor conveys his or her title to a trustee, who holds it as security for the benefit of the note holder (the lender); also called a *deed of trust*.

trustee One who as agent for others handles money or holds title to their land.

trustee's deed A deed executed by a trustee conveying land held in a trust to the beneficiary.

undivided interest See tenancy in common.

unearned increment An increase in the value of a property caused by increased population, development, or demand for which the owner is not responsible.

Uniform Commercial Code A codification of commercial law, adopted in most states, that attempts to make uniform laws relating to commercial transactions, including chattel mortgages and bulk transfers. Security interests in chattels are created by an instrument known as a security agreement. Article 6 of the code regulates bulk transfers, that is, the sale of a business as a whole, including all fixtures, chattels, and merchandise.

Uniform Residential Appraisal Report (URAR) Standard Fannie Mae Form 1004 used by appraisers.

Uniform Residential Loan Application Report (URLA) Standard Fannie Mae Form 1003 used by loan originators.

unilateral contract A one-sided contract by which one party makes a promise to induce a second party to do something. The second party is not legally bound to perform; if the second party does comply, however, the first party is obligated to keep the promise.

unity of ownership The four unities traditionally needed to create a joint tenancy—unity of title, unity of time, unity of interest, unity of possession.

urban renewal The acquisition of run-down city areas for purposes of redevelopment.

useful life In real estate investment, the number of years a property will be useful to the investors.

usury The practice of charging more than the rate of interest allowed by law.

valid contract A contract that complies with all the essential elements of a contract and is binding and enforceable on all parties to it.

valid lease An enforceable lease that has the following essential parts: lessor and lessee with contractual capacity, offer and acceptance, legality of object, description of the premises, consideration, signatures, and delivery. Leases for more than one year also must be in writing.

value The present worth of future benefits arising from the ownership of real property. To have value, a property must have utility, scarcity, effective demand, and transferability.

variable rate mortgage A mortgage loan that contains an interest rate provision related to a selected index. Under this provision, the interest rate may be adjusted annually either up or down.

variance An exception from the zoning ordinances; permission granted by zoning authorities to build a structure or conduct a use that is expressly prohibited by zoning ordinance.

writ of attachment The method by which a debtor's property is placed in the custody of the law and held as security, pending the outcome of a creditor's suit.

Notes

Notes

Notes

Notes

Notes

Notes

Notes